4-13

MOJO ⚡ HAND

BRAD AND MICHELE MOORE ROOTS MUSIC SERIES

MOJO HAND

THE LIFE AND MUSIC OF

LIGHTNIN' HOPKINS

TIMOTHY J. O'BRIEN AND
DAVID ENSMINGER

UNIVERSITY OF TEXAS PRESS ⋁ AUSTIN

Requests for permission to reproduce material
from this work should be sent to:
Permissions
University of Texas Press
P.O. Box 7819
Austin, TX 78713-7819
http://utpress.utexas.edu/about/book-permissions

The paper used in this book meets the minimum requirements
of ANSI/NISO Z39.48-1992 (R1997) (Permanence of Paper). ♾

Design by Lindsay Starr

LIBRARY OF CONGRESS CATALOGING-IN-PUBLICATION DATA
O'Brien, Timothy J. (Timothy Joseph), 1962–2011.
Mojo hand : the life and music of Lightnin' Hopkins /
by Timothy J. O'Brien and David Ensminger. — 1st edition.
pages   cm — (Brad and Michele Moore Roots Music Series)
Includes index.
ISBN 978-0-292-74515-5 (cloth : alk. paper)
1. Hopkins, Lightnin', 1912–1982. 2. Blues musicians—United States—
Biography. I. Ensminger, David A. II. Title.
ML420.H6357O27 2013
781.643092—dc23
[B]
2012031552

doi:10.7560/745155

Frontispiece: Lightnin' Hopkins, 1972. Photo by Philip Melnick.

Dedicated to
Kyong Mi O'Brien
and
Yuna O'Brien

CONTENTS

Tim O'Brien, Houston, Texas, April 2011. Photo by David Ensminger.

P R E F A C E

How Two Hearts Can Beat As One

OVER A BOISTEROUS DECADE, Tim O'Brien and I attended the same gritty rock 'n' roll shows, wrote high-energy music reviews and previews for papers like the *Houston Press*, and navigated academia, where we attempted to bridge our concerns for social justice with pop culture and an intensely felt sense of "living history." O'Brien pursued an exemplary focus on African American Studies and the blues, while I leaned toward examining punk rock culture's democratic impulses and multiculturalism. As a tough-minded, redheaded, fiery-tempered researcher of Irish descent, he could enumerate issues with rapid-fire aplomb, stitching together elements ranging from labor history and death penalty abolition to affordable urban housing, historic preservation, and fair trade movements. I would sit on his couch, simply trying to match the rigor of his thoughts, though I admit his sheer gusto often overwhelmed me.

For decades, when not pressing his ear to the feedback-drenched gyration of garage rock bands like the Dictators and Guitar Wolf, both bands whom he had befriended, he had immersed himself in the blues, especially at clubs like Antone's in Austin, Texas, and Fitzgerald's and The Continental in Houston, where he snapped eager photos of wise older players and young turks who filtered the past into their raucous sets with charm and panache, skill and fervor. He contributed articles about them to local papers and submitted entries on Sun Ra, Chuck Berry, and Art Blakey to the *Encyclopedia of African American History*.

He eyed Lightnin' Hopkins endearingly, knowing this unparalleled bluesman had not been researched and scrutinized fully. This robust Texas legend soon became the subject of his dissertation, approved by Dr. William Ferris, professor of history at the University of North Carolina, and Dr. Douglas Henry Daniels, professor of African American history and jazz at the University of California, Santa Barbara. Upon completion, that work soon morphed into this book. O'Brien was compelled, seemingly deep in his DNA, to capture Hopkins's often raw-boned, sizzling, and incantatory oeuvre. O'Brien also understood that Hopkins's tunes effortlessly fused inveterate woe, fecund joy, and nuanced sociohistorical observations. And O'Brien collected at length.

Mining 135 secondary sources, he combed archives with eagerness and delved into Library of Congress collections, record company files in Berkeley, California, privately held collections, census and social security records, and probate court and police records. He unearthed elusive informants deep in Houston and logged endless hours tracking down musicians on the road who were willing to share their stories, eventually conducting 130 oral interviews.

O'Brien was no arcane musicologist. He wanted to create and carve out a concisely woven, close-to-the-ground, insightful, and heavily detailed social and cultural history of Hopkins. Together, we edited his dissertation, wrote query letters to publishers, and began assembling this version. We intended the book not merely to appeal to a core audience of musical enthusiasts and others piqued by the text's links to Southern, African American, and American studies, but also to include cultural history readers. We believed the text would appeal to those interested in folklore, performance, and urban studies, and to social justice audiences as well.

Other recent work has also focused on the legacy of Hopkins, such as *Lightnin' Hopkins: His Life and Blues* by Alan Govenar. I believe O'Brien's primary research tends to be much more wide-ranging and inclusive, including the commentary of Grammy winner Dave Alvin and twice-Grammy-nominated Peter Case, well-admired Americana artists. Whereas Govenar might be considered more poetic and romantic, O'Brien aimed for historic depth and breadth. He desired to expose the modern ripples of the subject, tracing how current artists explore the "usable past" of the blues to address their own artistic concerns and themes.

The book debunks several myths. For instance, Hopkins did not refuse song royalties and record only for cash payments. It also illustrates and explains his idiosyncratic business practices, such as shunning professional bookers, managers, and publicists. We discuss recording sessions at length and also elucidate his lyrics, which embody a keen sense of poetry that transforms mundane aspects of life, from beans to telephones, into vibrant tropes. His diverse song content far exceeds rudimentary blues themes; he readily grasped issues of the day, such as space exploration, the Vietnam War, and lesbianism. In addition to surveying rock 'n' roll guitar players such as Jimi Hendrix and Stevie Ray Vaughan, the narrative recounts Hopkins's influence on Miles Davis, John Coltrane, Tom Waits, and Bob Dylan, who based his tune "Leopard Skin Pillbox Hat" on a Hopkins song.

Hopkins's music style mutated and adapted to the era of rhythm and blues. After recording alone on acoustic guitar for years, he grabbed an electric guitar and gyrated to the new beats, delivering a modern blues idiom. By the late 1950s, though, rock 'n' roll overshadowed country blues, burying Hopkins's career. Starting in the 1960s, he enjoyed a storied second career as a folk blues artist who gained worldwide acclaim and booked international tours. Indeed, Hopkins helped pioneer the folk and blues revivals of the 1960s, even grafted his music onto the rock scene while performing with and influencing notable bands such as the Grateful Dead and Jefferson Airplane. This inventive decade is discussed by performers such as Ramblin' Jack Elliott, Barbara Dane, and Mose Allison. Last, Hopkins's appearances at important nightclubs like the Ash Grove in Los Angeles, the Village Gate in New York City, and the Armadillo World Headquarters in Austin, Texas, paint a picture of an American music world yet again on the cusp of change.

While investigating the pained history of sharecropping in Texas, and becoming familiar with the heavy-handed Houston police force that maintained order in Houston during the height of the civil rights movement, O'Brien chronicled Lenwood Johnson, an activist who had fought courageously for a local housing development called Allen Parkway during the 1990s. O'Brien and Johnson fought to preserve and revitalize Freedmen's Town, a historic free black neighborhood near a Jewish cemetery that O'Brien called home and Hopkins once frequented.

O'BRIEN BECAME ILL WITH CANCER IN 2009, and the outlook was immediately worrisome. Tenaciously, by monitoring his health closely and adopting a strict diet, he was able to fend off the worst symptoms for nearly two years. In the spring of 2011, the cancer had spread, the treatments were limited, and the manuscript languished, mostly complete. I openly encouraged O'Brien to tackle the final chapters and finish the manuscript that could become his signature piece of writing. With relatives nearby, I came to his side, helping him type the last portions. Deep pockets of his memory remained intact: he could recall Hopkins's contracts and concert details with ease, yet he experienced difficulty sending an e-mail or cutting and pasting a portion of text. The cancer's journey through his brain was mysterious. Yet he never complained. His rectitude was unwavering. He thought of his wife, his child, and Lightnin' Hopkins.

When he died, friends and family gathered at his home to hear radio broadcasts of news events in which O'Brien had participated, including his efforts to end the death penalty in Texas, to push the University of Houston to affiliate with the Worker Rights Consortium, to found UH Students Against Sweatshops and UH Students for Fair Trade on campus, and to publicize and lobby on behalf of the Free Man's Neighborhood Association. This side of O'Brien somewhat surprised his immediate family, who were more familiar with his role as father, student, and music writer. I knew of those struggles, too, but I was more gripped by his writing and love of music.

Ironically, the man whose sentences I helped finish had organized two major fund-raisers during recent years. On behalf of Alejandro Escovedo, suffering from acute hepatitis, and Peter Case, who was nearly struck down from a severe heart attack, O'Brien had gathered a coterie of talents—Joe Ely, Gurf Morlix, and James McMurtry—to provide thousands of dollars in medical relief. As O'Brien slipped away, we closed the envelopes full of Hopkins news clippings and Xeroxes, filing away his research, and I recalled such volunteerism.

He was more than just a chronicler of history, an honest and invigorating music fan and friend, and a complex community leader. He was a comrade who understood that more than music was at stake. Telling the story of Hopkins is telling the story of America, writ large into the fabric of one person's hardscrabble life. It is the story of art that perseveres despite flawed economic systems, of songs that penetrate past the built-in obsolescence of music fads and fashions, and of stories that evince the historic wounds of America, even when told spontaneously, off-the-cuff, slightly tipsily, and maybe, in any given version, for one night only.

DAVID ENSMINGER
December 2011

MOJO HAND

O N E

The blues is born with you. When you born in
this world, you were born with the blues.
LIGHTNIN' HOPKINS, 1967

"I WAS WORKING TRYING TO TAKE CARE OF MY WIFE, me and my mother, six bits a day and that was top price. I'd come in in the evening it look like I'd be so weak that my knees be clucking like a wagon wheel. I'd go to bed and I'd say, 'Well baby I just can't continue like this.'"[1] Sam "Lightnin'" Hopkins's recollection of his life toiling in the fields for seventy-five cents a day is one example of farm laborer misery and fortitude in the Deep South during the 1920s and 1930s, when agricultural laborers in Hopkins's East Texas environs endured the backbreaking work of planting and harvesting crops. Long after the Civil War faded, the scorching Texas sun beat down on such African Americans. Hopkins's early life, in fact, did not differ much from his grandparents'—slaves in the very same fields. The family seemed tethered to the land of Centerville, Texas, which sits halfway between Dallas and Houston, just east of present-day Interstate 45. Hopkins's subsistence living and small-town upbringing in this rough-and-tumble agrarian society deeply impacted his personality and music, shaping both his lyrics and banter.

In the pre-emancipation days of 1860, Leon County had fewer than seven thousand residents spread out over 1,078 square miles. The Navasota River forms Leon County's western border with Robertson County, while the Trinity River, the eastern border with Anderson and Houston Counties, drains two-thirds of the county. Freestone County lies north of Leon County, and Madison County borders it to the south. Folks like the Hopkinses planted the rich, rolling East Texas land with cotton, corn, and peas. In 1860, only three Leon County families farmed more than five hundred acres. Half of Leon County's seven hundred families worked less than fifty acres. Land not used for agriculture was thick with oak, elm, hickory, and mesquite trees. Some of the trees were harvested for fuel, fencing, and buildings by numerous small sawmills, which met the demand for lumber.

In 1872, workers completed the International and Great Northern, Leon County's first railroad. Entering the county at the northeast corner, the tracks traveled in a southwesterly direction. Financier Jay Gould backed the project, which spurred several important changes. For one, trade on the Trinity River soon collapsed; thus, the population shifted from older towns like Centerville and Leona to upcoming towns established along the train's route, such as Buffalo, Jewett, Oakwoods, and Marquez. Buffalo and Jewett quickly became substantial centers of commerce and trade.

The Trinity and Brazos Valley Railroad and the Houston and Texas Central also ran thirty or so miles through the county, connecting the towns of Normangee, Flynn, and Concord. Another transportation option was the Tri-Weekly Hack Line, which ran between Jewett and Hopkins's hometown. The five-hour, one-way trip cost travelers one dollar. By 1909, companies started exploiting coal deposits west of Jewett. One of Hopkins's most important influences, Alger "Texas" Alexander, was born near Jewett in 1900. Alexander worked on the Leon County railroad tracks and as a farm laborer in Leon County.

In the nineteenth century, Texas teemed with slavery. In 1860, 2,620 slaves made their home in Leon County alone. Almost half of the seven hundred white families in the county owned at least one slave, but most owned fewer than ten. At the outbreak of the Civil War in 1861, Texas was home to almost 200,000 slaves.[2] Although Centerville did not see any Civil War battles, several notorious outlaws did pass through the town during the conflict.

Toward the close of the Civil War, a band of twenty guerillas commanded by the notorious William Clark Quantrill showed up on the Centerville town square. Quantrill's men were Confederate partisans who often operated behind enemy lines. They provided intelligence for Confederate troops and pillaged Union sympathizers. The infamous outlaw Jesse James, his brother Frank, and Cole Younger rode with Quantrill. Union troops shot and killed Quantrill in June 1865, but his men became outlaws after the war. By all accounts, Quantrill's raiders quickly dispersed from the town of Centerville.

Texans learned late that President Abraham Lincoln had granted slaves their freedom. On June 19, 1865, Major General Gordon Granger arrived in the port of Galveston and issued his General Order Number 3, which proclaimed, "All slaves are free." From that day on, in Texas, June 19th became known and celebrated as the Juneteenth holiday. Born into slavery in 1844, just six miles west of Centerville on the McDaniel plantation, Willis Anderson remembered the day that the slaves in Centerville learned of their freedom. In an interview for the Works Progress Administration slave narratives project, Anderson recalled that the news of freedom came to Centerville when Yankee soldiers traveling through the town told the slave owners to free their slaves.[3]

During Reconstruction, two companies of Federal soldiers occupied Leon County. The seventy-five troops camped in tents on Beaver Creek one mile outside of Centerville. There was some talk by the local citizens of a rebellion against the Yankee occupiers, but after Richard Coke took the Texas governor's office in 1874, the reasons for dissatisfaction eased because he restored antebellum political conditions. Meanwhile, most of the freed slaves stayed in Leon County and became sharecroppers. The former slaves usually worked for one-half or one-third of the crop they raised.

Abe Hopkins, Sam's father, worked as a sharecropper in Leon County. The elder Hopkins was born in Leon County in 1873. Although not born into slavery, he endured the far from ideal conditions typical for African Americans just eight years after emancipation. As the son of a freed slave, Abe's lifestyle was that of a dirt-poor sharecropper who lived from crop to crop. Sharecropping consisted of a cycle of work and debt heavily tilted toward white landowners. After working the land day in and day out from sunup to sundown (or "can to can't"), at harvest time sharecroppers sold the cotton or other crop they had raised and applied the proceeds to pay back the amount their landowner had advanced them for supplies.

Hence, the sharecroppers were at the mercy of both the merchant, who set the price, and the landowner, who kept the books, and a firm grip, on what a tenant owed. If the sharecropper was illiterate, he was even more vulnerable to being swindled by unscrupulous white plantation owners. After a season of backbreaking labor, sharecroppers often ended up earning less money than they had been advanced for their supplies. This exploitive system bound the sharecropper to the land for yet another season, continuing the cycle of hard-bitten poverty. As Navasota, Texas, songster Mance Lipscomb noted, sharecroppers felt little difference between sharecropping and slavery: "I was in slavery right up to 1942 . . . sharecropping, yeah."[4]

Furthermore, the end of slavery did not mean that Southern whites' racial attitudes toward African Americans underwent a radical change. Abe Hopkins's neighbors frowned on race mixing, in particular. Examples of such racial attitudes are evident in a column Amos Keeler penned for the *Jewett County Messenger* newspaper in 1889. Upset about whites attending black festivities in Buffalo, a town about seventeen miles north of Centerville, he evinced distaste:

Well, who would have thought it! Some of Buffalo's respectable people were at the negro festible [*sic*] a few nights ago. Now, I think if people study the matter a bit they are bound to admit that they had better stayed at home. Such places are not fit for anybody to go to. That's what makes the blacks so forward and sassy with the white people, just because whenever they have a meeting of that kind some white people are there.[5]

Abe Hopkins, meanwhile, made his home in Centerville, managing to eke out a tumultuous life of drinking, gambling, and fighting. Eventually, his reckless lifestyle caught up with him, and he was charged and convicted in a homicide case. After being released from the penitentiary, he returned to the Centerville area. By the turn of the century, he had met fifteen-year-old Frances Washington. Minister Moses Clark married them on May 9, 1901.

On February 3, 1902, Frances gave birth to their first son, John Henry. Abe and Frances worked as farm laborers. By 1910, they supported a growing young family of six. John Henry was now nine and worked as a farm laborer to help support his younger siblings: Joel, seven, Abe Junior, four, and Alice, two. Sam Hopkins was the baby of the family. Although scholars do not dispute his birth date, March 15, the year is still not certain. When the 1920 census taker counted the Hopkins family in their precinct on January 29 and 30, 1920, he reported Hopkins's age as eight years old, which suggests 1911 as his birth year. However, mistakes by census takers were not unusual: they only record information respondents gave them. For example, the age of Frances, Hopkins's mother, was listed as twenty-five on the 1910 census, which was recorded on April 28, 1910. Yet, on the 1920 census taken in January 1920, Frances Hopkins's age was recorded as thirty-six. Less than ten years had passed, but Frances Hopkins had managed to age eleven years. Hopkins himself claimed he was born in 1912. In the Houston-based recording *Goin Back and Talk to Mama* from 1949 or 1950, he mentions his birth date: "I was born March 15th—man the year was 19 and 12."[6] The social security death register puts Hopkins's birth date as March 12, 1911, while his death certificate lists March 12, 1912, as his birth date. When Hopkins received his social security account, he also listed his year of birth as 1912.

Hopkins's rural roots exposed him to what would become his lifelong hobby—fishing: "I was born down by the river, they call it Warren's Bottom."[7] "I was born on the banks of the river, that's the reason I'm a fisherman from my heart. I was born on the banks of the river that's true, water flowing I guess. . . . Cuz that was on the Red River."[8] Unfortunately for Sam Hopkins and his family, the calming and lazy flowing river through Leon County did nothing to soothe Abe Hopkins's wild ways. After he fathered a family, Abe Hopkins continued drinking, gambling, and shooting guns. Sometimes the elder Hopkins's gambling winnings were paid in cotton. Another time his winnings amounted to a mule and a wagon.

Sam Hopkins might have been old enough to notice friction between his mother and father due to his father's carousing, because later he recorded a song called "Mama and Papa Hopkins":

> I wonder why my mama don't love my papa no more
> I guess my daddy been doing something wrong . . .
> Oh yea caused my mom's heart to ruin[9]

In 1915, when Hopkins was about three years old, his father was murdered. Minus a breadwinner, the Hopkinses' family life quickly became hardscrabble. His mother Frances kept the family mended and supported as best she could, but she soon came to understand the difficulty of feeding and clothing five children all by herself. In addition to the dangerous racial climate, Frances lived in a time when women suffered second-class citizenship. For example, a nearby newspaper, the *Grapeland Messenger*, carried an item on May 20, 1915, that read, "Hats off to Houston! She is the first city in Texas to start an organized movement against women's suffrage."[10] Unfortunately, women like Frances were years away from benefiting from the freedoms promoted and pioneered by suffragettes.

Right after Abe Hopkins died, the oldest Hopkins boy, John Henry, left the family and Centerville, saying he had to leave so he would not harm the man who killed his father. I will not be coming back, he told his family as he left.[11] In turn, the rest of the Hopkins family moved about nine miles south from Centerville to Leona.

Sam Hopkins was raised in a dangerous Jim Crow racial climate. Similar to many other towns in the Deep South, Centerville experienced incidents of racially motivated vigilante justice on a regular basis. Stemming from white supremacist ideology, the violence instilled palpable fear in the African American community while enforcing and maintaining the rancor between races and the racial status quo. Like all African Americans, Hopkins's family lived under the threat that at any time they faced death or injury. The Hopkinses also understood that the justice system would not be able to protect them. Even long after Hopkins became a world-renowned musician, his friends noticed his lifelong fear of the police.

For instance, in Centerville, the hanging tree, or the "tree of justice" as the locals called it, stood in front of the courthouse square. During the early days of Texas statehood, General Sam Houston traveled from Huntsville to Centerville and stood under the hanging tree to speak to Leon County citizens. Racists used the hanging tree to lynch African Americans from the Civil War until 1919. During Reconstruction, one black was hanged from the tree and left to swing for two nights and a day before his stretched-out body was finally cut down. The complete record of all the folks who met their fate on the Centerville hanging tree does not survive, but the legacy of terror likely victimized twenty thousand black men in the whole post-Reconstruction South, inspiring haunting songs like "Strange Fruit" by Billie Holiday.

The account of one Centerville incident is preserved in an article written and published by editor G. R. Englelow in the November 27, 1919, edition of *The Record*, a Centerville newspaper. At daybreak on a Monday morning, two gunshots were heard. News got around that the dead body of Jim Sinclair, an Anglo, had been found. Sinclair had been murdered in his home. Sinclair's mother suspected that the murderer was an African American tenant farmer and preacher who lived on their property. The tenant farmer had been angry with Sinclair. Deputy Sheriff Wade Lowrance searched the African American suspect's house in vain. After Sheriff Cobb was summoned from his mother's bedside in Normangee, he rounded up a posse and some bloodhounds in Madisonville. The suspect was tracked to the farm of Joel Leatherman. After a chase of three or four miles, the suspect surrendered without resistance and was placed in jail. Wednesday morning the suspect was found swinging from a limb of the large oak tree in front of the courthouse. Billy Bizor, Hopkins's childhood friend, could point it out: "Used to sit right in front of the jailhouse, big old oak tree. If there been gangsters in those days like that, they'd come out of the jailhouse and swung on a limb and come down the trees."[12]

Another newspaper account claimed that the dispute that caused the killing stemmed from a disagreement about cotton. Sam Hopkins, however, remembered a different reason: "They hung him cuz god damn he told a white man to stop from fucking with his wife. And he just kept on doing it and he said man, well if you keep that up, I'm gotta do something to you . . . it would have been a hell of a thing to see that man the way he was hung."[13]

The school in Centerville closed on the Monday of the murder because of the incident. Everyone in the area, including young girls, tried to see the body of the accused killer. A song was even written about the event. That episode of racial terror served to underline the fact that whites were firmly in control. African Americans had better stay in their places, incidents like these symbolized, lest they be dealt with in a similar manner. The niceties and legality of a jury trial would not be afforded to African Americans accused of a crime. A noose served as their judge and jury.

By the time Hopkins was seven years old, his father had been killed, his oldest brother, only fourteen, had left home, and at least one local African American had been yanked from the town jail and lynched in the town square. In addition, Hopkins's grandfather, a slave, met a violent death. "My granddaddy hung hisself [sic] to keep from having those hard times. He'd rather be out this world. He'd rather be in another world, to keep from having hard times."[14] The violence demonstrated by these incidents was common, immediate, and significant. Racial terror was an everyday aspect of African Americans' lives.

The Hopkins family was poor, but they kept themselves entertained by making music. Hopkins's brothers and sister played guitar, and his mother could play a hymn on the accordion. One of Hopkins's childhood friends remembered, "Him and his brothers, his sister, all of them, you know, could play. He was a boy then. And . . . I used to enjoy listening at him. We wasn't nothing but kids but I like the music. We was just kids together but we were having a good time."[15]

Hopkins taught himself to play guitar by borrowing his brother John Henry's instrument when he was not home. One day John Henry came home, caught his brother on the instrument, and asked him to show what he could play. After Hopkins strummed out a tune, his brother approved and asked him where he had learned it. Hopkins replied, "Well, I just learned it." A friend from Hopkins's youth remembered such self-taught style, "He didn't have to practice. He picked it up and played it. . . . He could pick up a guitar and jump it. He was just like a lumberjack on that dancin'. Don't fool yourself and think he couldn't dance or play that guitar."[16] Hopkins's natural musical ability eventually freed him from the sharecropper fields.

In an interview for a documentary film, Hopkins recalled his childhood: "I was eight years old when I made my first guitar. I got the screen wire off the screen door to make my little sound on my little box. I made it out of a cigar box, I kept champing on it and I'd ask my brother to let me play his guitar. He said, no boy, you can't play this guitar. He never did decide to let me play his guitar. So he told me one day, boy don't you fool with my guitar. But it wasn't hanging too high from the wall. I got a chair and got it down. One day they went to the field. They come in and I had it down on the floor, laying on the floor but I was picking a tune, and he heard the guitar and he walked in and it was playing so good he just stood there and listened. He liked it so well he said didn't I tell you not to bother that guitar? His name was John Henry. My brother, oldest brother, so he said you can have it. So that's how good the music sounded to him."[17]

In addition to his family, one of Hopkins's early musical influences was Albert Holley, a local blues musician he heard singing a song to his widowed mother Frances. "I heard him play; he was sitting on the foot of the bed. He was saying, 'Baby come sit down on my knee I got something to tell you keeps on worrying me.' And he was saying that to mama. I just listened. I just picked up on what he was saying. The song appealed to me, and made me feel good. I just walked by 'em and by 'em. That was one thing he was saying that I do remember to this day. 'Baby come sit down on my knee.' He was right back on the foot of the bed pickin' the guitar looking at mama. . . . I was seven years old. So that give me some ideas how to sing too."[18] Hopkins, already an astute observer of human nature, later developed that key ingredient of songwriting, mustering songs offhand, spontaneously, and fluidly from sundry details of life.

When Hopkins was young, he also heard his mother's cousin, Tucker Jordan, a fiddler, and Jordan's wife Rose, a guitar player. Years later Hopkins used a lyric creatively culled from the Jordans, "Don't the sun look pretty going down," as a lyric to his song "Shining Moon": "I know it was pretty music and that gave me an idea. I never did learn the fiddle, but I learned the guitar. That's the way it happened."[19] Hopkins realized his musical talent was "a gift. . . . There was an old lady told me, said son, it was your mother had music in her heart when she was carrying you. You know what that means don't you? Well alright, then. Well she must have cuz when I come in this world I come in doing this [plays a chord]. . . . I swear to God."[20] Hopkins soon realized his innate, idiosyncratic, indelible style, allowing him to forge, after some threadbare struggle and profound patience, a brazen route ahead.

T W O

The blues didn't come to Texas by themselves.
I brought them here.

LIGHTNIN' HOPKINS, 1981

IN 1920, HOPKINS ACCOMPANIED his family to a meeting of the General Baptist Association of Churches in Buffalo, Texas. Black Baptists gathered every year to worship and fellowship at the Buffalo Association camp meeting. In 1972, Bill Ingram, a railroad agent in Buffalo, told *Dallas Morning News* columnist Frank Tolbert that in the old days, thousands would gather at the Association grounds to camp out and enjoy gospel singing and blues music. According to Tolbert, the Association grounds were about twenty acres "beyond a shacky suburb of Buffalo, Leon County."[1]

Hopkins remembered his experience at the 1920 Buffalo Association in an interview with folklorist Mack McCormick, "That's where all the delegates, preachers—they'd get there and they'd have a wonderful time. Church, they had a tabernacle there, you know? Well they'd have church in the tabernacle. And they'd sell sody water out on the grounds. . . . it'd last for days, long time."[2] The religious occasion provided Hopkins an opportunity to hear Blind Lemon Jefferson singing the blues.

In Les Blank's documentary *The Blues According to Lightnin' Hopkins*, Hopkins also discussed his experience at the Association: "I was eight years old and I'd go all up to those country festivals and go to the Buffalo Association. The Buffalo Association is a place that they have once a year. Which they gonna have it for forty years, they still having it up there. It's where the church people would get together, and they would have church, and a little music and barbeque and dinner, such things like that. They had a tabernacle there and people come from far and low for that, and they still do. So that's the biggest I know and preachers from everywhere. They used to have a preacher there. They called him Blind Butler and the same time they had Blind Butler there, they had Blind Lemon Jefferson there. Both of them were blind men. Jefferson had been hired to play for the picnic."[3] Hopkins's awareness of the religious tradition indicates his understanding of the role blues singers played in his rural society. Blues singers could coexist with traditional church-based social functions and even actually profit from them.

Throughout his life, Hopkins often told the story about meeting Blind Lemon Jefferson. "He had a crowd of peoples around. I was standing and looking at him playing and I just went [to] playing my little guitar what he was just playing," Hopkins told Sam Charters.

> So, he said, "Who's that playing the guitar?" So they said, "Oh that's just a little boy. He is knocking on the guitar." "No, he's playing that guitar," he said. "Where he at? Oh yeah, come here boy." I gone over where he was. He feel for me. I was so low and he raised me up, saying, "This here [was you] playing the guitar?" "Yeah" and he said, "Do that again." So I did a little note again, same one he done. He said, "That's my note, the same thing, boy you keep it up and you gonna be a good guitar player." So he went on and when he commence to playing, I was playing right on with him. Me and him, and we carried on. That excited me because I was so little. I was just picking what he said, I wasn't singing, but I was playing what he was playing.[4]

The importance of playing with Blind Lemon Jefferson at such an early age was not lost on Hopkins, since "Blind Lemon was the star of the whole wide world when I started playing."[5] The deep-down excitement Hopkins experienced playing with the most renowned country blues icon of the day validated and enriched his own sprouting musical efforts. Jefferson's encouraging words spurred, prodded, and shaped Hopkins's musical trajectory. Though Hopkins might have been too young to understand the full, candid meaning of blues when playing with Jefferson, as he grew older, he, too, experienced the monotony of unrelenting work in the fields, which yielded toil and hardship oft-associated with the genre, fostering the musical tone and lyrical terrain. Much of the American South resounded with such music.

Most blues scholars trace some of the roots of the blues to the field hollers and work chants that African American laborers sang while toiling, although Luc Sante challenged this in "The Invention of the Blues." Singing while working is common throughout many societies, for it fosters rhythm, alleviates boredom, and provides solace and hope. This was likely the case with the sharecroppers and tenant farmers in Leon County in the early 1900s. Picking cotton in the Texas heat consisted of raw, miserable work that wore down laborers, physically and mentally. Singing field hollers and other songs broke up the grueling tasks at hand, becoming an important component of the blues.

Nat Dove, a native Texan, musician, educator, and author, linked the blues to folk aesthetics: "The reality was that a war had been fought for their freedom and then there was no freedom. These people had reconstructed the country back to the way it was and in some ways even worse. So this is where the blues came from, the blues didn't come from some guy meeting some devil at some crossroads, that's crap."[6] For Dove, blues yielded stories about the ingrained, inveterate survival of persecuted people. Such songs reflect the muscle, blood, and spirit, constituting a narrative steeped in the African American experience.

Historian Larry Willoughby explained that the first slaves that came to East Texas in the 1820s "brought with them the Afro American heritage indigenous to other parts of the cotton kingdom. They brought their songs: the field hollers, the work chants, ritual shouts, chain gang moans and gospel rhythms. They brought their instruments: banjos, panpipes, mouth organs, recorders, three-string guitars and any cylindrical object to use as a drum. For the next century, the so-called race music in Texas existed in a state of incubation waiting to give birth to ragtime, jazz and rock'n'roll. With the exception of the Mississippi Delta, no geographical locale was as rich a spawning ground for the country blues and all its derivative musical styles as Texas."[7]

Unlike the Mississippi Delta area, East Texas is not known for myths about blues singers' skills. The well-worn myth about Mississippi Delta bluesman Robert Johnson suggests he sold his soul at the crossroads in exchange for guitar-playing abilities, an overblown fiction that overshadows the importance of culture and environment, which profoundly impact blues music. Hopkins's rural upbringing, the state of race relations in America, especially Texas, and Hopkins's later intrigues relating to urban life formed the nexus of his blues and persona. Hopkins's repertoire represents his keenly felt sense of home, place, and heritage within a strictly enforced and oppressive Jim Crow system. Hopkins understood the blues' uniquely African American status: "The white boys just don't have the voices for the blues. They're afraid to let go of themselves. . . . it isn't white man's music."[8]

Bob Wills, a mainstay and progenitor of Texas swing, was also an East Texas native. Born in 1905, just six years before Hopkins, he grew up forty miles west of Centerville in Kosse, Texas. Like Hopkins, Wills's family worked as sharecroppers, right alongside African Americans in the cotton camps of East and West Texas. When Wills was asked about African American blues he grew up around, he recalled, "I don't know whether they made them up as they moved up and down the rows or not, but they sang blues you never heard before." The Wills family also recounted blacks and whites in cotton camps listening to music and watching jig-dancing contests.⁹ Because radio was not popularized until the 1920s, sharecroppers witnessed musicians of that era create music on-site for weekend jamborees and celebrations.

Jefferson, Hopkins's primary influence, remains known as a seminal pre-Depression blues singer. Born in 1893 in Couchman, a tiny Central Texas town outside of Wortham, Jefferson was immersed in local church life, indelibly shaping his music. His family attended the Shiloh Primitive Baptist Church in Kirvin, Texas, where Jefferson first began to play guitar and sing. By the age of fourteen, Jefferson regularly visited town and sat in front of stores playing for shoppers. After singing and playing picnics and parties on nearby farms, he moved to Dallas as a teenager. He also played for tips on the streets of Groesbeck, Wortham, and Kirvin.

In Dallas, he frequently gigged in the black entertainment district known as Deep Ellum, a vernacular take on deep Elm Street. Texas singer and Hopkins contemporary Mance Lipscomb experienced Jefferson's performances in Dallas as early as 1917:

I knowed him from 1917. He was playing out on old [unintelligible] we called it the track . . . in Dallas, when I saw him. In those days the laws would put you out. They put you out off the street so that singing and going on wouldn't bother the people. . . . He was always standing there under that shade tree on a little bench and he had his guitar and people would come from far and near to hear him sing and that's how he made his living. He never did keep no time with his music.¹⁰

Meanwhile, influential Texas guitar player T-Bone Walker worked with Jefferson around the Dallas circuit:

He had a cup on his guitar and everybody knew him . . . and so he used to come through on Central Avenue singing and playing his guitar. And I'd lead him, and they'd put money in his cup. . . . Well, I was crazy about him. My whole family was crazy about him. He'd come over every Sunday and sit with us and play his guitar. They sang and they had a few drinks. At that time, they were drinking corn whiskey and home brew, things like that. Cause you couldn't buy any whiskey unless it was bootleg in those days. . . . Course Blind Lemon was a very good friend of my family. I used to lead him around a lot. We'd go up and down Central Avenue. They had a railroad track there, and all the places were clubs, beer joints. They wouldn't sell no whiskey no way. Beer joints, and things like that, we used to play them joints. Place upstairs called Tip Top. We used to play there. We'd never leave out of Dallas, no further than Oklahoma City, or maybe Tulsa, Oklahoma, and then on back to Texas and into West Texas, and Waco, Texas, and San Antone and all around.[11]

Jefferson met Huddie Ledbetter, better known as Leadbelly, in Deep Ellum. They traveled together on and off until 1918, when Leadbelly was indicted for murder. According to Leadbelly biographers Charles Wolfe and Kip Lornell, Jefferson's reputation remained regional until he met Leadbelly.

After parting ways with Leadbelly, Jefferson became one of the country's foremost practitioners of fecund country blues, deeply impressing Hopkins and popular audiences. Blues producer and writer Paul Swinton declared, "Throughout the '20s Lemon spearheaded a boom in 'race' records sales that featured male down home blues singers."[12] Although hard data for record sales are slim, renowned blues scholar and researcher Gayle Dean Wardlow ranted, "Blind Lemon Jefferson sold more records than God."[13] In 1926, the national edition of the *Chicago Defender*, an important African American newspaper, carried ads for Jefferson's records, labeling him as a "famous down home blues singer from down Dallas way."[14] Such notoriety quickly fanned across the country.

More than just a country blues singer and guitarist, Blind Lemon Jefferson epitomized *the* bluesman whose lifestyle and songs were chock-full of dark and violent imagery, often associated with so-called "devil's music." He often performed at country suppers "where men were hustling women and selling bootleg and Lemon was singing for them all night."[15] Songs like "Matchbox Blues" and "One Kind Favor" later gelled into blues standards that musicians adapted and performed decades after his death.

Some of Jefferson's songs describe the desperate poverty and the injustices permeating black life in the Jim Crow South. Tunes like "Hangman's Blues," "Prison Cell Blues," and "'Lectric Chair Blues" speak to the criminal justice system, while songs such as "Broke and Hungry," "Bad Luck Blues," and "Tin Cup Blues" reveal an uneducated blind blues singer scratching out a living.

Jefferson's blues themes did not dwell on death and despair alone. Approximately half of his repertoire invoked women, three decades before brown-eyed handsome man Chuck Berry duck-walked across stages, brandishing his electric guitar as a phallic symbol. He also prefigured soul singers, hip-hop pioneers, and gangsta rappers evoking their sexual appetites and bias. For example, Blind Lemon Jefferson boasted about his own sexual prowess in "That Black Snake Moan":

Mmmmm, black snake crawling in my room
and some pretty mama
Better come get this black snake soon.

In "Oil Well Blues," he grafted an oil well, important to local Texas economies, to the physicality of sex:

A mean reputation
And they call me Drilling Sam
When I starts to drillin'
You hear women hollering too black bad

The virile Jefferson was not always on top, though; in "Peach Orchard Mama," the woman plays him for a fool because Jefferson found "three kid men shaking down your peach-a tree." In "Deceitful Brownskin Blues," Jefferson's

Brown skin girl is deceitful
Till she gets you all worn down
She get all your pocket change
She gonna drive you from her town.

The braggadocio blues of Blind Lemon Jefferson, which chanted sexist power, resemble racist images concocted by segregationists: loose, sex-hungry black men present a constant threat to chaste white women. Anti-integrationists exploited those sentiments effectively as a weapon in their attempts to fight equality and civil rights during the 1950s and 1960s.

Jefferson did not make his first record until 1925. He was already an important and powerful bluesman, though, playing a unique homegrown blend, when eight-year-old Hopkins encountered him in Buffalo, Texas, in 1920. Notes are sung or played below pitch by Jefferson, a personal inflection besets the vocals, and a feeling of bare-boned personal narratives and idiosyncratic rhythm patterns shape the work. The spontaneous, haphazard, and irregular elements, adopted in Hopkins's music as well, exist as provocative, self-taught, and idiosyncratic gestures, delivered often without the backing of a band. The meeting with Blind Lemon Jefferson surely gave Hopkins the confidence to pursue music, though Hopkins's musically talented family stoked his interest as well. "Every last one of them were musicians, singers or dancers," revealed Ray Dawkins, who grew up around the Hopkins family in Leon County, where they had a band and performed together.[16]

Gospel music Hopkins heard in church impacted him as well. When film-maker Les Blank shot a documentary about Hopkins in the 1960s, he asked Hopkins if the music he heard in church influenced the way he played. Hopkins responded, "Sure." When Blank asked Hopkins if someone taught him the church songs, Hopkins intoned, "They didn't teach me the songs baby. Nuh uh, they made them up. Fact of the business the way it goes, they sang the songs and I played them. Whatever they sing, I played it. All they do is get into tune just like this [plays]. Now they say 'Glory Glory.' I never had played it on the piano but on the guitar I did. It goes like this [plays]. 'Glory glory hallelujah . . . as we go marching in.' But you see I wouldn't be singing. I just played the song. They'd be singing it not me. I just be playing it. When I 'posed to come in, I just play it. I do it now play it on the piano, guitar anything."[17]

Hopkins discussed his church-shadowed childhood with author and record producer Sam Charters: "Organ used to be the real family. We played on Sundays. If we didn't go to church, we had church at home. I was the organ player singing them good old Christian songs. I had to play them because that's what she [Frances, Hopkins's mother] wanted us to do. She want us raised in church. Fact of business was she did."[18] "I come up in Sunday school too. I played the organ in Sunday school and I played the piano too. I would open up the church with it. The songs you know, on the piano, yeah."[19]

This religious background and its gospel songs formed basic ingredients of Hopkins's oeuvre. For example, "Jesus Won't You Come by Here" was one traditional gospel song he played for many decades. When Hopkins recorded the song in 1964 at the Cabale Club in Berkeley, California, he asked folksinger Barbara Dane to join in. "He sat at the piano and he was playing 'Jesus Won't You Come by Here' and he asked me to harmonize and I did," Dane remembered. "He was dead serious with his religiosity too, which is not my bag, but I'll honor it if it's somebody else, if that's where they're at. Glad to harmonize with him."[20]

Though, for some, blues existed at the opposite end of the morality spectrum from gospel music and African American spirituals, Hopkins did not see any contradiction. Churchgoers often condemned blues songs, often sung in seedy and dangerous bars where alcohol flowed freely and fisticuffs often broke out, as vulgar and indecent. The Ten Commandments were likely not foremost in revelers' minds. However, the relationship between blues and gospel music is much more complex. One should not just dismiss the blues as secular and hold up spirituals as a form of godly praise. As author James H. Cone has shown, the blues *is* "secular spirituals." They are secular because they "confine their attention solely to the immediate and affirm the bodily expression of black soul, including its sexual manifestations. They are spirituals because they are impelled by the same search for the truth of black experience."[21]

Hopkins had a view similar to Cone's when it came to the relationship between blues and gospel music. "You go to church and a real preacher is really preaching the Bible to you, he's honest to God trying to get you to understand these things. That's just the same as singing the blues. The blues is the same thing. When they get up there and put their whole soul in there and feel it, it's just like a preacher."[22] "The blues and gospel are first cousins, in fact they are so close they are almost brothers," Hopkins opined.[23] In fact, Hopkins saw another parallel between his role as a blues singer and that of a preacher. "Course I'm like a preacher. I got to keep hearing that 'Amen!' from my congregation just the same as a preacher."[24] Hopkins's own words clearly testify: gospel music and church molded him as a person and a musician.

Another formative influence on Hopkins's character was the single-parent family situation resulting after his father's death. Hopkins discussed his earliest memories of his mother and his childhood with filmmaker Les Blank: "She didn't have no trouble having me. But the thing of it [is], she had the trouble after having me. I don't guess she had no trouble. She didn't have no trouble having me, it's as a way of speaking, you must have the wrong understanding. After my mother had me, there was no great thing at home, with me and my family, because I couldn't do no good there. So I left my home when I was eight years old with a guitar around my neck. And that's the God darn truth and you could have found that out today if you'd have asked any people, they would have told you."[25]

Hopkins often said he left home at the age of eight; likely, he went to stay with another family near his family's home. When Hopkins was young, he lived with a white family in Leona, a town less than eight miles from Centerville. He remembered, "See they was white people, but they was alright. . . . Their kids and me, we'd just get together and have a time. Riding horses, playing ball—you'd look out there, you'd see me and you'd think I was one of them. That's the way I was raised."[26]

Yet, the racial status quo in the Deep South was not lost on young Hopkins. "The way I come up, I did come up under the old peoples, but for white people same as my age or older I'd just say 'Yes, sir' or 'No, sir.' You know, natural polite like 'Yes, ma'am' and 'No, ma'am.' That was just it. I never did come up with that other, that 'Yow, suh' and 'Naw suh.' Never did that, like some of 'em had it."[27] Hopkins had been raised to observe the strictly reinforced racial hierarchy, but he did not act overly subservient. He performed the minimum in order to weather the Jim Crow system.

Another important part of Hopkins's personality was his independent nature. Hopkins showed such independence and concern for others' welfare by leaving home so that his absence would take some of the burden of child rearing off his mother. At the same time he sought to make his mother's life less of a struggle, he sought a better life for himself. Hopkins explained to Blank why he left home at such a young age:

Well I just know there was something in store for me. There wasn't anything on the end of that hoe handle for me, chopping cotton for six bits a day. Plowing a mule for six bits a day. That wasn't in store for me. I went on with what the good Lord give me with that guitar, on my singing and my blues. And I made it all my life with that guitar, never seen a hard day in my life with the guitar. I stayed around in Leona, that's seven miles from Centerville. I used to stay there, stayed in the back room of white peoples, the Thomases. And the first time I ever knowed anything about Galveston they came up there and brought me back to Galveston and brought me back to showed me around, a good time. I was a small kid, nine years old picking my guitar. I stayed with them.[28]

Hopkins supposedly took his first train ride when he was about nine years old, but he never discussed buying a ticket. Like a hobo, he caught rides on freight trains. He explained,

[I] went to Houston, Texas. Been riding the freight since I was about nine or eleven. That's right, we went to Houston, Texas. Well you know the train have been my friend. Just like I sing my song when I first started hoboing I take the freight train to be my friend. Fact of business I did. When we left out [of] Crockett, Texas, me and Billy Bizor, right there, I had a dime and he had a nickel and he had a harmonica and we hoboed our way from Crockett, Texas, to Clarksdale, Mississippi. That was pretty good. We was young at that time. We got put off the train one time and that was when we was in Vicksburg, yeah that's right.[29]

Crockett, Texas, the county seat of Houston County, is thirty-three miles east of Centerville. The town was named for David Crockett, the frontiersman and congressman who died fighting at the Alamo.[30]

Most of what is known about Hopkins's formal schooling comes from what he told others. Hopkins attended a school near Leona that only enrolled African Americans.[31] "We used to go to school. Well Alameda [Dixon] she's older than me, but we used to go to the same school and you know we used to dance, go [to] dances well it be four and five miles across the prairie but we'd walk it sometimes. We had a good time, long about then."[32]

Hopkins's formal education ended in the seventh grade. Early on, a girl was instrumental in getting him expelled. He explained:

You know the reason I didn't go no further than seventh grade? And I was doing fine. But [that] man want to whup me. And I know he whup me for nothing. . . . A girl wrote me a letter. I didn't write her none. But still, I was happy. And I laughed out in school. They didn't allow you to open your mouth. I laughed out [loud]. She got on there and said, "I love you," and I said, "Ha!" I laughed, "Ha!" So he said come here. Called me in there. I dropped the letter on the ground. Boy, they was strict. They accused me of this and that. He come back, he seen it in my hand. Thought I was reading it. He got it. He read it before the whole school. "Hopkins, I love you." But I tell you, you know how it is. I love you and I hope you love me and all that jive. Well I did love her. But the man got the letter and this ain't no lie, he read it before the whole congregation, school. But that didn't make me shamed but I knowed he was gonna punch the girl. Me too, I give it to him. That's what he thought he was going to do. I got fired from school.[33]

Hopkins was probably about twelve or thirteen when he got thrown out of school.

Whether he was living at home or nearby with a white family, Hopkins absorbed the music around him, learning his craft by carefully listening to the musicians he saw and heard and improvising his own versions. Instead of mimicking the finger movements, scales, and rhythm of others, he often created his own impure hybrids, adopting and adapting simultaneously. Hopkins demonstrated this to filmmaker Les Blank. "Now you want me to show you something? Now this is Blind Lemon Jefferson [plays and tunes guitar]. . . . Here's the way Blind Lemon done. Now, he did it from here. See but I made [this]. That's Blind Lemon, see, but I didn't do it that way. My beat ain't like that . . . everybody got their own way. Now, if you was to make it, I'll bet you make it different from me and him. You don't do what the other player is doing. . . . I caught his way of playing, and I did play like him, but I don't exactly. Just like the blues come to Texas loping like a mule [plays].[34]

That simile of the loping mule, an early bit of traditional anonymous lyric encountered by folklorist Alan Lomax as well, but in reverse order—"the blues came from Texas"—partly illuminates how blues migrates.[35] It does not come forceful and single-handedly. Instead, the blues is disseminated through song and utterance, from person to person, field to porch to roadhouse, absorbing and incorporating a cornucopia of song styles, especially in the fecund musical landscape of Texas and western Louisiana. In slow but steady degrees, blues was affected by Cajun and zydeco, Eastern European and German folk traditions, Mexican-flavored dance floor mariachi, and turn-of-the-century foot-stomping boogie-woogie, whose originators likely entertained midnight masses deep in the woods of the Gulf Coast region a handful of years before Blind Lemon Jefferson mastered "booger rooger"—boogie-woogie riffage played on bass strings.

Hopkins played his first paid public gig before he turned fourteen. One day he met Jabo Bucks near where he had first met Blind Lemon Jefferson, about two miles from the Buffalo Association grounds. On that day, no church service gathered. Bucks was a fiddle player who agreed to go with Hopkins in order to make some money playing music. Bucks followed Hopkins to nearby Buffalo, Texas, where they stopped in front of a small café. They laid their hats down to collect tips and started playing. Soon, a café employee invited them in to sit down and asked if they would play some more. Hopkins and Bucks put their hats on the table, and Bucks sang a song about "River stay away from my door" while Hopkins accompanied him on guitar. Their music "turned the town out," and although they played the same song for half the day, they each ended up with a handful of money. Hopkins and Bucks continued on to the nearby towns of Oakwood and Jewett, playing for tips too, sometimes successfully, other times to no avail. This trip started a pattern Hopkins would continue until he finally moved to Houston permanently several decades later.

Besides working as an itinerant musician in public places, Hopkins would "go around to the white people's houses and play piano for them. He was making ten or fifteen cents or a quarter."[36] As soon as he generated some revenue from his music, Hopkins also started gambling, a hobby that he would enjoy for decades. "That's when he started gamblin' with the grown men all around down what we called Keechow because his mother belonged to Keechow church," Hopkins's neighbor Ray Dawkins remembered.[37] Although playing music was an unstable way to survive, it provided Hopkins with funds for gambling and offered more freedom and flexibility than being tied down to the sharecropping life. Hopkins's first hoboing trip with Jabo Bucks was not enough to make him serious about music as a vocation, though, for he spent many more years farming just to survive.

Hopkins's first cousin (on his mother's side) Alger "Texas" Alexander indelibly impacted Hopkins as well. Alexander was born September 12, 1900, in

Jewett, Texas,[38] in Leon County, about twenty miles from Hopkins's hometown of Centerville, but little is known about his early life. His mother Jenny Brooks was supposedly rowdy. Due to such behavior, Alger and his brother Edell were sent to stay with their grandmother in Richards, Texas, a town so small that it is not even featured on maps from that time period. According to blues scholar Paul Oliver, Alexander worked for a time as a field hand.

Alexander did not play an instrument. He depended on an accompanist to play guitar behind his singing. He carried a guitar around in case he ran into somebody who knew how to play. In 1927, he moved to Dallas, where he worked in a warehouse. He supplemented his income by singing on the streets and in neighborhood bars in the Central Tracks area. Pianist Sam Price heard Alexander performing in this neighborhood. At that point, Price had already arranged for Blind Lemon Jefferson to record. Price was looking for new talent when he saw Alexander. Price said, "Texas Alexander had an uncanny voice but he couldn't keep time. . . . he could sing, he had a good voice but he couldn't sing in tempo."[39]

Price made arrangements to record Alexander, so the former field worker made his first recording in New York City with guitarist Lonnie Johnson on August 11, 1927. Okeh Records released Alexander's first record, which featured "Range in My Kitchen" and "Long Lonesome Day Blues." Due to high sales, Okeh released more sides from the sessions. Alexander's lyrical themes ranged from food ("Cornbread Blues") to prison ("Section Gang Blues") to work ("Farm Hand Blues"). As with Jefferson and many other blues singers, many of Alexander's songs focused on women, including "Evil Women Blues," "Yellow Girl Blues," "No More Woman Blues," and "Someday Baby, Your Troubles Gonna Be Like Mine."

Lonnie Johnson, a New Orleans native, told Oliver that Alexander "was a very difficult singer to accompany; he was liable to jump a bar, or five bars, or anything. You just had to be a fast thinker to play for Texas Alexander. When you had been out there with him you done nine days of work in one! Believe me, brother, he was hard to play for. He would jump—jump keys, anything. You just had to watch him that's all."[40] Hopkins, similarly, would later be known for his irregular, unique playing that did not conform to accompanists' expectations.

Alexander had a sonorous tenor voice that he used to testify about his surroundings. Songs such as "Farm Hand Blues," "Levee Camp Moan Blues," and "Bantam Rooster Blues" embody what folklorist Mack McCormick characterizes as rough blues shouts and field hollers, the purest form of the blues tradition reaching back to slaves and black railway workers.[41]

Hopkins said he first met Texas Alexander when he was singing at a baseball game in Normangee, Texas. The occasion was a game between the home team and one from nearby Leona. Texas Alexander was singing so well, "He almost broke up the ball game, people paid so much attention to him still at the ball game. They [were] interested in him."[42] As in his partnership with Jabo Bucks, Hopkins traveled with Texas Alexander to Crockett, Grapeland, Palestine, Oakwood, Buffalo, Centerville, Normangee, Flynn, and other small East Texas towns. Hopkins wandered around with Alexander off and on for years. Some of the songs Hopkins picked up from Alexander were risqué. Lines like "I got something to tell you baby make the hair rise on your head. I got something to give you darlin' that make the springs tremble on your bed" had meanings that were not immediately evident to Hopkins. "I just been hollerin' it out 'fore anybody . . . didn't know then what he was talking about, but now I know."[43]

Hopkins discussed Texas Alexander with Les Blank in the documentary film *The Blues According to Lightnin' Hopkins*:

He spoke good from his heart so the songs, some of them that I'm singing you understand, some of them old-timey songs is his songs that I was traveling along with him and got the results out of it and got the feeling that I knowed what it mean. And one of the songs is if you ever been on Brazos yeah nineteen-hundred and ten, boy drove ugly men I mean pretty women just like it did ugly men I mean, get me right. And I liked that it's been so long it kinda cuts into from the word I been speaking but I'm gonna speak it just like he speak[s] it. He said he asked the captain, said old captain for the time of day and he looked at me and walked away. That was Texas Alexander. You know all them songs that dwell with me [the songs] 'bout the best you can get. And right now I would like to bring them all back so people [could] understand what I'm talking about.[44]

Little data exist about Hopkins's life after he got thrown out of school in the early 1920s until sometime in the 1940s, when he moved south to Houston. Hopkins did some wandering around the East Texas region. Most of what is known about Hopkins's lean years as a young man before he got his first break in the music business has to be culled from Hopkins's own anecdotes.

THREE

BAD LUCK AND TROUBLE BLUES

You know, I often wonder, what in the
world is going to become of me.
LIGHTNIN' HOPKINS, 1960

FROM THE MID-1920S TO THE MID-1940S, Hopkins traveled and played guitar, trying to avoid working as a farm laborer. Despite his aversion to working as a field hand, sheer economic necessity forced him to spend some of his time toiling in the fields. Honing his musicianship, he supplemented his farm wages by playing dances and parties in the Piney Woods of East Texas. Hopkins discussed these early decades with preeminent blues scholar Paul Oliver:

Did a little plowin'—not too much, chopped a little cotton, pulled a little corn. I did a little of it all—picked a li'l cotton. But not too much. Because I just go from place to place playin' music for those dances. I jest keep going like that, pretty good. I didn't have to do too much cotton pickin'. I be out there most for that Friday night, Saturday night for those dances . . . Murray Farm . . . Maples Farm . . . Bruden's Farm. . . . I'd go from farm to farm every Saturday and every Friday night. They have them dances why, because they be lettin' the boys enjoy themselves, because they worked hard all week making them big crops, and bringin' in them good crops. . . . Be old sets, you know, them ole square dances. All you had to do was rap on your git-tar and they'd pat and holler. Ole sister would shout, "You swing mine an' I'll swing yours!" and all that. . . . Well sometimes they would have the blues played, but most was really dancin' you see. Have fast songs like "Oh, My Babe, Take Me Back," that [was] jumpin' at the time.[1]

Though the pay or prestige Hopkins earned as a local entertainer is not clear, he enjoyed the respite from sharecropping burdens.

Hopkins gave a more detailed description of these country dances to film-maker Les Blank:

> Well they played blues but that was most prompt, this fast old stop time where you'd get out there and dance. You know you see these plugs and how they do it, get to jumping that hillbilly thing, get to stompin'. Well that's the way everybody danced. You know when you get in there playing "Oh my baby take me back," or old stomp time. You'd be two or three out there dancing against one another. There'd be two men dancing against one and other. And the one [that] out dance[d] the other get four bits or a quarter, sometimes a dollar. [There]'d be pretty well off white guys around there with the biggest money you know. . . . they'd call that testing, see who could beat dancing. Buck dancing they'd call it, buck and wing . . . people dance to 'em Saturday night, Sundays they go to church, Monday they'd go to field.[2]

These dances were not mere trivial pursuits but ways to rejuvenate, bond, and regenerate a multiracial community in the pre–civil rights years. They were a hive of action and adrenaline, physicality and pleasure.

Houston club owner Ryan Trimble hired Hopkins regularly when he ran Liberty Hall in Houston during the 1970s. Hopkins told him about playing dances and private parties: "He told me that back then they didn't have night-clubs where they lived. They'd have parties over at people's houses, dance parties. . . . He told me he would have to play all night long. And I said, 'It must have been pretty hard on your fingers.' He said, 'I didn't have a choice. They would beat me up if I didn't play.' I'm sure he probably didn't play all night."[3] Possibly, Hopkins did play all night, because his contemporary, Navasota native Mance Lipscomb, attested he did as well: "Saturday night, I'd play all night 'til 11 a.m. Sunday morning and go right back and play for the white dance Sunday night and go to the field Monday morning."[4] In some form, the entertainment seemed to represent yet another form of heavy work and exploitation—being a house musician and working with sore hands for hours on end.

Tomcat Courtney grew up in Downsville, Texas, about eighty miles from Centerville, and remembers seeing Hopkins play all around East Texas. Courtney's experience picking cotton reflected the migratory lifestyle of farmworkers whom Hopkins entertained and worked alongside. Courtney remembered, "I saw him when I was very young. During that time, late '30s early '40s, most blacks' jobs was picking cotton. We'd do one farm and then go to another, like that. I used to see him play in those little places [on] Friday, Saturday nights. [I would see him play] from Waco, Texas, all the way down to Beaumont. Like you gather this crop here well then people would come and get you take you to another crop. He used to come to this place . . . out from Waco little towns near there [like] Waxahachie, we used to pick cotton there. All those places around Waco, not far from Dallas some of them . . . I used to see him play there then."[5]

Hopkins explored the whole territory of Central and East Texas, migrating toward gigs and work, letting the cotton trail lead him to audiences that were hungry for recreation after days of heat and toil.

In addition to singing and playing guitar, Hopkins was a skilled dancer whose talents even earned him a job with the circus: "Well I sure did, I used to dance with Ringling Brothers show, I used to dance pretty good and can do it now. I don't be jiving with you. You be thinking I'm lying. One day just get out there on the concrete with me, some taps on my shoes; I'll show you and give me some music. Old-time style show and my brother [John Henry] he used to be the leader of Waxahachie. He dead now. John Henry used to be the leader of Waxahachie."[6] If Hopkins's account of his stint in the circus is accurate, it parallels the experiences of other Texas bluesmen like Tomcat Courtney, who sang and tap-danced as a teenager with the Ringling Brothers Circus.

Hopkins continued to live near his birthplace of Centerville during the late 1920s and 1930s, marrying Elamer Lacy on September 22, 1928. He was eighteen years old, and she was seventeen years old. The marriage license, written in longhand, appears to spell her name Elamer; however, the birth certificate of their first child, Anna Mae, born on August 29, 1929, features her name spelled as Almer. At the time, Hopkins farmed and Elamer tended to their home in Middleton, Texas, about ten miles south of Centerville.

Despite his new status as a father, Hopkins continued to roam the country. Mississippi bluesman Skip James, known for his performances of "Devil Got My Woman," "I'm So Glad," and "22-20 Blues," met Hopkins when he spent a week in Jackson, Mississippi, in 1930. James claimed to have shown Hopkins some guitar tips, but Stephen Calt, James's biographer, said Hopkins only admitted to gambling with the fellow bluesman. James approved of Hopkins's lively personality, saying, "Lightning's kinda like myself . . . on the pimpy side." At one point, James lived with a prostitute and on other occasions had predatory relationships with women of ill repute.[7] Apparently, the bluesmen had more in common than just guitar playing.

On June 5, 1934, Hopkins's wife gave birth to Maxine. By this time, the Hopkins family was living on rural route number 2 near Crockett, Texas. The birth certificate lists the mother's name as Diamond, rather than Elamer, Lacy. Hopkins still farmed, and Elamer "Diamond" Lacy still occupied herself with domestic duties. When Lacy gave birth to her first child, she listed her age as eighteen, yet four years and nine months later she gave her age as nineteen.[8]

In addition, the State of Texas changed the certificate of birth form. In 1929, the form had a box for "color," and Elamer [Almer] and Hopkins were listed as "colored." In 1934, the form had been changed to read "color or race." Hopkins and his wife were listed as "negro."

Hopkins and Lacy split up, perhaps after Hopkins started venturing down to Houston with Texas Alexander and his childhood friend Billy Bizor. Hopkins told record producer Sam Charters about his first trip to Houston when they were recording the *My Life in the Blues* interview album in 1964:

First come into Houston, let me see it was around in the '30s. I don't know about '34 or something like that, but I didn't stay. Just went to Houston cuz I heard the name of Houston. You know what a town it was. Big cities I hadn't been used to. I'd been used to three or four little stores, and cars in Centerville, and Leona, and Madisonville. Places like that, little old places. Midway, about two stores there. All of my towns was small at that time. Hadn't [played] no big towns until I did go to Houston. I run up on a big place, see. So I gets there so there was a man over there carried us over to a broadcast station. Me and Texas Alexander and Billy Bizor. Billy was young, I was young and Texas was, he was a man you know. So you know we goes in there and we did 'em up that day. Come back and see what we could do. Cuz we was just broadcasting [on the] station, we wasn't cutting a record. People wanted it to happen. So we left, couldn't hang around no more. We left and went on back to Crockett. . . . Something happened, we wound up splitting up. We didn't go back to Houston for that engagement.[9]

Hopkins was silent as to the reason why he did not stay in Houston to continue the radio gig.

In 1934, Hopkins worked dances with Nathaniel "Bill" Barnes on the Murray farm in Leon County. Barnes was born in Mississippi in 1910 but moved with his family to Texas in 1911. When boll weevils ruined crops in Mississippi, George Murray moved about six hundred people, including the Barnes family, from Mississippi to Texas. Murray's farm was called Low Bottom and the Mississippi Hill because most of the people living there migrated from the nearby state.

Barnes's father taught him to play music when he was ten years old. He went on to play guitar in the Holiness Church, which was also known as the Church of God in Christ, located just off the Murray farm in Vistoula, Texas. Barnes stayed on Murray farm from 1911 to 1927. He then made a series of moves to various farms his father bought. By 1934, a drought wiped out his father's farm and mules. Barnes moved back to the Murray farm to work alongside his father, who had been hired as the boss. In 1939, Barnes headed to Houston, where he would eventually work with Hopkins again. In an interview with Louis Marchiafava, Barnes declared, "On the Murray Farm on the Low Bottom back in '34 we'd play for dances. Every third night they'd have dances and me and Lightnin' and Coon Spiller were the guitar players."[10] Barnes had a relationship with Hopkins from 1933 until 1942 or '43. In the interviews that Hopkins gave over the years of his professional career, he never mentioned Barnes or Spiller, so their guitar playing and singing likely had little, if any, effect on Hopkins.

Though Hopkins was likely not influenced by those cohorts, his performances at local country dances did, however, inspire others. Tomcat Courtney noted,

I was kind of a little interested in playing. I could dance. When I saw Lightnin', it inspired me more. He inspired me more than I think anybody. He was good, and he had a little gimmick. He could play those old boogie songs. . . . He'd have people dancing. He'd play a good slow blues. He made up a lot of songs right in them places. He used to do a song ["Cook My Breakfast"]. He'd used to do that when I was a kid. He'd say, "Baby I got this song here" [sings some lyrics]. He'd have some little gimmick with it. He was mostly teasing the women. He'd do it every time I'd see him. He'd use it a little different. . . . He was the best playing off the crowd. That's what inspired me so . . . if a crowd wanted to listen, he'd play the slow stuff. If they wanted to dance, he'd hop it up. He traveled around a lot, and he was younger than the other people that were playing.[11]

Hopkins's prolonged absences from home, and his first taste of urban life, may have contributed to marital strife. Why or when Hopkins's marriage dissolved is a mystery, but one clue may be present in his song "When My First Wife Quit Me":

When my first wife quit me,
You know she put me out on the road
. . . You know I didn't have nar a nickel,
You know I didn't have no place to go.[12]

Music provided a release from the monotony of his life, epitomized by the struggle to survive and the rugged, rural, and menial lifestyle of his family. Perhaps his first wife had little patience for those conditions.

Economic despair and ruin were almost always just a failed crop away. In the 1930s, Hopkins's mother, Frances, a sharecropper in Leon County, ran headlong into some financial difficulties. She almost lost two horses used for transportation and working the fields. Ike Dawkins owned a farm on nearby Nubbin Ridge and knew Frances and the Hopkins family. Dawkins did not want to see Frances lose those all-important horses, so he paid off the note and let Frances and Hopkins move onto his farm.

During such financial distress, people commonly pledged personal assets as security for loans. The loans were called chattel mortgages. Trinity County chattel mortgage records still survive. Trinity County adjoins Houston County on its south and southeast borders. Most of the loans listed in the Trinity County chattel mortgage records were taken out in the spring and summer and came due when the crops were harvested. For example, on July 11, 1911, C. H. Driskell borrowed $30 and pledged his "Entire crop grown by or under me, during year, 1911, except ⅓ rent to L. L. Friday." Driskell's loan was due on October 1, 1911.[13] Jim Boney's loan illustrated the value of horses. Boney borrowed $29.35 against "one mare." He signed the note on April 1, 1911, and promised to pay it back by October 15, 1911.[14] Hopkins's mother, Frances, probably took out a similar chattel mortgage by using her horses as collateral, but such records from Leon County chattel mortgages do not survive.

Tenant farmers also signed legal documents whereby they agreed to give a certain amount of the crops they raised in exchange for being able to farm the owner's land. For example, R. R. Thames and William McNally were tenant farmers on eighty acres of Virginia Collins's land in Houston County in 1932. They signed an "Acknowledgement of tenancy" document that declared, "We hereby agree to pay Mrs. Virginia Collins, as rent for said place, during the year of 1932 one-third of the corn and one-fourth of the cotton and cotton seed to be grown on said place during said year, 1932."[15] American farmers in the South were firmly bound to a system akin to feudalism, even as the twentieth century entered the New Deal period.

As Ike Dawkins's son, Ray, attested, Hopkins was around seventeen or eighteen years old when he first moved with his mother to Ike Dawkins's farm. "That's when I was a little boy then. That's when Lightnin' would be playing, he'd be playing late in the evening and I'd sit and listen to him play."[16] Dawkins's oral history provides rare corroborating evidence regarding Hopkins's life during that time.

After leaving the Dawkins farm, Hopkins and his mother moved to Guy's Store, another geographic speck in East Texas, where they resided on Herb Mannie's farm. Frances Hopkins lived in one house, and Hopkins and Ida Mae, a woman Hopkins had taken up with, lived in another. Scant information survives about Ida Mae, the woman Hopkins called his wife. They met near Grapeland, where, according to Ray Dawkins, Hopkins lived for a while doing farmwork and playing music.[17] If Dawkins's memory is reliable, this would have been around 1930, when Hopkins lived on Dawkins's father's farm. Although Hopkins called Ida Mae his wife, no record has proved they were legally married.[18] Nor do any prove Hopkins divorced his wife Elamer. Hopkins's music, though, could provide clues and shed some light on the relationship. For instance, in 1948, Hopkins waxed romantically about her in the song "Ida Mae."

> If you ever go down in Galveston
> Try to find that little girl they call Ida Mae . . .
> You know she ain't so good looking
> But I want you to know she sure look good to me.[19]

Hopkins's life during the late 1920s and the 1930s ranged from picking cotton in Waxahachie, Texas, to playing for six dollars a night in the market of Coolidge, Texas. Like most subsistence farmers, Hopkins led an arduous and draining physical life. "They was hard times, you can believe that. I was working trying to take care of my wife, me and my mother, six bits a day and that was top price. I'd come in in the evening it look like I'd be so weak that my knees be clucking like a wagon wheel. I'd go to bed and I'd say, 'Well baby I just can't continue like this.' Look like no sooner than I go to bed then I was ready to go catch that mule and that wasn't no bull corn."[20] The privation was deep, the work long, and the weariness worn like a second skin.

Working on a large farm in East Texas meant dealing with plantation owners holding old-fashioned views harking back to a pre-Civil-War-era racial status quo. For example, the treatment that some African Americans received on Tom Moore's plantation in Grimes County, a prison farm before Moore purchased it, was so harsh that Mance Lipscomb penned a song about it—"Tom Moore's Farm"—recorded in 1960. Prior to Lipscomb's recording, though, Hopkins changed Tom's name to Tim and recorded the song in Houston in 1948 for Gold Star Records:

> You know it ain't but the one thing this black man done was wrong. . . .
> Yes, you know I moved my wife and family down on Mr. Tim Moore's farm.

> Yeah, you know Mr. Tim Moore's a man, he don't never stand and grin
> He just said, "Keep out of the graveyard, I'll save you from the pen."[21]

The Moore brothers operated their twenty thousand acres with an iron hand. Mance Lipscomb's biographer Glen Alyn later wrote that the farm was a symbol of "all that kept African Americans in their place."[22] It was a concrete manifestation of lingering racism and inequality.

Knowledge about the Moore family's power in Grimes County was passed down through generations of African Americans. Ola Mae Kennedy was raised on her grandfather's farm in the 1930s and 1940s about forty miles from the Moore plantation: "If any of his people be living on the farm do something, if they could make it to the gate . . . the police couldn't come in there." Kennedy's parents lived on their own land but worked on the Moore farm. "Tom Moore would send a truck by to pick them up, take them over there to pick the cotton. In the evenin' time they'd take them back and drop them at the house."[23]

Mance Lipscomb also testified to Tom Moore's power over the police. "Well see, there's two of them go round. Mista Henry and Mista Jackson: that old fellow purdy tough too. He's the one that got in that mess with the police. Tuck the police's pistol, and the police shot hisself and kinda claimed *he* shot im. But Mista Mow an them got im out of it."[24] Moore might have stood up for his African American workers in some circumstances, but Moore would not endure criticism from such a worker.

One incident illustrates Moore's thin skin. According to Arhoolie Record Company founder Chris Strachwitz, after the Houston-based label Gold Star Records released Hopkins's song "Tim Moore's Farm," Tom Moore showed up at a dance in Conroe, a town just north of Houston and about forty-two miles east of Grimes County, where the Moore's farm was located. According to Strachwitz, Moore told Hopkins never to sing that song around there again.[25] In an interview with Mack McCormick, Hopkins confirmed this: Moore and his brothers gave him trouble when he first recorded the song.[26] Mance Lipscomb had an even more vivid anecdote about the owner and the farmer-cum-bluesman. Lipscomb recalled Moore saying, "Lightnin' Hopkins, from Houston. If I see that bastard, I'll kill him."[27]

Hopkins escaped the sharecropping life intermittently by playing music, but two decades slipped by before his career in the entertainment field really began to gestate. He could equate the life of a professional musician with material reward because he saw Texas Alexander riding around in a fancy automobile: "First Cadillac that I was known to be, one of them expensive cars you know, he went somewhere and he showed up in Normangee and that was the longest and most ugly car. Long Cadillac—one of those the first made you know. But it was new and everybody admired him you know. Cuz colored people they didn't even have T-Model Fords then. He come in a Cadillac. Texas was doing all right for hisself."[28] Hopkins must have understood that such glamour was not the result of toiling in the field, but of Alexander carving himself a niche as a songster riding the pulse of music trends.

While Texas Alexander was enjoying success, Hopkins ended up in legal trouble. Picking cotton in the Texas heat was a weary way to survive. Plus, the strain of living under the Jim Crow system of oppression in America contributed to Hopkins's frustration, pent-up anger, and inevitable hostility. His immaturity and defensiveness led him afoul of the law. "Then I tried to be a little bit rough too, you know? Mess with me a little bit; I'd start me a little fight in a minute. So they was throwing me on the rope and puttin' me in the joint and going on. I had to calm down. Wearing that ball and chain ain't no good."[29]

On one occasion, according to Hopkins, he got into a scrape in Grapeland. The result was common for the era: authorities sentenced him to serve time on the county road gang. In an interview with Paul Oliver, Hopkins attributed some of such legal trouble to his age:

> I had lots of trouble when I was, you know, young. Kinda mean. Kinda hard to get along with. Some things—some places I'd be where we had a few fights. One of them caused me to go on the road . . . ole boys say to the country road—bridge gang. I worked there for about a coupla hundred days. Working out on the road gang—it ain't no easy thing, I tell you. Every evenin' when you come in they would chain you, they'd lock you with a chain around your leg. And they had a tent made with a row of bunks on each side. So you had a bunk of your own and they'd lock you to a post . . . the next one to that post; all the way down, till they lock all o' ya up. So therefore you'd be locked up that night, and next mawnin' when you get ready to go to breakfast, man come to unlock you. You go out, eat breakfast, catch the mules, hitch the wagon, git right down to the work. Two hundred days. . . . What helped me some while I was there my wife come down there and she helped me for a while. She was cookin' for fifty cents a day. So I was workin' for fifty cents a day. . . . Late one day the boss man decided—judge at least—he decided . . . I could go, and told them to free me that day . . . ain't been back ever since.[30]

Hopkins also spoke about his criminal record with folklorist Mack McCormick, who recorded, managed, and interviewed Hopkins in the late 1950s and early '60s: "Had to cut an old boy and they give me time on the county farm. It wasn't the penitentiary but it was second to the bottom." In the liner notes to Hopkins's 1959 record *Country Blues*, McCormick explained, "The Texas penal farms dotting the Trinity and Brazos river bottoms are commonly known as 'the bottom.'" Hopkins said, "It was old Judge McClain—he's dead and gone I suppose—give me that time. Then he came and made them turn me loose, saying, 'That old boy didn't do nothing so much.' . . . Back in '37 or so. The judge comes and says turn me loose after I sung him a song about 'How bad and how sad to be a fool.'"[31]

Hopkins told a slightly different version of the captivity narrative in an interview with Andy Silberman of the Swarthmore College *Phoenix* in 1963: "I was in trouble. I had a hundred days down on the chain gang. But I was singing and most of the people just loved me. They would come around on Sunday and sit around like you all are here, and hear me play guitar. Of course I got lucky one day. The jailer came by and said 'Lightnin' Hopkins, I'm going to unlock this lock off your leg and let you go free. Will you be a good boy?' I said, 'Yes, I'll be a good boy. I sure will.' And that's what he did, and I have been free ever since and I just keep playing, everywhere."[32]

Several years after being interviewed by Swarthmore's paper, and while being taped in a studio while recording an album for the International Artists label in Houston in 1968, Hopkins also discussed running away from the chain gang, explaining, "I did some damage in Grapeland, Texas. One New Year's night about four people got on me and I managed to get my blade. . . . I had that guitar in front of me and every time they'd throw a bottle . . . well I did see, cut my nose hereabouts, see? . . . I tell you what, there were three brothers, a daddy and a sister on me, I ain't gonna lie. They was tough, I didn't think I was tough. I got a soda water crate and knocked two down in one. Then I knew I was going on there. Man I walked the board. Man come to me, put me in jail in Crockett. I did pretty good and I runned off, I hit the road jack. They come to the Trinity, got me out of the Trinity [River]. I wore a ball and chain. Man I can show you a scar on my leg. You see that there? That's from wearing that man's outfit." Hopkins also told folklorist Mack McCormick he ran from the Houston County chain gang, was later arrested in Leon County, and then returned to the chain gang to finish his stretch.[33]

No such records of his conviction exist at the Houston County courthouse in Crockett, Texas, whose books are intact back to the late 1880s. Therefore, Hopkins was likely not arrested and sentenced to the chain gang. Hopkins's story, however, does contain some elements of truth. Judge McLean [not McClain as McCormick's liner notes spelled it] did serve Houston County, appearing in court records starting in 1931, which matches the story Hopkins told McCormick. Hopkins also mentioned Arch Baker as sheriff. Indeed, an "Archie L. Maples" was elected sheriff on November 6, 1934, serving through January 1,

1939. Then E. H. Baker served as sheriff from November 8, 1938, until January 1, 1943. Hopkins's memory appears incorrect: he combines their two names.[34] A chain gang, meant for prisoners who could not pay their fines, did work stretches of Houston County. Constructing roads and bridges, they labored to pay off a dollar a day from their fines. When the county commissioners discontinued the chain gang in December 1937, the labor unit had existed for four years.

Hopkins's version of events is eerily similar to a well-known incident in Huddie "Leadbelly" Ledbetter's life. The court sentenced Leadbelly to a total of seven to thirty years after he was convicted in two separate trials for assault to murder and the murder of Will Stafford in Bowie County, Texas, in 1917. By 1920, authorities locked up Leadbelly in the Central State Prison farm in Fort Bend County, about twenty miles west of Houston. The prison, better known as Sugarland, was immortalized in the song "The Midnight Special," which Leadbelly recorded in 1934, after borrowing components from other popular prison ballads. In 1969, Creedence Clearwater Revival repopularized the tune, imbuing it with their rootsy pop style. The Canadian punk band D.O.A., in turn, reimagined it again in 1990 and shot a video for the song at a prison. Undoubtedly, the song embodies symbolism and sentiments that easily transcend eras.

When Leadbelly was locked up in Sugarland, the prison overseers quickly realized that giving Leadbelly the opportunity to showcase his musical talents was a good way to alleviate the monotony of the dreary workdays. Leadbelly's skills earned him extra privileges. The prison even allowed him to travel alone to different prison camps on Sundays. When Texas governor Pat N. Neff and his wife toured the state's prison camps in 1924, they saw Leadbelly perform. Neff requested some hillbilly songs, and Leadbelly played them. Next, Leadbelly improvised a song on the spot that pleaded for his release. The governor told Leadbelly that he would free him after a while, but he wanted to keep him locked up for now, so he could hear him play. Neff came back to the prison several times and watched Leadbelly perform. On January 16, 1925, Neff pardoned Leadbelly, one of just five pardons that he gave out in his final acts in office.

Due to a lack of evidence, Hopkins's different accounts about his early release from the county chain gang likely amount to mere tall tales. Furthermore, his interviews with historian Paul Oliver and Andy Silberman, the Swarthmore College reporter, were roughly three years apart, which may account for his offering disparate details: Hopkins told Oliver his sentence was two hundred days, but he informed Silberman his sentence was only a hundred. In the Oliver version, the judge freed Hopkins, but Hopkins told Silberman that the jailer made the decision to free him. The story is unstable and unverifiable.

Leadbelly sang his way out of prison and the chain gang. This story lured Hopkins, so he probably adopted it. McCormick, the folklorist, averred,

They say Texas Alexander did the same. . . . the story is told about most singers with any reputation at all. . . . These stories are probably true in most cases, for it is a time honored Texas tradition to release Negro prisoners who make an eloquent plea. . . . bear in mind that the concept of southern penology is not to punish the individual but to maintain a threat to an entire race [and to provide free labor]. Under this system it is easy for a Negro to be sent to prison and by the same token it is relatively easy for the individual to gain his release. One of the best ways is to make up a song pleading for release or justifying the crime, which is presented to a sympathetic judge or warden or governor. This is a privilege which is reserved for poor people since those with any money were required to purchase their pardons. Those in authority enjoy the sense of power they demonstrate by releasing a man or dropping charges merely on the strength of a song.[35]

Hopkins seems to have injected himself into such penal policy and lore.

Other details of Hopkins's time on the chain gang also conflict. In one of his concerts preserved on video, prior to playing "How Long Have It Been Since You Been Home" he tells the audience, "My daddy died when I was three." A few sentences later, he adds, "I got in prison once you see, and my mama called me and I answered, 'Ma'am.' She said, 'Son are you tired of working?' I said, 'Yes, I am.' Daddy called and I answered, 'Sir.' He said, 'Son, you tired of working?' He said, 'What the hell you going to stay there for?' See I couldn't just run away from the penitentiary."[36] As Hopkins notes, his father died when he was three, thus could not telephone later. Furthermore, prisoners rarely received phone calls while incarcerated in a Texas county jail in the late 1930s.

Hopkins routinely embellished his life experiences when discussing them. In his heart, he exuded an entertainer's gift for banter and anecdote, poetic license and stretching the truth. This story might have been meant as a form of loose, impromptu counseling, or even suggestion. Audience members should listen to their parents, he implies. He then sings "How Long Have It Been Since You Been Home."

How long have it been, since you've been home?
. . . Poor mama, still rocking by the window, since you've been gone[37]

This anecdote offers a glimpse into Hopkins's tender personality. In the 1960s, at the height of his worldwide acclaim, Hopkins's public and neighborhood image was that of a hipster character. He always wore dark shades and dressed extremely sharp, even when hanging out in his neighborhood. He wore jewelry and chain-smoked cigarettes. He was the image of a cool urban bluesman, driving around in a regal car with a pint of alcohol always within reach. Yet, for all the flashy accoutrements of a successful big-city bluesman, at heart, he was a born and bred country boy. When Hopkins sat in a television studio playing to a young white crowd, he was not afraid to reveal his inner core and character: he was a son who loved his mother and respected his father.

According to Hopkins, he was freed from the chain gang around 1938, though he actually probably lived as a farm laborer and itinerant musician. The Great Depression was in full swing, severely debilitating and destabilizing the economic climate. Hopkins traveled to Clarksdale, Mississippi, which is located in the Mississippi Delta. The region is famously interwoven with the blues. W. C. Handy, often called the father of the blues, moved to Clarksdale in 1903 to direct the Knights of Pythias Band. In 1912, he published the song "Memphis Blues," making him the third person in a few months to publish a song with the word "blues" in the title.[38]

Dockery Plantation is situated between Ruleville and Cleveland, Mississippi, and is about fifty miles from Clarksdale. Seminal blues pioneer Charley Patton lived on the plantation from his early teens until he was thirty-four. Later he moved near Clarksdale on Highway 61 and started recording at the age of forty. Some of Patton's most cherished songs include "Screaming and Hollerin' the Blues," "High Water Everywhere," and "Shake It and Break It," which inspired and catalyzed the likes of Howlin' Wolf.

Clarksdale is considered the epicenter of the delta blues, due to such icons. Yet Hopkins told McCormick he did not meet any such blues singers during his time in Clarksdale. "I was playing guitar over there. It was a nice spot. It wasn't long. 'Bout a month. My wife was over there—I was in a little trouble when she went over there. So after I got out of my trouble, I goes on over there. And I stays there awhile till they complete what they were doing. They was picking up cons. I'd had a little fight in Grapeland, Texas. I was kinda bound down at that time."[39]

Hopkins's reference to "picking up cons" back in Texas likely referred to lawmen's practice of arresting African American men around harvest time so that they could lease them out to plantation owners for crop harvesting. The convict lease system was outlawed by the Texas legislature in 1912. That system served to generate revenues for towns and to provide a cheap labor source for farm and plantation owners. Though the practice was illegal and outdated, Hopkins's statement insinuates the practice still existed in places like Houston County, where he felt threatened, despite having served his sentence and not committing any further crimes.

An uncredited front-page article in the September 16, 1937, edition of the *Grapeland Messenger* proves that Hopkins's concerns were valid:

> Constable G. W. Dickerson said Wednesday he intended to round up loafers who refuse to accept jobs as cotton pickers or otherwise. "The loafers had just well go to work because farmers are crying for hands," said Dickerson. He said Negroes and whites who refuse jobs alike would be taken to jail as vagrants. "There are a lot of them who hang around town just doing nothing," said the constable, "when they might as well be at work."

A significant amount of cotton existed in Houston County; for example, in 1935, over twenty thousand bales were ginned by mid-December. The threat of forced farm labor could have spurred Hopkins to leave. Plus, Texas farm wages suffered severely in the Depression. In 1929, Texas farmers paid laborers $1.29 a day without board. By 1935, this had dropped to $1.20. Cotton pickers in Texas earned $1.11 per hundred pounds in 1929, but only 60 cents in 1934 and 1935. These stark figures illuminate the strain of the massive recession and the lean economic conditions that propelled Hopkins toward the Delta.

Hopkins's traveling helped keep him far from law enforcement's illicit labor schemes in his East Texas stomping grounds. In an interview published in *Jazz Journal* in 1960, McCormick asked Hopkins if he traveled anywhere in the South besides the East Texas region. Hopkins replied, "Oh I did quite a bit. I went to Arizona, California. Practically near about everywhere. Mississippi. Tennessee. Louisiana. All around." Several decades later Hopkins wrote the song "Selling Wine" about his experiences in Arizona:

> This time I went to Arizona
> Pick that cotton
> Thought I could
> But I couldn't do no good.[40]

Wherever Hopkins traveled, cotton stood in tufts, reflecting his roots, his servitude to the land, and his ultimate dissatisfaction.

Arthur "Big Boy" Spires remembers seeing Hopkins in Yazoo City, Mississippi, about 110 miles north of Clarksdale. Spires was a lesser-known bluesman who only recorded four sides. Born in Yazoo City in 1912, Spires did not learn to play guitar until the 1930s. He told blues researcher Pete Welding, "About 1939 or '40 Lightnin' Hopkins began coming into Yazoo City to play for house parties and at the Beer Garden that Mr. Crowder operated there. That was about the only place there you could go then. Well, I was good enough then to second behind Lightnin'. He used to come through there fairly regularly."[41]

Hopkins roamed as far to the east as Georgia, according to Edward Lee "Buddy" Durham, who was living around Ashburn and traveling from town to town, playing guitar. In an interview with Kip Lornell, Durham recalled how he met Hopkins, "It was about 1937 or '38, I can't remember exactly. It was after the storm came through in '36. He came in sometime around cotton picking time; last of June, first of July. He stayed around there until the fall. He played for the people around their houses and for frolics and things. He was good. . . . I learned two or three songs from him. You know, he weren't making no records then. Somehow he got hooked up with my auntie [Sarah McCray], and they stayed together." According to Durham, Hopkins and his Aunt Sarah moved to Chicago and stayed there for a while when he visited them for a few weeks.[42]

By the late 1930s, Hopkins ventured to the Houston area at least once, where Mance Lipscomb encountered him: "I first met Lightnin' in nineteen thirty-eight, I believe. In Galveston."[43] Lipscomb recognized Hopkins's talents, stating, "No one in the world ever played none of Lightnin' Hopkins's songs. Never will play it. . . . Cause he's got his own way of playin' it. He picks up his own style. And he knows his own time."[44] In another account, Lipscomb added, "He's a good songster and what he play, I like it. . . . I know Lightnin', you gonna know him from his music when it start. Just like here [plays a Lightnin' lick], every song he play is in that tune. But he can really sing and he make up songs. And he made lots of money off his singing. But he don't play in any chord but E and A."[45] "That rascal can sang. . . . He can play them songs and mix them up so bad you'll thank he playin' five thousand songs. But you know how many songs he singing? Don't y'all tell im cause I might see im an he'd kill me. He's sangin' two songs! Cause words don't mean music: music gotta be changed by different codes."[46]

As Hopkins recalled the era,

So I goes back again in round about '38 or '39. And I [was] stuck around there for a while . . . playing up and down around Dowling Street there. After that I began to get around and I began to ride the buses for free. The bus driver'd stop and pick me up anywhere he'd see me with that guitar.

And I had a big time see on that bus, I'd pick up quarters, halves, and dollars, he'd even share me a couple of dollars. And one thing that bus driver did, and God in heaven knows I'm not lying. He knowed that I drink, he'd stop at the liquor store at the corner of Dowling and Leeland at his own . . . risk. Sent me in that liquor store and got me a half a pint of liquor. And that's true, waited 'til I got back and he takes on off . . . every day I'd catch that same man. And that's the way I'd ride them buses and didn't pay nar a dime. . . . one night I looked for us all to get arrested, they had a dance on the bus, I got to playing and they had one of those little schoolgirls. They all got up and went to swinging on the bus. Bus driver driving slow and he's just having as much fun as anybody. Didn't anything happen.[47]

Post-emancipation African American history in Houston centered on the Freedmen's Town section of the Fourth Ward. In 1860, slaves made up 22 percent of Houston's population. In 1865, when the slaves were freed in Texas, many freedmen in the Houston area started moving to Freedmen's Town, which stretched out along the southwest area of downtown. Buffalo Bayou ran along Freedmen's Town's northern border, and San Felipe Street formed an east-west corridor from downtown to the farms on the city's outskirts. Immediately following emancipation, the Fourth Ward was Houston's only black settlement.[48]

The Fourth Ward epitomized the economic and cultural life of black Houston in the late nineteenth and early twentieth centuries. One section of the Fourth Ward earned a titillating nickname—Houston's Harlem. The January 27, 1940, edition of the *Houston Informer*, a black newspaper, carried a story about the upcoming performance of African American bandleader Jimmie Lunceford and his orchestra at the Pilgrim Temple at 222 West Dallas Street [formerly known as San Felipe Street] in the Fourth Ward. Lunceford's band, featuring players such as Sy Oliver, Willy Smith, and Trummy Young, waxed hits like "Organ Grinder Swing," "It Ain't What You Do (It's the Way That You Do It)," and "Lunceford Special." The neighborhood that freed slaves settled right after emancipation had become an epicenter of African American culture.

Starting as early as the 1920s, though, the Third Ward began to displace the Fourth Ward as the center of black culture; in turn, black property ownership in the Fourth Ward began to decline. The Great Depression contributed to this erosion as well. By 1938, gentrification began to destroy the Fourth Ward's history, heritage, and culture. For example, the city built the one-thousand-unit San Felipe Courts housing project on land in Freedmen's Town just south of Buffalo Bayou that had been home to some of the oldest Fourth Ward churches and schools. When Hopkins rode the bus back and forth between the Third and Fourth Wards, he traversed a ward in the early stages of decline to burgeoning West Dallas Street neighborhoods, the new entertainment district.

By 1940, Hopkins returned to East Texas. On January 24, he applied for a social security account number and listed his occupation as "unemployed." At twenty-seven, he had two children, ages six and eleven, and was still married to Elamer Lacy. He listed Elamer, spelled Elina, as wife on the social security application. Later, when Hopkins became internationally famous, he always said he was from Centerville, but on that day he listed his birthplace as Leona, which is seven miles south of Centerville. Both are in Leon County. During the years of World War II, Hopkins probably spent most of his time around the small towns of Grapeland, Leona, and Crockett, and in the nearby vicinity.

When Tomcat Courtney saw Hopkins perform during this time period, he remembered how farm laborers were ready to relax with some live entertainment after a hard week working

from Monday to Friday . . . they'd always have Friday night and Saturday night off. Every Friday evening they'd settle up [pay] with everybody. They'd be ready to party. . . . People would make that homemade beer and wine. . . . You was a hundred miles from the law. The man that ran the plantation didn't want the law there no way unless he called them. He didn't care what they did as long as they weren't killing nobody out there and was able to go back to work Monday. So the people that run the places hired him [Lightnin']. They'd give him a little money and tips too. Plenty to eat, fried chicken, plate of pork. . . . At harvest time on Friday and Saturday everyone had two or three dollars to spend. Everyone would donate, wouldn't be a lot cuz there'd be a hundred people around there. He had a little old guitar with a pick up on it. He still had the same guitar but he had a pickup on it. He had an amp. . . . He had this piano player and they was singing through it and playing through it. Before he made a record. Just a little before. . . . When they got someone like Lightnin' people [got] real enthused as to what he was doing. He was real good.[49]

While millions of Americans were going off to fight Hitler in the "good war," Hopkins played these boisterous plantation weekends and avoided military service due to a stabbing he suffered. Apparently, his injuries prompted the armed forces to reject him. The fight itself was precipitated by his love for gambling: Hopkins won money in a craps game, and one of the losing players wanted his money back. After Hopkins bought the other gamblers a fifth of whiskey with his winnings, he headed out the door, where one of the losers was waiting for him. Although the police found the perpetrator, he beat the case because Hopkins refused to file charges. Not one to get the law involved in settling his scores, Hopkins had other plans. He said, "I was gonna get him but I think someone else got to him before I did. I didn't want the police to do nothing to him."[50]

After some prodding from a relative, Hopkins finally transitioned from tenant farmer to a city dweller, following the larger economic trend—the Texas African American tenant class shrank from more than fifty thousand in 1935 to fewer than twenty-four thousand in 1945.[51] Hopkins's relocation from rural Leon County to Houston reflected a larger migratory pattern. From the beginning of World War I through the end of World War II, an estimated forty-four thousand African Americans migrated to Houston from small towns in Texas and Louisiana. According to historian Bernadette Pruitt, the promise of a brighter economic future in Houston attracted black migrants as the rural racism and poverty pushed them to the city.[52]

F O U R

THE WAR IS OVER

*I never was born with a dime, nothing. But I got to hustling
and learned how to knock up on a little change.*

LIGHTNIN' HOPKINS

ON SEPTEMBER 2, 1945, Japan surrendered unconditionally to the United States. That act ended a war that cost 405,399 American lives. Over one million African Americans served in the armed forces in World War II, yet when black veterans returned to the United States, they faced an oppressive Jim Crow system limiting them to inferior schools, neighborhoods, and jobs. In nearly every facet of their lives, they were treated as second-class citizens, despite so many risking their lives for the country.

Although not a military man, Lightnin' Hopkins faced this racial climate every day when frequenting Houston's Third Ward. Its segregated confines provided no exception to the national racial status quo. For example, in August 1946, shortly before Hopkins got his big break, an entire area of Dowling Street was placed under martial law. Two white policemen were driving down Dowling just after midnight and claimed they witnessed a "free-for-all" at a business called Jack's Cleaners. One of the officers, Thomas Hambey, rushed into the building. When he heard shots outside, Hambey "fought his way through the crowd" out to the sidewalk and discovered his partner dead and the "body of a Negro man [lying] across him." Shortly thereafter, Officer Hambey claimed, "Six or eight Negro men and women grabbed at me and began to tussle with me. They took my pistol and flashlight away and beat me. Then they got down and stomped me."[1] White police officers were much-disliked symbols of official racist oppression in the South. The suspicious death of an African American in the presence of such officers was a spark, enraging an already unruly group of people.

The slaying of the police officer apparently led the Houston police department to send out an all-points alarm because fifty to sixty law enforcement personnel from various agencies quickly showed up, "seizing 19 suspects, all Negroes, and holding them in Café Zanzibar, next door to the cleaning establishment for questioning, while more than 300 Negroes milled around outside."[2] The Dowling Street entertainment district, teeming with illicit activities, provided Hopkins plenty of venues in which to ply his trade and indulge in gambling. However, in addition to opportunities for women, alcohol, and gambling, the possibility of violence also lurked, as the Jack's Cleaners incident demonstrated.

Still, most of the Third Ward was a warm, tight-knit community, according to Horace Tapscott, the legendary avant-garde pianist, trombonist, and composer. Tapscott, born at the segregated Jefferson Davis Hospital in the Fourth Ward in 1934, grew up in the Third Ward. He had fond memories of his youth there:

Everyone was family. . . . There were no locked doors. It was the kind of neighborhood where everybody knew each other. . . . in those days, people were always in the street socializing, and there wasn't any crime to speak of. We were raised in such a way that there wasn't everyday crime against people—knocking them down, snatching purses, those kinds of things. . . . If you did something wrong in the community, like hurt some kid, the community would beat you up. Everyone took care of everyone else's children. . . . the emphasis was on trying to maintain a certain quality to our race, where you gain some respect as a whole people. . . . every once in a while there'd be fights over women. Cats would cut each other, but those kinds of things just involved a few people personally. . . . what crime there was had to do with gambling, rum-running, things like that, those kinds of crimes that brought in the white police. The worst that would happen in segregated Houston was the racist attacks, the black male getting away from the white policeman, getting away from a lynch mob.[3]

Since Hopkins often spent his time hustling money with his guitar on Dowling Street, he often ran the risk of getting caught up in such racial violence.

By the time Hopkins settled in Houston permanently, the city featured three mainstay black enclaves—the Third, Fourth, and Fifth Wards. No city ordinance segregated the city, but these three wards offered a small-town, neighborly feel to black citizens. Longtime Fourth Ward resident Ola Mae Kennedy remembers that in the late 1940s and early 1950s, "Fourth Ward was nice, everyone got

along good. [We had] churches, stores, beauty shop, barbeque, cab, we had law-
yers. What I mean by it being nice, people didn't bother anybody. People didn't
break in your house. Everybody give you respect, yes ma'am and no ma'am. I
know one Saturday we went all the way to my home [in Washington, Texas,
about eighty miles from Houston] when I was staying on West Dallas [Street]
in an old shotgun house. I left the door standing wide open, didn't get back till
that night. Just like I left that house, that's the way it was, didn't nobody go in.
. . . they didn't bother nothing."[4] This cohesion—easygoing pride and robust
dealings—fostered Sam Hopkins's blues as the segregated city continued to
maintain the status quo in the pre-civil-rights era.

Before he became a recording artist, Hopkins worked at least one day job in
Houston, described in a documentary, *Artists in America*, made by the University
of Houston in 1971:

I used to work right here in Houston for Sheffield Steel out there. I was
working there for a month or more and I'd tote those rails and I'd tote them
cross ties. . . . I used to line track, yeah I did that. . . . and the boys like for
me to sing you see, and late in the evening when the sun began to fall down
a little bit, it began to cool off a little bit. I'd go to hollering cuz I'm glad it
won't be long from quitting time. So I'd jump down with my little bit of it
and make everybody happy and so long fore we'd be going home you see.
We used to stop down on Dowling . . . it be about fifteen of us, we'd stop
in a joint . . . where they'd be selling beer. We'd pull us up some tables you
know, fifteen people at that time could buy lots of beer for a little money.
So we'd just get high, go on home and go to bed, next morning go on back
to work.[5]

Hopkins claimed he worked in law enforcement in the dirt-poor Acres Homes
enclave. First developed around the time of World War I, Acres Homes was an
unincorporated African American community northwest of the city of Houston. No independent verification of Hopkins's one-year stint in law enforcement
has survived. Thus, the veracity of his claim, relayed to Les Blank, is unknown:

I was a cop in Acres Homes. That's in Houston. I arrest me one man. He
was up on the truck stealing iron, putting it on another truck, and I held
him until the cops come and got him. But that now I went and got him out
of that. . . . If you want to be a cop you'd have to get away from me. Cuz I
wasn't no good, ha. . . . I was just a cop so I could keep them from bothering
me man. I tell ya it ain't nothing but a racket no how anyway. . . . A good cop

he arrests you for anything you do that's a violation. . . . I wouldn't arrest you for nothing less I see one of them good ones coming up and then I'd arrest you . . . yeah I'd hold you. Cuz I was just as deep in it as you were. Ha![6]

Hopkins's reason for working as a cop—"So I could keep them from bothering me"—underscores the police harassment African Americans faced in Houston. The fact that he only arrested people if another "good" cop was around showed his sympathy for blacks in a country that lacked equal justice before the law. Even if it represents a tall tale rather than a truth, the story unveils his sympathies.

Hopkins's show business break occurred in 1946 while he was playing his guitar and working up and down on Dowling Street, which retained the same vigor and reputation that Hopkins experienced there in the late 1930s. Word spread regarding Hopkins's guitar playing and singing. Before long, Lola Ann Cullum, a talent scout, tracked him down. Hopkins was at home shooting craps with some buddies when a friend told him that a lady outside was honking her horn and asking to speak with him.

Hopkins remembered,

When the lady came to my house, I was on my knees shooting penny dice and she came there and said, "Do Mr. Sam Hopkins live here?" and the boy told her yeah, and the boy told me someone out there wanted to see me. So I was shooting for a five then about six cents a point, so I said tell her to wait a minute, I went ahead and made my five[.] I got up and went to the door, she said, "Bring your guitar and come here for just a minute, man this is worthwhile to ya." I went back and put a shirt on and got my guitar[.] [S]he said[,] "Man I been looking all over for you, are you Mr. Sam Hopkins?" I said, "Yes, yes." She said, "You is losing the biggest chance of your life fooling around here." She said, "I'm a talent scout and I could get you plenty of money if you will leave this place and go with me[.] I'll get you plenty of money." She said, "I'll give you a thousand dollars cash now to put in your pocket and then you get the rest of your money on your tour." And so man you know how I felt. I already forgot about dice.[7]

After Hopkins played one song for Cullum, she promised to arrange for him to record. As Hopkins told her, "I'm gonna have a thousand dollars, so she give me the thousand dollars."[8]

By the time she discovered Hopkins, Cullum was very accomplished: she became the first African American woman to file for the bar examination in

Oklahoma; she operated oil well leases in Oklahoma and Texas; she was one of the first African American women to model for Kaufman's Art Gallery; and she earned degrees from Wiley College and Blackstone College for Girls. After moving to Houston in 1930, she soon married Dr. S. J. Cullum, Jr., a dentist. As a staunch Democrat, she worked on Franklin Delano Roosevelt's campaign. In June 1941, Roy Hofheinz appointed her as the manager monitoring black voters for the Lyndon Johnson Senate campaign.

In the 1940s, Cullum discovered Houston singer and pianist Amos Milburn. She began managing him and pitching his tunes to record companies. After they recorded some demos, they took a train to Los Angeles to seek record companies. First, they approached Modern Records co-owner Jules Bihari, who liked the demos they brought, but Bihari and Cullum could not agree on a price.

She then sought out Edward Mesner of Aladdin Records. Edward and his brother Leo Mesner founded Philo Records in 1945 and experienced some success with releases of Johnny Moore's Three Blazers and Helen Humes. They soon ran into a conflict with the Philco Company over their name. So they changed it to Aladdin and adopted a genie lamp as their logo. Charles Brown, formerly one of Moore's Three Blazers, earned eleven top-ten R&B hits while recording for newly established Aladdin.

Eddie Mesner was hospitalized at the time that Cullum sought him out. Aladdin was making records for the black jukebox market and becoming one of the most successful independent labels in the country by the late 1940s. Legend states Cullum took a portable tape player to Mesner's hospital room, where Mesner liked what he heard. He immediately signed Milburn for three times the amount that Modern Records offered. Milburn's first recording session for Aladdin in September 1946 yielded three singles, selling over 50,000 copies. The sales numbers turned Milburn into a viable artist and inaugurated Cullum as a legitimate manager. Cullum eventually booked Milburn into many famous nightclubs across the country, including the Apollo Theater in New York City and the Million Club in Los Angeles.

Amos Milburn credits himself for introducing Hopkins to Lola Cullum:

I was in an accident with a taxicab . . . so they put my leg in a cast. At the time I was living with my grandmother and one night around 12:30, 1 o'clock I heard this lonesome guitar down the streets and said "Who is this guy, this guy sounds good." And it was like, Lightning Hopkins. So I got to the window and called him over and from that night on for about five nights a week he would come to my window and . . . he would sing the blues for me and it was kind of nice. When I got the cast off I went over to talk to

Lightning Hopkins. At that time he had a partner playing piano with him, Thunder Smith, so I went to this lady doctor [Cullum] who had taken me to California and brought Lightning to her to let her hear him. She was inspired also so we all packed up and took a train to California. Then we got Lightning started.[9]

When Cullum tracked Hopkins down, she repeated the steps she had taken as manager with Milburn. She bought Hopkins his first amplifier and made some test recordings of Hopkins at her house. Then Cullum made arrangements with the Aladdin Record Company for Texas Alexander and Hopkins to journey out to the West Coast to record for it.

According to Chris Strachwitz, Cullum was afraid to travel with Alexander because he had recently been released from prison. However, Texas prison records do not reveal an Alger Alexander in the custody of the corrections system at any time. Alexander tried to convince Cullum to take him along, since he had previous experience recording music in the 1920s. Unimpressed by the story line, Cullum refused to take him to Los Angeles. To replace Alexander, Hopkins lobbied Cullum to bring Wilson Smith, a barrelhouse piano player and singer. Again, Cullum felt Smith did not demonstrate or offer enough talent.

Hopkins described the incident in his interview with Sam Charters: "So she was kinda across the fence on that. She didn't know whether to try that double up there. She knowed I knowed my way. . . . She said, 'Well, Mr. Hopkins, I don't know about Mr. Smith. I don't know if I can take Mr. Smith. . . . I said, 'Well look, you mean you don't want to go.' She said, 'No, I'll just take you this time you know and take him later.' I said, 'No, if you can't take him, I ain't goin'.' When I say something I pretty much mean that. So she looked at me and said, 'Well Mr. Hopkins, you gotta go.' And I said, 'No, I ain't neither. I'm under no obligation to go.' She said, 'Well, just in case you won't go I'll take Mr. Smith too.'"[10]

Hopkins's first recording session provided the basis for one story line regarding his nickname "Lightning." To do so, he spun a yarn about Wilson Smith: "Thunder Smith, well I wished they'd call him Thunder. Named Wilson Smith, just like they named me Lightnin' you know."[11] In this version, Hopkins and Wilson were at their first recording session for the Aladdin Record Company at Radio Recorders in Hollywood on November 9, 1946. Smith was dubbed "Thunder"; thus the Aladdin management team named the duo "Thunder and Lightning."

In 1960, Hopkins held a radio interview with folksinger Barbara Dane for her show *Barbara's Blues*. She asked him, "Didn't you start using the name Lightning when you were with [Thunder]?" Hopkins replied, "That's right, Lightning and Thunder were named the same day."[12] This testimony, often repeated, rings valid, since marketing personnel, in cahoots with record companies, grafted catchy names onto their performers.

However, Hopkins later told *Dallas Morning News* writer Frank Tolbert, "Blind Lemon said when I played and sang I electrified people. He was the one that started calling me Lightning."[13] Hopkins's experience with Blind Lemon pre-dated his California recording trip in 1946. In a third version, Hopkins's nickname originates from a story he told Texas drummer Doyle Bramhall, who backed him on some gigs around Texas and Louisiana in the 1970s. Bramhall, a Dallas-born solo artist who cowrote songs with Stevie Ray Vaughan, remembered sitting backstage when Hopkins asked him, "Doyle, do you know how I got my nickname Lightning? I was sitting on my porch and got hit by lightning."[14] All these variations reflect Hopkins's sense of jest, his ample felicity for storytelling, and his earnest pursuit of recasting himself.

As a result of Hopkins and Smith's sessions in Los Angeles, Aladdin released four 78-rpm records. Aladdin 165 was credited to "Thunder and Lightnin'" and featured Smith's vocals on the songs "West Coast Blues" and "Can't Do It Like You Used To." Aladdin 166 was a Thunder Smith release, but Aladdin 167 was credited to "Lightnin'" Hopkins and featured "Katie Mae Blues" on one side and "That Mean Old Twister" on the other. The tunes "Rocky Mountain Blues" and "I Feel So Bad" were released on Aladdin 168, also credited to "Lightnin'" Hopkins. Hopkins's discs had the phrase "accompanying himself on guitar" and "rhythm background" inscribed on the red-and-silver record label. All four songs on Aladdin 167 and 168 credited Hopkins as the writer.

"Rocky Mountain Blues" told the story of a man leaving his sweetheart and heading out west. One line describes a funeral: ". . . they carried my baby there and they throwed clay dirt in her face." Hopkins told friend Ray Dawkins back in Centerville, Texas, he witnessed a funeral traveling through West Texas on his travels to Los Angeles, which inspired the tune.

"Katie Mae Blues" showcased Hopkins's witty lyrics. The main character is a woman who ". . . Walks just like she got oil wells in her backyard . . . While some folks say she must be a Cadillac . . . She must be a T-model Ford." The instrumentation on the country-flavored blues of "Katie Mae Blues" included Hopkins's guitar work and Smith's piano and drums. Lola Cullum was probably the inspiration for "Katie Mae Blues," since she had an oil well in her backyard and drove a Cadillac, according to bluesman David "Honeyboy" Edwards.[15] Hopkins's signature guitar style—playing both rhythm and lead, picking the bass and rhythm lines with a thumb pick while exploring solos with his bare index finger—helped expand the sound.

Texas Johnny Brown described Hopkins's approach: "I would think it would be more real traditional blues, the real thing that started the blues that set the tone for the blues, and the more natural thing because what he did was just like picking up an instrument and having it to do what he wanted it to do without really knowing what the instrument consisted of. . . . He knew the chords, but it wasn't a chord structure because he played the type of guitar that he ad-libbed. . . . He carried the melodic line and the bass line all at the same time. You know like finger picking? He did that finger picking. He used those little picks that you put on your fingers. . . . Today, I don't think there are that many people [that play that style]."[16] Rooted in rural traditions, Hopkins's guitar style—primitive and vernacular—maintained an evocative and unique edge.

Hopkins's first recording sessions signaled a new era. Ray Dawkins remembered this transition: "When he came back [to visit Centerville], . . . we was on Jack Marshall's farm down there. . . . he was sitting on Mr. Brown Marshall's porch playing guitar . . . singing 'Rocky Mountain.' . . . that's when he told us that that song would be coming out in about two, three weeks and that we would get to hear it. He said, 'I finally made it.'"[17]

Tomcat Courtney confirms, "He come out with 'Katie Mae,' oh man everyone was playing it, dancin' off it, listening to it. It got known outside of Texas. It was real known. That really made him a hit. Got him proper, real proper." Even in those early days of his career, Hopkins's wardrobe exuded flair. "He was a real fancy dresser. He always dressed fancy, even when he was young," Courtney added.[18]

"Katie Mae Blues" spun frequently in Houston jukeboxes, catalyzing Hopkins's fame across town; consequently, he worked a series of weekend dances and juke joints around the city, earning perhaps three dollars a night, like Amos Milburn did in 1946.[19] Lola Cullum continued to manage Hopkins. Houston guitar player Texas Johnny Brown comments,

She did quite a few things for us, kept us working, even went so far as clothe us if we didn't have the correct clothing or anything, then she would see that we got that. She was a good personal manager. We kind of stayed around her house. She had . . . a garage apartment. I stayed there for quite awhile and I think he stayed there awhile too. Miss Cullum had more than one thing going on. She gave me the title "Texas Johnny Brown." She had three in one, she had myself, she had Lightnin', and also had Amos [Milburn]. . . . Amos would be going back to California to do his recording with Aladdin. . . . when he'd be gone she'd book me into certain places. And she'd book Lightnin' in certain places. Lightnin' did a lot of . . . house parties and smaller places, smaller cafés. It was a little time before he got into doing festivals. But he did manage to do some and travel some.[20]

However, blues guitarist Goree Carter did not share such fond memories of Cullum. As a Houston native, he started playing guitar when he was thirteen. His family hosted backyard jams featuring Texas tenor saxophone player Arnett Cobb, Illinois Jacquet's older brother Russell Jacquet, and Eddie "Cleanhead" Vinson. "My mother used to cook a pot of beans for them and they'd play out in the backyard all day, practicing. I was so small I didn't know too much. But I always loved music."

Carter played some floor shows at clubs, including the Eldorado Ballroom on the corner of Elgin and Dowling in the Third Ward. Cullum heard Carter playing with I. H. Smalley at the Eldorado: "She discovered me, heard me at the Eldorado one night, and then got me booked in Nashville, Tennessee with Lightning Hopkins, and we had a battle of the blues up there. She was so grouchy after money, she gypped me a whole lot, like she done in Nashville. She took me there and dropped me like a hot potato and come on back. Just left me on my own. I was young and didn't know my way around or nothing."[21]

Carter and Hopkins "battled" at the Club Arrow in Nashville. "I won that engagement," Carter insisted. "Me and Lightnin' used to sit down and practice together in Nashville. I was trying to play like him, and he was trying to play like me! It was a style you could just sit down and play, you didn't need a band."[22] Such battles were common. The performer who got the most applause "won." Hopkins went back to Houston, but Carter stayed on in Nashville because the club extended his contract another six weeks. Promoters wanted Hopkins to travel like this to support his records, but he preferred to stay rooted down in Houston. A frustrated Cullum finally gave up on trying to help him.

When Hopkins started his recording career, several other Houston artists stirred the music business too. By 1948, Milburn was scaling the rhythm and blues charts with "Chicken-Shack Boogie," hitting number 1 for the Aladdin label in November 1948. Milburn would have eight top-ten hits between 1946 and 1949. Recording under the Amos Milburn and the Aladdin Chickenshackers moniker, Milburn scored eleven more top-ten R&B hits from 1949 through 1954.

Besides Lola Cullum, Fifth Ward native Don Deadric Robey helped launch the careers of several Houston-based recording artists as well. He operated the Harlem Grill nightclub in Los Angeles for three years; next, he opened the Bronze Peacock ballroom in Houston in 1945 in the Fifth Ward at 2809 Erastus Street. An intrepid businessman, he also owned a liquor store right next door to the Bronze Peacock. National artists such as T-Bone Walker, Louis Jordan, and

Lionel Hampton entertained at the dining and dancing establishment. Robey followed up by opening a record store at 4104 Lyons Avenue, a commercial strip in the Fifth Ward similar to Dowling Street in the Third Ward.

From at least the late 1940s, Robey lived with his wife in a typical narrow, shotgun-shack-style house in the Fourth Ward. Robey's house, located at 1517 Andrews Street, featured fancy "brick"-style glass. Two large concrete lion statues (Robey named his music publishing company Lion) still flank the front porch. Jacqueline Beckham lived with her husband James and their family at 1308 Gillette, directly across from the private rooming house Robey operated on Gillette Street. Beckham recalled witnessing, or hearing accounts from her in-laws, about superstar black entertainers like Buddy Johnson, T-Bone Walker, Louis Jordan, B. B. King, and Dakota Staton visiting the Robey-owned rooming house.[23]

John Hightower grew up in the Fourth Ward in the 1940s and 1950s and remembers seeing entertainers pass through his neighborhood as well. Big Mama Thornton also lived in the Fourth Ward at that time. Hightower recalled:

You'd see some of them. . . . Don Robey lived on Robin [Street], you'd see them passing through, they'd have gigs at the City Auditorium downtown. Fourth Ward was kind of a hub for that kind of thing. West Dallas [Street] was a busy place with clubs [and] lounges, so they'd be in and out of those places. You'd see them in their cars. We'd see Louis Jordan frequently. He was one that got more attention because he had records out. Mama Thornton used to give us quarters to go to the movies. She was really big mama then. She was big. Whenever we knew she had a show downtown, we would go down to West Dallas and she'd give us a quarter apiece, and we'd go to the movies. She would always stress, "Now get your lesson in, do your schoolwork." She had an Oldsmobile station wagon those days. She had Hound Dog painted on it after she recorded it.

Hightower also remembered seeing Hopkins hanging out in the neighborhood and on the porch of his next-door neighbor; however, people considered Hopkins rather pedestrian compared to the big national acts that regularly populated the neighborhood:

When I saw him, he was on the porch strumming the guitar, it probably on the weekend. That's basically where we saw him. Our address was 1016 [Arthur Street] so it must have been 1020 Arthur. It was a big house . . . had a porch that went around the front and the side. I guess he was just practicing some licks. . . . We'd be playing in the street and we'd see him there. We'd speak to him in passing. We had no sense that he was anyone famous or extraordinary or anything like that. He was just another character in the neighborhood. There were a number of guys that would come through there that Don Robey was promoting then. You would see Louis Jordan and people like that, and we'd think they were something special. But Lightning Hopkins was part of the community fabric, so he didn't get anything extra whatever. Our parents told us who he was and that was about it.[24]

Robey's Bronze Peacock club often played host to modern electric blues guitar pioneer and Oak Cliff, Texas, native Aaron "T-Bone" Walker. Walker, like Hopkins, traveled around with Blind Lemon Jefferson during the 1920s. Walker's clean and jazzy lead guitar style influenced B. B. King, Pee Wee Crayton, Pete Mayes, and numerous others. As a flamboyant entertainer, he played the guitar behind his head and performed the splits too. When Walker was inhibited by an ulcer attack midway during a set at one of his Bronze Peacock gigs in 1947, twenty-three-year-old Clarence "Gatemouth" Brown jumped on stage, grabbed Walker's guitar, and led the band through "Gatemouth Boogie," a tune he improvised on the spot. Brown's spontaneous act led to his self-made break into the music business.

Robey witnessed the impromptu show, impressed with Brown's performance. A day later Robey bought Brown a guitar and some suits. By August, Robey took Brown to Los Angeles to record for Aladdin. After the Aladdin records failed to sell, Robey considered starting his own recording label. By early 1949, Robey recorded six Gatemouth Brown tracks. Those recordings constituted the three initial releases of his Peacock label. By 1950, Robey's label had also waxed sides by R. B. Thibadeaux, Edgar Blanchard, Memphis Slim, Floyd Dixon, and Clarence Green. The label soon acquired a strong national presence in the era of independent labels.

Robey also pushed Willie Mae Thornton's career to a pinnacle. In 1948, the young Alabama-born Willie Mae "Big Mama" Thornton traveled through Texas working for the Hot Harlem Review, when she quit and stayed on in Houston. The hefty Thornton settled in the Fourth Ward, where neighbors remembered seeing her walking around "always dressed in overalls."[25] The first time Honeyboy Edwards saw Thornton, "She was walking down the street in the Fourth Ward, wearing big blue jeans and a man's hat cocked on the side of her head. She was big then, too, good-sized. . . . she was a damn good harp player—she was hell with that harp."[26] Robey ran across Thornton when she was working a gig with Ike Smalley's band at the Eldorado Ballroom. After

Robey signed her under contract, Thornton cut the tune "Hound Dog" in 1952 in Los Angeles for his Peacock label. Thornton heard it on the radio for the first time, after its release in 1953, while touring in Dayton, Ohio, with the ill-fated entertainer Johnny Ace. The song further skyrocketed, though, in the hands of Elvis Presley.

In addition to Robey's Bronze Peacock ballroom, other Houston venues featuring rhythm and blues acts included Shady's Playhouse, the Diamond L Ranch, Club Matinee, and Club Savoy. Houston also had numerous no-name dives where Hopkins and other like-minded players harnessed a gutbucket style of music, contrasting with glitzy show bands and the posh jazz orchestral style favored in larger and more upscale venues like the Eldorado Ballroom.

Although Hopkins lived in the same city as Robey and his rapidly expanding music businesses, Robey never released any of Hopkins's records. The bluesman's down-home country blues did not mix well with the pre-rock 'n' roll, R&B, and gospel vinyl that Robey issued, yet guitarist and vocalist Texas Johnny Brown remembered going with Hopkins into a studio Robey often used. "He was out there a few times; he never really got on that label. We did some demos and you know I never knew what happened with those demos. I don't know who's got those. I don't know what happened to them."[27]

After Aladdin issued Hopkins's first records, he gigged locally, resisting Lola Cullum's efforts to book him into nightclubs and dancehalls on the rhythm and blues circuit. In contrast, his peers Amos Milburn, Gatemouth Brown, and Big Mama Thornton toured the country, capitalizing on the attention their recordings amassed. Milburn was particularly successful financially. By his third Texas tour, begun in 1950, he reaped almost $50,000 in just ten one-nighters, setting records for grosses all across the state, including the Houston Coliseum, where Milburn drew $8,279 at the box office.[28] Hopkins could have seized the opportunity to tour with Milburn, with whom he shared a manager, but he remained blatantly local, rarely leaving Houston.

This failure to capitalize on the momentum his music generated through record sales and jukebox plays remained a consistent trait throughout the rest of his career. Hopkins did not concern himself with longevity and long-term profit, even though his first recordings were successful and lifted him out of obscurity. Instead of maximizing such newfound attention, his lifestyle remained centered in the Third Ward. A sense of place remained vital to him; seeking a larger audience was not a key concern or motivation.

After he became a recording artist, Hopkins also continued his gambling habit. The Houston police picked up Hopkins on June 14, 1947, charging him with "gaming." Justice of the Peace records show James Routt was arrested with Hopkins. Each paid a fine of $1.00 plus court costs, for a total of $13.50.[29] The records do not reveal the location of the offense. Hopkins tapped the income from Aladdin to help supply his gambling hobby.

After his minor brush with the law, Hopkins made a West Coast recording trip with Thunder Smith in August 1947. The recording session yielded six more sides for the Aladdin label. Just as in their first session, Hopkins and Wilson recorded with a drummer whose name is not preserved on the record. "Short Haired Woman" is the seminal track, and different versions and variations of it became a mainstay of Hopkins's repertoire until the end of his career. The song featured just Hopkins's guitar and his moaning vocals.

> I don't want no woman
> If her hair ain't no longer than mine
> . . . she ain't no good for nothing but trouble

In the documentary made by the University of Houston, Hopkins explained,

> Well the way that "Short Haired Woman" come about, I got on the bus, right there on Dowling, I got on the bus with my guitar, the man let me in the back cuz it was full. There was a little old girl sitting up there, she had on a wig, and she looked back there and [said], "There's the man with the guitar." While she's standing up there talking to me, she went to sit down, you know how those seats on the bus are, well she missed the seat and she fell and the top of her hair come off, her wig came off, see I ain't never seen that before, so I'm figuring about the girl all the time. So when her wig fell off her head it come to me. *I don't want no women, no hair no longer than mine.*[30]

Hopkins provided a more detailed version of his inspiration for the tune when Skip Gerson and Les Blank shot their documentary about him:

> You know the reason, because a woman walked on the bus and she walked down the aisle and she seed me with a guitar. She said, "Hello T-Bone." Talking about T-Bone Walker. I said no baby you got me a little bit wrong this ain't T-Bone Walker this is Sam Lightnin' Hopkins. She said, "Oh well T-Bone my man." She didn't have no hair on her head looked just like a little old and you ever see that, you know. She goes on back to sit down and she missed her seat and she fell on the floor. And I made this song I don't want no woman with her hair no longer than mine. Cuz I know if they all do like

her they gonna do like she do they gonna do wrong, they gonna talk wrong. So I made that song. From that day to this I been singing that song.[31]

One important feature of the lyrics to "Short Haired Woman" is Hopkins's use of third person to refer to himself, ". . . poor Sam he woke up about the break of day / I even found a rat on the pillow where she used to lay." This portion is the first recorded instance of Hopkins mentioning himself by name and bemoaning his fate in third person. Hopkins soon used "poor Sam," and later "Po' Lightnin'," constantly throughout hundreds of songs and in gig banter, providing a certain ironic distance from the narration, an arm's length from the core of the story, despite the subjects being firsthand and personal.

"Lightnin' Hopkins is not coming from any sort of angle that can be even slightly considered commercial," explained singer-songwriter Peter Case.

> He's not trying to make pop records. Later on in his career, he's not even trying to make popular blues records, R&B records, or race records. Early on, he did, and he made some beautiful records, like "Shining Moon" (1947). As he went along, he went deeper, and the words got tougher and more detailed. Mance Lipscomb is connected to the Texas tradition of song that goes back through Blind Lemon Jefferson and Texas Alexander. So is Lightnin', but Mance is more connected to the individual songs of the tradition. Lightnin' is more connected to the feelings and the whole idea of making up songs. He constantly made up new songs, and he really wasn't learning anybody else's songs correctly. When you hear Lightnin' Hopkins do a cover, he'll maybe use the title of it, but he'll make his complete own version of it. He doesn't care really. He's just there to express Lightnin' Hopkins.[32]

As Case noted, Hopkins's songwriting benefits not solely from his keen observations of human nature. He also fluidly refashioned existing songs, like reinventing "Short Hair Blues," a song Kid Stormy Weather cut in 1935, as "Short Haired Woman."

Another notable aspect of Hopkins's early recording career is the brevity of each track. His early songs clocked in at three minutes or less because the 78-rpm format featured time limitations, forcing Hopkins to keep his songwriting and musical accompaniment concise.

"Short Haired Woman" also preserved Hopkins's guitar playing technique. Billy Gibbons, guitar player, singer, and songwriter for internationally renowned Houston-based ZZ Top, described Hopkins's style for music journalist Jas Obrecht: "One of the most distinctive elements of Lightnin's sound is that turnaround in [the key of] E. It's a signature lick that he did in just about every song he played. He'd come down from the B chord and roll across the top three strings in the last two bars. He'd pull off those strings to get a staccato effect, first hitting the little open E string then the 3rd fret on the B string and the fourth fret of the G string. He would then resolve on the five chord after doing his roll. It's a way to immediately identify a Lightnin' Hopkins tune."[33]

Texas guitar player Jimmie Lee Vaughan, older brother of Stevie Ray Vaughan and founding member of the Fabulous Thunderbirds, summarized Hopkins's influence in an unreleased documentary about Hopkins, "Whenever you hear this [plays a Lightnin' lick], that was Lightning Hopkins. Never did anyone else do that, like folk guys did it later, but it was Lightning Hopkins. . . . I don't think there could be a B. B. King, or a Buddy Guy, or a Jimi Hendrix or a Stevie Ray Vaughan without Lightning Hopkins."[34] SugarHill Studios engineer and chronicler Andy Bradley detects Hopkins's influence on the contemporary work of Keb' Mo and longtime Houston natives like bluesman Bert Wills, who sometimes emulates Hopkins's narrative style.

"Probably everybody who tries to play blues guitar, has used, or should use, some of [Hopkins's] ideas. [It] seems like he played everything in [the key of] E, and it always had 3 chords, and he did the same little licks and turnarounds over and over, but his stuff had a magic to it,"[35] argued Denny Freeman, a guitar and piano player who grew up in Dallas, Texas. He joined Bob Dylan, Taj Mahal, Jimmie Vaughan, and countless Austin, Texas, bands on stage. Freeman was also an important member of the Antone's nightclub house band in the 1980s, where he backed blues luminaries like Albert Collins, Buddy Guy, Junior Wells, Otis Rush, Eddie Taylor, Jimmy Rogers, and Lazy Lester.

Hopkins continued recording for Aladdin through 1947. Though "Short Haired Woman" was a "hit," it did not propel him to tour. Another track Hopkins recorded during his Aladdin tenure was "Whisky Headed Woman." Texas Johnny Brown remembered Lola Cullum's input during this period: "She helped him a lot with writing some of the songs he did, what was it 'Beerhead Woman'?" [probably referring to "Whisky Headed Woman"].[36] Similar to his "Short Haired Woman," Hopkins didn't want a "Whisky Headed Woman":

Didn't want no woman
I have to buy liquor for all the time
Yes you know every time you see her
She lit up like a neon sign.

At some point in 1948, Hopkins discontinued his relationship with Aladdin and started recording for the Gold Star label. Although why Hopkins stopped recording for Aladdin is still unknown, "Everyone seems to agree that its owners, the Mesner brothers, were a bunch of rats."[37] One example of Aladdin's suspicious business activities is Edward Mesner filing burglary and grand theft charges against pianist Charles Brown because Brown took a copy of his own contract from the Aladdin offices to make a photocopy of it. The district attorney did not pursue the charges; in turn, Brown filed a lawsuit against the Mesners asking for over a half million dollars in damages for malicious prosecution.

Aladdin did not pay Hopkins any royalties, most agree. A recording artist could generate money from two different streams: mechanical royalties based on record sales and performance royalties from record plays. According to music historian John Broven, contracts at that time were written to exclude performance royalties. Broven cites a standard Aladdin contract from 1952 to illustrate his point. The contract included the phrase, "no performance royalties to writers."[38] Songwriting and song publishing royalties were in addition to mechanical and performance royalties.

Even if independent record labels made it a practice to pay royalties, Hopkins had no way to be assured that he was getting a fair accounting. No evidence suggests he employed any music business professionals to guide his career or audit record company books. Aladdin, the Los Angeles–based label, controlled its accounting records. Nothing prevented Aladdin or other record labels from collecting and pocketing the mechanical royalties on songs that artists such as Hopkins recorded. Aladdin's practice was to give Hopkins the credit for songwriting on the physical record itself. Under the song title, in parentheses, Aladdin printed (Lightnin' Hopkins). The text also credits Hopkins Singing And Accompanying Himself On Guitar. Broven summed up the financial situation of that era, "The personal acquisition of song copyrights has been another damning accusation levied against record men generally. But who knows what deals were struck behind closed doors?"[39] Hopkins got the one thousand dollars Cullum promised him for the trip to Los Angeles to record, but the data do not exist to show whether Aladdin or publishing companies ever paid Hopkins anything for his songs or if Aladdin actually paid him mechanical royalties.

Brownie McGhee recorded for the Newark, New Jersey–based Savoy Records label during the era when Hopkins started recording for Aladdin. For every four sides he recorded, McGhee was paid sixty dollars as a lead man or thirty dollars when he played as a sideman. Savoy wanted the publishing rights and gave McGhee fifteen dollars up front against future royalty payments. In

1947, when McGhee had a hit with "My Fault," he approached Savoy and said, "I want a hundred dollars a side plus twenty-five advance on my tune." McGhee received the rate he wanted.[40] Hopkins, likely unaware of the pay that his fellow artists were getting, probably took whatever amount Aladdin offered.

After Aladdin, Hopkins signed with Gold Star Records. Bill Quinn owned the Houston-based label. Hopkins likely started recording for Gold Star before his Aladdin contract ran out, because although the "Option on Contract for Unique Services" he signed with "Quinn's Recording Company" on May 7, 1948, refers to a contract Hopkins was bound to until May 21, 1948, the record suggests Hopkins's first Gold Star record was recorded in 1947. The Gold Star contract that Hopkins signed states that for $150 Hopkins agreed to "Perform and make recordings for" Quinn's Recording Company "as stipulated in the regular ARTIST'S CONTRACT." The contract gave Quinn "SOLE AND EXCLUSIVE" right to Hopkins's unique services. The signatories to the contract were Sam Hopkins and W. R. Quinn.[41] Quinn would soon learn that the words "sole" and "exclusive" would not have much value when featured on a contract signed by Hopkins.

Lola Cullum stopped managing or helping Hopkins during this time. No surviving records show whether Hopkins sought professional advice before signing the contract with Quinn. In 1951, Cullum went on to form her own record label, Artist Record Company (ARC), to push her artists. She used Gold Star Studios and ACA Recording Studios in Houston to cut artists like Lester Williams, Percy Henderson, Vivianne Greene, and Honeyboy Edwards. ARC profited very little, leading Cullum to jettison the music business altogether.

No Hopkins recordings were released by any other company between the time Hopkins's records for Aladdin were recorded and the time his Gold Star material was recorded and released; therefore, the contract between Aladdin and Hopkins is likely the contract mentioned in Quinn's "Option on Contract" with Hopkins. Whether Hopkins had an in-depth understanding of the ins and outs of entertainment contracts is unknown. The contract was notarized, but nothing else—a personal manager, booking agency, or attorney—survives in the record. Such a decision not to hire professional management fits perfectly with his business protocol for the rest of his career.

Bill Quinn's recording studio was the first established in Houston, possibly the first in the Deep South. As a self-contained, vertically integrated music businessman, he recorded artists, pressed up the records, and sold them regionally. Starting in 1942, he opened a small studio at 3104 Telephone Road in southeast Houston and learned, by trial and error, how to process, master, and press records.

During this era, big corporations controlled the pressing of most records. An independent record company owning its own record-pressing machine was unusual. Quinn ran his company during the shellac shortage of the war years, but he was able to purchase small amounts of the scarce materials. He would print up a few thousand records, though he sometimes endured problems finding the right mix of ingredients to place into the pressing machine to get a good-quality 78-rpm record.

Quinn debuted the Gulf label in 1944, but shut it down and started Gold Star in 1946. Gold Star had a regional hit with Cajun singer Harry Choates's recording of "Jole Blon." Quinn licensed the song to the Bihari brothers, who owned Modern Music, a West Coast independent label. With the Biharis' promotion and distribution, "Jole Blon" became a national hit, making Choates's song the first Cajun record to achieve national acclaim. Quinn now acquired access to a larger, national independent record label that he could use when the demand for Hopkins's records exceeded his capital and distribution.

In 1947, Hopkins's first Gold Star record, another version of "Short Haired Woman" backed with "Big Mama Jump," became the label's first blues release. Barely two years into Hopkins's recording career, he established a pattern he would emulate throughout his entire life: he rerecorded songs in multiple versions for a wide variety of record labels. According to charts, "Short Haired Woman" sold between forty thousand and fifty thousand copies. It resonated nationally, appearing on a list of top-ten jukebox hits in Los Angeles. On August 14, 1947, the *Los Angeles Sentinel* reported "Short Haired Woman" tied for number 7 with Amos Milburn's "Money Hustlin' Woman."

Curtis Amy was Hopkins's neighbor during this era. "Lightning Hopkins lived in an alley a block away from my house. I'd come home from school, and I'd come through the alley, and Lightning Hopkins and all his guys would be out on his front porch. Playing. Every day," he fondly recalled. ". . . I was into bebop, you know. So he called, someone told him that I played, because I was playing with Amos Milburn. . . . I was a young cat. I was afraid of them; you know, because of all of that alcohol, all of that whiskey and stuff. They'd be drunk and cussing and, you know what I mean? But the music would be, man, it was heavy to hear those cats."[42] Amy saw Hopkins at his natural best, in his stomping grounds, with his friends, creating music spontaneously.

Hopkins made a West Coast tour in 1947 or '48, according to Amy: "Well, during that period I was at home one afternoon, and this guy came down from Lightning's house and said, 'Hey, Lightning wants to talk to you.' I said, okay. So, you know I must have been eighteen, nineteen. Right. Well, this was right after I got out of the army. . . . I said, 'Shit, I don't want to play with no Lightning

Hopkins, man. I want to play with Bird [Charlie Parker] and Diz [Dizzy Gillespie].' So I went down, and the cat offered me a job. They were coming to Los Angeles, and he asked me would I go with him and make this tour with him, and I gave him some kind of excuse about my mother or something. . . . Now I realize, but no, it wasn't the right step. It wasn't the right move at that time."[43]

Around this time, Harrison D. Nelson, Jr., later known as recording artist Peppermint Harris, met Hopkins. "I met him and L. C. Williams. I saw them down on Dowling Street and said, 'Are you Lightning Hopkins?' They both 'spread it to the side' like cowboys. And I told him who I was and what I wanted. From that day on, we were very very close friends. I used to go to his house early in the morning. I was washing dishes all night. I'd get off in the morning around 7 or 8 o'clock. I'd go by Lightning's house, and then I'd go to school in the afternoon. Lightning, he'd try to teach me how to play, but I didn't want to play like him."[44]

In Harris's view, Hopkins inhabited the Third Ward like an embittered client of the blues. "Back then, Lightning played and sang on Third Ward street corners, on Dowling Street, for tips, but most passersby gave him a hard time. He'd get so damn mad that he'd roll up all the windows of his car and lock his guitar inside, then he'd stand back in the alley hoping somebody would steal it so he could shoot 'em. Well, he never shot anyone, but I could understand his attitude. When I started, . . . the bluesman's life was tough. Hopkins told me that playing the blues 'Was like being black twice.'"[45] Hopkins soon introduced Harris to Bill Quinn at Gold Star. "Lightning took me to Gold Star, but Mr. Quinn never showed up. Finally we left because Lightning had a gig at a rural café. I remember they were serving chicken, beer and whiskey."[46] Eventually, though, Harris recorded for the label in 1948, waxing "Peppermint Boogie" backed with "Houston Blues."

That same year, after cutting forty-four sides for Aladdin, Hopkins began recording for Bill Quinn and his Gold Star label in earnest. Even though they did not all translate into national hits, all Hopkins's Gold Star releases reportedly sold forty thousand copies apiece. On February 12, 1949, Hopkins's song "Tim Moore's Farm," recorded for Quinn on the Gold Star label, hit the *Billboard* magazine charts—the first time one of Hopkins's songs appeared on a national chart. Although it remained listed for a week only, earning the number 13 slot on the "most-played juke box race records" proved Hopkins's national appeal.

The song details a sharecropper treated shabbily by "Tim" Moore. The name actually referred to Tom Moore, who owned a plantation in Navasota, Texas. Hopkins told Chris Strachwitz that he heard Texas Alexander sing the song.[47]

Yes you know I got a telegram this morning boy it read It say "Your wife is dead"
I show it to Mister Moore he said "Go ahead nigger
You know you got to plow old Red"

Like the racial slur contained in the lyrics, this type of regional, topical song was rare on record, yet it became commercially viable. Topping the "Juke Box Race Records" chart the same week of "Tim Moore's Farm" entry were two versions of "Bewildered," one version by the Red Miller Trio and the other by Amos Milburn. Detroit bluesman John Lee Hooker's best-known number and first hit, "Boogie Children," held down the number 4 spot, and Pee Wee Crayton's "Texas Hop" was number 6. The fact that Hopkins recorded "Tim Moore's Farm" at all shows that he had a lot of courage, considering the tense state of race relations.

Print ads offering his records for sale in various record stores across the country helped elevate Hopkins's national profile. For example, Harlem Hit Parade, a record store in Brooklyn, New York, ran an ad in the July 23, 1949, national edition of the *Chicago Defender*. Just under Louis Jordan records, the ad listed four Lightnin' Hopkins records: "Tim Moore's Farm," "Short Haired Woman," "No Mail Blues," and "Lightnin' Blues." The 78-rpm records retailed for seventy-nine cents, and the record store offered one free record for every four purchased, plus a free picture of the buyer's favorite artist and a free "hi-fidelity" needle with every order.[48] Essex Records in Atlanta ran an ad in the *Atlanta World* that listed "Short Haired Woman" in a roster of records by such artists as Duke Ellington, Dinah Washington, and Glenn Miller.[49] Other stores also regularly took out ads featuring Hopkins's records, while Aladdin Records simultaneously touted Hopkins's latest releases in print, too. During the fervor of Hopkins's first appearance on the charts, his national success remained unabated. On October 8, 1949, "T-Model Blues" made the same most-played jukebox record chart as "Tim Moore," eventually hitting number 8.

Billboard ran its first review of a Hopkins Gold Star record in its June 4, 1949, issue, giving "Unsuccessful Blues" a solid write-up and describing it as "Southern market blues if feelingly executed," but the magazine was less enamored of the flip side. "Muddy and unorganized blues side with hybrid styling," summarized the unnamed reviewer's comments on Hopkins's "Rolling Woman Blues."[50] *Billboard* continued its reviews of Hopkins in its August 13, 1949, issue for Gold Star Records 662, featuring "Jail House Blues" backed by "T-Model Blues." The reviewer liked the A-side, discerning in it "An old-style sorrowful blues, warbled and guitared in the ancient manner. Staple fare for the Deep South market." As Hopkins entered his third year as a recording artist, his music was described by this influential magazine as "old style," replete with "ancient" guitar style. The B-side was described in the same review as "A provocative double entendre slow blues in the Hopkins authentic manner."[51] The writerly tropes are obvious: Hopkins represented the primitive, authentic, and old Deep South.

Hopkins's Gold Star record number 666 included a song called "Automobile" backed with the zydeco-tinged "Zolo Go." As folklorist John Minton points out, the latter features Hopkins playing "an electric organ instead of his usual guitar, imitating an accordionist at a 'zolo go' ('zydeco') dance" and may be the first time the term "zolo," found on the single's label, was used in print. The song, featuring a basic three-line stanza and twelve-bar progression, both reflects Hopkins's indelible blues background and seems to "embody contemporaneous trends in Creole music as well."[52] The A-side was Hopkins's answer song to Memphis Minnie's (Lizzie Douglass) "Chauffeur Blues." Having recorded for a variety of labels for over four decades, she is considered iconic. Chris Strachwitz, founder of Arhoolie Records, insists, "In my opinion, Memphis Minnie was without a doubt the greatest of all female blues singers to ever record," surpassing Bessie Smith and others. On "Chauffeur Blues," Minnie pleas:

> Won't you be my chauffeur
> . . . I wants him to drive me downtown
> Yes he drives so easy, I can't turn him down

In turn, Hopkins answers Minnie:

> I saw you ridin' 'round
> You ridin' in your brand new automobile
> Yes, you was happy sittin' there
> With your handsome driver at the wheel

Hopkins's wry wit easily takes shape in the lyric, like an offhand conversation with an artist finding her own limelight in the blues tradition.

Hopkins continued to find success in the early 1950s. Apparently, he was satisfied with his business relationship with Quinn's Gold Star label from 1948 to 1950, because he signed another contract with the Quinn Recording Company on December 16, 1950. The contract ran for two years. As an improvement to the one Hopkins signed with Quinn in 1948, the contract provided that Sam Hopkins, professionally known as "Lightnin' Hopkins," would receive "two hundred dollars advance at each recording session at which four sides are

Mojo Hand

recorded" [as opposed to $150 for an indeterminate amount of sides in his first contract]. His first Gold Star contract did not provide for any royalties, but his new one declared that he would receive "a royalty of 1.5 cents for each side of the record which is used for his recordings; or if both sides of the record carry his recordings, he will receive 3 cents per record royalty," less his advance. "The Company" designated agreed to provide the artist with a statement showing all the records it manufactured and sold during the preceding quarter within forty-five days after each quarter, along with a royalty check.[53] Whether Hopkins ever actually received any royalty checks is not preserved. The contract stipulates that the artist will produce ten songs per calendar year and that the company will advertise, promote, and distribute the recordings in a "proper and business-like manner."[54]

Quinn leased and sold Hopkins's recordings to other labels as well. The Modern label version of "Tim Moore's Farm" hit the charts in February 1949, but Gold Star originally released it. At least twelve sides Gold Star recorded and released appeared on the Modern record label. "T-Model Blues" on the Gold Star label hit the charts eight months after "Tim Moore's Farm" on Modern made the charts. Hopkins's recordings actually competed against themselves. Because Gold Star was a regional label, Quinn made a deal with Modern to release them on a national basis. Even Hopkins himself could not keep up with the different pressings. In response to Barbara Dane's radio interview question about what label the songs "Sad News from Korea" and "Questionnaire Blues" were on, he said, "You know I don't know, they change those labels. It was first on Aladdin and they change 'em. Lots of times you ask me about those records well they be done sold out to another company."[55]

Hopkins's next chart entry was in September 1950 with "Shotgun Blues," a track he had recorded for Aladdin two years earlier. Unlike his first two chart entries, which dented the "most-played jukebox" listing for a week, "Shotgun Blues" made the "best-selling retail race records" charts for four weeks, peaking at number 5, Hopkins's highest position yet. The cut included a couple of haunting lead guitar solos played by Hopkins on his acoustic guitar. "Shotgun Blues," like most of the other songs Hopkins waxed in this period, illustrates Hopkins's creative powers in his zenith period. It begins with an instrumental lead, after which Hopkins sings:

> Yes I said go bring me my shotgun boy bring me back some shells . . .
> . . . You know my woman trying to quit me and I ain't done nothing wrong
> You know she done put me out of doors and I ain't got no home

Hopkins's composition echoed three common blues themes, just like those of his mentors Blind Lemon Jefferson and Texas Alexander: women, bad luck, and violence. From the tune's viewpoint, Hopkins's destiny amounted to bad luck and trouble; his woman unjustly quit him, so he is loading up his gun to address the losing hand fate has dealt him.

While Hopkins was waxing his blues records, other Houston artists and labels impacted the national scene too. Charles D. Henry and his wife Macy Lee Henry owned Macy's Record Distributing Company, the largest wholesale distributor in Texas. In 1949, they started Macy's Recordings, "Queen of Hits." They cut most of their artists at Bill Holford's ACA Studios, where Hopkins would also record. Lester Williams began his recording career for Macy's Records. In April 1949, Lester Williams cut his debut record, "Winter Time Blues," the first release on Macy's R&B series, which became a huge hit that Williams rode for years. Although Williams was not able to duplicate that success, he did cut several more quality tracks, including "Dowling Street Hop," a paean to Houston's equivalent of Harlem's 125th Street. The *Houston Informer*, a weekly African American paper, named Williams the "King of the Blues" in 1952.

African American music filled Houston clubs, auditoriums, and radio airwaves. In February 1950, Jax beer, the "Best Beer in Town," inaugurated the Doctor Daddy-O show *Jivin' with Jax*, run by KTHT. The show broadcast live starting at 4:55 p.m. from the Bronze Peacock club on Monday, Wednesday, and Friday and from the Eldorado Ballroom on Tuesday, Thursday, and Saturday. The show featured interviews with local and national guests.

In the April 8, 1950, edition of the *Houston Informer*, the "Night Lifer" column led with an item stating, "Club Matinee has become the Small's Paradise of Houston and every person of note visiting the city makes a visit to the spot a 'must' on their agenda." The following week the *Houston Informer* carried "T-Bone Walker at City Auditorium Next Thurs." as a bold headline on its amusements page. Further down the page, a short article and picture related events at the Eldorado Ballroom. "Playing the El Dorado Saturday and Sunday nights, Big Joe Turner, singer of the blues, known from Coast to Coast, was honored by the presence of Louis Jordan." However, despite Hopkins's Los Angeles record deal, the Houston black press lacked coverage of Hopkins, as if his music was under-the-radar and too much down-home country blues to rate a mention in the black press, which tended to focus on the tastes of the black bourgeoisie.

In September 1951, Quinn sold thirty-two unreleased sides by Lightnin' Hopkins and Texas country bluesman Lil' Son Jackson to Modern Records for $2,500. Modern immediately started releasing the Hopkins sides on its RPM subsidiary label. Modern formed RPM because many of its distributors would not take all the releases on the Modern label. So Modern started to send its new distributors releases on its RPM label. The RPM label's talent roster was to be different from the artists on Modern, but both labels released rhythm and blues. Quinn shut down his Gold Star label shortly after selling the Hopkins and Jackson sides to Modern. However, Quinn continued to operate his recording studio.

Although Hopkins's records were absent from the charts for the next seventeen months, his next hit "Give Me Central 209" proved his staying power. The song, also known as "Hello Central," stayed on the charts for six weeks, reaching number 6. By this time, Hopkins was recording for Bobby Shad's label Sittin' In With. Hopkins made a recording trip to New York City in 1951, where he cut at least eight sides.

During the time Hopkins was recording for Shad, Mississippi-born bluesman David "Honeyboy" Edwards arrived in Houston. Earlier in his career, Edwards played with Delta blues legend Robert Johnson and Big Joe Williams and had heard much talk of Lightnin' Hopkins, T-Bone Walker, and Gatemouth Brown. Edwards reminisced,

> I first met Lightning . . . in Galveston on a Sunday morning. I knowed of him, but I didn't know him personally. Down in Galveston taverns open at ten o'clock on a Sunday . . . selling whiskey, and beer, start playing blues Sunday morning. Lightning drove up there, him and his sister all of them with alcohol, whiskey, son of a bitch drink a lot of whiskey. . . . he was driving a '51 Kaiser . . . pretty new car at the time, drunk as hell. . . . we started playing blues in there and I started talking to him. His sister was drunk, his brother was drunk, all three of them son of a bitches drunk. I got drunk afterwards but those sons of bitches come there drunk. That's the first time I met him. Then I started seeing him around the Fourth Ward. Then Thunder Smith, his piano player recorded with me. . . . they was playing together every once in a while . . . not too often, just in and out. Lightning was playing a lot of stuff by himself.[56]

On the weekends, Edwards worked out of town: "On Friday nights I would drive twenty miles over to Pearland, I found a little job out there. My wife would play with me there . . . and every Saturday Lightning Hopkins played the same place. We had a night apiece . . . it was a good time. I'd listen to Lightning play the blues and I felt good. Didn't nobody have a sound like Lightning Hopkins. He had that Texas road blues, real country, way-down-in-the-country blues. He played a lot different from Mississippi blues players. When I listened to Lightning play the blues and when I played, sometimes I stopped thinking about where the blues would take me. We wasn't making no money then or anything, but just listening to Lightning made me feel good, and I felt good playing."[57] Edwards eventually left Houston for a while, only to return the next year.

By 1952, Edwards hooked up with Hopkins's old manager Lola Cullum and made some records and money under her direction: "Miss Cullum hooked me up with a band. I had Thunder Smith on piano, an old half-Mexican boy on tenor sax, and a drummer named Shorty. Thunder Smith, Wilson Smith, he got to be a good friend of mine. We called him Smiley. Miss Cullum gave him the name Thunder to go with Lightnin' Hopkins because he was Lightnin's piano player for a while. We'd rehearse over at his house . . . him and Lightnin' had fell out and wasn't working together at all."[58]

Calvin Owens, a Houston trumpet player and B. B. King bandleader, played with Lightnin' during the Gold Star rush: "He did play little honky tonk joints, you know, little joints, that was about the size of it. I don't know if anything was done, I do remember doing some recordings with Lightning, when I had just start playing. Because what happened was Gold Star, Bill Quinn, they would just bring people in the studio, you know, and of course I don't think I was drinking at the time, but I do remember these things like they'd have two or three fifths of whisky and about that time everybody got to feeling good. 'So OK boys, let's try something,' . . . Lightning is one of the cats I remember best."[59]

Hopkins's Gold Star contract from 1950 to 1952 contained a clause that prevented him from allowing "His talents to appear in connection with any other phonograph record enterprise," but that clause did not stop Hopkins from recording tracks for Bobby Shad and his Sittin' In With label. Hopkins's first label, the California-based Aladdin, probably paid him cash for recording and no royalties throughout their relationship. Modern Records, owned by four brothers, also likely avoided paying Hopkins any royalties after making deals with Quinn to purchase Hopkins's Gold Star recordings. In turn, Lightnin' displayed no qualms about violating contracts he signed. Each side commonly pursued immediate profit, not preserving long-term legacies.

Hopkins's business dealings with Bobby Shad proved to be contentious. Hopkins refused to sign a contract with Shad and would not accept a royalty arrangement. Certainly, if Hopkins had been receiving a steady stream of royalties from Aladdin, Modern, and Gold Star, he would not have insisted on this condition with Shad. By this stage in his career, Hopkins chose not to stand idle and let the white-owned and -operated music industry shape the terms of his business dealings. Bobby Shad remembered his dealings with Hopkins: "He had to be paid cash. Not only that, he had to be paid after every cut. Yes, you had to pay Lightnin' after every song. Before he started a new one, I'd pay him a hundred dollars. He did another, I gave him another hundred. He refused to work any other way." Shad's memory is very emphatic, as his statement "He refused to work any other way" shows. Hopkins later told Houston bluesman Big Walter Price his feelings about record company contracts, "[Lightnin'] would tell you . . . he wasn't too particular about contracts with record companies. He said the same thing I always know, they wasn't going to treat you fair just like me and Little Richard. They been taking money from us since they've been out there." When the interviewer asked Price if Hopkins was angry regarding record companies' treatment of him, Price replied, "That's right. Very much."[60]

Hopkins worked like a human jukebox. Instead of companies putting money in, then hearing a song, Hopkins played the song, and then he received the money. If Hopkins recorded ten songs and waited until he was finished to request payment, he risked losing money. By stopping after every song to get paid, Hopkins limited his exposure to exploitation, or so he thought. Earlier in his life, Hopkins labored on farms. Although no incidents or anecdotes survive about his wages during that hardscrabble period, he likely experienced mistreatment, both physical and economic, when dealing with the sharecropper system. As noted earlier, after Hopkins was released from the county chain gang, he left town so he would not be forced to pick cotton or other crops. So when Hopkins could exercise some amount of control over selling his labor, all those prior life experiences, particularly sharecropping, informed his actions.

As was true specifically in Hopkins's early recording career, whites more generally dominated the blues and jazz recording and production industry, while blacks tended to dominate the talent pool. As historian Frank Kofsky maintains, "The leading innovators of jazz have always been black, whereas the ownership of the music—places where it can be played, that is, and of the channels through which it is distributed—have always gone to enrich whites."[61] Hopkins was not immune to that often one-sided division of profits.

At this early stage of his music career, all of Hopkins's recording employers were white, from the Mesner brothers who owned Aladdin to the Bihari brothers at Modern Records who bought his recordings, to Bill Quinn at Gold Star, up to and including Bobby Shad at the Sittin' In With label. Hopkins was discontented with payments that he received, or did not receive, from royalty agreements, like the ones he signed with Quinn. Therefore, he changed to his cash-on-the-barrelhead method. His bitterness toward those who employed him both in the cotton fields and in the recording studio needs little explanation. Yet evidence suggests Hopkins did not let the decades of white oppression taint his view of an entire race. For example, white record producer Aubrey Mayhew came to Houston five times during the 1960s to record Hopkins and quickly found out that "There was no color line with Hopkins . . . once you gained his trust you were all right with him."[62] After Hopkins dictated business terms to his advantage, he worked with Shad for a couple of years in the early 1950s.

Hopkins's song "Give Me Central 209" backed with the mostly instrumental "New York Boogie," with its recycled John Lee Hooker–style riff, constitutes Hopkins's third release for Shad's company. In the lyrics of "Central," Hopkins tries to get ahold of his baby on the telephone because the buses are not running, the trains won't allow him to ride anymore, and even the ticket agent says Hopkins will not ride again.

Aladdin continued to release Hopkins's work, which attracted national press repeatedly. E. B. Rea's "Encores and Echoes" column in the January 20, 1951, *Baltimore Afro American* noted, "Lightning Hopkins' 'Honey, Honey Blues' backed by 'Moonrise Blues' are poised for terrific juke box biz."[63]

Journalist Phil Johnson praised the sides Hopkins recorded for Shad in 1950 and 1951. Writing in *The Independent* (UK) more than fifty years later, on the occasion of a rerelease of some of the Shad sides, Johnson claimed, "What makes this collection a must is one incredible rockabilly number, 'Buck Dance Boogie' [also issued as 'Papa Bones Boogie']. Yes, four full years before Elvis and Scotty Moore, a Texas 'primitive' had gone and invented rock 'n' roll."[64] "Buck Dance Boogie" would fit nicely alongside any number of ravers by artists such as Gene Vincent, Carl Perkins, or Eddie Cochran.

Hopkins's music, particularly his guitar style, preceded what became known as rock 'n' roll. The Muddy Waters and Brownie McGhee song title "The Blues Had a Baby and They Named It Rock and Roll" encapsulates Hopkins's role in American music history nicely. Hopkins became one of the fathers of rock 'n' roll. "Buck Dance Boogie" and several other songs Hopkins recorded for Bobby Shad, along with songs he recorded for Herald Records shortly thereafter, prove Hopkins's style of country blues music catalyzed another genre just as American popular music appetites stirred, hungry for something new.

Hopkins's last chart hit in the first segment of his two-stage career was also released on the Sittin' In With record label. "Coffee Blues" entered the most-played jukebox charts on March 29, 1952, just five weeks after "Give Me Central 209" first made the charts. "Coffee Blues" remained on the charts for two weeks, stalling at number 6.[65] It was backed with his third recorded version of "New Short Haired Woman," this time entitled "New Short-Haired Woman." "Coffee Blues" placed Hopkins's upbeat acoustic guitar and boogie styling at the center of the song. The rather tepid lyrics describe papa being mad at mama because she did not bring any coffee home. Hopkins's method of improvising lyrics on the spot while in the recording studio often yielded fairly subpar results, such as this coffee drone.

In contrast, "Bald Headed Woman," a single also from 1952 on Sittin' In With, retains flair and distinction too. Still another song about black women and their hair, it reveals Hopkins's keen observation skills, especially regarding black women's beauty habits:

> Give me—I'm gonna take it—back that wig I bought you woman,
> Oh Lord, let your doggone head go bald

Hopkins's fixation on short-haired and bald-headed women invokes more than just a superficial meaning in African American culture.

The importance of hair has roots in Africa. In West African societies, hairstyles indicate marital status, age, religion, ethnic identity, wealth, and rank within the community. Slave owners often described Africans' hair as woolly, likening it to animal hair, and this dehumanizing practice emotionally scarred the slaves. When African Americans saw that straighter-haired and lighter-skinned African Americans received better treatment and more opportunity, many tried to straighten their hair in hopes of receiving similar treatment. Although Hopkins's lyrics do not directly address the hair-straightening issue, the frequency with which he recorded "Short Haired Woman" throughout his career seems to indicate an awareness of hair care and the aesthetics of beauty in black culture. Ironically, despite his criticism of black women and their hair issues, Hopkins himself would invest quite a bit of time and money in hair, for he straightened his own throughout most of the 1960s.

Hopkins did not have a presence on the national charts for the rest of the 1950s. His songs "Give Me Central 209" and "Coffee Blues," chart-busters in early 1952, were part of a larger national trend, which Billboard "Rhythm and Blues Notes" columnist Hal Webman noted in his February 9, 1952, column:

> For the first time in many months, the down-home, Southern-style blues appears to have taken a solid hold in the current market. Down-home blues had been taking a back seat to the big city blues, good rocking novelties and vocal quartet ballads for quite a while. However, the Southern blues appears to have opened up to its widest extent in some time, and the lowdown stuff has been cropping up as bestselling of late. Such artists as B. B. King, Howling Wolf, Roscoe Gordon, Fats Domino, Sonny Boy Williamson, Lightnin'

Hopkins, John Lee Hooker, Lloyd [*sic*] Fulson, Billy Wright, Muddy Waters, etc., have taken fast hold in such market areas as New Orleans, Dallas, Atlanta, Los Angeles, etc. Even the sophisticated big towns, like New York and Chicago, have felt the Southern blues influence in wax tastes.[66]

Nineteen fifty-two marked the height of Hopkins's national recognition. After his success early in the year, he increased his recording pace. In 1951, he only recorded about ten sides, but in 1952 he cranked out at least thirty sides for the Sittin' In With label and its subsidiary Jax imprint.

In 1952, Hopkins toured the West Coast with Amos Milburn. In an interview for Barbara Dane's radio show on KPFK in Los Angeles, he spoke of that 1952 tour: "Yeah, I came here on a tour then, long about '52, I was with Amos Milburn. I imagine you heard of Amos. Well we did a tour here for about a month. And we played around here and so at last one day I caught the blues. I caught The Sunset Limited, yeah, right back [to Houston]."[67] Hopkins's comments reflect a lifelong displeasure concerning staying away from home.

In addition to touring the West Coast in 1952, Hopkins also received the attention of Brownie McGhee and the Blockbusters, who released the song "Letter to Lightnin' Hopkins" on the Jax label. One member was Sonny Terry, who later joined McGhee in a duo that lasted for many decades. Walter "Brownie" McGhee hailed from Knoxville, Tennessee, and started working as a guitarist and pianist in a Baptist church choir in Lenoir, Tennessee. He met Sonny Terry in North Carolina in 1939, and they worked together almost continuously from that point. McGhee's lyrics reveal his musical debt to Hopkins's lyrics, sarcasm, gumption, and attitude.

> I'm going to Houston, Texas
> Lightnin' Hopkins is the man I want to see
> . . . Well, if you can't stand my jiving
> Sam I'm gonna give you the 3rd degree

McGhee's song playfully disrespected Hopkins, proving Hopkins's popular reputation, which compelled McGhee to pen a tune that acted as a one-way version of playing the dozens, in which African American men exchange insults about family members or their mothers. McGhee's taunts also prefigured hip-hop feuds that became popular forty years later. The final verse even calls out Hopkins's hit song "Give Me Central 209," for McGhee sings, "The reason you didn't get no answer, when you called Central 209, because the line was busy she was calling me Sam, all the time." Hopkins never answered with his own song about McGhee, but he did go on to record with McGhee and Sonny Terry eight years later.

Hopkins also met and began mentoring Luke "Long Gone" Miles, a young man from Shreveport, Louisiana, who moved to Houston in 1952. Miles entered the music community because he heard about Lightnin': "What really got me to sing was I heard so much about Lightning. And I have heard a lot of his records and after I found out he was in Houston, Texas and I was in Shreveport, which was about 200 miles [away]. I went there in '52, and stayed, and me and him were together just about everyday and night from '52 til I come out here in '61. . . . the first song I ever sung was behind his playing. The first thing I did was drop the mike. I wasn't nervous . . . I was just scared. But Lightnin' told me I had a good voice, but I still had a lot to learn about singing in front of people."[68]

Miles continued, "He's the one that give me the name of Long Gone. The first day he met me he named me that. Well, first he named me Long Tall. He said 'I don't like that name I'm gonna take that back.' I guess there's no man on earth I'd rather be with than him. The day I left Houston to come to the West Coast, Lightnin' sat on his front porch and watched me all the way down the street until I disappeared. Somewhere in the back of his mind I think he thought I was his little boy, and when I told him I was leavin' he just couldn't believe his little boy was goin'."[69] While Hopkins introduced Miles to the scene, he also signed a deal with Bobby Shad to record for Decca.

The August 22, 1953, edition of the *Pittsburgh Courier* reported that Bobby Shad was now working for the Decca record label, thus boosting its rhythm and blues roster. The *Courier* also reported Shad adding such artists as Benny Green, Little Esther the Peterson Singers, and Lightnin' Hopkins. In 1953, Hopkins cut back on his recording. He made only eight sides for the Decca label, recording the sides in a Houston studio in July. Two of those songs offer holiday themes, "Merry Christmas" backed with "Happy New Year," which comprised Decca release number 48036.

Even though Shad recorded and signed Hopkins to his Sittin' In With label, its Jax subsidiary, Decca Records, and Mercury, Shad maintained a sense of ambivalence toward the bluesman's talent. Lightnin' did not know how to play the blues, nor was he a good guitar player, Shad argued after recording him. In fact, according to Shad, Hopkins hardly played at all. In later years, Hopkins learned how, admitted Shad, but the producer still did not understand Hopkins's status. Shad made those comments to blues writer Ted Berkowitz during an interview in Shad's office in Rockefeller Center in 1968.

In 1954, Hopkins ramped up his recording pace again. He moved to yet another label, this time recording for New York–based Herald Records. Fred

Mendelsohn founded Herald Records in Elizabeth, New Jersey, in 1952. Previously, Mendelsohn had cofounded Regal Records with the Braun brothers in Linden, New Jersey, in 1949. Regal was an R&B label that recorded the likes of Larry Darnel, Paul Gayten, Ann Laurie, and blues singer Chubby Newman. After a tax dispute with the government, he dissolved Regal and struck out on his own with Herald Records. Eventually, he joined forces with Al Silver and Silver's brother-in-law, who continued Herald after Mendelsohn left.

Hopkins was now playing an electric guitar when he recorded, plus he added a rhythm section, a bass player, and a drummer. Bass player Donald Cooks and drummer Connie Kroll worked some Sittin' In With sessions with Hopkins, too, and continued working with Hopkins on his Decca sessions in 1953.

When Hopkins played gigs around Houston in the 1950s, Earl Gilliam sometimes joined him:

I had my band in Fifth Ward and I moved to Third Ward and that's when I played with him, in the '50s. [We played] Shady's Playhouse, Hamilton Inn on Wayne Street in Fifth Ward. He was all right, just a guitar player. I would make the changes but him playing by himself, he just changed when he get ready, you just have to follow him. . . . He made up songs, in the same beat; it'd be in the same beat, just a different key. He'd be mostly answering himself. He [was] something like John Lee Hooker, he'd say anything. You asked him what he'd say on a song, he'd tell you he didn't know. Something like James Brown, he be saying all that stuff, you just tell a story about something, make it rhyme. He was good at it. He dressed nice, he had that old Cadillac. He used to drink that wine; he'd make up some songs.[70]

According to Gilliam, Hopkins epitomized a local musician when they worked together in Houston. As Hopkins recorded less, his national profile faded away, and American popular music trends, record buyers, and Hopkins's mostly African American audience moved on to fresh, inchoate styles of song.

Meanwhile, the Jim Crow system continually impacted the streets of Houston. Rhythm and blues pioneer Ray Charles lived in Houston's Fourth Ward in 1954. On one occasion, the Houston police stopped Ray's Oldsmobile that his friend, saxophone player David "Fathead" Newman, was driving. The "legitimate" reason for the stop seems to be the police were suspicious of African Americans driving an expensive car. Newman wore his hair straightened. After the white cops discovered Ray was blind, they informed him, "Well you better find a way back, because we're taking this other nigger and his fucked-up hairdo down to the station." The cops left Charles alone on the side of the road and beat Newman up on the way to the police station.[71] Such humiliating and random police violence threatened many African Americans in the city.

By the time Hopkins cut his first session for Herald in Houston in April 1954, sweeping changes immersed popular music. Black R&B, which was rooted in slave songs, baptized by gospel influences, and often pigeonholed as ghetto music, began to cross onto predominantly white pop charts, just like countrypolitan crooners displaced honky-tonkers. Early in 1954, vocal groups like the Ravens and Orioles nibbled at the bottom of the pop charts. The Chords' song "Sh-boom," which appeared on the pop charts in July 1954, signaled a siege: twice as many R&B records crossed over in 1954 as the previous year. Six years after *Billboard* magazine derided Hopkins as "old style," his music faced these broad, sweeping changes to the American musical palate.

Not long after black R&B started becoming more popular with young white record buyers, Mississippi-born truck driver Elvis Aaron Presley ventured into Sam Phillips's Sun studios in Memphis and recorded some revved-up hillbilly music. On July 5, 1954, Presley and his band cut three tracks, including "That's All Right," a track first recorded by bluesman Arthur "Big Boy" Crudup in September 1946. Two days later Memphis disc jockey Dewey Phillips blasted Presley's take on "That's All Right" on his *Red, Hot and Blue* radio show. Presley's hip-shaking, hiccupy song style helped launch a genre that almost buried the music of bluesman Hopkins and his peers.

The Herald label released twenty-eight sides, showcasing the forty-two-year-old Hopkins's ability to execute finely chiseled, top-notch songs over a snarling three-piece combo led by his now-electrified guitar. "Hopkins Sky Hop" was a raucous instrumental guitar ripper that bore little resemblance to his solo acoustic country blues sides cut for the Aladdin label. The unhitched intensity and speed of Hopkins's guitar on the tune foreshadowed Link Wray, the eventual father of the power chord, and other white guitar rock 'n' rollers who followed Hopkins, like the Jon Spencer Blues Explosion decades later. Hopkins's Herald sides constitute primitive garage rock 'n' roll before the term gained popularity.

Texas guitar legend Stevie Ray Vaughan later appropriated "Hopkins Sky Hop," as an instrumental too, calling it "Rude Mood." During the 1980s, Vaughan briefly became an internationally renowned guitarist on par with Jimi Hendrix. Like ZZ Top and others, he did not hesitate to mimic, reinvent, and build on guitar licks he borrowed from black music, including that of Hopkins, Albert King, and others. Following in the footsteps of Eric Clapton's guitar imitation of Albert King on Cream's song "Strange Brew," Vaughan also incorporated heavy strains of Albert King, particularly when playing on David Bowie's album *Let's Dance*. Vaughan, like many more who preceded and followed him, believed that African American music provided a wellspring of inspiration. He paid homage to a richly woven musical heritage, though critics feel chagrined by his lack of attribution. Like most rock 'n' rollers, he failed to give full credit to hybrid compositions culled from other tunes.

At one point, Albert King borrowed a substantial amount of money from Vaughan. King dropped by one of Vaughan's recording sessions. When Vaughan was ready to leave, he told King, "I was wondering if I could get back the money I loaned you," to which King replied, "Money? Money? Come on now son, you know you owe me, don't you?" King left without paying Vaughan.[72] According to the *All Music Guide* database, at the time of this writing, Vaughan's song "Rude Mood," based on Hopkins's "Hopkins Sky Hop," has been released no fewer than twenty-three times.[73] The sales of the compact discs with "Rude Mood," though, do not benefit the Hopkins estate.

Some artists, for example, the Grammy-nominated songwriter and folk artist Peter Case, did not short Hopkins or his estate of royalties. When Case, a Buffalo, New York, native, cut a song he called "Icewater" for his solo debut album in 1986, he credited the music to Lightnin' Hopkins and added his own lyrics. Case remembered how his song came about:

I got up to Boston one night, I was over in Cambridge, and it was winter. I had about five bucks. It was winter and it said Lightnin' Hopkins [on the marquee] and I went in and saw him play. It wasn't packed, maybe a hundred people there, a little theater. He played electric, he played "Your Rolling Mill Is Burning Down" ["Mister Charlie"], telling a lot of stories, it was fantastic. . . . I really got into Lightnin' Hopkins and learned how to play that stuff. He became a hero to me, along with Mississippi John Hurt. I remember loving his record *Lightnin' in New York* at that same time he might have played some of those same songs. He also played "Lightnin's Piano Boogie," "Come Around Here," and ["Jesus Won't You Come by Here"], that gospel thing.

Years later, when I was in L.A., I got this album *Lightning Hopkins Sings the Blues*. It was an incredible album. It was rereleased as *Jakehead Boogie*. It just blew me away. It's just a great record. It's got "Jakehead Boogie" [on it]. I just got obsessed with it when I was in the Plimsouls. One day I put my guitar in G tuning and played [Lightnin's song] "Tell Me Pretty Mama." I've been told by people like [Bruce] Bromberg that [Lightnin'] didn't play in tunings, but on that song it sounds like he was playing in a G tuning. I copped it the best way I could in G tuning. Nobody ever showed me. . . . I figured out the words for it when I was here in Texas over in Fort Worth staying with T-Bone Burnett in '85. . . . One morning I woke up and wrote a new lyric for it. He liked it, and we cut it. Played it with a thumb pick, just playing that Lightning boogie the way I learned it. I thought I learned it off the record as best that I could.[74]

By the 1950s, Hopkins's stylistic shift was not solely a reaction to the shifting tastes on the R&B charts. When he played live, Hopkins amplified his sound in order to be heard over noisy Houston ghetto-based juke joint crowds. The patrons who frequented these joints wanted to dance, which required Hopkins to swing with a churning, up-tempo beat. While his lyrics and musical style clearly embodied the blues vernacular, most of the songs he recorded for the Herald label evoke a more rough-hewn, husky intensity than his earlier work. Some of the choice instrumentals on Hopkins's Herald sides are "Grandma's Boogie," "Lightnin's Boogie," "Moving Out Boogie," "Early Mornin' Boogie," and "Lightnin' Special." Every one of those songs exhibits the potential to prompt dancers to fill up a floor quickly.

Hopkins did not record very often for the rest of the decade. In 1955, he cut four sides for the San Antonio–based TNT label, which provided Hopkins $350 to record. The TNT acronym stood for Tanner 'N Texas. The label released sides by Big Walter Price and recorded acts such as Santiago Jimenez, the Texas Tophands, and Harry Choates. The label disappeared eventually, and by the 1960s Tanner was running a studio and pressing plant on Poplar Street in San Antonio, Texas.

On January 14, 1955, disc jockey Alan Freed produced the Rock 'n' Roll Jubilee Ball in New York City, his first event in the "Big Apple." The lineup included Fats Domino, Clyde McPhatter and the Drifters, Ruth Brown, and Big Joe Turner. In March, the movie *Blackboard Jungle* debuted with the song "Rock Around the Clock" by Bill Haley and His Comets playing over the opening sequence. Bo Diddley's song "Bo Diddley," backed by "I'm a Man," entered the *Billboard* charts in early May. On May 21, Chuck Berry waxed "Maybellene" for Chess Records. In June, Buddy Holly opened up an Elvis Presley concert in Holly's hometown of Lubbock, Texas. Down in New Orleans, Little Richard wailed his way through his song "Tutti Frutti" in Cosimo Matassa's J & M Studio. In late December, hillbilly bopper Carl Perkins recorded "Blue Suede Shoes" in Sun Studios in Memphis. The scene was now crowded with Presley, Holly, Diddley, Berry, Little Richard, Carl Perkins, and many more. This left little room or interest in Hopkins's Texas country blues.

The onslaught of rock 'n' roll and trend-following music consumers did not alarm Hopkins, who enjoyed Houston's humid neighborhoods and stroking the blues in no-name beer joints, which supplied him with enough money for alcohol, cigarettes, and rent money. He also enjoyed spending a lot of his time fishing, as Barbara Dane discovered in 1960, "I like fishing for those croakers there in Houston and them reds. We goes out in deep water there, and those flounders there are the best fish. . . . I work practically every night that way when I wake up in the day I be lonesome. All my little friends they have a job, they be working. I just jump in my car and run on down there and rent me a boat and go out there a little piece. But I don't go out there very far cuz I'm scary, I'm scared to go in the water by myself."[75]

By 1956, Hopkins's recording talents were not in demand. He only cut two songs in one year, this time for the Chart label. Hopkins's career slid into obscurity. Hopkins did not return to the recording studio in 1957–1958, though record companies had enough of his product to go on releasing singles through 1959. For example, the March 2, 1957, edition of *Billboard* magazine ran a review in its R&B section of his Herald Records release "Please Don't Go Baby," backed with "Remember Me." The reviewer's assessment of the B-side was "Similar to the flip—Southern blues with the authentic folk quality. Great for those who dig territorial wax."[76] *Billboard* reviewed Hopkins's Shad records release of "Mad as I Can Be," backed by "Hello, Central" in its October 26, 1959, issue. The anonymous reviewer saw some crossover potential in the A-side, writing, "The authentic folk blues artist gets off a lyric which tells a story. Sound may appeal to pop deejays as a change from usual fare."[77]

Despite Hopkins's fading recording career, in the late 1950s the city of Houston teemed with entertainment performers just about every night of the week. For example, the weekly entertainment publication *Inside Houston* boasted ads to see Houston resident Clifton Chenier, the King of Zydeco, performing at the Eldorado Ballroom on Labor Day, September 2, 1957. Etta James was also on the bill, performing her hit "Roll with Me Henry." Another option for Labor Day festivities included catching the twin bill of B. B. King and Louis Jordan and their bands performing at the Coliseum, located downtown. Before catching a band, hungry fans had an array of choices in Hopkins's Third Ward neighborhood. They could enjoy a steak dinner at the Black Cat Tavern on the 1800 block of Dowling, have some seafood at the Delicado on Wheeler Avenue, or stop by the Groovy Grill on Tierwester near Texas Southern University. Record buyers could stop at either of King Bee Record and Barbershop's locations, on Dowling Street or Lyons Avenue in the Fifth Ward, and pick up their favorite R&B twelve-inch LPs for $3.98 or $4.98.

In January 1958, Houstonian Johnny Copeland and his orchestra worked at Club De Lisa, while local guitar man Albert "Freeze" Collins and his orchestra held forth at Walter's Lounge. The Eldorado Ballroom's January 1958 schedule included Charles Brown and his orchestra, Lowell Fulson and his orchestra, James Brown and the Flames, and Little Willie John, while the City Auditorium featured Bill Doggett playing hits like "Honky Tonk" and "Rambunctious."

Ironically, as Hopkins recorded less, the national music press heralded "a great day for the blues." Ren Grevatt wrote the "On the Beat" column for *Billboard*, which covered rhythm and blues and rock 'n' roll. In his April 14, 1958, column he noted, "The resurgence of the blues, even in the pop idiom was noted as early as last fall in the stories in *Billboard*. At the time, particular note was taken of the appearance of the blues in the singles field. Now, the trend seems apparent in an even more notable way in the package field. There have been a number of albums of late dedicated to the blues."[78] By August 1958, a *Billboard* article entitled "Diskeries in Blues Switch" reported, "Observant deejays are programming blues. . . . The big upsurge in blues is most interesting on the package level . . . the increase of blues in the album field followed the singles upsurge. . . . It is unlikely that this is only a passing phase. Blues is one of the only American musical forms and in its variations blues can be simple or relatively sophisticated."[79]

The African American music scene in Houston was packed with high-quality acts near the end of the 1950s. However, Hopkins's black audience was slim. Since his recording debut in 1946, Hopkins had recorded over two hundred sides that made it to the marketplace on fifteen different record labels. His name appeared on best-selling record and R&B radio charts; his song "Short Haired Woman" sold more than one hundred thousand copies. Artists as diverse as Bob Dylan and Miles Davis were deeply inspired by him. The former confessed that Hopkins influenced his song "Leopard Skin Pillbox Hat," while the latter admitted he borrowed the chord structure for his song "It Gets Better" from Hopkins.[80]

Near the dawn of the 1960s, popular music tastes and styles soon swept Hopkins up into a different world—one of new technologies, audiences, and larger, international venues. Hopkins, the "King of Dowling Street," would soon reign over a whole new kingdom.

FIVE

FOLKSINGER BLUES

BY THE LATE 1950S, the near-destitute Lightnin' Hopkins was living in a rooming house in the Third Ward. The rise of rhythm and blues and rock 'n' roll, combined with Hopkins's failure to record and tour over the previous several years, severely lowered his national profile. By the late 1950s, Hopkins played small dive bars around the city for a few dollars a night.

At the end of the 1950s, fortunately for Hopkins, a folk music revival began to gather steam. For instance, Barry Olivier started presenting concerts of local musicians at the University of California in Berkeley in 1956 and 1957. By 1958, Olivier convinced the university to let him organize a summer folk festival, the genesis of what became known as the Berkeley Folk Festival. Farther down the coast in Los Angeles, Ed Pearl opened the Ash Grove nightclub on Melrose Avenue in 1958. Although Pearl presented various styles, acts like the New Lost City Ramblers, the Limeliters, and Buddy Travis appealed to the same audience that supported folk artists like Ramblin' Jack Elliott, Odetta, and Guy Carawan in their earlier Los Angeles appearances. The Ash Grove earned a reputation as an important showcase venue.

On the East Coast, *New York Times* music critic Robert Shelton wrote columns in 1958 and 1959 praising records by folk artists Pete Seeger, Burl Ives, Josh White, and Carolyn Hester. Shelton's articles also discussed music that influenced popular modern-day folkies, including a Sam Charters–produced reissue of a Blind Willie Johnson record for Folkways Records. In the Greenwich Village neighborhood, Izzy Young ran the Folklore Center on MacDougal Street, which attracted performers and folk music fans. When the weather permitted, Washington Square Park in the Village hosted amateur musicians creating their own scene, hanging out singing and strumming guitars, banjos, and mando- lins. Farther uptown in Manhattan, a folk/blues revival concert was held at the Carnegie Recital Hall in April 1959, featuring Chicago bluesman Muddy Waters backed by pianist Memphis Slim and harmonica player James Cotton.

Not long after Olivier's pioneering West Coast folk festival promotions, mu- sician and promoter George Wein and artist manager Albert Grossman pro- duced the first Newport Folk Festival in Rhode Island on July 11–12, 1959. The festival featured Odetta, Peter Seeger, Brownie McGhee and Sonny Terry, the Stanley Brothers, Barbara Dane, the Kingston Trio, and many more. Robert Shelton, an advocate for the revival, called the Newport Festival "perhaps the most ambitious attempt . . . at delineating a cross-section of the nation's folk music."[1]

England experienced a renewed interest in traditional forms of American music too. Briton Lonnie Donegan recorded a skiffle version of Huddie Led- better's "Rock Island Line," a big hit in the United Kingdom. Skiffle musicians blended blues, traditional jazz, and Anglo folk songs in easily imitated forms. Donegan's hit crossed over the Atlantic, charting to number 13 on *Billboard*'s The Top 100, proving consumers' interest. This steadily increasing appetite for "authentic" folk music coincided with a much-needed professional and financial revival for Hopkins.

The folk revival was accompanied by or spurred the blues revival. According to author Francis Davis, "The impetus for this blues revival was the publication of Sam Charters's mythopoeic *The Country Blues* in 1959 and his 'rediscovery' of the Texas blues singer and guitarist Lightnin' Hopkins that same year."[2] The book contained an entire chapter on Hopkins. In a positive review for the April 24, 1960, edition of the *Washington Post*, Ray B. Browne delineated blues singers as "rude poets," and Hopkins was "the last of the great."[3]

Houston folklorist Mack McCormick and New York author Sam Charters became jointly responsible for bringing Hopkins back into the limelight and repositioning him for a second career in the folk music and coffeehouse scene of the late 1950s and the 1960s. With the help of McCormick, Charters, and several music industry professionals, Hopkins transitioned successfully from a Southern country blues chanter to a folk blues artist. In less than two years, he would play Carnegie Hall, constituting one the best examples of a forgotten blues singer "discovered" by mainly white college crowds, affluent listeners, and record buyers who appreciated "authentic" folk music. During the height of the turbulent sixties, the blues bard of the Third Ward performed at several 1960s hotspots, such as the University of California's Berkeley campus and the 1965 Newport Folk Festival, where Bob Dylan plugged his guitar in and angered the folk purists.

Sam Charters stimulated Hopkins's career rejuvenation. In the late 1950s, Charters lived in New Orleans and managed a picture shop on Royal Street. He joined friends who also deeply enjoyed rhythm and blues music at a restaurant and bar called Bourbon House, located at the corner of Bourbon and St. Peter Streets. One day, while Charters and his pals were discussing Lightnin' Hopkins, one of the cooks overheard their conversation. The cook informed the group Hopkins was his cousin and lived in Houston. This bit of information eventually led Charters to rediscover Hopkins.

Charters published his first book, *Jazz: New Orleans 1885–1957*, in 1958. The publication begat Charters's broad name recognition and opened up professional opportunities. He starred on a radio program in New York City with the composer Gunter Schuler and jazz critic Nat Hentoff. Afterwards, Hentoff probed Charters's enthusiasm for blues music and his concept for a book on the subject. To encourage Charters, Hentoff suggested Ted Amundsen at Rinehart might be interested in such a work. Charters dropped off a short sample at Rinehart on a Thursday afternoon, and by the next Monday Charters received a telegram at a sculptor studio on Broadway Street in Greenwich Village, where he resided, asking him to sign the contract because an English publisher desired the book.

Charters received a small advance, which he added to some of his own accumulated savings, so he packed some personal belongings, including a professional recording machine used on prior field trips, and began the research trip. Before leaving New York, he contacted Mack McCormick, who offered to let him stay at his house when he arrived in Houston. McCormick had been scouring Houston for Hopkins. When Charters arrived in Houston in January 1959, he spent some time with McCormick searching for Hopkins around Dowling Street. However, few folks in the neighborhood offered help. Charters and McCormick, two whites scouting black neighborhoods in the Deep South, likely aroused local suspicions.

The duo drove around the Third Ward ghetto looking for Hopkins, finally tracking down a pawnbroker who held Hopkins's guitar. His files contained an address for Hopkins. They could not locate Hopkins at that address, but they did meet a young boy at the premises who directed them to Hopkins's sister. She sent them to his landlady, who, in turn, directed them to two or three bars Hopkins frequented. Charters and McCormick still lacked luck, though.

The next morning, when Charters drove down Dowling Street and stopped at the first red light, a car pulled alongside his. A thin black man wearing shades rolled down his window, leaned toward Charters, and said, "You lookin' for me?" "Are you Lightnin'?" Charters replied. "That's right," said Hopkins. "Lightnin', I sure am." Charters rode alone that day due to McCormick's job duties. After Charters and Hopkins spoke on the street corner, Lightnin' agreed to record that afternoon—January 16, 1959. Since Hopkins's guitar rested in the pawnshop, they drove around for an hour looking for a guitar to borrow, finally choosing an old acoustic guitar to rent in a pawnshop. The next stop was a music store for a new set of strings and then the liquor store for a bottle of gin.[4]

Charters, Hopkins, and a friend settled in at 2803 Hadley in the Third Ward, where Charters rented a room. Charters had his portable Ampex recorder with an Electrovoice microphone set up to record the session. Over the next few hours, Hopkins sang eleven songs accompanied only by the rented acoustic guitar. Having finished by four o'clock, Hopkins signed a simple release and Charters paid him three hundred dollars in cash for his performance. At forty-seven years old, Hopkins didn't realize his circumstances were changing: recording that afternoon became the first step to the internationally successful second phase of his musical career.

Later that day, Charters sent a letter to Marian Disler at Folkways. His letter showed the significance he attributed to Hopkins:

I've found and recorded the legendary Lightning Hopkins. It's been a hell of a struggle, but I got an LP out of him. . . . He's used to the kind of recording fees that the major outfits have paid in the past—he's recorded on Gold Star, Aladdin, Herald, and Score—we had a long weary afternoon. I was able to get him for $300 [over $2,200 in 2009]. It took nearly every cent I had, but it was nothing compared to what he used to get from Gold Star and Aladdin.

. . . He's got this sudden reputation among the folk singers, which the Score LP has helped, even though it's the old Aladdin material. He's the best, without question; so I'm not going to record anyone else. If anyone's interested in managing him; let me know. There's money here. . . .

. . . I think you should get this out as quickly as possible. . . . He's pretty hot at this moment, and after we listened to the playback we both agreed he's never sung better.[5]

That night, Charters headed back to McCormick's house, where they listened to the tapes. At the time, McCormick's keen interest included the music of blues artist Huddie "Leadbelly" Ledbetter, who had died in 1949. Because Hopkins's songs were dissimilar to Leadbelly-type material, he was disappointed. However, that sentiment did not stop him from quickly following in Charters's footsteps by recording Hopkins himself in 1959.

Beginning on February 26, just a little more than a month after the Charters recording, and continuing through July 20, McCormick captured Hopkins's tunes on six different occasions, and acting as Hopkins's de facto manager, started setting up gigs. A hootenanny presented by the Houston Folklore Group at the Alley Theater in downtown Houston was the first important gig McCormick arranged. McCormick, who chaired the Folklore Group, founded in 1951, scheduled the "Hootenanny at the Alley" for July 20, 1959. Ben Ramey, an attorney and member of the Houston Folklore Group, emceed the midsummer hootenanny, which featured performers John A. Lomax, Jr., Kyla Bynum, Jimmie Lee Grubbs, Jim Lyday and Howard Porper, and Hopkins. Porper and Lomax were also founders of the Folklore Group.

This Alley gig amounted to the first occasion where Hopkins played for a mainly white audience, since he usually performed in the black community. Chris Strachwitz, the founder of Arhoolie Records, recalled witnessing Lightnin' playing in a juke joint in Houston in 1959, "They weren't really bars, they were houses . . . and they were selling beer. . . . the amplifier was on top of the table and there was a refrigerator behind him, the drummer was in the corner. It's amazing. It was this real house party, improvising on the spot and people would yell back at him, 'You don't know what you're talking about.' And he would respond, 'Baby I know what I'm talking about.'"[6]

Texas barrelhouse piano player R. T. Williams, better known as the Grey Ghost, saw Hopkins perform at a venue on Airline Drive in Houston: "He used to play at a café right across the street where I lived. He'd be over there with his hair conked and his amplifier sitting up on another soda water case. Him sitting on a chair with one case in this chair, and that's where he played. That's where I met him."[7]

Hopkins's performances in these small juke joints and dives were characterized by their interactive nature. The tradition of an audience orally reacting to a performer is rooted in the gospel music performed in African American churches. Identified as call and response, one example is found in the turn-of-the-twentieth-century Pentecostal churches, which used congregational singing to achieve climactic events, usually spiritual experiences. Characterized by shouting, spiritual possession, and a holy dance that signaled that a person was filled with the Holy Spirit, music drove the rhythm of sermons, which accompanied the high point of ceremonies. Members of a congregation often met a reverend's exhortations with an emphatic "Amen!" Hopkins had grown accustomed to such interactions when he played for black audiences. Thus, Hopkins remained apprehensive before the Alley concert.

For the July 20, 1959, performance, McCormick wanted Hopkins's performance to be akin to the bluesman playing on the streets of a black neighborhood. He asked Hopkins to come out singing when he walked onto the stage.

Hopkins obliged and entered the stage of the sold-out two-hundred-seat venue singing. McCormick recalled, "The audience had never seen it before and it was awkward for a while, but he found himself." The culture clash was evident:

> At the . . . time he said something to me that I'll never forget, it was during a song, he said, "Well a preacher don't get no amen in this corner," meaning people are clapping but they're not saying anything during the song, you're not hearing "Tell it man, you got it." That's what he's used to hearing.
>
> And when he said, "The preacher don't get no amen around here," the audience had no idea what it meant. I had to think about how strange it was when you come out and do your thing, and everybody was quiet. Particularly quiet in the Alley, a small box room. The tendency there is for everyone to breathe at the same time, otherwise it's too noisy. You get applause, and he got very good applause along with shouting, but nothing during the song, which is especially hard on him. It's hard on a lot of performers. Blues performers have an awfully hard time with the crowd silent.[8]

Hopkins was clearly a hit with his newfound audience and with critics. In a *Houston Chronicle* review, Frank Stack wrote, "Lightning Hopkins, a Dowling St. Negro folksinger who makes up his own songs, in the grand old ballad tradition from his own experience, overshadowed everybody else on the program with an easy personable style."[9] Reviewer Bill Byers, writing in the *Houston Post*, the other Houston daily, became even more effusive, writing that Hopkins's "personality electrified the overflow audience." Byers described the material Hopkins sang as "Concentrated on his own anxieties in life—the trouble he was having with a shorthaired woman, and the miseries of tornadoes sweeping into East Texas."[10] After the Folklore Group paid $75 in expenses, it split the remaining $325 box office proceeds fifty-fifty with the six artists. Hopkins's cut amounted to $20.

Charters brought the tapes to Moe Asch, the founder of Folkways Records, a figure well known in folk music circles since he previously founded the Disc Records label after World War II in an attempt to capitalize on the niche market for folk music. Disc Records lasted from 1946 to 1949 before collapsing into bankruptcy court. The experience served Asch well as he moved on to his next venture. After Disc folded, Asch started Folkways on May 1, 1949, under the nominal ownership of Marian Disler. In 1952, Folkways released the boxed set *Anthology of American Folk Music*, produced by Harry Smith. The anthology, a recording of songs from 1920s and 1930s, introduced thousands of listeners, including a young Minnesota resident, Robert Zimmerman, later known as

Bob Dylan, to American folk music. Folkways became the seminal label of the American folk scene. In 1959, Folkways issued the recordings Charters made under the title *Lightnin' Hopkins*, the first Hopkins album recorded specifically for the 33⅓ rpm format. It was not just a compiled collection of previously released 78s, like *Lightnin' Hopkins Strums the Blues*.

The Score record label issued the album *Strums the Blues* in 1958. The Mesner brothers started the Score label as an offshoot of Aladdin Records in 1948. *Strums the Blues* contained songs that Hopkins recorded for Aladdin from 1946 to 1948, including "Short Haired Woman" and "Katie Mae." The record jacket featured a cover painting with a white flannel-clad arm playing an acoustic guitar. Apparently, the decision-makers at Score Records thought revealing Hopkins to be an African American was not wise. The unsigned liner notes, just two paragraphs, barely hinted at his race and clearly positioned Hopkins as a true folkie. The author attempted to draw out the appeal of Hopkins to a white audience.

Of course, Hopkins's songs *are* emblematic expressions of the South, probing the essence of his people's culture, including their joys, triumphs, difficulties, and oppression. Yet Hopkins's work exudes a universal quality too, an everyman conceit and vibe. He emotes the personal sadness, pathos, and ecstasy of people in easygoing cadences and tremors of expression. Like great folk artists such as Burl Ives, Lightnin' improvised easily, the Score liner notes assert: "A chance sunlight—a glimpse of a railroad—the play of moon on the water, all turn his talent into a quick, fluent outpouring of feeling in wonderful accompaniment to his rich guitar. So long as folk music endures so long will Lightnin' Hopkins be played."[11]

Comparing Hopkins's improvisational ability to Burl Ives's may be suspect, but it does reveal the author's intent to make Hopkins's black blues safe and consumable for a white folk audience. Posthumously, Ives is perhaps best known for his narration of the perennial Christmas television show favorite *The Rednosed Reindeer*. In 1958, when Hopkins's first album was issued, Ives already had a storied career under his belt. He hit the record charts in 1949 with "Lavender Blue (Dilly Dilly)." In 1951, Ives followed up with his version of "On Top of Old Smoky," which entered the top ten of the charts. He recorded an album of Mother Goose rhymes for Columbia Records, published the book *The Wayfaring Stranger*, acted in Broadway plays, and appeared in movies and on television. He was a known, bankable figurehead. The comparison to him was no mistake.

In Hopkins's career, the Score record was the first example of a label remarketing his blues, originally meant mostly for a black audience, as folk music for a white audience. The album became a first step toward repackaging Hopkins's music into the long-playing format of 33⅓-rpm records as well. The music business underwent a shift in technology. Up to this point, Hopkins's records had been issued on 78s. The newer formats—the long-playing (LP) album, issued on twelve-inch discs that played at 33⅓ rpm, and seven-inch extended-play discs (EPs), more commonly known as 45s—were introduced in the United States in 1948–1949, but steadily gained ground in the market.

During the 1959 session, Charters explained to Hopkins he needed ample songs for the long-play format. "This was a continuing source of edginess between us because he never ever thought of doing an album," Charters admitted. "He'd always done singles and so when I kept asking for another song he got more and more concerned, but then he finally realized that he wasn't going to make any money at all until he finally did what I wanted."[12] The liner notes on the Folkways release recounted Charters's hunt for Lightnin' in Houston earlier that year, but contained no information illuminating the ten songs featured within. The cover was a colorful collage of Hopkins wearing a light-colored suit, with his shirt buttoned up, and donning his trademark dark shades.

Prior to his recording session with Charters, Hopkins's last large body of recordings amounted to the ferocious, primitive blues-based rock that he recorded for Herald. On those recordings, he played an electric guitar and was accompanied by a bass and drums lineup. The twenty-eight songs Hopkins recorded in 1954 for the Herald label were steeped in the blues, but included some raw, paint-peeling numbers that starkly contrast with the spare acoustic blues Charters committed to tape on that January afternoon in 1959.

Charters rented Hopkins an acoustic guitar because the folk crowd desired an unvarnished, somewhat fossilized rootsy version of the blues. For instance, the traditional blues song "Penitentiary Blues" started off the Folkways album, which contained some songs Hopkins recorded earlier in his career. Three fast-tempo guitar boogies, "She's Mine," "Come Go with Me," and "Fan It," showed off Hopkins's dexterity, though. One spoken-word track, "Reminiscences of Blind Lemon," paid tribute to Blind Lemon Jefferson, whose tune "See That My Grave Is Kept Clean" Hopkins revisits as well.

The Folkways release and the Alley Theater performance generated media coverage of Hopkins. On August 23, 1959, a little more than a month after his appearance, both the *Houston Post* and the *New York Times* ran feature stories on him. John Wilson wrote the *New York Times* article, entitled "Lightning Hopkins Rediscovered," recounting Charters finding and recording Hopkins in Houston. Wilson gushed, "Mr. Hopkins must be counted as one of the best (possibly *the* best) of the unalloyed country blues men still singing." According to Wilson, the excellent quality of the recording was important, but more significantly,

"Mr. Charters has rescued from obscurity a singer who seemed to have committed suicide by trying to adapt to rock 'n' roll standards."[13] Wilson was clearly not enamored of Hopkins's records made during the height of his R&B phase in the mid-1950s.

Journalist Charlotte Phelan wrote the lengthy piece about Hopkins that appeared in the *Houston Post.* The article, entitled "Song Maker," featured a profile and interview that were accompanied by a large photo of Hopkins sitting on his bed wearing a snazzy hat, a plaid flannel shirt, and a small white towel draped around his neck. With an acoustic guitar cradled in his lap, he looked skyward. In the piece, Hopkins expressed pleasure about playing the Alley hootenanny. The article also mentioned the increased interest and commercial opportunities stirring Hopkins's newly rejuvenated career. Harold Leventhal, a well-known New York promoter and the manager of the Weavers, contacted McCormick, offering to book Hopkins at Carnegie or Town Hall in New York City. The article also mentioned negotiations for a European tour.

According to Phelan, Hopkins's daily routine included drinking two beers for breakfast and more drinking throughout the day. In the article, McCormick described Hopkins as innocent, isolated, and oblivious to contemporary life to the point that he was unaware of long-playing records, even though an LP reissue of his earlier recordings was for sale within a block of his home. Considering Hopkins had recorded an album for Charters earlier in the year, McCormick's comments seem open to question. However, McCormick's observations imply Hopkins suffered social and financial isolation.

In regard to drinking, drummer Robert Murphy, who backed him throughout the summer of 1961, professes, "I never saw him drunk and trying to play. Some guys would fall off chairs. Lightnin' would get a little tipsy, because everybody got like that. But he never got out of control. When he'd get a little tipsy, that's when he would extend his chord pattern and things." About traveling and keeping abreast of modern life, Murphy observes, "He didn't care about traveling. He was from the country country, way back in the woods country. He wasn't used to it. I don't really think he thought that he was that good, like B. B. King."[14]

Still, on November 26, 1959, Hopkins's girlfriend Antoinette Charles handwrote a letter on behalf of Hopkins to Folkways Records, complaining about the financial arrangements surrounding the release of Charters's tapes:

I was thinking I was going to get a share of the money that was made. and that would be right I think any that sell your records they are supose [*sic*] to give you part of the money made. if you dont [*sic*] agree I ask you to stop the records. This company doesn't have the contrack [*sic*] like they should. And they don't have my permision [*sic*] to be selling my songs & my singing on records. they didn't send me a copy of my records I did think they would send me one. I have a nother [*sic*] record coming out that is paying me Roaltes [*sic*] so I see no reason for not getting a share from you all.[15]

McCormick's guiding hand was likely behind this piece of correspondence. When Hopkins executed business with Bobby Shad and his Sittin' In With label a few years before, he insisted on cash payments only, no royalties. Yet, on this occasion, Hopkins wanted royalties after taking cash payment from Charters. At the time Charters recorded Hopkins, though, he explained he was providing the entire payment for the recording.

Although the secretive McCormick does not discuss the issue, he might have informed Hopkins that getting only three hundred dollars, and no royalties whatsoever, did not reflect a sound economic decision. During the time McCormick tried to help Hopkins wrangle better terms from Folkways, he leased tapes he made of Hopkins to different record companies. Regarding Hopkins's records on the Tradition label, McCormick maintains, "I wrote Tradition and said I had an album I'd like to produce for you and they said fine and leased the material for 3 or 5 years. They paid me a royalty and I turned around and paid Sam a royalty."[16] McCormick's intercession on behalf of Hopkins helped him gain Hopkins's trust; as a result, he could manage and book Hopkins. This should have served Hopkins's interest, since his professional career lacked guidance in the first place.

Moe Asch handled Hopkins's letter. Writing back, he told the bluesman that Folkways in no way assumed the rights to his songs, but asked him not to provide them to another record company. As for Hopkins's insistence on royalties, Asch batted away that line of inquiry: "We are not a large company and the $300.00 represents a lot of money to us. We could have made this money part of a royalty agreement if you had received $100.00 advance and the balance to be paid at the rate of 25¢ per record sold. However, you did receive the $300.00 and we think this covers the lifetime of the record."[17]

Hopkins replied to Asch with a letter signed by him but typed and drafted by Mack McCormick. In the letter, Hopkins asked Folkways to remove the record from sale. Hopkins also explained how he got $350 for recording four songs for the San Antonio–based TNT record company and that "It was my original idea that I was to recieve [*sic*] my standard fee which would have been $200 for two songs. I was trapped into thinking this and did not find out otherwise until the recording had already begun." Further, he detailed his contract for leasing some of his sides for a limited-edition record available only by mail order in England. Hopkins laid out an offer to Folkways that mirrored the one he had with the English company. Finally, he explained how Mack McCormick had written Folkways almost two years ago saying he was prepared to produce a blues record but that McCormick never did get an answer.[18] McCormick also verifies he had written Folkways, wanting to do a record with Sam Hopkins, then Charters showed up.[19] McCormick might have been upset that Charters recorded Hopkins first.

Instead of finding and documenting Hopkins on his own, he waited for two years until Charters came to town to research his book on country blues. After Charters recorded the material, Folkways released the record, and McCormick finally took up the cause on Hopkins's behalf. Charters remembers Moe Asch telling him about the lawsuit by Mack on behalf of Lightnin' Hopkins over the record, but he supposedly never heard any more details: "Moe was continually in trouble with someone or other and it was simply part of an ongoing situation. And all I know is what Moe told me. I did not see the papers and I was not involved in the legal solution, discussion." The Harris County, Texas, court records do not preserve a copy of the lawsuit or its outcome.

Ed Badeaux, a photographer and Mack McCormick's brother-in-law, worked for Moe Asch and Folkways at the time. Folkways never paid any royalties, Badeaux recalled:

He didn't like to pay royalties. . . . Moe had his records pressed in a little New Jersey plant and he ordered them ten and twenty at a time. He didn't order them like the big record companies did, and the man who owned the pressing plant would come by and have his limousine parked in front of Moe's building. . . . he would send the doorman of the elevator to announce he was there. He wouldn't go up himself. And Moe would come down with the money for that day's pressings. And he would give him a 100 or 150 of maybe twenty different labels that he had pressed.

Moe kept his stock at Sam Goody's and the deal with Goody was that whenever Goody . . . ran out of a Folkways record they would go off and just take it off Moe's shelf. . . . This is why Moe Asch was not set up to pay royalties. And he didn't really sell enough to pay royalties. I remember John Lomax did a record for Folkways, and he got all tied up that he didn't get any royalties. . . . Moe got a living off of what he did, but he never got that much money off it. The man worked, he was down there in the morning from five thirty or six o'clock at his office, and he'd work till eight or nine, go home and sleep for a while, come back at three in the afternoon and work till sometimes ten or eleven at night. . . . In the days before computers, little operations like that couldn't keep track of what they sold. There was just no way.[20]

Bess Lomax said Asch balanced his nonpayment of royalties with acts of kindness. "He went bankrupt and started back again. He never paid us a cent of royalties, but if you were really flat—and most of us were—you could always drop by to see Moe, and he would invite you to lunch. . . . Moe would give you a couple of dollars, saying . . . 'Just so you can take a taxi home.'" According to Pete Seeger's biographer, when singer Earl Robinson complained that he did not get royalties, "Moe threatened to drop his records from the catalog. Asch had an explosive temper and was not above manipulating artists; depending on where one stood in his hierarchy, he was a benevolent or a callous godfather."[21] The Folkways files reveal that some releases were paid royalties ranging from seven to twenty-five cents per album. Other albums, such as *Folk Songs of New York City*, *Eskimo Songs from Alaska*, and *Been in the Storm So Long*, received no royalty payments. Sam Charters received fifteen to twenty-five cents royalty per record for the albums he produced, though.

However, Folkways and Hopkins did arrange an agreement. In October 1960, Hopkins signed a contract that provided him with twenty-five cents royalty for each record Folkways sold. According to the surviving Folkways documents, Hopkins never received royalties. A very incomplete record of royalties preserved in the archives of the Smithsonian Institution, which now owns the Folkways label, shows that release number 3822, Hopkins's record, sold sixty-four copies from July through December 1960, which would have earned Hopkins a total of sixteen dollars if all the records were sold after he signed the October 1960 contract. The Folkway Records royalty reports only show sales for the years 1960, 1961, 1963, 1973, 1974, 1975, 1976, 1977, and 1978 (see table).

McCormick arranged to have two Hopkins records released in England. 77 Records released *The Rooster Crowed in England*. Tony Dobell, owner of a jazz record store at 77 Charing Cross Road in London, founded 77 Records. The package included two pages of liner notes from McCormick, including this admission:

Until only a few months before making these recordings, Sam Lightnin' Hopkins knew of England only vaguely as a place "over across that water." A place he'd heard of thru friends who'd visited there while in the army. He was startled and dubious when I told him some of the greatest enthusiasm for the blues was centered in those places "over across that water."

Previously he had more or less believed, and operated in his terms of his belief, that his music had a following only in his native environment the East Texas "Piney Woods" and the Negro wards of Houston . . . [where] his raw, deeply rooted lore and unique personalization of the blues has made it's deepest impact and earned him a special kind of fame and affection that comes not thru publicity, but thru personal encounter and word of mouth celebration. Among the rural bred people who now dwell in the city working as longshoremen, truck drivers and yardmen, Lightnin' is regarded as a personal friend, a spokesman for their own joy, bad luck, and trouble. They granted have granted him a royal position: Lightnin' Hopkins occupies the throne vacate by Blind Lemon Jefferson.[22]

TIME PERIOD	COPIES SOLD
July–Dec 1960	64 copies
1961	230 copies
July–Dec 1963	11 copies
July–Dec 1973	18 copies
July–Dec 1973	48 copies (re-issued version)
Jan–June 1974	12 copies
Jan–June 1975	2 copies
July–Dec 1975	16 copies
Jan–June 1976	18 copies (re-issued version)
July–Dec 1976	4 copies
Jan–June 1977	3 copies
July–Dec 1977	1 copy
Jan–June 1978	4 copies
July–Dec 1978	9 copies
Jan–June 1978	32 copies
July–Dec 1978	4 copies

SOURCE: Unmarked, uncataloged ledgers from the Moses and Frances Asch Collection, Smithsonian Center for Folklife and Cultural Heritage, Washington, DC (assembled by archivist Jeff Place).

The *Journal of American Folklore* called this record a "highly personal docu-ment—improvisation, burlesque, humor, sex."[23] The combination of humor and improvisation was a long-held practice of Hopkins, a deeply ingrained part of his character, especially during gigs. "He'd sit out there on a chair at the edge of the stage. People would get up from tables and everybody would be crowded all around the front of the stage. Lightnin' would just make up song after song right there," drummer Robert Murphy attests. "If someone came up and said, 'Hello Lightnin'', blah blah blah,' he might ask them a question, like 'Are you married?' 'Oh no, I'm divorced.' He'd make up a song right there about some-one getting divorced. He was good at that. They just loved him for that kind of thing. Nobody was as spontaneous as Lightnin'. I've never played with anybody that spontaneous." In his style of humor, "He was so unassuming. He was dry, if you want to put it that way. He had very dry humor. You know how some of these comedians crack a joke? It's a dry joke and their face never breaks out with any smile. He was a very dry and unassuming person. He was."[24]

It would be four more years until Hopkins reached European concert halls, but that did not prevent aficionados from snapping up his release on Dobell's new label. Hopkins's *The Rooster Crowed in England* was the label's first release, and, according to author Roberta Freund Schwartz, it sold well and was praised as one of the best albums of the year.

The second English release arranged by McCormick came out on the Heri-tage imprint, a label owned by Tony Standish. The disc was split between Hop-kins and his older brother Joel. The record contains a song called "Look Out Settegast Here Me and My Partner Come," which references Hopkins's girl-friend Antoinette Charles. She was married to someone else during her rela-tionship with Hopkins. In the liner notes to *Smokes Like Lightning*, from 1963, McCormick indicates Hopkins "had been the pampered daytime pet of a mar-ried woman for 14 years. She often accompanies him on trips out of town, and is then introduced as his wife, but in Houston a triangle is maintained with everyone keeping carefully to their own corner."[25]

Despite the usual music business hassles, Hopkins's comeback gained strength. A survey of the many articles published on Hopkins during 1959 and 1960 reveals the extent of his rapidly rising fame. One revealing article includes an interview Mack McCormick published in the *Jazz Journal* in three parts from November 1960 through February 1961. In the interview with McCormick, Hopkins discussed his early music experiences and life growing up in East Texas.

The interview revealed how little Hopkins's daily routine had changed, even with such notoriety and a busy recording schedule. Hopkins discussed his working life, such as playing on the street. In addition, he would gig at clubs in the Fifth Ward area of Houston, another night he might work in Richmond, a town southwest of Houston, and the next he might play in Sunnyside, a black neighborhood in south central Houston.

McCormick also inquired about Hopkins's audience. "It's an entirely different sort of thing to play for dancing," the bluesman replied. "No they're not paying attention—not like they would if I'm playing out in the street. Out there, they'd stand and listen. But now they got me in these [juke] joints—so you know the biggest majority want me to swing out." Asked if he preferred sitting audiences, including the Alley, Hopkins replied, "That's way better— anytime I can get people to listen to what I'm doing. But still and all I don't want to go out begging on the street, you understand."[26]

During 1959, Hopkins busily worked in the studio. He recorded at least sixty-five tracks. McCormick produced and recorded two-thirds of these tracks. His financial dealings emulated those of Charters: McCormick paid Hopkins a flat fee for the sessions and retained ownership of the master tapes.

One track in particular is worthy of discussion. Apparently, McCormick arranged, according to the booklet that came inside, "an informal song-swapping session with a group of Texans, New Yorkers, and Englishmen exchanging bawdy songs and lore, presented without expurgation."[27] The record was released in a plain white jacket with no printing on either side. Inside the package was a twelve-page booklet and record, both entitled *The Unexpurgated Folk Songs of Men*. Both the record and booklet indicated that the songs were "collected by Mack McCormick." The record label itself listed fifteen songs on each side but did not mention any of the artists' names. One singer is John Lomax, who helped Hopkins get the Berkeley gig. Lomax sang a selection called "Change the Name of Arkansas." The collection of "bawdy" material included "Cocaine Bill and Morphine Sue," "The Merry Cuckold," "Take a Whiff on Me," and "No Balls at All." The album carried the name Raglan Records—a front name for a nonexistent company. The session was recorded in Texas in 1959, the booklet informs, and copyrighted in 1960 by Mack McCormick, who collaborated with Chris Strachwitz to release the record.

McCormick recorded enough unexpurgated material for two records. In a long letter to Strachwitz, he explained the various marketing possibilities:

Now realistically we both know that this is going to be bought and sold not as folklore, but as pornography. In no respect however tiny should we pander to this interest so far as presentation in packaging. But we are free to take advantage of the well-established market for erotic poetry, privately printed books, and other such quality pornography.

Traditionally material in this field is very expensive for like us they sell in small quantities and avoid problems of mass sales and distribution with the tide of attention that brings. For a boxed set anything from $10 to $25 retail might be possible.

. . . But make no mistake I think this set is entirely defensible as a work of reputable folklore. But for practical considerations we want to avoid legal complications by not operating on such a scale that it attracts attention. There is an enormous amount of arty filth that passes around (morocco bound, etc) that no one bothers as long as it remains an expensive item for specialists. We have to stay in the same category simply because it's a bit expensive to take a case to the Supreme Court.[28]

On the record, Hopkins performed a short version of "The Dozens," leading off with the introduction "Get your black ass out of here fellow . . ." Then Hopkins launched into the dozens:

> Your old mama died with the measles
> And your old grandma died with the whoopin' cough
> Your old pa died with his old horse rounding the goddamn curve
> And that son of a bitch was shitting a long, long turd

This recording embarrassed Hopkins later in life. When Texas drummer Doyle Bramhall did some gigs with Hopkins in the 1970s and asked him about the record, Hopkins told him never to mention it again. McCormick leased some of Hopkins's less shocking material to the Tradition Records Company, which released two albums in 1960, *Country Blues* and *Autobiography in Blues*.

Music critic Robert Shelton in the *New York Times* gave *Country Blues* a positive review, characterizing it as an "impressive album that . . . is of great interest." Although Shelton complained about the sound quality, he noted the authenticity of the performance: "One gets the feeling of listening to a sensitive man reflecting on a hard life with pathos, not sentimentalism, and meaning every word he sings."[29] The *Country Blues* album featured the instrumental song "Gonna Pull a Party." Hopkins later explained the song to folksinger Barbara Dane: "That was after we went and made a little piece of change. I think I had beat a man out of about $400 dollars and I was gonna pull a party and I just grabbed this guitar and went on and talked about how we were gonna have that party."[30]

The Folkways and two Tradition albums marked the first wave of what would become a surge of Lightnin' records released during the 1960s. Record companies of all sizes and stripes quickly began their attempts to profit from the rediscovery and remarketing of several once-forgotten African American blues singers. At the time, performers commonly released several albums a year in many music genres. For example, Frank Sinatra, arguably the most influential singer of the twentieth century, released four albums, including a Christmas and soundtrack album, in 1957. Other icons of the industry during that era, such as Elvis Presley and the Beatles, also released three albums a year during the prime of their careers.

The labels that recorded Hopkins in the 1940s and 1950s capitalized on the new audience for Hopkins's material by repackaging and rereleasing collections of 78s on long-playing albums. From 1958 through 1960, these reissues included the albums *Strums the Blues* on the Score label, *Lightnin' and the Blues* on Herald Records, and *Lightning Hopkins: Last of the Great Blues Singers* on the Time label. Hopkins never saw any money from these reissues, one can assume, because his standard practice during the 1940s and 1950s was to charge one hundred dollars cash for recording a two-song 78-rpm record.

The music industry, however, was not entirely made up of unethical businessmen exploiting back catalogs that did not require the payment of royalties. Chris Strachwitz was a music lover first and a businessman second. He started off his business as a mail order operation and went on to build an impressive catalog of zydeco, Cajun, spirituals, polka, Tejano, blues, and more. Many of his titles would barely recoup their costs because their appeal was so small and virtually none of his releases had any commercial potential. Strachwitz's name would never show up on any songwriting credits; the same could not be said for the proprietors of many record companies for which Hopkins would record. His fair treatment of Hopkins does not fit the stereotypical image of many underhanded music industry types.

Strachwitz was a German immigrant living and teaching German at a high school in Berkeley, California. He received a postcard from Sam Charters in 1959 saying, "I found Lightning Hopkins." Charters also offered Mack McCormick's address in Houston. Strachwitz set off driving across the country to meet Hopkins. When he arrived in Houston, he got the cheapest room he could find, at the YMCA. He contacted McCormick, and they rode over to Hopkins's room on Hadley Street. Hopkins told Strachwitz where he was playing that night, a small bar called Pop's Place, and invited him to come down. Strachwitz walked into the place, and Hopkins pointed his finger at him and greeted him with, "Whoa! This man came all the way from California just to hear poor Lightning sing." Hopkins worked that line into the song that he was singing.

The intensity of the performance shook Strachwitz: "It was just ferocious electric guitar and bellowing into that microphone with a crappy speaker. I was listening to him and Jesus . . . so that's how I got to meet Lightnin'. . . . I decided there and then that by God someone's got to document this man in these beer joints the way he does that, and I told Mack that I wanted to start a record label just to do that. I remember we talked about the name. I had thought about Gulf Records or Southern Records or Down South Records or something and all of a sudden Mack said how about Arhoolie! I said ar what? Well that started it."[31] That gig inspired Strachwitz to make a return trip to Houston the next year in hopes of documenting Hopkins's performances in the juke joints of black Houston. Strachwitz went on to become a good friend of Hopkins and released several of his albums over the coming years.

The local press continued to cover the "Negro guitar player," demonstrated by an article Ann Holmes, the fine arts editor of the *Houston Chronicle*, published on May 12, 1960. It summed up Hopkins's recent fame and attention. Supposedly, Hopkins's New York agent sent him an offer to play England, and promoters were offering two plane tickets and a two-thousand-dollar fee, which Hopkins declined. Sitting on the porch of his shotgun house in the Third Ward, strumming his guitar, Hopkins told Holmes, "Course Lightnin' is not going. Not just yet. Heah, I can be broke and hungry and walk out and someone will buy me dinner. It ain't always like that in a strange place where you don't know no one. Yet an' still, I'll be going someday. I'll be goin'."[32] Hopkins voiced similar sentiments in an article in *Down Beat* magazine: "I stay with my own people. I have all my fun, and I have my trouble with them."[33] This sentiment is supported by Andy Bradley, music historian and head engineer for SugarHill Studios, formerly Gold Star Recording Studios: "He was definitely a down-home guy. That's why he didn't want to get on airplanes or ships and go to England. It was too much hassle. It wasn't close to his roots and what he was used to. Of course, he had his vices, and his vices were close to his house."[34] Hopkins's habit of staying in his Third Ward neighborhood playing for a few dollars or a few tips instead of taking up opportunities that offered him thousands to play remained consistent throughout his life.

Bill Greenwood was a teenage student in Houston when he attended a high school party in 1959 in a subdivision near River Oaks. Greenwood remembered,

We had a guy named Robert Cook that was a musician and a guy named Fred Airheart. . . . They got to know Lightnin'. He had a drummer named Spider who was the skinniest guy walking and they played at the party. It was $150 or $200 and a bottle of whiskey was what the fee was. Lightnin' was very, very good. . . . This was Kincaid High School. He [Cook] got to be friends with Lightnin' and Fred Airheart did too. Lightnin' was very friendly with us. This was an all-white audience. . . . We used to go to places he was playing and we'd be the only white ones there. If you were friends with Lightnin', you were as good as if you were friends with [Muhammad] Ali. I only went to places once or twice. We never had any problems. The one place I remember, it wasn't in the world's best part of town. You could walk in if you were with Lightnin'.' It wasn't any problem. It was a nice house, not an auditorium. I remember him being there, a normal house, and Spider sitting there next to him drumming. . . . I do remember Robert Cook was learning to play guitar and asked Lightnin', and he just said watch my fingers. He wanted to make sure there was a bottle of whiskey included. He seemed like a nice guy. Spider didn't really talk. Lightnin' seemed to like us. He didn't seem like these are a bunch of white kids that I'm going to exploit.[35]

Mack McCormick was not the only person trying to get Hopkins gigs. John A. Lomax, Jr., who performed with Hopkins at the Alley Theater gig, also actively promoted Hopkins's career. Coming from a family of folklorists—his father and uncle made field recordings for the Library of Congress—John started his career in investments and banking. After a move to Houston, he cofounded a construction company that specialized in building residences. Singing folk material was a hobby. Although Lomax had no financial stake in Hopkins, he worked to get him a slot at the Berkeley Folk Festival, by then held annually over several days at the University of California campus, featuring many folk music workshops and several concerts.

Barry Olivier started, coordinated, and promoted the Berkeley festival for its entire fifteen-year lifespan from 1956 to 1971. After some correspondence with Olivier and his staff, Lomax came to an agreement for a fee of four hundred dollars for Hopkins's performances at the festival. Lomax's letters to Olivier and B. J. Connors, the secretary of the Committee for Arts and Lectures at the University of California, express his frustration in dealing with Hopkins. Lomax wrote to Connors:

If Lightning's presence adds the rich flavor to the Festival I believe it can, I wish you to know that I will be due at least a large pink rosette for my extra curricular duties with him. Largely, he lives each day to itself. . . . You might be surprised at the number of conversations and meetings I have already had with him to get the proceedings to this point. I had to agree to stay with him at all times thruout [sic] the trip; this includes his performances too.[36]

Lomax had to ease Hopkins's trepidations about traveling to California. His experiences mirrored what McCormick described in a letter sent to Charters in May 1959: "[Lightnin'] wants to go play for people that will listen—but, on the other hand, he is terrified by the unfamiliar. And to Lightnin', who in many ways is the sheltered innocent, the whole world beyond Texas is alien territory."[37] Such incidents help explain Hopkins's reluctance to tour when he was just beginning his recording career in the late 1940s.

Grover Lewis drove down from Dallas the summer of 1960 hoping to meet Hopkins. After bugging bartenders, passersby, and store clerks, he was directed to Spider Kilpatrick, Hopkins's drummer, and eventually found Hopkins, who told Lewis that he was supposed to go to California with Lomax but that he was afraid of "molly-trotters" (airplanes). "Why one of those flimsy little outfits could crash and burn up in a minute, and then where'd you be?" Hopkins told Lewis.[38]

While hanging out with Hopkins, Lewis witnessed an ugly incident of racism, at Zito's Jungle Hut in the Third Ward, which he described in one of a series of articles that the *Village Voice* published:

When Hopkins approached the bar and ordered, the waiter answered tonelessly, "We all outta beer today, man." Looking steadily at me, the barman mumbled, "I told you fellow, we ain't got no beer today." . . . Stunned, Hopkins spun around and motioned curtly for me to follow, plunged back out into the sunlight. Shuffling from foot to foot, he tried to dismiss the incident as a joke, but the more he talked about it, the angrier he became. The episode seemed to trigger some edginess in him, and in the moments that followed, he grew increasingly morose, only occasionally breaking into abrupt unprovoked fits of hyper tense laughter. "One thing that man's still got to learn," he grumbled darkly, inspecting the ridged hairless skin on the backs of his black hands. "This here stuff don't rub off one way or another, you know what I mean?"[39]

Lomax, Jr., and Hopkins flew to San Francisco on June 30, 1960.[40] Lomax's sister, Bess Lomax Hawes, lived in California and was involved in the folk music scene. The siblings arranged for Hopkins to play a few club gigs after the Berkeley festival dates of July 3 and 4, 1960. Alfred Frankenstein, reviewing the festival for the *San Francisco Chronicle*, called Hopkins a "Great, authentic folk artist . . . whose gorgeous bass voice, colossal rhythm, and subtly shaded delicacy in guitar-playing provided the festival with one of its most distinguished moments."[41]

While Hopkins was on this tour, the Ash Grove nightclub on Melrose Boulevard in Los Angeles booked Hopkins. Ed Pearl, the founder, owner, and manager of the club, remembered how the gig was arranged:

Bess knew Lightnin' and Sonny and Brownie for twenty years. So the Ash Grove presented various musics from the very beginning. A couple of years later her brother John, one of Alan and Bess's older brothers, was coming out with Lightnin', so Bess arranged for Lightnin' in an afternoon concert and he came. . . . Brownie was the mainstay and always a solid audience, and the glamour was coming after the Kingston Trio, people like Buddy Travis, the Limeliters, a very big group, who recorded their first album, number one in the country, at the Ash Grove. Some people were beginning to make it right at that time. For some reason, the Lomaxes, at least John, Sr. and Jr., sort of patronized him. So when Lightnin' showed up, he was wearing a red shirt, he might have been wearing coveralls, the thing I remember was this red plaid shirt, really country and a straw hat . . . that's how Lightnin' showed up.[42]

Folksinger Barbara Dane remembered Lomax's dressing up Hopkins like a country bumpkin:

The first time I met him he came to California with John Lomax. . . . He admired [Lightnin's] work, and he wanted to help him out, but he also thought of him as a protégé, or not even, like a pet. Bringing him to California so he could get some credit for showing him off and getting him some jobs. The funny thing is that Lightnin' had been here before and played on his own and was pretty well known. . . . Old John Jr. was an old-fashioned Southern white guy. He had Lightnin' wearing a plaid flannel shirt and jeans and bringing him to California to get him a job at a folk club. As if that was necessary. It was ridiculous. . . . The Ash Grove . . . opened people's minds up to what could be done and what culturally was healthy, exciting, and interesting. Ed . . . had two different acts on that would draw two different crowds, and that would help people open up their vision. . . . Mr. Lomax was making [Lightnin'] put that outfit on, and Lightnin' was kind of cooperating because he wanted to break into that scene too. . . . I understood right away that Lightnin' was embarrassed by this. That immediately made for a good friendship between us.[43]

Pearl had fond memories of Hopkins's first appearance at his famed nightclub:

That was 1960. So I talked with him and he'd played acoustic. I asked him would he like to come back. The thing that really surprised me was that it was a Sunday afternoon, and the place was packed, like 250 people or something, and the response was phenomenal. . . . People were bringing meaning to pop music. . . . Brownie and Sonny were great blues performers, but their material was couched to play to the existing audience. Lightnin' didn't at all. Big Joe Williams had come earlier than Lightnin' and had played to very small crowds. He's from Mississippi and . . . you could barely understand him, but I did it. But Lightnin' came, and it was amazing cuz the audience was younger. . . . I knew it was going to thrill a lot of other people if I could present it right. And it works. It's worked my whole life. It doesn't matter what field it was, flamenco to anything. I asked Lightnin' if he'd like to play, and he said, "Yeah, but do I have to wear the shirt?" And I said, "No, don't you always wear the shirt?" And he said, "No, I never wear the shirt and I don't wear this hat."[44]

Hopkins also recorded one studio album while he was in California after a get-together at Bess Lomax Hawes's house. Ed Michel produced the record. After Hopkins played a gig at the Ash Grove nightclub in Los Angeles, Sonny Terry and Brownie McGhee showed up. Michel's liner notes for the album pick up the story:

Things adjourned to Bess' home to settle into an all-night-long mutual confrontation. Some eighteen years before, Brownie had recorded a "Letter to Lightning Hopkins," in an attempt to woo him from Houston to New York, but until the Monday night session, the two had never met, although each admitted to being the other's devoted admirer. With an alternate goading and refereeing of Sonny Terry, and to the delight of the by-this-time-stunned-numb group of remaining musicians and fans, . . . the session drove through the night, all three men playing individually and together, and with each of the two guitarists even taking an occasional whack at the piano in the corner, culminating in the awesome conversation which began with Brownie's "sweet letter" to Lightning, and its verse-by-verse answers. . . . Somehow everyone managed to make it into the World Pacific Studio by eleven the next morning, at the encouragement of Ed Pearl. . . . The date was first set up as an audition, but it took about four bars of the opening warm up to convince everyone that the best idea was to turn on the tapes and not waste anything.[45]

For his part, Brownie McGhee remembered,

> I was the guy that got that together. I went to Ed Pearl and another club
> owner and a record company and I said, "Do you know what's happening
> today? Lightnin' Hopkins from Texas, Big Joe Williams from Mississippi,
> Sonny Terry from Chicago, and Brownie McGhee from Tennessee is all in
> the same town. And you guys are going to let it get away? Somebody ought
> to put something together and get a record—a record of us live. Cut it in
> the studio. We can do it."
>
> We walked into the studio to rehearse, and out of the rehearsal become
> Down South Summit Meeting. You looked under my chair you saw a bottle
> of scotch. Under Lightnin's chair you saw a bottle of whiskey. Under Big
> Joe's chair you saw a bottle. Under Sonny's you saw a bottle. . . . we created
> our songs from what we were talking about—what we thought—the meet-
> ing. That's the way the album happened. It wasn't nobody suggestion what
> we sing about.[46]

The recording turned into a loose, frenetic, and totally impromptu jam. One of
the highlights of the six-track album was "If You Steal My Chickens, You Can't
Make Them Lay," which featured Sonny, Hopkins, and Williams trading verses.

> . . . Lord I found out my baby left me this morning
> Lord when the clock was striking four
> Joe Williams she left me this morning
> Yes, when the clock was striking four

The day after the recording, Barbara Dane invited Hopkins and Lomax, Jr., to
her KPFK radio show *Barbara's Blues*. Dane's interview revealed how important
family was to Hopkins. "I understand too," she observed, "that one of the reasons you like to stay close to Houston is because your family is all still around
there." Hopkins replied,

> That's right, I have a sister and she live[s] next door to me. My brother he
> lives in Dickinson, Texas . . . that's just only 28 miles from Houston. And
> my mother she lives in Centerville, Texas. She's a living right up there close
> to me. She's a hundred and thirty miles, which I can jump in my automo-
> bile when I think about and run up there. And this far when I think about
> it, I be too far to make it in a hurry when I think about it in a hurry. Cause
> she's getting old now and I kinda gets worried about it. When I get worried

about it I'm quick to go. Just round up sister and brothers throw them in the car and we hit the highway, go up there and give the old lady a good time. She's 72 years old.

I'm gonna stick around just as long as she live or I live you know what I mean. She'll pass and I'm liable to go England and live forever. Cuz I won't have too much to worry about. That's my biggest worry, that's my mother right now, . . . when you lose your mother, you lost it all. That's about all in this world that I could say, chording that, I am hitting on a guitar string, because she is the mother and I thinks cuz about she raised all us kids. Little things . . . she's a mother and a father in a way cuz my father got killed when I was three years old. . . . We children could get together and she'd put us on the back porch and we'd have all the fun we want. She'd didn't pay us no mind as long as she knew her children were having a good time and anybody's child is her child she is a mother. That's what I love about her.[47]

Hopkins's comments are deeply endearing and revealing. Though vices often pulled him hard, so did the tugs of family life.

Shortly after Lomax and Hopkins returned to Houston, Lomax wrote a letter to Berkeley festival organizer Barry Olivier about his experience touring the West Coast with Hopkins:

At various times the trip was a considerable ordeal. I had promised Lightnin' (in order to get him to agree to make the junket) to stay with him at all times and to bend every effort to get him home with as big a bankroll as possible. Being the King of Hadley Street, he has an assortment of women at his beck and call (incl. a wife—common-law) to the end he has come to expect that all the small domestic problems of life are automatically done for him; therefore I went ahead and did things at the moment that had to be done and smoothed the path ahead on a basis that I would not have endured save that I had somewhat impetuously agreed to bring him and determined to bring it off successfully. Lightnin' is most immature in the ordinary complexities of our times so that I had to gear my entire time down to his level in order to keep him relaxed enough to perform as he should (and did). Margaret and I in talking over the trip agree that we could think of no one locally save myself who had the necessary specialized experience and general background who would have undertaken the matter . . .

. . . We finally had some harsh words when one of his shows at the Renaissance Club on Sunset was not well handled and poorly received; he began to cut on me. I thought to myself: "Well, what the hell am I doing here anyhow at 1 a.m. and beat to a frazzle!" I let him have it, which did change his tune for the time being. I couldn't help but recall Mark Twain's description of one of his characters: "He had every attribute of a dog except gratitude." But maybe one of his type of his race can't ever say thanks in a way that we understand.[48]

Lomax's letter reveals his difficulties helping and traveling with Hopkins. Despite such gripes, while he was on Barbara Dane's radio show, he admitted, "Well I'm very happy to be here and to have made this trip. Lightnin' has been with me all the time and I just want to say that I've had a lot of personal enjoyment out of it. From my own singing, in a small part, and from helping Lightnin' to make this trip."[49]

Hopkins expected his tenders to take care of trivialities such as travel and housing arrangements. Like Lomax, Mack McCormick complained about Hopkins as well:

It had something to do with a child trying to get away with something mischievous . . . that's not the word for an adult. I can give you example after example. He and I were constantly going over the same little ground. One time I went by to pick him up and take him somewhere. He had kind of an entourage, hangers-on. What happened is I'm getting myself ready to walk into the building, and I assumed he was getting himself ready, and I turned and looked and his guitar case is sitting there and his amplifier is sitting there. And he's standing waiting for somebody to pick them up. So I just went on in. It was part of that little thing he was always trying to turn people into servants. Because of his entourage, he never had any trouble with that. When the folk thing came along, he had more people, and his entourage was well-integrated . . . earlier it was just black."[50]

After his stint along the West Coast, Hopkins headed to New York City alone. Mack McCormick helped facilitate the New York trip by answering New York promoter Harold Leventhal's entreaties. McCormick also attempted to book Hopkins in England. Leventhal arranged for Hopkins to play Carnegie Hall on October 14, 1960, for a benefit for the folk music magazine *Sing Out!* The bill contained several important folk artists of the day, including the renowned Pete Seeger, the Clancy Brothers, Tommy Makem, Elizabeth Knight, Jerry Silverman, the Harvesters, and nineteen-year-old Joan Baez. Robert Shelton covered the concert for the *New York Times*, devoting much of his review to Hopkins, praising his "gifts of wit and flair and improvisatory skill" when he played a verse-swapping song with the host Pete Seeger. Shelton also contextualized

Hopkins's journey, noting the long distance from his normal stomping grounds on a street corner in Houston's Third Ward to the Carnegie Hall stage.[51]

Hopkins's six-week-long trip to New York City was very productive. After his gig at Carnegie Hall, he appeared on a *CBS Television Workshop* program in an episode entitled "A Pattern of Words and Music." The other guests included folksinger Joan Baez, harmonica master John Sebastian, and Michael Kane, who read prose. The CBS promotional material for the show, dated November 4, 1960, described Hopkins as "An exponent of the talking blues" and "A street corner minstrel of Houston, Texas who lives in a jukebox world and has made over 200 recordings of his original works."[52]

John Sebastian, Jr., a child when Hopkins taped this television appearance, attended the show with his father. "I had kind of a special beginning with Lightnin' because of my father and he did a television show . . . called Robert Herridge presents . . . and it included my father and Lightnin' and an unknown nineteen-year-old folksinger named Joan Baez. I sat underneath a [television] camera and watched them film this show, and in effect got the camera's-eye view of Lightnin' doing his three or four songs that he could come up with that day. It was just incredible. I had already heard a Lightnin' Hopkins album, but to see Sam in person, just to see what a tremendous musical kind of a freight train he could present while he would toss off this great spontaneous lyric. Sometimes some of the songs had lyrics but sometimes he was working extemporaneously, and for a lyricist, I think it was a jumpstart for me."[53]

Hopkins performed four songs on the CBS television show: "Baby, Come Go Home with Me," "Going Down Slow," "Bunion Stew," and "Let's Pull a Party." Wearing a light-colored linen suit and a white towel around his neck, he played an acoustic guitar while sitting on a high stool in a darkened studio. He also sported a pair of dark sunglasses, his trademark look, and when the television camera zoomed in, it caught the glint of gold on his teeth.

His spoken introduction to "Bunion Stew" revealed how he turned an everyday event like making a pot stew into a song:

Papa said every time the ground cry, he gets a tater, he looked around behind him and she had a tomato. He said, "Old lady what you gonna do with that tomato?" She said, "Old man what are you gonna do with that potato?" "I just figure to make a soup," he said. "That's what I figure, I was just gonna meet you in the soup and we'd be all messed up together." She said, "Son, how do you feel?" [I] said, "OK mama." She said, "I want you to play us a little something." Say I'm gonna swing this one a little, said alright we gonna have a stew.[54]

Hopkins's portion of the show ended with him performing "Let's Pull a Party." During this tune, Joan Baez sat next to him on a stool and watched. Hopkins also called out to his friends, Luke "Long Gone" Miles and Mack McCormick, while he played the "Pull a Party" boogie.

Hopkins recorded four full-length albums during his stay in New York. Nat Hentoff produced a solo album with Hopkins playing guitar and piano. The record was entitled *Lightnin' in New York*, released on Hentoff's Candid Records label. Almost fifty years after the recording, Hentoff remembered little about his onetime recording experience with Hopkins, whom he described as "Calculating, he was meticulous about mike placement and things. He knew what he was doing."[55] Hentoff's liner notes say, "Hopkins traveled to the city alone and was booked into a drab hotel room in Harlem. When Hopkins asked for another room, he got another dreary place in a Greenwich Village basement. Hopkins said, 'There's no light down there. There's no sun, so I don't know what time it is. I just sat down on the bed and played my box awhile.' Finally, Leadbelly's widow, Martha Ledbetter, took him into her apartment."[56]

Hentoff recorded Hopkins singing the song "Mr. Charlie," which became a staple of Hopkins's live set. The song is about a boy with a stutter. Hopkins would go on to rerecord it, but he recorded it for Hentoff first. The phrase "Mr. Charlie" is usually used as a disparaging term for white people. The song, which has a long spoken introduction, is an example of a cante fable.

Filmmaker Les Blank asked Hopkins if he wrote "Mr. Charlie":

Sure that's mine. . . . Now a guy gave me an idea, cuz it's true he could not talk. He have to pat himself to get his words out, thump his finger. He trying to tell you something . . . my momma said, it's true . . . he stutters. Well, now that's when a person go to ch ch like that. He's stuttering, he's trying to say it. It look pitiful to me. It looks like it hurt him. He can't get his words out. . . . And I say, Mr. Charlie say if you can't talk it sing it. Now you take a man that stutters. John Lee Hooker you heard him, he stutters, you know he do. But put him to singing and see do he stutter. He don't stutter on nar a song he sings. He just sing it. Well that's the reason I figure Mr. Charlie say sing it if you can't talk.[57]

Although Hopkins talked about the song in its simplest terms, a homeless boy who stutters and a man who owned a sawmill, the song serves as an allegory for slavery. The mill owner represents a patriarchal slave owner, and the boy represents the slave who cannot take care of himself on his own, so he needs the mill or plantation owner to provide for him. Even after Mr. Charlie loses his sawmill, he still provides a home for the boy, or slave. Sawmills were common where Hopkins grew up, so the song definitely culls from Hopkins's environment and everyday experiences. However, Hopkins's use of the "Mr. Charlie" slang is trenchant. Despite being raised by a white family for a time, he grew up black in an unequal America. By the time Hopkins recorded "Mr. Charlie," he had endured plenty of oppressive whites, or Mr. Charlie types, in the fields, streets, and music business.

While Hopkins was in New York, music business pioneer Bobby Robinson produced *Mojo Hand*, the most historically significant record album of Hopkins's career. The title track, "Mojo Hand," first released as a single on Robinson's Fire label, became Hopkins's last charting song and a staple of live performances for the rest of his life. Robinson started his music business in 1946 by opening Bobby's Record Shop on 125th Street in Harlem, situated next to a nightclub where icons such as Duke Ellington performed. Frank's Restaurant, a popular place for show business people, glittered right up the street from Robinson's record store. Performers at the famed Apollo Theater, which featured seven shows a day from noon to one a.m., passed by the record store too. Because Robinson knew the performers, his national reputation spread. Ahmet Ertegun of Atlantic Records asked Robinson for advice about records produced by Atlantic. Other music industry folks, like the Bihari brothers, stopped at the store when they were in town from California, as would the founders of Chicago's Chess Records, Leonard and Phil Chess, when they were in town.

Eventually, Robinson started closing at eleven p.m. instead of midnight so that he could rehearse groups in his store. He founded the Red Robin label in 1951, but shut it down in 1954. He had a label called Whistlin' Disc Records for a time, though he soon closed it and formed Fury Records in 1957. In 1959, Robinson and his Fury label hit with Wilbert Harrison's recording of "Kansas City," which moved one million copies immediately and eventually wound up selling four million copies. By 1959, Robinson started Fire Records.

In an interview with music historian John Broven, Robinson remembered his experience recording Hopkins:

I did that record with just Lightnin' Hopkins, acoustic guitar and a drum, Delmar Donnell. . . . he was one of those little local guys that was always around rehearsing with me, he wasn't a professional drummer or anything. . . . we recorded altogether different from the way it was released. . . . he played a solo for about two minutes, just a guitar and all that, so I sat down with my stopwatch one night at home, and I worked on it for about two hours, and I timed it so many seconds to this point, then I had to leap this much, cut it out, and then we'd start back at this point. So I made what I called a guide sheet, a road map, and went into the studio, I had it down to just how many seconds I wanted, the introduction was the end of the solo . . . and I got it down to three-and-a-half minutes from about eight minutes. Of course the rest he was just doing the same thing over. Well I looked him up, he was in New York playing a little club in the Village somewhere.[58]

Robinson explained the recording session arrangement:

He was so unorthodox, you never knew which way he was going to go. . . . I knew I couldn't put a band behind him, it's very hard to do a guy like that with a band. . . . I said this is so earthy and authentic I'm not going to add anything. . . . I brought Delmar down with me, I said, "Listen, all I want you to do, wherever this guy goes, you follow, where the hell he goes you follow, just keep that beat going and follow whatever he does." So we ran it down and he got the feel of it, he'd put a book on his drums for a muffled sound and playing along with the brushes. . . . I said, "Lightnin' you just do it the way you did it for me yesterday," so he got a tall chair, cigar stuck in his mouth, crossed his legs and I set another mike on his acoustic guitar and another mike for him to sing. I sat him on a tall stool so that his vocal mike was in front of the other one, we didn't have an amplifier so I had to set the mike at an angle right near the box, that way we could divide it with drums. . . . it was like an instant record.[59]

Music-business entrepreneur Marshall Sehorn was working for Robinson as a promotion man in the South when he was making the Hopkins record. Sehorn got his start with Robinson in the late 1950s, piquing Robinson's interest in Wilbert Harrison, who ventured to New York to record "Kansas City." In an interview with music historian Broven, Sehorn recalled the *Mojo Hand* sessions:

I was down South on a promotion trip and was gonna have Christmas with my folks. Bobby called me from New York. "I just cut a mother." I said, "What do you mean?" And he played it for me over the phone. And we discussed it. It was very long, it had a lot of things going, it was good, but it wasn't *good*. So we made a few suggestions back and forth on the phone. The next time he called me he had done a few of the things we talked about. Like there were three or four solos in the song, which made it too long, so we spliced a couple of those and shortened it down and made it into "Mojo Hand."[60]

Mojo Hand

Robinson released "Mojo Hand" as a single with the tune "Glory Be" on the B-side. *Billboard* agreed with Robinson's assessment about the song being a "mother," writing in its January 23, 1961, issue, "Hopkins is at his very best with these two monumental efforts. Topside is an uptempo blues—a story of women, love and superstition. Flipside is a slow, dirge-like blues also spotlighting drums and the singer's own guitar. Two great sides."[61]

Hopkins's transformation from a blues singer making records for the black jukebox market to a folksinger performing for a white crowd neared completion by the end of 1960. In a larger context, the music industry and American consumer tastes changed from the time Hopkins was rediscovered until his repositioning with a new audience. The *Cash Box* (a music industry trade publication similar to *Billboard*) singles chart over this time period shows the flux.

For the week ending January 17, 1959, when Hopkins was recording what became his comeback album on Folkways, the number 1 song on the top 100 singles chart was "Smoke Gets in Your Eyes" by the Platters. The rest of the top ten included the throwaway novelty "The Chipmunk Song" at number 2, while folkies the Kingston Trio's "Tom Dooley" held down the number 4 spot. Elvis Presley occupied two spots in the top twenty, and Latino rocker Ritchie Valens was at the ninth spot with his ballad "Donna." The top spot of 1959 charts was occupied by the country stylings of Johnny Horton's "Battle of New Orleans" for nine weeks, the Broadway show tune "Mack the Knife" done by Bobby Darin for eight weeks, and teenybopper heartthrob Frankie Avalon's "Venus" for five weeks. The only number 1 song in 1959 that could fit into the R&B or rock category was Lloyd Price's revved-up take on the traditional blues folk number "Stagger Lee," which occupied number 1 for three consecutive weeks in February.

By the end of 1960, *Cash Box* charts reveal the resilience of rock 'n' roll, whose artists, along with rhythm and blues acts, crowded out traditional pop artists like Percy Faith and teen idols like Frankie Avalon. Faith and his orchestra held down number 1 for eight weeks with the instrumental "Theme from 'A Summer Place,'" but the top of the pop chart was owned by two Elvis Presley songs for a combined fifteen weeks, the Drifters' "Save the Last Dance for Me" for six weeks, the Everly Brothers' "Like Strangers" for five, and Chubby Checker's version of the Hank Ballard song "The Twist" for four weeks. The blues impact on American pop culture revealed itself through the popularity of rock 'n' roll rooted in rhythm and blues. Hopkins is a prime example of those roots.

Hopkins's well-received performances at the Berkeley Folk Festival and at Carnegie Hall, the nation's most storied performance venue, marked his transformation from a forgotten country blues singer into a vital and renowned performer in the folk and blues revivals. From January 16, 1959, when Charters recorded Hopkins for Folkways Records until late November 1960, when Hopkins returned from New York City, he recorded no fewer than seven full-length records, played several high-profile gigs in California and in New York City, and received favorable write-ups in numerous daily newspapers and magazines, including the *New York Times*.

Hopkins's Folkways release in particular garnered sheaves of press. The *San Francisco Sunday Chronicle*, *Santa Clara* (California) *Journal*, *Esquire* magazine, *High Fidelity*, *New Yorker*, *Audio*, *Down Beat*, *Rogue*, and *The New Record* offered positive reviews. Furthermore, Charters's book, which jumpstarted the blues revival, featured an entire chapter on Hopkins, enabling Hopkins to begin one of the most tumultuous decades in the twentieth century in a position where he could capitalize on his decades of strife and struggle as a black man in Texas.[62] Hopkins gripped a mojo hand that soon changed his luck, again.

S I X

TOO MANY DRIVERS

Baby you got too many drivers, Lord when you ain't got but just one wheel . . .
Yes you know out of all them drivers you've gotten, you're
lucky if you don't get someone killed.

LIGHTNIN' HOPKINS, 1949
(FROM BIG BILL BROONZY, 1939)

THE THIRD PHASE OF Hopkins's career set sail at the beginning of the 1960s. Nineteen sixty-one started with positive press for his new single on Bobby Robinson's Fire label. In late January, *Billboard*'s review of "Mojo Hand" waxed, "Hopkins is at his very best with these two monumental efforts. Topside is an uptempo blues—a story of women, love and superstition. Flipside is a slow, dirge-like blues also spotlighting drums and the singer's own guitar. Two great sides."[1]

A mojo hand is a good luck charm. Hopkins's lyrics partially explain the meaning:

> I'm goin' to Louisiana, and get me a mojo hand
> . . . I'm gonna fix my woman so she can't have no other man

The mojo theme had been prevalent throughout blues history. Some of the artists who used the theme were Ida Cox, who recorded "Mojo Hand Blues" in 1927 for Paramount; Blind Lemon Jefferson, who recorded "Low Down Mojo Blues" for Paramount in 1928; J. B. Lenore [later Lenoir], who released his combo's "The Mojo" in 1953 for J.O.B. Records; and Muddy Waters, who popularized a version of Preston Foster's "Got My Mojo Working" in 1956 for Chess Records.

Hopkins's song shared some lyrics with Ida Cox's "Mojo Hand Blues," which begins:

> I'm going to Louisiana, to get myself a mojo hand
> 'Cause these backbiting women are trying to take my man

Ma Rainey's "Louisiana Hoo Doo Blues" (1925) invoked the same theme two years prior to Cox:

> Going to the Louisiana bottom to get me a hoodoo hand Gotta stop these
> women from taking my man.

Texas Alexander also wove a mojo hand lyric into his "Tell Me Woman Blues" (1929):

> I'm going to Louisiana, get me a mojo hand
> Just to see when my woman got another man

Hopkins imbued the familiar lyric, or blues theme, of Cox, Rainey, and Alexander with his own sauntering style, successfully penetrating the market more than thirty years after Ma Rainey recorded her version.

Hopkins's contemporary, Mance Lipscomb, explained the mojo hand trope, "They say a mojo hand can change your person and give you good luck. If you twistified there ain't nothing you can do except get you a good Mojo Hand. They ain't no better Mojo Hand than a sparkle stick, you know off a farkleberry tree. The Indian people down in Polk County put a lot of store in the power of a sparkle stick."[2]

Hopkins's mojo hand related to his gambling luck:

> Well gamblin' is just another part of my life. . . . I'd go play a dance and then
> the ladies, it's time for them to go home, and then the men . . . We'd get
> on there and shoot some craps. That was mostly in that time dice shooting.
> And I would sit right there with them and shoot with them, old and young,
> and I gets lucky and I win me a little bit, you know. . . . They all said I had
> something. That's the reason I made that mojo hand. They said if you get a
> mojo hand you can win. And that's what I must had cuz I sure did win. I'd
> pick up a pair of dice on them old peoples and I wouldn't fall off. When I'd
> fall off everybody would be broke. They'd be asking, "Hey son, let me have
> a dollar." I'd let them have it you know because I'd know there was going
> to be another game. And when it come up I wouldn't have to worry about
> it cuz they'd give me my dollar back and I still could gamble. Well we'd be

shooting about ten, fifteen cents and then sometimes one of them big shots come in there with about fifteen or twenty dollars. Then they'd try to win out real quick cuz they'd bet two, three dollars and I was just the guy who caught them. I caught all I had in my hand. And they'd count it up and I'm doing very well. And I'm doing that all the time.[3]

Hopkins's single "Mojo Hand" marked his final appearance on the national record charts, entering the *Cash Box* singles chart February 25, 1961, for five weeks, peaking at number 26. His everyday lifestyle did not markedly change. More opportunities to perform in better venues ensued, but the business became more complicated. Due to Hopkins's increased income and a largely new white audience, more people involved themselves in the revenue stream that his music and performances generated.

McCormick, an astute folk commentator and avid researcher, signed an exclusive deal to represent Hopkins in 1959. He was not an experienced music business professional like Harold Leventhal in New York City or Bobby Robinson in Harlem. While McCormick apparently wanted the white folk music audience to appreciate Hopkins's talents, he was a novice in the music industry. His lack of business experience might have hampered the career of Hopkins, the only artist he represented during this era. Sam Charters went as far as describing him as "a leech on Hopkins' side" in a letter he sent to Folkways founder Moe Asch.[4]

In a letter to Arhoolie Records founder Chris Strachwitz, McCormick wrote about his frustrations regarding the music business he was attempting to enter:

In a sense I'm counting on you since I've been thru every potential folklore record company in the U.S. and England. With only the exception of Dobell's 77, I find they are a corrupt and nasty bunch of people who don't know their own mind nor have any real sense of conviction. This applies to the crass commercial peddlers as well as the operations, which pretend to some honesty in their material. It has been a frustrating two years for me, frustrating because months and months of hard work have ultimately wound up at the mercy of such stupid jokers. Companies and people who make deals and fail to follow thru; those that ask for dubs and never return them; those that rearrange material without permission; or cheat on payment. I've dozens of hard luck stories—and after talking with a number of other people I have learned these are typical incidents. It's just a nasty business all the way.[5]

On June 12, 1961, Hopkins signed a ten-record deal with Prestige Records. Kenneth Goldstein, an important figure in the folk revival, signed the contract on behalf of Prestige. He was the first student to graduate with a doctorate in folklore from the University of Pennsylvania. He worked as a professor at Penn, where he chaired the graduate program in folklore for two decades and built the prestigious program. According to an obituary in *Dirty Linen*, Goldstein "served as folk music director for Stinson and Riverside records, and as folk and blues director of Prestige records, issuing over five hundred LPs of various kinds of folk music, on which he was listed as editor, producer, or both."[6] Some of the albums with which he was associated were by artists such as Ewan MacColl and A. L. Lloyd, Jean Ritchie, the Reverend Gary Davis, Sara Cleveland, and the Clancy Brothers. Goldstein's integrity was well established.

The founder of Prestige, jazz fan Bob Weinstock, entered the music business in 1945 with a mail order operation. In 1948, he opened the Jazz Record Corner, a retail outlet on 47th Street in Manhattan. Next, Weinstock founded the New Jazz label, which began by issuing "Subconscious Lee" backed with "Judy" on a 78. The record was released under the name of blind pianist Lennie Tristano and tenor saxophone player Lee Konitz. *Down Beat* and *Metronome* magazines gave the disc rave reviews. Not long after, Weinstock shut the New Jazz label down and started Prestige, which is widely regarded as the second-most-successful independent jazz label after Blue Note. By the time Weinstock sold his interest in the label in 1971, he built a formidable catalog boasting releases by jazz heavyweights John Coltrane, Coleman Hawkins, Miles Davis, Thelonius Monk, Rahsaan Roland Kirk, Sonny Rollins, Dexter Gordon, Gil Evans, the Modern Jazz Quartet, Eric Dolphy, and Jack McDuff.

The recording contract with Prestige (which released some Hopkins records on its Bluesville imprint) provided Hopkins with twenty cents in royalties for each double-sided twelve-inch record. Royalties were computed on 90 percent of records sold. Prestige only paid royalties on 90 percent of the records it sold because it was customary in the record business to allow a certain percentage for breakage. That custom came from 78-rpm records, which were more fragile than the new LP format. Record companies also designated that a certain percentage of records manufactured would be given away for promotional purposes. Royalties were not paid on promotional copies.

The contract called for Hopkins to be paid a five-hundred-dollar advance for each record payable within two weeks upon the completion of the record. According to Goldstein, "[Black performers] preferred being paid a flat amount rather than a royalty, and we worked out the details of what they should be paid. . . . the least I think we ever paid someone was 250 dollars as an advance. I think Gary Davis got the biggest advance outside of Sonny Terry and Lightnin' Hopkins; all got paid 500 dollar advances."[7]

The five-hundred-dollar advance was charged against royalties; therefore Hopkins's records had to sell 2,750 copies to recoup the advance before he saw any more royalty payments. The contract also contained language concerning exclusivity: "You will not perform any musical compositions recorded hereunder for any other person for the purpose of making phonograph records within 5 years after our recording is made; and you acknowledge that your services are unique and extraordinary." Such provisions did not trouble Hopkins.

The bottom of the one-page contract also contained the following language:

> The artist hereby appoints (according to terms of a pre-existing agreement) Mack McCormick, 1608 Haver Street, Houston, Texas, as his sole authorized agent under the terms of this agreement to collect and receive all monies due to him, and declares that the receipts of said Mack McCormick shall be a full and valid discharge, and therefore requests and directs Prestige Records, Inc. to make such payments as are due to him through said Mack McCormick.

This part of the contract was signed by Sam Lightning Hopkins as "Artist" and Mack McCormick as "Agent." The potential for problems with this agreement is evident in the language. Hopkins essentially signed away all his rights to payments from Prestige Records to McCormick. Therefore, Hopkins would have a difficult time getting paid by Prestige because the contract language clearly stated "that the receipts of said Mack McCormick shall be a full and valid discharge, and therefore requests and directs Prestige Records, Inc. to make such payments as are due to him through said Mack McCormick."[8]

Just like the contracts Hopkins signed with Bill Quinn and his Gold Star label, Hopkins did not consult any legal representation when he signed the ten-record contract. The clause giving up his interests to McCormick eventually became problematic because no enforcement mechanism existed for Hopkins to use.

Correspondence between McCormick and Chris Strachwitz reveals much about McCormick and Hopkins's business relationship. In addition, McCormick's statements about Hopkins hint at bitter feelings about Hopkins, "He lived in an unhappy world. He couldn't figure out why it was that way. He was unhappy, let's put it that way, he was always unhappy, something was always displeasing him. Did not enjoy life and unlike most any musician did not enjoy performing. He didn't enjoy performing. Take any actor or musician and put them on a stage where the audience is hollering for more that person will be thrilled, and . . . will give more another encore or perform longer or whatever, and usually afterwards he'll go out and sign autographs. This is why so many performers keep running from city to city—to get love from different cities. That's . . . the way performers are. Sam was not like that. Sam would perform as little as possible and harass people for hours. [Hopkins] did not enjoy life."[9] McCormick's relationship with Hopkins still struck a sour note many years after it dissolved.

An undated letter McCormick sent to Chris Strachwitz casts some light into McCormick's opinions and attitudes when it came to paying performers or songwriters. McCormick wrote to Strachwitz:

Don't fret about copyright and song clearance *until you are selling 10,000 copies of each release* [underlined in original]. When publishers want royalties they'll let you know but most of them don't bother with small releases simply because it isn't worth the trouble. No one in the publishing business cares about limited appeal material for collectors. You're in no legal jeopardy using copyrighted material for there is a compulsory license provision in the copyright act, and when they want payment, they'll let you know. Chances are it'll never come up.[10]

McCormick essentially advises Strachwitz to ignore copyright laws until someone catches him. However, McCormick's advice contrasted with his actions on Hopkins's behalf. For example, McCormick certainly dictated or suggested the content of Hopkins's girlfriend's letter to Folkways owner Moe Asch demanding royalties, which resulted in a better deal on paper for Hopkins's Folkways material. However, due to slow sales, poor record-keeping, and Folkways' failure to actually pay royalties, Hopkins never saw any more money from Folkways despite McCormick's beneficial assistance.

McCormick claimed he paid Hopkins royalties on the records he arranged for the Tradition and 77 labels to release, and he was able to help renegotiate Hopkins's Folkways deal favorably. Yet at the same time, McCormick advised Chris Strachwitz not to worry about paying royalties on copyrighted material when Strachwitz released records on his Arhoolie Records label. With a ten-record deal with Prestige at hand, McCormick and Hopkins saw more money at stake. In addition, McCormick expected a percentage for acting as booking agent. McCormick recalled, "He made an enormous amount of money at times. And he'd come back, one time he came back from a trip to New York, I gave him $2,700 he had earned on that trip."[11] However, Hopkins did not have a good way to ensure that $2,700 was an accurate accounting of his earnings.

Hopkins's experience with Bobby Robinson, if in fact Robinson's version is correct, is one way that Hopkins sought to protect his interests. Hopkins told Robinson to pay him cash for the songs he recorded and to forget royalties. Certainly, Hopkins disliked royalty-only record deals, so he chose onetime cash payments instead. Yet when he signed a ten-record contract with Prestige Records, his pay was linked to the number of copies of records sold. Therefore, Hopkins faced two filters to getting his money from Prestige. First, he had to depend on Prestige providing an accurate accounting of how many records it sold, and, second, Hopkins needed to seek money from McCormick. Hopkins's signature on the Prestige contract is dated June 1961, and the contract itself is dated May 1961.

He recorded two records for Prestige: the *Lightnin' in New York* album for Nat Hentoff and the *Mojo Hand* album for Bobby Robinson's Fire label. Legendary recording engineer Rudy Van Gelder recorded the two Hopkins sessions in his Englewood Cliffs, New Jersey, studio. Van Gelder was an optometrist by trade who began his engineering career in a home studio at his parents' house in Hackensack, New Jersey. At the beginning of his career, he learned how to engineer sound by recording local musicians on nights and weekends. By the late 1940s, professional musicians started showing up at his studio. Pianist Billy Taylor, one of the earliest Prestige artists to record with Van Gelder, worked with him to improve his recording techniques. Van Gelder started engineering records in 1953 for the Blue Note label, the most renowned independent jazz label in American history, and later became famous in the jazz world as the creator of the "Blue Note Sound." "See the main thing about him, he wasn't a bullshitter," Prestige owner Bob Weinstock mused about the engineer. "He loved the music . . . so it wasn't just some guy doing it for the money. He put his heart and soul into it."[12]

In 1959, not long before he first recorded Hopkins, Van Gelder moved his studio from his parents' living room in Hackensack to Englewood Cliffs. He also shut down his optometry practice in order to concentrate on engineering records full time. By the time Hopkins entered his studios on October 26, 1960, Van Gelder had already recorded tracks for Blue Note label jazz milestones, such as Jimmy Smith's *Home Cookin'* and *Back at the Chicken Shack*, Horace Silver's *Blowing the Blues Away*, Hank Mobley's *Soul Station*, John Coltrane's *Blue Train*, Art Blakey and the Jazz Messengers' *Moanin'*, and Sonny Clark's *Cool Struttin'*, and many more.

Bass player Leonard Gaskin and drummer Belton Evans joined Hopkins for his first Prestige recording session. Sonny Terry also played harmonica on a few tracks. The production was mysteriously credited to "'The Sound of America," of which little is known. The thirty-two-page booklet that accompanies the compact disc reissue entitled *The Complete Prestige/Bluesville Recordings* does not shed any light on the identity of this producer or producers either. Gaskin, however, kept meticulous records of the sessions he worked. His notes reveal that he received a check for seventy-five dollars for the October 26, 1960, session for Sound of America with Sonny Terry and Lightning Sam Hopkins.[13]

With Rudy Van Gelder working the soundboard, Hopkins experienced the skill sets of an expert sonic sculptor. By this stage of his career, Hopkins's recordings had been supervised by various music professionals, including producers in Los Angeles, Bill Quinn in Houston, and Bobby Shad in New York. With Kenneth Goldstein's nominal participation, plus Van Gelder's skills, the session signaled that, for expertise in production, Hopkins had arrived at the top of the jazz recording field.

The Prestige production team made a good choice when it hired Gaskin and Evans, because both were well-seasoned musicians. Bass player Gaskin had a particularly sterling résumé. Before he settled into working as a full-time session man in 1960, Gaskin played with Dizzy Gillespie, Max Roach, Thelonius Monk, and Erroll Garner, and toured Europe with Eddie Condon's Dixieland band. After the session with Hopkins, Gaskin went on to record with Bob Dylan and many others, including Little Richard, James Brown, and Marvin Gaye. Belton Evans's credits included sessions with King Curtis, Clyde McPhatter, Sunnyland Slim, and Big Joe Turner. He also drummed on Elmore James's songs recorded for Bobby Robinson's Fire label.

Hopkins's idiosyncratic, self-taught style sometimes befuddled sidemen, but for this studio date Gaskin and Evans stayed right in the pocket and provided a solid rhythm foundation. Since Charters rediscovered Hopkins in January 1959, Hopkins had recorded hundreds of songs. Yet Hopkins easily devised fresh material. Decades of developing his craft in East Texas and fifteen years playing professionally in Houston proved this, but Hopkins chose to rerecord some of his best songs by reaching back into his catalog and revisiting some older numbers.

Prestige released the October 26, 1960, Hopkins session as *Last Night Blues* and credited it to Lightnin' Hopkins with Sonny Terry. For this studio date, Hopkins rerecorded "Rocky Mountain," first recorded for Aladdin Records in 1946, the second record released under his name. The first time Hopkins cut "Rocky Mountain," he recorded solo, but this time the song benefits from Sonny Terry's hooting and hollering and harmonica. Mack McCormick's liner notes tell the story behind the song:

This song has its basis in Lightnin's trip to Arizona on a cotton-picking contract back in the 1930s. He had seen pictures of the mountains but had "never believed they were true." Coming from the prairies of Texas, his first sight of the giant peaks impelled him to make this song. While in Arizona, Lightnin' quickly wandered away from the terms of his labor contract and was soon found south of the border, playing guitar in a Nogales whorehouse. From there he extended his activities to bootlegging Mexican wine and whiskey into the Papago and Gila River Indian Reservations. Touching on this nefarious activity, one verse expresses whimsical compassion for the Indians and contempt for the Federal Prohibition Law that rules their reservations.[14]

The verse McCormick discusses reveals Hopkins's often-ignored role as social commentator.

> If you ever go out in Rocky Mountain
> Will you please stop in Arizona town
> You know they won't sell them Indians nothing to drink
> And they don't hardly allow them around

Hopkins told Les Blank about selling liquor on an Arizona Indian reservation:

I was in Arizona with a bunch of liquor, but when I was selling liquor, I didn't feel like I was going to get caught. Which I didn't, but I knowed this one thing, I knowed that you wasn't allowed to sell it to Indians and Indians come by once you sell him one pint you might as well sell it to him as long as you got whiskey or wine. Wine is what he wanted. Now this particular guy, his name was Big Ben. Now me and him would go out together and me and him would ride together and I would sneak him a little drink and he would get to talking to me, you know I'm a good man, and the next thing you know he slapped me on the shoulder, Big Ben want a drink. I said well I ain't got no more Ben. Yeah you got more wine and Big Ben fight. Well that mean you and me gonna fight then and he hauled off and slapped me and I jumped out of the car and run around there and I hauled off and I knocked him almost down. Now you make Big Ben mad, Big Ben gonna fight. Yeah well I said Big Ben gonna fight by himself. I'm gone. So I lit out. I hit him with all I had, what I'm gonna stay and fight him some more for? And he couldn't catch me. I made a circle big enough for I could get back to the car, and when I got back to the car he's way over there somewhere and I took off. I would go to his house. I didn't go to his house no more after that.[15]

As an African American living in a racist and segregated society, Hopkins certainly identified with the plight of Native Americans. By now, Hopkins had made several references to racial injustice in lyrics, most notably in "Mr. Charlie," but this constituted the first time he recorded a song with lyrics chronicling racial injustices against nonblacks.

On November 9, 1960, Hopkins returned to Van Gelder's studio with Gaskin and Evans, but this time without Sonny Terry. Gaskin noted in his records that he received a check for $103 for working the session.[16] This was Hopkins's second session for the Prestige label, but it would be released first, titled *Lightnin'*.

Hopkins rerecorded "Automobile Blues," which he first recorded as "Automobile" for Gold Star and as "Automobile Blues" for Jax Records. Hopkins reinvigorated another old song, "Katie Mae," a cut from Aladdin in 1946, the first record ever released under Hopkins's name only, after two records credited to Thunder Smith and Lightnin' Hopkins. Hopkins also cut another version of "Shinin' Moon," which he had originally taped for Modern Records. The record featured Hopkins playing acoustic guitar on mostly slow and mid-tempo blues. Evans played the drums with brushes, which provided a sympathetic accompaniment. Hopkins varied the pace of the set with "Walking Blues," an up-tempo shuffle, and a version of Arthur "Big Boy" Crudup's "Mean Old Frisco," for which Hopkins claimed the songwriting credit. Crudup was known for writing classics like "Rock Me Mama," "My Baby Left Me," and "That's Alright (Mama)," the third released by Elvis Presley in his first step to superstardom in 1954. After recording in New York, Hopkins returned to Houston with four more albums under his belt and the boost of "Mojo Hand." Hopkins's profile continued to surge.

Ed Badeaux, Mack McCormick's brother-in-law, took the cover photo featured on *Lightnin'*, a profile shot of Hopkins playing an acoustic guitar used for decades after it first appeared on the Prestige/Bluesville album. Badeaux recalled photographing Hopkins: "Mack was managing him for a brief time and got me to take pictures of him, so . . . I went out to where he was living in one of those white box houses out there in whatever ward [Third] it is. . . . I think Lightnin' only played an electric guitar, so I brought out an acoustic guitar to pose him with. Our interests were mainly in acoustic. . . . He walked out and posed on the railroad track. This was a color roll of film. . . . Lightnin' was a remarkable musician. He had his own sense of phrasing and timing, and it was quite unique, and it can't really be successfully imitated. . . . He seemed to me, I won't say a lonely individual, but he drank a lot and he smoked like a chain smoker. [He] spent nights, when he could get booked, in these smoky clubs around town."[17] But it was not the smoky dives Hopkins normally played that propelled his career to the next level.

Hopkins's Folkways record and the hootenanny gigs he played in Houston in 1959 and 1960 were the keys to his career's revival. The stories that those performances generated in the local daily papers kept Hopkins's name in the public eye and started to generate dividends. His single "Mojo Hand" charted on the radio for February and March 1961. Mack McCormick and John Lomax, Jr., helped him book profitable gigs detached from his usual Dowling Street and other neighborhood haunts, though Hopkins did not relinquish his humidity-streaked neighborhood nights at the juke joints.

In 1961, Hopkins also appeared on the Pete Seeger album *Sing Out with Pete!*, released by Folkways Records. Hopkins joined Seeger on the song "Oh, Mary Don't You Weep." The cut was recorded when Hopkins worked with Seeger at Carnegie Hall in 1960. The record was a compilation of Seeger sides recorded at, besides Carnegie, Yale, University of Chicago, and the Village Gate nightclub.

In February 1961, Mack McCormick landed Hopkins a gig at Rice University. African Americans were not permitted to attend Rice, the exclusive private university located in a tree-shaded area between the museum district and the medical center area of Houston, yet Hopkins and his childhood friend, and ace harmonica player, Billy Bizor hit the stage on February 17, 1961. The Rice University paper reported that three hundred attended the show in Will Rice Commons, and concert producer Mike Buckley said it was a "smashing success."[18]

Professional musician Ezra Charles, a student at Rice, recalled, "I went to Rice [in the] early sixties . . . '63. Occasionally, we'd bring someone into there. At Rice, you have residential colleges, something like a cross between a dormitory and a fraternity, and I was at Hanzen College. Occasionally on Sunday afternoon, they'd bring someone in to put on a little concert in the commons, which was the dining hall. And I remember Lightnin' Hopkins coming in for one of the shows one time, and it was the old give him $50 and a bottle of Jack Daniel's and he'll sit there and play for two hours kind of thing. That was the first time I ever saw him or heard of him and was too ignorant to know what it represented. But I thought it was OK."[19]

Drummer John Turner, later known professionally as Uncle John Turner, also first encountered Hopkins at Rice University. "The first time I ever saw him was at Rice University. He was still in scholarly circles. Him and his cousin [were] playing an afternoon concert for students," recalled Turner,[20] who eventually backed Hopkins on drums in the 1970s.

Hopkins's next gig was the Texas Folklore Society's annual meeting. In late March, Hopkins and Bizor worked the meeting in Austin at the University of Texas, which, unlike the University of Houston and Rice University, had been desegregated for years. Hopkins and his band played at the student union auditorium on March 29, 1961. The day of the show, the university's student newspaper, the *Daily Texan*, hyped Hopkins's appearance in a three-column article on the front page of the Amusements section. The writer, Bill Hampton, romanticized Hopkins and included plentiful biographical errors in his piece. However, Hampton did note Hopkins's influence correctly: "Lightnin' is the pinnacle. He is the unsurpassable master of his song. Just as great entertainers so widely known, such as Duke Ellington and Count Basie, look to Ray Charles, the popular blues singers such as Charles look back to Lightnin' Hopkins, Muddy Waters, and the late Bill Broonzy. . . . Where they got him, or what he'll sing, it will be in the music of a people that knew misery, and Lightnin' know it as well as any."[21] Hampton had a loose command of Hopkins's biographical details, but he was astute enough to grasp the larger picture: Hopkins and a select few built the musical foundation that groundbreaking entertainers like Ray Charles used when overlaying their innovative sounds of soul and rhythm and blues.

Gilbert Shelton, who later became known as the creator of the cartoon strip the *Fabulous Furry Freak Brothers*, wrote a review of Hopkins's show for the *Daily Texan*. Shelton excoriated Bill Hampton's piece from a day earlier and gave the correct biographical context for Hopkins's performance. Shelton noted, "Many of the overflow crowd in the Union auditorium Wednesday didn't know what to expect, but scarcely any were disappointed. Audience enthusiasm was high in the informal lights-on atmosphere of the auditorium, and they gave a standing ovation at the end of the show, at which Hopkins remarked, 'There, you've made me feel a little bit better even.'" Shelton noted that Hopkins and Bizor played for over two hours and played some old songs, improvised some on the spot, and injected humor into the performance. The crowd was most pleased with "Short Haired Woman" and "Mojo Hand" and several that Shelton did not recognize and Hopkins did not identify.

Like the student reporter Hampton did in the article of the previous day, Shelton noted Hopkins's influence on others: "Harmonica player Billy Bizor, accompanying Hopkins during much of the show and playing a couple of solo numbers, is admittedly a product of 'Lightnin's' own talent—Hopkins raised him and taught him music. Bizor both plays and vocalizes—sometimes simultaneously, singing right through the harmonica."[22]

After his gig at the University of Texas, Hopkins, in April 1961, played another venue frequented by a white audience, the Playhouse Theater on Main Street in downtown Houston. The Rice University student newspaper carried a listing showing Hopkins played a midnight and one a.m. show. Don Sanders, later a well-respected folk artist, was a teenager at the time. Sanders energetically recalled his early encounter with Hopkins:

There was a guy called himself Pucho, and he had a place called the Purple Onion on South Shepard. He was a wannabe beatnik. This was [April 14, 1961]. Pucho staged a bunch of midnight concerts at the Playhouse Theater. . . . it was the first in-the-round theater in Houston [and it was] owned by Bob and Marietta Marich. They were connected with Channel 2, the TV station. . . . My parents were strict Baptists, and I don't know what I told them to get out to a midnight jazz concert starring Lightnin'. I went down there and there weren't many people there. Lightnin' was playing an old Harmony Sovereign, an acoustic guitar with a D'Armond pickup in the sound hole. That was kind of weird for me. I was a folkie and hadn't seen anyone play a guitar with a pickup in it. . . . At the break, 12:45 or one o'clock, I followed Lightnin' [out of the venue]. He didn't go to the dressing room. He used to walk out in front of the theater and stood under the marquee, and I stood around hemming and hawing, not really saying anything, and he finally said, "Hey, hey, wanna sip of this?" And he pulled a pocket flask, a hip flask, out of his pocket and gave me a shot of whiskey, my first shot of whiskey, exactly what my parents probably were afraid of. I remember him being very cordial and nice at that point, and that's the only time I ever remember Lightnin' as a nice person. Pretty much every time after that I encountered him, he seemed like an angry person. That may have been the guise he took on around white musicians or wannabe on the scene type of people.[23]

Later, in the summer of 1961, on July 13 and 26, Hopkins was back in the studio recording for Prestige. This time, Hopkins recorded at home in Houston. On July 13, Hopkins cut four tracks with a band that were not released until 1962. A couple of weeks later, on July 26, McCormick joined Hopkins at ACA Studios, where he cut tracks for a solo album that Prestige released as *Blues in My Bottle*. McCormick and Kenneth Goldstein were credited as producers, and McCormick, as usual, provided excellent liner notes.

Goldstein remembered the significance of his involvement in Prestige's Bluesville line: "My own direct and most important involvement in the Bluesville series was with the singers I knew well, had a hang up on, such as Sonny Terry and Lightnin' Hopkins. Lightnin' Hopkins had been recorded earlier but had been given a very commercial sound. I wanted to go back with a country thing with him. So when I took over the Bluesville series . . . all the stuff from then onward was produced essentially with my concept of the country blues. . . . Lightnin' was a pro from the get go. He knew exactly what he wanted to do."[24]

Blues in My Bottle opens with Hopkins's version of Texas Alexander's song "Buddy Brown's Blues." McCormick's notes provide some history:

According to the story that Texas Alexander told on himself, his career had been interrupted by having been sent to jail for singing "a bad song." Though the incident has never been confirmed, it is entirely possible that some local law officer may have taken offense at Alexander's unrelenting sense of life. In any case, the story is widely known and, having heard it from the older man himself, has instilled in Lightnin' reluctance to record anything he regards as questionable.[25]

Hopkins's reluctance to record "questionable" tunes is a telling comment on racial tension in Houston, Texas, circa 1961. Alexander offended the white supremacy system, resulting in incarceration, while Hopkins's own "Tim Moore's Farm" stirred malevolent feelings as well. Consequently, he hesitated, unwilling to give law enforcement, or any other white people, a reason to threaten or harass him.

McCormick's annotations provided more insight into Hopkins's recording of Alexander's song: "Included [here is] . . . Lightnin' doing a vivid impression of Alexander's 'trembling' vocal style. The song is a portrait of 'that lazy Buddy Brown that let his women do all the work'—a famed character around Crockett, Texas some years ago. . . . Lightnin's apprehension of a 'bad song' still haunted him. He was tempted to omit its most memorable verse."

> I got something to tell you make the hair rise on your head
> Well I got a new way of loving, make the springs scrunch on your bed

Hopkins also recorded several cover songs that day that were released on the album, including: Sticks McGhee's 1947 R&B hit "Drinkin' Wine Spo Dee-O-Dee"; a version of "Going to Dallas to See My Pony Run," which, according to McCormick, was a traditional Texas blues that had not often appeared on record; and the title track, "Blues in the Bottle," originally a sharecropper's song, from Blind Lemon Jefferson.[26] Some of the most interesting songs Hopkins recorded were autobiographical, reflecting his values and personality. "Beans, Beans, Beans," a spoken word piece accompanied by an occasional strum on the guitar, illustrated Hopkins's time spent with Missouri Pacific Railroad in the 1930s:

> Little country town they call Centerville, Texas and that was my home
> When I left there, I was picking cotton and I was pulling corn
> But when I got on that railroad, I thought I should have stayed home

Hopkins worked on the railroad with Texas Alexander. According to McCormick, that particular stint of manual labor inspired Hopkins to forge a career in music.[27] Hopkins also recorded the first version of "My Grandpa Is Too Old!," on which he played an upbeat tempo blues while invoking respect for an elder:

> I want all you young peoples to know what to do
> Leave my grandpa alone because he got old too
> . . . Sweetest man I ever saw
> I ain't jiving, I ain't joking

Hopkins's respect and concern for his grandfather do not strike a familiar blues theme in his canon, but family, undoubtedly, mattered a great deal to him.

Hopkins continued work gigs outside of Houston. Robert Murphy played drums with him on a tour in the summer of 1961. He remembered,

> [The] summer of '61 . . . we were on the road . . . with Lightning, Clifton [Chenier], [and] Sonny Boy Williamson. Clift, Sonny Boy and Lightning, we all rode in separate cars. Clifton and the band in mine, and Lightning and his lady in his. Sonny Boy Williamson carried a turtle in the back of his car. Some nights I'd play with him and some nights he was a loner, he was not a band man. He wasn't particular about accompaniment. He knew he was subject to do most anything. He did it by himself it was good, but if he did it with others, he'd look bad. I remember we played between Dallas and Forth Worth, the mob or somebody had some clubs up in that area and they would all raid each other's clubs for bands. We heard about this and got kind of scared . . . but nothing happened. . . . Some nights we drove all night. He'd just play for a little while and then he'd tell the folks, I don't think me and this drummer are going to make it. I wouldn't say a word. Just go backstage and he'd want to play by himself.[28]

Murphy also remembered that Hopkins played a cheap department-store guitar. "Did anyone ever tell you what kind of guitar he had? He had a Sears Roebuck. At the time I knew Lightning he had a Sears Roebuck and a speaker and amplifier. He liked that Sears Roebuck guitar. He wouldn't play nobody else's guitar. Some of the other guys would ask him wanted to play their guitar. He'd say no, I don't want to play that thing. The whole time I knew Lightnin' I didn't know him to have a Fender or a Stratocaster or a Gibson. The only thing I knew him to have was a Sears Roebuck."[29]

Murphy's roots were in the Deep Elm (later known as Deep Ellum) and Thomas and Hall Street sections of Dallas, where his father was a well-regarded entertainer. Having attended both UCLA and Xavier University, after his father derailed the young man's desire to hit the road with Ray Charles, Murphy was an all-around learned talent who could play percussion as well as piano, violin, cello, bass, and mandolin.

"Hopkins was not a 'musician' who was trained in chord patterns and all that," Murphy averred.

He didn't play with a clamp. He just played by ear, just like most of the old-time bluesmen. He wouldn't pay much attention to whether it was an eight-bar blues or a twelve-bar blues, just as long as it fit what he was singing and doing. Sometimes he'd go and stick to the pattern. When he was playing with Clifton and me, the three of us had a thing going. We even had afternoon jam sessions over there right where Lightnin' used to live. . . . There was a two-story house on this particular street, and they converted it into a beer joint club. Lightnin' would come over and join Clifton and me, and we would have a jam session. You would not believe what we would play during those sessions. . . . Clif liked the way I played. He wanted to mix zydeco with the blues . . .

Well, I was able to adapt to the zydeco thing, even though I wasn't used to it. Clifton wanted to play like Jimmy Smith. I said, "I'll tell you what, I'll teach you to play like Jimmy Smith if you will teach me the left hand on that accordion!" I could always play the piano, so the right hand was no problem. So, he did. . . . Lightnin' would come over and we'd have a jam session. You know what they mean by saying, taking fours, right? Well, we took fours. We'd start a tune and we'd take fours soloing. Man you'd never heard such a thing in your born days! . . . We'd [Lightnin', Clifton, and I] take a popular song. . . . We could do the fours if they knew the chords. If they didn't know the chords, I'd give them the chords.[30]

Increasingly, Hopkins benefited from the renewed popularity of R&B. Following up on his well-received California performances of 1960, he began to tour the West Coast regularly. In August, Hopkins headed out to Los Angeles to play Ed Pearl's Ash Grove with Brownie McGhee and Sonny Terry. Hopkins had played a one-off Sunday afternoon gig at the Ash Grove in the summer of 1960 when he was in California to perform at the Berkeley Folk Festival. The Ash Grove nightclub became his West Coast touring base. Hopkins played there regularly until it closed in the 1970s. As musician Taj Mahal characterizes it:

The Ash Grove was the focus of folk music in L.A. . . . a gathering place for people knowledgeable about folk and ethnic music. The aficionados. It was a family-oriented type of place, in the sense that the regulars there, the people who hung out, felt like a family. . . . The whole place had that lived in feel. . . . The music and political tone was set by Ed. It was very progressive toward all people. There were lots of grassroots politics and grassroots music going on at the Ash Grove and at the center of it, real music from all over the place. People gathered for conversations, drifted in and out from the performance scene to the conversation scene. . . . On any given night there'd be conversations about Tolstoy, Jung, Martin Luther King—all kinds of people talking politics, art, philosophy. Cesar Chavez and the farmworkers had their meetings in one of the rooms during the time they were organizing into a union. I could hear the old-time music from the Appalachian-European tradition or the Afro-American tradition, plus Balkan music, Slavic music, music from all angles. . . . The place was packed, packed out every night.[31]

The space Ed Pearl provided gave Mahal and others the chance to earn the approval of the most renowned performers in the field:

Howling Wolf and Lightnin', they checked me out. They didn't say, "Look, do it this way or that way," and I didn't say, "Now, Mr. Lightnin', this is the way to play it?" It wasn't done that way. They would watch, not saying anything. That's how they told me I was doing all right. When I started listening to Lightnin', I said, "Okay in order to listen to this music, or be part of this music . . . I've got to go with the way the music goes . . ." Other musicians often said that "You can't play with Lightnin' because Lightnin' change when Lightnin' do." Well all right so don't rush it. I used my ears. I never counted by the bars. Let him lead, as long as you get in the right relationship with it, you can play with it, you can play with him. You got trouble when you start deciding that you know what guys like Lightnin' are going to do before they get there.[32]

Mahal's thoughts perfectly summed up how to play on stage or in the studio with Hopkins: the trick was to let Hopkins dictate where the song went, not to strictly adhere to a set twelve-bar blues pattern.

Mahal pointed out the unique blend of politics and music that existed at the Ash Grove. The mixing of traditional country or bluegrass musicians such as Bill Monroe with the blues of Lightnin' Hopkins stretched many boundaries and created a hybrid, inclusive, and democratic space for the audience. Hopkins was just one generation away from the founding of the country blues, but his direct connection to Blind Lemon Jefferson, the root of country blues, allowed the audience to experience the real roots of American blues music that East Texas blues encompassed. Performers like Bill Monroe, who was widely credited as being the father of bluegrass, showed the audience another important branch of American roots music.

Ed Pearl recalled Hopkins's importance to the Ash Grove: "He quickly developed an audience. It was very clear that people were starved for something that was really authentic. . . . I learned from Bess [Lomax Hawes] about Leadbelly and Brownie and Big Bill Broonzy and people like that and white people. For me, it was like a total revelation of hearing real music in their own voices by Cajuns, Texas blacks, Molly Jackson, you name it and many, many black performers. . . . To me, that was very encouraging. To me that solidified the beginnings of my politics and what I wanted to do. So, Lightnin' very quickly began changing the culture of the club. Lightnin' was critical to that."[33]

Ed Pearl's younger brother Bernie hung around the Ash Grove and learned to play guitar by playing with Hopkins: "I was smitten immediately—that image of him with his gold tooth shining, his hand raised up singing some beautiful phrase. So, it's all one thing wrapped up. That's how I met Lightnin'. . . . He would come through three or four times a year. When he was at the Ash Grove, he'd be doing four and five and six days engagements, so he was not there and gone the next day. He was there for a while. There was some visiting. Sometimes I'd just bring him his half pint of Gordon's gin and we'd talk and he'd show me stuff. Shortly after that, he started asking me to go onstage and back him. And essentially that's how I learned to play."[34]

Grammy Award–winning musician Dave Alvin hung around the Ash Grove as a teenager. His recollections of Hopkins remain vivid too:

First time I saw him at the Ash Grove he was wearing a sharkskin suit, shades, a tie, and later, then it would be a turtleneck, the shades were always there, the hair was always greased, processed, pompadour, the quasi-Lightning pompadour. He just exuded cool and confidence and authority. Seeing him live you also got the sense of the old Native American mythological trickster. . . . he could turn around and do something to tug at your heartstrings. Tell a story about his mother or something and then play something spiritual, make you forget that he was a trickster or a hustler. When you saw him live, mainly at the Ash Grove, they'd bring him in for like five nights. He'd come in like four times a year, so we'd at least go two nights each time, and they would have it set up as two shows a night and usually the first show would be sold out, packed. . . . Sometimes on Sunday nights you could be . . . close to him. . . . it was . . . very powerful. He'd made so many recordings. Not all of them are great, but some of them are transcendental. . . . I was twelve or thirteen years old, I didn't know there were transcendental men, but that was what you got.[35]

Alvin recalled that Hopkins's behavior toward him changed as Alvin grew up: "Because we were kids, you kind of had a free pass. I never realized that until 1979 when I saw him playing the Lighthouse in Redondo Beach. We'd all grown up, and the free pass was gone. When we were kids, he was very friendly, but I wouldn't put him down as gregarious. Big Joe Turner was gregarious. . . . As friendly as some of them were, . . . there was a boundary around all of them, and don't cross that boundary, whether due to racial issues or whatever. I live in bars and rightly or wrongly . . . there's a boundary you don't cross with me. I'm at work. You want to keep a little bit of your personal shit personal. He wasn't unfriendly either. He valued his space."[36] Watching performers like Hopkins play at the Ash Grove deeply impacted Alvin, who penned a song called "Ash Grove," the title track of his 1994 album:

> I used to slip away
> Down to the Ash Grove
> To hear the old blues men play
> There was Big Joe and Lightnin'[37]

Horizon Records released one of the Hopkins, McGhee, and Terry Ash Grove performances from August 1961 later that year as *Blues Hoot* and gave Hopkins the title billing. The record begins with Hopkins's spoken introduction to "Big Car Blues":

> Excuse me miss
> . . . But what can your good man be
> Sugar, I know I'm a funny looking fella
> Whoo! But if I clean up won't you have a little pity on me[38]

Alvin remembers this as the first Hopkins song he heard: "That was like a nine, ten-minute monologue that had a little bit of a song. I first heard that when I was twelve years old. Just his voice, it was so musical. He does some singing in it. It's kind of like 'Mr. Charlie,' but 'Mr. Charlie' is a folktale. 'Big Car Blues' is

'I saved up this money, got this car and this woman stole it.' . . . the musicality of the speaking voice . . . was rhythmic. . . . even to hear him talk to somebody ordering a drink or some food at the bar, it was the same musicality . . . you just couldn't separate the two [art from person], . . . Whether it's Ralph Stanley or Miles Davis, it's just the same thing: you're either born with it or play it so much it becomes second nature. . . . a lot of his power was the one-man band thing."[39]

Hopkins used the type of spoken-word introduction from "Big Car Blues" in many of his songs. However, Mack McCormick had a different opinion about the entertainment value of Hopkins's speech between his songs: "He started doing something quite early on, and it was a white/black thing, he started talking a lot on stage, sometimes incoherently and endlessly. But I think . . . why he started talking so much [was] because in his talking so much he got more constant reaction—laughter. I think that's the seed of it. . . . I feel that's where it came from, and people started objecting to it because it's like an hour and a half concert with like three songs, and an hour and fifteen minutes of talking. And his talking wasn't that entertaining. Know the way he talks his way to introduce 'Mr. Charlie'? 'Your rolling mill is burning down.' That's fairly well organized, but most of what he did is not well organized. . . . it got to be very incoherent at times."[40] Others, like W. L. Bane, who saw Hopkins several times in Houston in the 1960s, felt the banter did not detract from his performance: "What amazed me was how he could start talking on some drab subject and then swing in on that rhythm . . . right into a song."[41]

By the fall of 1961, Hopkins was back in California for an extended run at the Ash Grove club. Hopkins played from October 17 through November 5 with Ramblin' Jack Elliott and Hugh Romney, better known as Wavy Gravy. Elliott had acquired an impressive musical résumé since he first appeared on the American music scene in the 1950s. After spending time traveling with Woody Guthrie in the early 1950s, he moved to Europe in 1954. He returned to America in 1961, when he met Bob Dylan while visiting Woody Guthrie in the hospital. The folksinger Odetta claimed her mother gave him the nickname "Ramblin'" because he told unrelated stories before he got around to answering a question.[42]

Elliott remembers the bill with Hopkins:

I remember that Lightnin' wore a towel around his neck like boxers do like when they're resting. His hands perspired a lot and he would wipe the sweat off the strings and his hands to keep them dry. He wore shades all the time. I think he was drinking whiskey. I couldn't hardly understand a word he said. Maybe it was just that Deep South Texas black-man dialect that he spoke was just impenetrable for me. I couldn't understand the words he sang in songs either. I just loved the way he played guitar and the way he spoke and sang. It was all just music to me. I'd been hanging around with other black bluesmen before: Sonny Terry and Brownie McGhee, and I hung out with Mississippi John Hurt, Big Bill Broonzy, and Muddy Waters. . . . Lightnin' I only met him two or three times, and I was utterly in awe of him. . . . He seemed . . . kinda shy and off into some kind of cloud of his own making. I didn't want to pierce his envelope, bust in on his dressing room, and violate his privacy. I was honored to be the opening act for him. . . . I began to like the Ash Grove immediately when I heard Lightnin' and did my first gig.[43]

Variety magazine published a review of Hopkins's October 20 performance at the Ash Grove, which it called "a rare excursion from the Negro district of Houston, where the master of the blues has grown into a legend." The reviewer wrote a highly favorable review:

Hopkins is the epitome of true blues, delivering in a spontaneous style. As a performer, he is important but his music depends greatly on the listener, as well. Ash Grove customers are listeners, quiet, contemplative, and interested in the material. There is an immediate empathetic rapport that allows honest expressionism without any attempt at commercialized styles.[44]

Hopkins clearly suited the audiences at the Ash Grove; thus, this club anchored his West Coast tours.

Bruce Bromberg, a later producer of a Hopkins record, experienced the bluesman's craft at California State University's Northridge campus: "My best experience of seeing him was in the '60s. When he first started out, they put him out there . . . he did his thing. It was hard to understand him. He just came out, sat down, had a towel around his neck, and he just did it. He didn't tell stories, didn't tell jokes, he said a few asides. It was very difficult to understand. Plus, he played acoustic. I like him on electric. It was just an acoustic guitar. It was early in the blues renaissance, where these guys were just thrown in front of an audience. Sometimes it was bad, but that particular time it was good. He was always good when I saw him."[45]

After his gigs at the Ash Grove, Hopkins headed north up the coast and played Barbara Dane's San Francisco club, Sugar Hill, "Home of the Blues," from November 14 to 25, 1961. The club had just opened in May 1961. Sugar Hill was on Broadway in the North Beach district. According to writer Lee Hildebrand, the venue was the first blues club located outside of an African

American neighborhood. The walls were covered in burlap and painted white, and they were lined with red vinyl booths. The club sat 150 people and did not have a cover charge or a drink minimum.

Hopkins shared the bill with Dane and her band, pianist "Good News" Whitson, and former Duke Ellington bass player Wellman Braud. The bill included jazz pianist and songwriter Mose Allison as well. Gene Robinson, who wrote a column called "On the Beam" for the *Sun-Reporter*, a daily paper in San Francisco, singled out the gig as "ANOTHER BEST BEAM BET." Robinson called Hopkins "Another famed blues artist from Houston . . . Sam, a lean, worn man, who wears dark glasses and sings with a towel around his neck, has served time on a chain gang, and brings his blues laments a strange poignancy not often found in present day singers. Hopkins appeared last year at Carnegie Hall and the Village Gate but it is Dowling Street in Houston where he is most at home."[46]

As Mose Allison tells it,

I always liked his stuff you know. I was listening to him when I was down South in the '50s. . . . I had been a fan of Lightnin' ever since he did "Tim Moore's Farm." I always said that was worth five hundred pages of sociology. . . . His stuff was always humorous. . . . He wasn't the best guitarist, I don't think, but he was good, and the songs he wrote were fantastic, but they were completely different than anybody else. He wrote one about having a cold or the flu or something, "I'm Achin' All Over" [recorded for Herald Records as "Sick Feeling Blues"]. That's one of the tunes I remember. I don't think he played any of those things. . . . I guess he played stuff that went over in a nightclub. I talked to him casually. I was the featured artist. I had a trio. He played with just a drummer, I believe. We switched sets. It was mostly a young crowd at the time.[47]

A day after Hopkins finished his performance run at Sugar Hill, he ventured across the San Francisco Bay to Berkeley to record for Chris Strachwitz's Arhoolie Records.[48] By November 26, 1961, when Hopkins walked into the Sierra Sound studio to wax another record, an abundance of Hopkins's albums had swept through the marketplace. Between 1955 and 1961, fourteen Hopkins albums were released in America or England: *Strums the Blues* (Score), *Lightnin' Hopkins* (Folkways), *Lightnin' and the Blues* (Herald), *The Rooster Crowed in England* (77 Records), *Last of the Great Blues Singers* (Time Records), *Country Blues* (Tradition Records), *Autobiography in Blues* (Tradition Records), *Down South Summit Meeting* (World Pacific), *Lightnin'* (Prestige/Bluesville), *Joel and Lightnin' Hopkins* (Heritage), *In New York* (Candid), *Last Night Blues* (Prestige/Bluesville), *Blues in My Bottle* (Bluesville), and *Sings the Blues* (Crown).

Mojo Hand

Even the prolific John Lee Hooker only had ten albums released during the same time period. Hooker, like Hopkins, also recorded for anyone who paid him. However, in an attempt to duck contractual restrictions, Hooker recorded under pseudonyms such as Texas Slim, Birmingham Sam, John Lee Booker, John Lee Cooker, Delta John, Johnny Lee, Johnny Williams, Little Pork Chop, The Boogie Man, and John L'Hooker. Hopkins saw no need for subterfuge and recorded only under his real name.

While record buyers had a lot of Hopkins's records to choose from when flipping through the record bins during the 1961 Christmas shopping season, Arhoolie Records founder Chris Strachwitz spent the Sunday of the Thanksgiving holiday weekend recording Hopkins. They completed their recording session for Arhoolie at the end of the week, on Saturday, December 2, 1961. Strachwitz recorded some songs with Hopkins solo and others backed by Gino Landry on bass and Victor Leonard on drums. Unlike on the four albums Hopkins recorded in New York, Hopkins played electric guitar on the Arhoolie sessions. On one track, "Do the Boogie," he played piano.

On January 23, February 17, and February 20, 1962, Hopkins returned to Houston to record for Prestige Records with McCormick, who penned liner notes for all three of the records generated by the sessions: *Walking This Road by Myself*, *Lightnin' and Company*, and *Smokes Like Lightning*. Kenneth Goldstein produced *Walking This Road by Myself*. The record featured a cover photo of Hopkins walking down the sidewalk in a black neighborhood, probably the Third Ward, with houses to his left and a couple of young boys playing on the sidewalk to his right. Although his pose was casual, with his left hand in his hip pocket, and his right arm straddling an acoustic guitar and electric cord, his image amounted to iconic urban cool. A cigarette dangled from his mouth, and his hat was cocked back at a rakish angle. He wore sharply creased dress pants and a striped dress shirt unbuttoned to his waist, which revealed a white muscle T-shirt. He sported his ever-present dark shades, and instead of the usual white towel around his neck, he wore a handkerchief. His two-tone white-and-black loafers with dark socks set off the outfit perfectly. Hopkins looked ready to entertain passersby on the corner, or likely to walk into a juke joint, plug his box in, and get a party started.

For this session, McCormick recorded Hopkins with his pals Spider Kilpatrick on drums, Buster Pickens on piano, and his childhood friend Billy Bizor on harmonica: "This is the first time that Lightnin' has been accompanied on record by a group of the musicians that regularly play with him in Houston. . . . the sound here suggests what can be heard nightly in the city's dance halls sans the uproar and frenzy of the audience. 62-year-old, 132-pound powerhouse drummer Spider Kilpatrick is Lightnin's most regular companion at such events.

Harmonica player Billy Bizor, pianist Buster Pickens, and bass man Don Cook work with him spasmodically as they have been doing for more than a decade. Since Lightnin' is a self-determined instrumentalist, recognizing no orthodoxy save his own, it is difficult for most musicians to accompany him. In his hometown he has built up a select group of men, taught them, warped them, or instilled in them the ability to anticipate his next move." While some complained about the quality of these sessions, Hopkins's companions likely helped him shape an accurate reflection of a Hopkins performance during that era.

The songs Hopkins recorded included his usual mix of fresh ones, a few previously recorded ones, and a handful of covers. McCormick's liner notes paint a vivid picture of Tuesday, February 20, 1962: "Lightnin' Hopkins came to the recording studio . . . direct from his landlady's TV set where, in step with most of America, he'd spent the morning spellbound by John Glenn's orbital flight on Friendship 7."[49] John Glenn had just become the first American to orbit the earth.[50]

McCormick's notes continued:

At one point, [Hopkins] asked for a piece of paper and, with a nod at the Gettysburg Address legend, a torn envelope was provided. His making notes for the song was essentially a symbolic act, for a half hour later the envelope only contained three marks resembling hex signs. Nonetheless, he insisted on propping it up in front of him as he took his place beneath the microphone. In some way the cryptic marks identified for him the incidents he wished to touch upon, and with it in place, he was ready to extemporize. He called for a last minute conference to confirm Glenn's first name and whispered his question because, child-like, he intended to surprise those present . . . with the song's subject. The surprise and first take were ruined by a sudden short in the guitar amplifier. It had been a moody blues set to the same tune as the bitter protest "Tim Moore's Farm." While repairs were in progress, Lightnin' read a newspaper account of Glenn's flight and there seems to have altered his concept for when he launched into the song again, it was definitely a happy blues. As a reporting historian, Lightnin's bias is deeply personal.[51]

Later, McCormick claimed to *Houston Chronicle* reporter Allan Turner that he co-wrote the song: "We were at ACA Studios down on Fannin and I went outside during the break and I saw the *Houston Chronicle* and the headline said John Glenn circles the world three times. So I bought a copy and I started thinking of a song in blues, put some verses together and then Sam Hopkins and I worked on it for a while and recorded it as a two part record which Prestige Records put out as a single and it sold very well."[52]

Billboard reviewed the single in its April 14, 1962, issue, noting the "Relaxed personable reading by Hopkins of talk-blues with amusing topical lyrics saluting astronaut Glenn. Solid programming for R & B stations and pop jocks searching for something off-beat."[53] The lyrics demonstrate Hopkins's improvisational acumen and knack for contemporary lyrical forays. With a fast blues shuffle as the soundtrack, Hopkins sang about Glenn for almost five minutes:

> People always said this morning
> With this on their mind
> Said ain't no livin' man go around the world three times
> But John Glenn done it

After the three days of recording in January and February 1962, Hopkins went back to playing live performances throughout the spring. On March 15, 1962, on his fiftieth birthday, he played at the Jewish Community Center (JCC). Jim Franklin recalled, "I got to go up to see it. I did drawings of him while he was playing. There were about ten of them, ink drawings. Then afterwards I got him to sign them. And he couldn't sign. The only thing he knew how to write was his name. He even got that wrong. L-I-G-H-N-I-N and he went back and put the T in. It was remarkable."[54]

The JCC was located in Hermann Park in Houston and supported a lively folk scene. Ed Badeaux remembered the JCC as the first meeting place for the Houston Folklore Group after he helped to found it:

In 1951, the Weavers came to the Shamrock Hotel. They played two weeks or something. I was corresponding with Pete Seeger. I wanted to learn to play banjo. . . . I went to see the Weavers. . . . So when they got in town, Pete Seeger phoned me and invited me out and he and his wife Toshi were living out in a motel across the street from the Shamrock. While he was here, I lent him my car. . . . The Weavers also gave a completely free concert at the JCC at the spur of the moment.

Anyway four of us together, John Lomax, Jr., Harold Bellikoff, Chester Bauer, who worked for the United Fund, and we kind of thought of having a regular folk song group, not society that sounded a little uppity. So, we called it the Houston Folklore Group, and it met from I imagine, 1951, 1952 once a month, usually at the JCC cuz that's were everything started in those days. The Center was, in those days, on . . . 2020 Hermann Drive. Then it was a public service group. I had a guitar group there . . . we'd meet once a month swapping songs. We'd work up one or two songs to impress our friends with that kind of thing.[55]

Badeaux started booking shows at the JCC. "I was the producer, I'd contact the people to perform. I didn't bother the performance. I went to the newspaper with stories, that kind of thing." Hopkins did not get a guaranteed minimum payment when he played the JCC. "He would get whatever came through the door. None of us got much money. Lightnin' probably got more money than any of us. I remember he drew about 140 people there, which was big for that room. This was a big empty room. It was good for this kind of thing. It didn't have an elevated stage."[56]

In 1960, the JCC hosted a hootenanny featuring some of the same performers previously cobilled with Hopkins at his Alley Theater hootenanny performances. Throughout the 1960s and 1970s, the Jewish Community Center continued to showcase blues artists such as Juke Boy Bonner, King Ivory Lee Semien, and D. C. Bender. Folkies John A. Lomax, Jr., Ed Badeaux, Jerry Jeff Walker, Townes Van Zandt, and Guy Clark also performed there, and Clark also gave guitar lessons. Mance Lipscomb was another featured performer.

Two days after his birthday gig, on St. Patrick's Day, 1962, Hopkins starred in another hootenanny production. This performance took place at the University of Houston, another segregated institution of higher education. John Lomax, Jr., Mance Lipscomb, and several other performers joined Hopkins in that production. Ed Badeaux also played on the gig, held at the Cullen Performance Hall:

I remember on the last one [hootenanny] he was mad at Mack, and Mack and he wouldn't have anything to do with each other, and I guess he found his own way there. I don't remember driving him. I may have, but I don't remember him. I remember going up to Navasota [to pick up Mance]. I betcha Lightnin's girlfriend Antoinette brought him.

. . . We did a hootenanny out at the University of Houston. . . . We had both Mance and Lightnin' on the program. . . . When other parts of the program were going on, they were sitting in kind of a stairway, trying to one-up each other . . . it was fascinating. I didn't want to go watch the program, I wanted to stay there. I wish we had recorded it because it was really neat. They came up with things trying to top one another even [though] Lightnin' was primarily a blues singer, and Mance was what I call primarily a ballad or kind of a country singer. He didn't sing much blues, but his sound was very interesting. Both of them were fabulous people. Mance, I think, lived a better lifestyle than Lightnin', as far as healthier and not playing clubs. . . . he worked around his farm and he took care of his grandkids. . . . But Lightnin', he had a girlfriend who I believe was married. But anyway she would satisfy that part of his nature, but he drank a lot and he smoked a lot.[57]

Badeaux remembered that the hootenanny show almost filled Cullen Performance Hall, the largest venue on campus, with a capacity of over two thousand: "The [Houston] *Chronicle* had given us the cover of their little entertainment thing the Sunday before, a big article and sign on it, or the *Post* [the other daily paper] had done that. The *Chronicle* had a story on it, plus the fact it was just coming in nationally, folk was [becoming very popular]. So that, coupled with the buzz that erupted from the Alley show the year before, got us the interest. We pretty damn near filled the place. I didn't go out and look [at what race was in the audience]. . . . At that time, Houston wasn't that integrated."[58]

By now, McCormick and Hopkins's strained relationship was evident, Badeaux testifies: "That's when they had their big falling out, cuz he booked Lightnin'. Lightnin' never gave him any of the money he got on the booking." McCormick eventually got the money he felt Hopkins owed him. "What Mack did was pocket the money that he got from records that Lightnin' made," said Badeaux. "Lightnin' got furious and broke off their relationship, and I don't think he ever spoke to Mack again."[59]

After working the hootenanny gig at the University of Houston, Hopkins headed to New York City for a six-day run at the Village Gate. The New York shows ran from March 20 to March 25, 1962. Flamenco guitarist Sabicas headlined the first few nights. The ad copy in the *New York Times* billed Hopkins as a "Great Country Blues Singer" and "One of the Greatest Country Blues men still singing." Further down the bill was the Roy Haynes Trio. By March 23, the John Coltrane Quartet replaced Haynes and his band, which pushed Hopkins down to third billing.

As pianist McCoy Tyner relates, "When Lightning played, he would move to the dominant [chord] whenever he felt like it and not at any particular bar. Trane realized that, in his own work, form had taken precedence over content, and what was also of importance was the use of the five-note (pentatonic) scale in all its derivations and the fact that the 'blues scale' had emerged with the secular music arising from early work-songs and spirituals, *not* the subdivision into specific categories. It was an intense realization, one which immediately became evident in his music."[60] Hopkins's approach influenced Coltrane, an extremely technically skilled and formally trained musician who won scholarships for performance and composition as a young man. Coltrane's saxophone playing and groundbreaking innovations in jazz may seem distant from Hopkins's country blues, but seeing Hopkins helped Coltrane focus even further on his own methods.

At least one more contrast can be gleaned. In Robert Shelton's review of Hopkins's Village Gate dates with Coltrane and Sabicas, published in the *New York Times* on March 31, 1962, he noted that Spanish native Sabicas played a seven-hundred-dollar guitar while Hopkins used a seventy-dollar Harmony model. Shelton also noted a change in Hopkins's performance since he first played New York:

Aware that his fame has spread far from his home Houston, Mr. Hopkins seems much more expansive on stage, and the audience seems more receptive to his subtle showmanship and wry humor. The raw material for Hopkins' songs are as wide as life, but he gravitates towards the many faces of trouble. He wrote an unusually lighthearted "Happy Blues for John Glenn," after watching television reports of the astronaut's trip around the world. Or in a dark smoldering voice with tension, he will turn bitter or sardonic. In such numbers as "Corrina, Corrina," he uses the guitar as a second voice to discourse with his own. A craftsman of folk poetry at its best, Mr. Hopkins peers through his dark glasses at audiences less forbidding than those he faced two years ago.[61]

As Hopkins settled into the third year of his comeback as a folk blues artist, Shelton's review highlights his established nightclub career in New York. Since Hopkins already established a base at the Ash Grove in Los Angeles, he could draw sizeable crowds in the two largest and most important cities in North America.

After a week off, Hopkins gigged at the Village Gate for three more nights from April 6 to 8, again with Sabicas headlining and the John Coltrane Quartet getting second billing. Hopkins closed the month of April 1962 playing the Village Gate with Nina Simone, described in her autobiography:

The Village Gate was the jazz center. Politics was so mixed in with what went on at the Gate that I remember it now as two sides of the coin. Comedians like Dick Gregory, Bill Cosby and Woody Allen opened for players and it was all part of the same thing—the music and the comedy, the jazz and the politics, it all went together. . . . Shot through everyone in the [Greenwich]

Village was the excitement with what was going on and a hunger to be the first one to discover what was coming next. The folk kids were discovering blues players that the jazz people knew so well they regarded them as old history, nothing to do with what was happening; but to the white kids it was somebody else's history they were hearing, so it was new and exciting. And the jazz players had their ears to and minds open to other influences—they had to or they wouldn't have been able to play like they did.[62]

Hopkins's shows were diverse, multicultural affairs building bridges between cultures and people, politics and poetry, and humor and humanism.

After working two nights in Boston during the first week of May, Hopkins played at the Second Fret, a coffeehouse in Philadelphia on May 17, 1962. Prestige recorded the set and released it a couple of years later as *Hootin' the Blues*. On the LP, Hopkins remade Ray Charles's hit "What'd I Say," with its signature organ lick, into an acoustic guitar tune. Calling the song "Me and Ray Charles," Hopkins took the songwriting credit for himself. After his late-spring 1962 East Coast tour, Hopkins returned home to Houston.

The summer of 1962 found Hopkins touring the West Coast again. In July, he worked a three-week stand at the Ash Grove with the Angelaires, a gospel group. For this engagement the *Los Angeles Sentinel*, an African American newspaper, presented Hopkins with plenty of attention. In a piece previewing his Ash Grove run, an unequivocal *Sentinel* reporter wrote, "Lightnin' Hopkins, one of the last great country-blues singers who has greatly influenced Dixie and Modern Jazz, and who has become a legend in his own time, begins a three week engagement at the Ash Grove Tuesday July 2. . . . those that have had the pleasure of hearing Lightnin' will attest to the powerful, deeply moving experience a singer of his stature creates."[63] After closing at the Ash Grove, Hopkins traveled up to San Francisco, where he worked for two weeks at Barbara Dane's Sugar Hill nightclub.

By May 1963, Hopkins returned to New York City for a two-week engagement at the Village Gate, booked from May 16 to May 31. The venue became Hopkins's regular gig in New York. John Sebastian, Jr., an enthralled teenager when he saw Hopkins perform for a television program during his Fall 1960 New York visit, made regular trips to the Village Gate to see him:

Lightning . . . began to work the Village Gate, and I began to go to watch him and eventually became kind of an unofficial guitar carrier, the guy who talks to the club owner, the intermediary kind of guy. . . . eventually, since my roommate from prep school had an apartment four blocks from the club, and several other clubs that Lightning could work, I became his home away from home because we'd move out of the bedroom so Lightning could have the bedroom . . . let him sleep and bring him breakfast when he wanted it, so it became his regular stop. . . . He was a good houseguest. He never complained, but then again he trained us well. We would bring him two eggs, coffee, and a jelly glass of gin, and that was how his day would begin. . . . I think he even stayed at my mom's house. So, for maybe three years I was kind of the go-to guitar carrier. I say that because I wasn't exactly a road manager. Lightning was the road manager, but I was sort of the guy who would help him schlep around in New York City. As time went on, he would sort of depend on me to say to make sure the back seats get filled up or make sure you get the full thing [amount of pay]. It was kind of a black and white thing, but [by] virtue of my father and his connection with Sonny Terry . . . I became a person who had the privilege of walking between the two camps.[64]

Sebastian, a musician himself, paid close attention to Hopkins's performances and analyzed Hopkins's song-creating methods: "He'd play 'Baby Please Don't Go,' 'Automobile Blues,' 'Katie Mae,' [and] 'Don't the Moon Look Pretty Shinin' Down through the Trees.' Those are ones that I'd hear him do fairly frequently. But there was another type of tune that I became aware of—loosely based forms around [which] he could construct new things. And they would change from time to time. Sometimes they were mildly topical or sometimes they would just be a funny story, 'I saw my girl with somebody else, or I saw my pal with some[one].' You could tell that those particular things were being made up on the spot around a rougher frame."[65]

Hopkins's May 1963 Village Gate gigs included singer Valentine Pringle, and for one night, the Jimmy Smith Trio. Sebastian remembered how Hopkins helped him get a break into show business: "That [Hopkins and] Jimmy Smith gig, I remember going to that. There was a gig he had an opener called Valentine Pringle. That week marks the beginning of my professional career, because at that show I went backstage and talked Valentine Pringle, a kind of baritone folksinger Harry Belafonte protégé, into having me play with him because he was having trouble with his accompanist. . . . I stepped in front of another musician and spoke to Val and said, I can play better than that, and if you don't believe me go ask Sam [Hopkins]. Val was the new guy in town. . . . he had great reverence for Sam, every bit as much as any white guy [did]. Sam vouched for me. Yeah, he knows what he's doing. He never let me play on stage with him, but he heard me play at the house."[66]

Mojo Hand

Sebastian also recalled that Hopkins's performances at the Village Gate were different than his gigs at the more traditional folk clubs: "[The] crowd was a better racial mix. That was a more integrated scene. . . . There was a duality to Lightning performances. Sometimes when he played for white folks, he could sound more humble than he sounded when he played the Village Gate. At Village Gate, he was more anecdotal. But, in a lot of these folk clubs, he was conscious of the fact that he needed to draw his audience along to understand what he was doing. So, some of those stories explaining the blues, that kind of stuff at the beginning of songs, a lot of that was directed to kind of help the white kids to understand what the guy sitting on the chair was. . . . often it was the big jazz act that was the focus of a lot of those evenings. Lightning was kind of a bonus. . . . Places like the Fillmore West and East were booking all his contemporaries that had been more in the electric blues field."[67]

In 1963, Prestige Records continued the flood of Hopkins vinyl, releasing the *Smokes Like Lightning* record. Mack McCormick's acerbic liner notes testified to the state of his relationship with Hopkins, which had soured over the dispute about fees, according to Ed Badeaux. McCormick recorded that Hopkins material during January and February 1962 sessions in Houston, which also yielded material for the *Walking This Road by Myself* and *Lightnin' and Company* albums. Three of Hopkins's friends, drummer Spider Kilpatrick, pianist Buster Pickens, and Billy Bizor, backed him on the LP.

The extremely critical liner notes, which at times launch into a personal attack, reveal McCormick's version of Hopkins. The notes read in part:

. . . as mentor and monster maker I am continually asked: "Has he changed much?" In the minds of some critics a notion has solidified to the effect that the college and coffee house crowds have corrupted him. While it is true that these audiences rarely bring out the best of Lightnin', it is hard to credit them with the general effect when one considers the other, devastating forces at work on him. Also it should be appreciated that this new fame is merely an extension of the exalted position he has long enjoyed in Texas. . . . Lightnin' now knows of Hollywood nightclubs, Harvard University, and the State of New Jersey, all of which have meaning for him as locales where songs may be exchanged for money.

But in direct reply to the question: No, he has not changed. He is just the same as he has been all his adult life: a natural born ease man, consumed by self-pity and everlastingly trying to persuade the world that it is his valet.[68]

McCormick's full notes paint a picture of Hopkins as a cruel, gambling, self-pitying, selfish, and pathetic man who ignores his daughter in jail facing a murder rap and neglects his mother and brothers living in poverty. This characterization of an artist is not what most record companies used to promote the sales of their product. The fact that Prestige printed this diatribe, true or not, breeds questions concerning the relationship among Prestige, McCormick, and Hopkins.

Years later in an interview with Allan Turner, McCormick explained:

> I was getting disgusted with him personally because he'd given me letters from his daughter who was in jail in Fort Worth and I said, "Sam why don't you let me take a couple of hundred dollars out of your next payment and send it to her or get her a lawyer?" He wouldn't let that happen. He just wanted me to do something. I got so irritated with him. At that time he was making $1,500 a week when he went off to nightclubs and $500 when he played here. So he was paying no taxes. He was doing very nicely and could have easily done it. So I just got disgusted. I wrote some album notes telling about this. . . . the fans said you can't do that to my sweet boy, you can't do that. I had written about 15 album notes on this same guy, and I was getting to the point were it was time to get into peripheral things, and even did little headers on each song, but even that was getting hard, and some of the songs were repetitious.[69]

Sam Charters, who produced Hopkins's comeback album for Folkways Records in 1959, started working for Prestige in 1963 when founder Bob Weinstock hired him to take over what was left of the blues and folk lines. As Charters remembered the liner notes, "We're [Prestige] sending money to Mack, who was promising us recordings and we're not getting recordings, so we had letters from Mack telling us about the difficulties."[70] In a 1963 letter to Mack McCormick, Sam Charters voiced his approval of the liner notes: "I particularly liked your notes to 1070. I can't think of a set of record notes from anything else to touch them."[71]

Charters insists, "We had so much trouble with the artists. We were dealing with heroin. We were dealing with petty theft. At one point, we were trying to get permission from a prison warden to be allowed to bring in recording equipment to record the sax player Gene Ammons. So I think that kind of entered into it [the decision to print McCormick's caustic notes], . . . somebody was finally telling it like it was. And also we had so much trouble with Lightnin'. So many whinings over the phone about money, and Mack was tricky too. . . .

I think that Ken Goldstein or whoever was behind actually printing them was very aware, said the hell with it, let's do it. They're unique."[72]

The correspondence in the Prestige Record company files reveals the dispute among McCormick, Prestige, and Hopkins. A letter from Mack McCormick dated October 1963, addressed to Prestige's attorney, states the case. McCormick also sent a letter to Prestige Records owner Bob Weinstock in New Jersey, in all capital letters, declaring, "Lightnin' Hopkins accepting exclusive contract major label. Any obligation due Prestige needs to be completed by October 15. Please advise."[73] No evidence of a "new contract" in place for Hopkins, prohibiting him from fulfilling his Prestige contract that was already in effect, surfaced.

The correspondence in the Prestige Records internal files shows that McCormick wrote to Sam Charters in February 1963, complaining about missing royalties. However, the Prestige files show royalty statements prepared and paid on a regular basis. Furthermore, the Prestige files contain a 1963 tax statement for Hopkins showing Prestige paid him $1,700 for the year. In response to McCormick's letter, Charters checked the files and wrote McCormick informing him that Prestige paid Hopkins directly, a violation of the Prestige/Hopkins/McCormick record contract.[74] Therefore, McCormick's October 1963 letter to Prestige's lawyer, whom the company turned McCormick's complaints over to, contained valid concerns. Prestige circumvented McCormick, paying Hopkins even though the contract decreed that Prestige must pay McCormick directly.

After some correspondence, Prestige agreed in November 1963 to advance McCormick $1,200 for the last four records remaining on the ten-record contract, plus $800 more to be paid out in monthly installments of $100.[75] The contract called for a $500 advance for each record, so the $2,000 represented the amount due according to the contract. After an agreement was reached, McCormick wrote to Charters from Mexico, saying he had booked a Houston studio for December 1964. At the time, McCormick was traveling back and forth between his house in Houston and Mexico.

As Charters recalls, "We were endlessly under pressure to get the recordings from Lightnin'. And all we knew was that we were sending the money, a thousand dollars [actually $1,200] and the recording costs, to Mack, and I knew he was going in and out of Mexico. And we were really hurting. For us, a thousand dollars was a lot of money. And we didn't know where the hell the tapes were, and we had promised the releases. . . . In my youthful inexperience, I wasn't getting any answers from anybody, so I simply said to the Houston police, 'I don't want this guy to go to Mexico with my thousand dollars.'"[76]

On February 27, 1964, Charters sent a letter to Mack McCormick stating:

Your letter reached me in time to delay the issuing of a warrant for your arrest in Houston; however, if I don't hear from you concerning the money you have received for the Lightning Hopkins sessions I will consider some kind of action. I managed to stop payment on the second check of the monthly installment agreed upon, so the amount in question is $1300. Lightning H, for whom the money was sent to you as agent, stated verbally, to Mr. Patterson of Gold Star Recording Studios, that he did not see you at any time before you left the country, and that the money sent on to you was not turned over to him. He also stated that he knew nothing about a pending exclusive contract with a major label and denied that poor health is interfering with his playing ability, the two reasons which you gave us for completing his contract at the present time. We have advanced a further $1,000 to Lightning Hopkins through Mr. Patterson, who has recorded two LPs of Hopkins for us.[77]

"And so whatever happened out of this I have no idea, but Mack and I have never spoken since," Charters admits. "I don't know if he ever wants to talk about that. Mack did a very important service by recording Lightnin' as best as he did, and he was holding a comet by the tail. And thanks to Mack we got a lot of wonderful things we wouldn't have gotten any other way because he worked with him so closely. Lightnin' was tough in the studio."[78]

McCormick must have known Hopkins did not take record contracts seriously. The correspondence between McCormick and Chris Strachwitz preserved in the Arhoolie Record Company's files makes a convincing case: McCormick was well aware of dishonest business practices prevalent in the music industry. Furthermore, McCormick attempted to straighten out Hopkins's copyrights and compile his discography, so he knew Hopkins rerecorded the same songs over and over again for various labels, often while under an exclusive contract that prohibited him from doing so. Paper contracts meant little to Hopkins; therefore, McCormick's desire for Hopkins to honor a contract with him is naïve. Perhaps McCormick thought Hopkins owed him special treatment. In the scathing liner notes on Hopkins's *Smokes Like Lightning*, he identifies himself as a "mentor." While there is no evidence that McCormick, a nonmusician, mentored Hopkins musically, McCormick obviously felt he aided, guided, and supported the bluesman.

For his part, Hopkins felt extremely irate when McCormick pocketed the money that Prestige advanced him to give to Hopkins. Several years later, when Les Blank was in Houston shooting a documentary, Hopkins discussed McCormick's actions: "See a lot of people coming round you but you can't tell what they up to. See right now I got four bits in my pocket. I'd rather swallow it and go to the doctor and try to get it to operate me and get it out before I see somebody take it from me. I ain't joking neither. Every day I walk out this door if I got me five dollars outta my pocket I got that .38 on my side and you just be careful how you walk up to me mister. I don't care who you is or where you come from Lightning don't go for that. . . . If I got something to offer, say hello, have a drink with me. Other than that, don't act like you approaching me for business, you gonna get exactly what you're lookin' for. . . . I went on the coast, man, I had a thousand dollars sent to me, the other man spent it. I don't like that."[79] When Blank asks for the man's name Hopkins responds, "I don't have to tell nobody who it was. But he know who it was. . . . Just don't do me like that. Cuz in cases like that, I don't play that. He did it, and he's happy, but he don't know how happy he is, I know.[80]

Houston bluesman Juke Boy Bonner remembered Hopkins telling him about McCormick's money management: "Mack came by and told me a lot of junk. He came by one night and wanted to record and all that stuff. Boom, boom, boom with all the hot lines. But Lightnin' had told me about him. Him and Lightnin' had a big run-in about how he went to New York and cut two albums in one day. One for Fire and one for Candid. He got 800 dollars out of one thing, and when one company found out that they had been beat on a record, they felt like they had been cheated. When Mack went to Lightnin' about the money, Lightnin' wouldn't have none of that bullshit. They parted ways right there."[81]

McCormick's statements about his modus operandi for recording are a good insight into business practices: "When I was recording musicians, knowing that many of them knew about the record business and heard these stories, I would tell them, let's assume that I'm going to take your record, I'll give you some money now but you'll never get another cent from me. I'm just gonna steal it. Let's start with that and then there won't be any bad feelings. You won't be able to say you were cheated but you will be able to say you've got a record and it's being played or sold and that's a start if you want to go into show business, which I don't recommend. And that helped often. Of course if it was a royalty deal I'd see that they got the money later."[82]

Sam Charters, however, had a different experience working with Hopkins:

I like hanging out with him. With only having short times with him, I continued to hold him in high regard, not like Mack who had to deal with him day to day and had to put up with the other side of him. He could be very picky. So Lightning was a pain in the neck for everybody. It was a situation,

which people wanted something from him, which he could give very easily without [causing problems]. He could have done an album a day like
Memphis Slim, Big Joe Williams. They could do it, and so he just did it.
Since it came to him as natural as breathing, I don't think he valued the
artistic side. . . . I've worked with everybody, Muddy Waters to Lightnin'
to Buddy Guy . . . their standard was not our standard. They're working
in a society where James Brown and Sam Cooke and the fact that they sell
a few thousand records and get to sing at a coffeehouse gathering at a university actually doesn't mean anything. They know where James Brown is
performing, and they listen to the radio . . . and they are very realistic about
where they fit into their own community and the fact that some white kids
not very well dressed show up in shabby cars and think they're wonderful
essentially doesn't mean much, not in any real way. So that this was very
complicated.[83]

While the business mess with Prestige and McCormick was being settled, Chris
Strachwitz, founder and owner of Arhoolie Records, traveled to Houston. On
Sunday, February 16, 1964, Strachwitz stopped at the Hadley Street boardinghouse in the Third Ward where Hopkins lived. He picked up Hopkins and his
brother Joel, who lived in Dickinson, a small town about thirty miles southeast of Houston. Hopkins's mother joined them, and they all rode up to Waxahachie, a small town about thirty-three miles south of Dallas. They were in
search of the oldest Hopkins brother, John Henry. Several months before, Hopkins had heard his brother was living there, and Hopkins's mother Frances also
wanted to see her oldest son. Strachwitz hoped to record all of them.

After some inquiries in the African American part of town, they located
John Henry's residence. Strachwitz's liner notes to the record *Lightning Hopkins
with His Brothers Joel and John Henry and with Barbara Dane* describe the scene:

It was a small hut in back of a larger house and I felt a bit the intruder as
everyone was crowding in the tiny room. John Henry had not been well
and was still very weak from a long illness. Everyone soon got happy and
it was a very moving reunion. However, Lightning, who was very anxious
to make this recording with his brothers, asked everyone to leave the room
for a while until they finished a few numbers. While the neighbors enjoyed
themselves in the yard, I attempted to tape what went on inside. The tape
recorder was standing in front of the door since there was barely enough
room for the microphone and myself. I moved the microphone from one to
another as the three brothers took turns singing. . . . John Henry Hopkins, I

was told, was the best of all the Hopkins brothers when it came to playing the guitar and everyone said he was better than his "baby brother" when it came to making up songs, and even Sam agreed.[84]

In Strachwitz's view, the scene soon darkened: "They had this weird reunion and started drinking. Lightning got awful nasty at the end when I tried to pay everyone off. I'll never forget when I gave John Henry his money, Lightning said, 'Man, you owe me a hundred dollars from back then,' or some damn thing. John Henry finally threw it at him and said, 'You motherfucker.' It was just disgusting."[85]

The recording trip to Waxahachie remained fresh in Strachwitz's mind decades later:

> They hadn't seen each other in thirty years. They all got drunk, probably my fault. It was just really nice. Joel was always this nice simple guy. And John Henry, apparently they all said he was the real showman of the family, except he was sent to the penitentiary way back and Lightning had just heard he got out. I had no idea how he was surviving. It was like some poor dog being let out of a kennel. That's the kind of life I had no experience with. That's why [there are] relatively few numbers. I recorded hours and hours of shit, but it was really bad. They were not together or they were too drunk and messing up. I think I recorded Joel later on again just to get one or two numbers from him. I forget what I put on the CD or LP. For a long time, I didn't want to issue the stuff. I thought it was so bad. It was one of those things I got this idea: here's the whole Hopkins hierarchy, the mother and the three brothers.[86]

Two days after Dr. Martin Luther King spoke in Houston on May 17, 1964, to a crowd of over one thousand people listening to him exalt the passage of the Civil Rights Act, Hopkins played his semiregular Tuesday night gig at the Jester, a folk music venue on the west side of Houston at 4800 Westheimer. According to John Davis, writing in the University of Houston *Daily Cougar* about the folk music craze, "In 1963 there were two nightspots catering to lovers of unfolk nonmusic; the Jester Lounge . . . and the Balladier. The Jester was the first and still is the most popular. The small club crowds up to 10 entertainers into a night's program and packs customers in like sardines."[87]

Founded in 1961, the Jester, previously a private club, had a capacity of 172. "The club drew a mixed crowd. It was one of the few places that served blacks," club promoter Mack Webster revealed. "People with money were all the same color to me. They'd get treated right. When I was first here, I didn't have any ads at all and no phone. It was the first folk club [in Houston], the only good one. The rest of them didn't know what they were doing, didn't know how to sell. That was the place to play. You'd be surprised how many people crammed in there. All I had to do was keep the quality up. People came to hear it."[88]

Hopkins's friend John A. Lomax, Jr., characterized the club as a "folk music mecca . . . that has blazed a successful name among Houston's entertainment spots and is gaining national recognition. This accomplishment is not due to mere trial and error. Mack and Barbara Webster, the genial host and hostess of the Jester, deeply appreciate good folk music and have the staunch courage to present it in an intimate manner most rewarding to the performer and satisfying the audience."[89] John Carrick remembered the performers at the Jester forging a real sense of community.

Hopkins had been playing at the Jester at least since January 1964. Webster booked him:

I went through [John] Lomax [Jr.] the first time to talk to him, but he wouldn't talk. Then I went over to a club he was playing. I said, man, I sure would appreciate it if you would come play at my club. You're a big star in Houston and everyone wants to hear you. He said, I don't want to listen to that crap. I told him you could bring anyone you want, any black folks, white folks, purple folks, and if anything comes up, there won't be any hassle. I'll take care of it. He said you sure about that? I said, I'm positive. He was playing black clubs. He didn't want to play any white clubs. He didn't want to play two or three sets. He talked about himself in third person. [He'd say], "Don't work Lightnin' too hard." He'd stay on the stage all night. He'd play until you called him off. I'd give him the door, and I'd keep the register. [The first time he played] he had this guy counting the door. The guy went to sleep. . . . He lost count. Lightnin' said you owed me so many bucks, and I said no, "I owe you more than that." He said, "What?" I said, "Yeah your guy lost count. Here's how much I owe you." After that we were tight. I never had any trouble getting him to come.[90]

The club even released an album at the beginning of January 1964 titled *Look, It's Us*, containing songs by the regular Jester performers, including Hopkins singing "Trouble in Mind." Other performers on the album included Kay Oslin, who later became country music star K. T. Oslin, Frank Davis, and Guy Clark. Webster, however, did not have any distribution for the record, so he sold it out of the club: "Hell, I lost eighteen hundred dollars on it. I paid [Hopkins] a hundred bucks for the record. Anybody else was supposed to get paid off the record, but they were a bunch of ne'er-do-wells. They thought they were big stars. The only one that had any true capabilities was Kay. She was a fireball. They wouldn't help me sell it to the shops. I went to New York one time trying to sell a sampler I made. This guy in New York said man let me show you something. It was a big record company. He had a big vault of tapes. He said every time Lightning comes to New York, I pay him a hundred bucks apiece for songs. Some day when he's dead, I'll be rich off all this. He said [Hopkins] won't make a contract and he won't do certain things. He knows what he wants."[91]

Darryl Harris worked at the Jester as a dishwasher and flamenco guitar player. "The Jester was a little cinder-block building. The Jester was the club that was responsible for every one of those Houston guys making a living, Guy Clark, Kay Oslin, Frank Davis, Ken Roberts and Judy Steward, Sarah Wiggins, Carl Snyder. It was the first place any of those people made a living. At one time he had twelve entertainers, each doing one twenty-minute set. They got ten dollars a night, which in 1963 they lived on. Mack Webster supported that whole crew. It was an amazing place. John Denver played there. Judy Collins came out and did a set one night. Some of the New Christy Minstrels came there and hung out one week. When Lightnin' played, he had his own night. He packed them in. . . . [Hopkins] was totally influential in that part of the folk scene, those that saw him."[92]

While Hopkins was playing to white audiences in the Houston folk clubs, he was also playing clubs in black neighborhoods, where he tended to play more spontaneously. His cross-cultural appeal and ability could not be duplicated by many other black Houston bluesmen. Webster saw Hopkins play in black clubs, altering his performance: "He played over in the Third [Ward]. I once set up the sound for him and Dusty Hill, those guys, his brother Rocky played bass [for Hopkins]. We went over to a black club. Man, it was a different story. There was only black folks. They didn't want us there. He said, I don't want any of these guys getting any trouble, one of them is my soundman and one of them is playing bass for me. They were so proud to have him, and man did he play a different set. It was like another world. I said, 'Man, that was not like you do at my club.' He said, 'I couldn't get that off at your club, too many people don't like blacks. . . . I don't want to put up with that foolishness.'"[93]

After his gig at the Jester, Hopkins headed out to play at the Cabale Club in Berkeley, California, from May 26 to 31, 1964. Rolf Cahn, Debbie Green, Howard Ziehm, and Chandler A. Laughlin III founded the short-lived Cabale, which opened in January 1963. The club was located at 2504 San Pablo Avenue. Eric Von Schmidt, a folksinger who was at the forefront of the folk movement in

Cambridge, Massachusetts, in the 1960s, recalled the scene around the Cabale: "Phil and Midge Huffman . . . were folk aficionados and social workers who didn't have to leave the job at five o'clock and took all sorts of strange people under their wing. That was a house where you'd wake up, and while you had been asleep, Lightnin' Hopkins and Sonny Terry would have set up shop in the living room and would be drinking whiskey and blowin' blues at 7:30 in the damn morning. So, you would wake up to some strong hangin' out. For anyone that was into the blues, it was the place. K. C. Douglas, Black Ace, T-Bone Walker. All the people connected to Arhoolie Records. Chris Strachwitz was in charge there, and he funneled it all through that house. And Rolf Cahn was real tight with the Huffmans, and it sort of went from the club to their house and back."[94]

Hopkins's contract, arranged by Chris Strachwitz, provided that he got paid a $350 guarantee against 50 percent of the door take. The contract also stipulated that Hopkins get a room and be picked up at the station and that arrangements were to be made for his trip to Los Angeles.[95] Strachwitz often helped Hopkins get gigs when he came to California to play at the Ash Grove:

I knew we could get him gigs. . . . We'd hire all these little theaters and go put up the posters. We were real hustlers in those days. . . . I also had him booked at the Continental Club, a black club [in Oakland]. It was owned by . . . a local R&B gangster. He got killed a few years after that. He got shot by somebody, I don't know why, not paying somebody. I remember him saying, he was a black guy, and he told Lightnin', "Boy I can use you around here." Lightnin' said something, "No, I don't want to" or something. Then when we got back here, I said I don't think you want to work for this man. He's got a bad reputation. He's one of those guys that rips off the chitlin circuit artists.

Then we went to Richmond. . . . If you go out there now, it's horrible, nothing but deserted shacks and run down, nothing but dope pushers out there, it's terrible. But it was a booming area during the war, Chevron and all the shipyards nearby. There were a lot of blacks living there. It had a record store, Ollie Freeman's Jazzland. [It] would sell Reverend Franklin 78s and Lightnin' records. He was a wonderful man, Ollie Freeman. There was this really neat down-home joint, the Savoy Club, but Jimmy McCracklin, Lowell Fulson, they all played there. I remember when Lightnin' and I walked in, this woman said to him, "Are you the real Lightnin' Hopkins?" He said, "You better believe it, baby."[96]

Eventually former Ash Grove employee Carroll Peery gained majority owner-ship in the Cabale Club, hosting Hopkins at the club and at his home: "When I moved up to Berkeley and was at the Cabale, he started staying at my house every time he was in Northern California and that went on until he died. . . . Lightnin' had played there before I got there. And when I got there I got him to play whenever I could talk him into it. Whenever he came from Houston to the Ash Grove, he'd come to the Cabale also. I think he was paid . . . a hundred dollars a night and sometimes two hundred dollars a night. But that was a very special occasion. Sometimes he would want a drummer to work behind him in a very subtle and controlled way. If he wanted that, I'd get him a little drummer. Actually once Barbara Dane's son Jesse backed him up."[97]

After a week at the Cabale, Hopkins headed to Los Angeles for a gig at the Ash Grove on June 2, 1964. Barry Hansen, later known as disc jockey Dr. De-mento, started working at the Ash Grove around this time:

I went to work for the Ash Grove as an usher and a light man and an emcee and just about anything Ed Pearl needed me to do. One of my jobs was to make sure the performers were ready to go on stage. That they were pro-vided for as best we could. I would also get up in the light booth and say, "Ladies and gentlemen, the Ash Grove proudly presents Lightning Hop-kins." So I got to know him a little better. He knew when he came to the Ash Grove I would probably be the guy who tells him, "Five minutes, Light-ning." So, one of my tasks, Lightning would always have the room full of people. He'd welcome people who'd want to say hello to him before the show. But I got to know that he enjoyed a few minutes of privacy before the show so he could have a nip of gin. So one of my jobs was to shoo people out of the dressing room. . . . he was certainly one of the better-drawing blues players. . . . [His audience was] mostly young adoring white blues fans. But I kind of recall him bringing friends of his, the ones he was stay-ing with.[98]

Hansen, a graduate student in folk studies at the University of California at Los Angeles, also founded the small publication the *Little Sandy Review*, where he wrote about roots music. Lightnin' "performed at the Ash Grove two or three times a year in those days. Ed Pearl really believed in him and would bring him in frequently. He was obviously improvising. He wasn't doing the same set at every show. There was always something different. This would be a little later, but I happened to see him the day Martin Luther King, Jr., died and he made up, he improvised a song about that."[99]

Hansen recalled that his friend Bernie Pearl, younger brother of Ash Grove owner Ed Pearl, arranged to interview Hopkins: "Bernie set that up. . . . Bernie could play guitar and Bernie certainly wanted to know more about how Lightnin' played, so it was Bernie's idea to set this whole thing up. . . . Bernie called me up. I had a tape recorder. . . . Bernie said, 'I'm going to see Lightnin' . . . where he's staying in South L.A.' and 'Would you like to come along and please bring your tape recorder?' . . . I think we spent about an hour and a half there. A lot of it was talking and a lot of it was giving Bernie a guitar lesson. . . . I remember Bernie wanted Lightnin' to play on a Martin [brand guitar] and Bernie really wanted Lightnin' to play that, but Lightnin' wouldn't. So, Lightnin' had a Kay electric guitar which wasn't plugged in, so he insisted on playing that. Perhaps so we wouldn't get anything out of it that would be suitable to release commercially."[100] Evidently, Hopkins was concerned about people recording his performances and profiting from unauthorized record releases.

On Thursday afternoon, June 18, 1964, Hopkins dropped by the Cabale Club to play with folksinger Barbara Dane for an Arhoolie Records live recording: "I was making my farewell. I was getting ready to move to New York in 1964, and I was recording my thing by myself. I was in there in the afternoon. Carroll Peery brought some friends by and one of them was Lightnin'. He sorta crashed the party, which everybody was delighted with. I thought the record is kinda called off and we're just having a little jam here jiving back and forth with the blues, and it got recorded. That's how that album happened to be."[101]

After the impromptu recording with Dane in Berkeley, Hopkins headed to Los Angeles, where he taped an appearance for *The Steve Allen Show* on June 24, 1964. Allen, a multitalented television personality, created and then hosted the *Tonight Show* for NBC from 1953 to 1957, which made him one of America's most popular TV personalities. By 1964, he was hosting for Westinghouse a syndicated show with the same variety format that he had developed on the *Tonight Show*. Hopkins's performance aired in August 1964.

Hopkins was joined on Allen's show by British movie star Laurence Harvey, Don Sherman, Bernie Kopell, singer Renee Roberts, and Dr. Bergen Evans. Though Allen did not interview Hopkins, the bluesman swung through two songs after Allen gave him a fluffy introduction: "One of the best, most authentic of the blues singers . . . he's considered by many people in the folk music field, the king of the blues. He's been playing guitar since he was 8 years old."[102]

Hopkins looked every inch a movie star, with a fresh conk in his hair, dark sunglasses, pinkie ring, white shirt, narrow dark tie, and a sharp dark-colored suit with narrow lapels, the fashion of the era. Sitting on a stool, he played his Gibson acoustic guitar with a mike in the sound hole through a small amplifier.

Mojo Hand

The name Gibson was blacked out on the headstock of his guitar. Two very conservative-looking white men, probably from show's house band, Don Trenner and his orchestra, backed him, one on stand-up bass and one on a small drum kit.

Hopkins played "Katie Mae," one of the first songs he ever recorded, as the band followed along gingerly. After receiving a round of applause from the live studio audience, Hopkins introduced his next song, somewhat unintelligibly: "This is [?] on Ray Charles, I ain't got no business doing it, but I'm gonna do it."[103] Hopkins did a version of "What'd I Say," which he released as "Me and Ray Charles" on his *Hootin' the Blues*. This time the band is right with him, dropping out and coming in at the right places. Hopkins clearly enjoys the limelight, and the crowd responds in kind, offering jubilant applause when he is finished.

On July 13, 1964, Hopkins worked the KHFI-FM Summer Music Festival in Austin. Rod Kennedy, who later founded the Kerrville Folk Festival, promoted and organized the free festival, which ran from July 13 to 18 at the Zilker Hillside Theater. Hopkins played to a record crowd of five thousand and shared the bill with Carolyn Hester, Mance Lipscomb, John Lomax, Jr., Segle Fry, and Mickey and Marty. Folksinger Carolyn Hester had good memories of Hopkins: "Lightning was a pleasure to hear and always kind and warm hearted when I saw him. I was very happy for his success. Brilliant!"[104] However, the respect Hopkins received from young, white folksingers like Hester did not necessarily translate into respect from white conservatives like the promoter Kennedy.

Rod Kennedy held a decidedly different view. In his autobiography, Kennedy wrote disparagingly of Hopkins's drinking habits before the gig, even though he put on a well-received and well-reviewed performance:

Lightning . . . was a hard-drinking performer who, most of the time, played blitzed. Dressed in a black suit, he ate dinner with John Lomax and me at the hotel, where we could keep an eye on him before the performance so he could appear sober. Lightning got up from the table to get some cigarettes from the drugstore in the hotel and neither Lomax or I remembered that the drugstore in the hotel had a small liquor department. But when Lightning got in the van and breathed on us, it was obvious that he had imbibed quickly on a pint in his coat pocket. So much for careful supervision. . . . Lightning's show, while interspersed with long stories about long black cars with big white-wall tires, was filled with great music and the crowd loved it.[105]

Despite Kennedy's disapproval of Hopkins's personal habits, he remained in demand by promoters.

The blues revival was still going full swing in 1964, especially packaged in overseas tours. According to author Bob Groom, the trend began in 1962 with the first annual American Folk Blues Festival tour of Europe. Horst Lippman and Fritz Rau founded the festival, which toured Austria, Belgium, Britain, Denmark, France, Germany, Holland, Sweden, and Switzerland. The festivals received a lot of media coverage on both radio and television. In October 1964, Hopkins toured Europe for the first time. Strachwitz helped Hopkins go on tour with the 1964 American Folk Blues Festival:

> [The promoter of the festival] Horst Lippman contacted me and he had heard that I got along with Lightning pretty good and his French promoter told Horst, "You've got to get Lightning Hopkins on this next tour." So he wrote to me, "Could you meet him in Houston?" I'll go there and we'll see if he'll go.
>
> . . . In October we flew out of Houston on a regular airliner, American Airlines. Then in New York we transferred to Air India to go to Frankfurt. Boy, I remember Lightning sitting next to me. It was an airliner where you walk in from the back and the flight personnel walks through to the front, and as they passed, Lightning said, "Are these people gonna fly this airplane?" I said yeah. I didn't think that much more about it at the time, but later on when we landed in Frankfurt he couldn't play and he could hardly talk. We called a doctor and had him examined. He couldn't find anything the matter with him.
>
> Then this nice lady, Stephanie Wiesand, a photographer, . . . kind of babied him along. I remember we visited her house and Lightning sat there and had a little drink and just relaxed. After a whole week, we were there a week to do the TV show in Baden-Baden for the Southwest German TV network. They put him on the last day and finally he was able to play. I think he had a nervous breakdown. . . . [He] regained his senses and could finally play. You have to remember that the only East Indians Lightning ever met were fortune-tellers, and his belief in mojo hands was very strong! I am sure he felt they would make the plane crash. In Frankfurt, I guess it was two nights later, [after] we left Baden-Baden, he made up a song about that airline trip from New York.[106]

Hopkins talked about this episode later. "I was on a plane, thirteen hours in the air. Tried to get drunk, couldn't. That's right. I would say that I was just too scared. I had me a pint and a fifth. And man, I was drinking it just like water. Didn't do nothing but make me sick. I was just as sober as I am now when I got off, but I was just sick. That's just the way . . . we got off in Baden-Baden. Well I laid up there and got a doctor. . . . I laid up there three days. You know tried to get over that scared. Why I don't like that. I don't know how I ever got started to flying. You know what I mean about flying on no airplanes. I goes to California but that's only two hours or better. That thirteen hours or some like to got me."[107] "I was all shook up. They tried to get me to eat but I was just too shook up. Every flight I was scared. One especially where we were ducking and dippin'."[108]

Wiesand, the photographer, witnessed Hopkins's condition when he arrived in Germany: "He had a mysterious illness, which made it impossible for him to play his guitar. Today one would probably call this 'psychosomatic' since at that time no physician could come up with a clear diagnosis. During the TV recordings in Baden-Baden I was looking after Lightnin', who spent quite some time at my kitchen table and on a sun chair on my balcony. Lightnin' recovered under my supervision, after providing him with his beloved soul food (steaks, etc.)."[109]

The tour's stop in Baden-Baden, Germany, was recorded for television. Bob Koester, founder of Delmark Records and the Jazz Mart in Chicago, was also on the 1964 American Folk Blues Festival tour and recalled, "They stayed a week in Baden-Baden. They shot this film. I've been on a lot of Hollywood sound stages and this thing was bigger than most of them. At one end of the sound stage, a singer whose name I forget performed . . . then at the other end a kind of a concept thing. One side depicts a saloon, a German concept of a blues joint. The other side of the wall is a front porch for the country singers to sing. Hopkins sang out on the porch. It was supposed to be the porch of a house. It looked a lot nicer than I saw black people living in on my tours of the South. . . . Sonny Boy Williamson was the hit of the tour. I think Wolf felt kind of bad about that. Personal feelings, inescapable among musicians. They don't hate the other guy, just wish they had done as well."[110] In turn, Hopkins wrote "The Jet" about his trepidations on the trip:

> I couldn't hear nothing but the motor
> Singing a song back at me
> You know I was scared
> Just as scared as any man can be

As Koester explained, "Lightning Hopkins . . . had this big macho thing going [but] he was scared to death of flying. It just didn't really go with the guy you know from the music. He didn't go ape shit or anything but he always got nervous at takeoffs and landings."[111] Hopkins's music and personal style made an impression on Koester: "He seemed very debonair for someone who is classi-fied as a country blues man. He was kind of a class act. He dressed to the nines, at least in Europe. One of the Lightning songs I really liked was 'Tim Moore's Farm.' He's awfully good. He's got his own style."[112]

The American Folk Blues Festival tour included dates in England. Simon Napier peppers his review with praise describing Hopkins's performance on October 25, 1964, at Fairfield Halls, Croydon [a borough in South London]. "The climax of the first half was Sam Hopkins, probably the greatest living blues singer and the most-recorded to present. Lightnin' ambled on giving the crowd a friendly wave, settled down in a chair, plugged in his guitar and com-menced to talk about himself and his songs. Casual listeners must have prob-lems understanding this man. . . . '3 o'clock blues' opened his set and at once he became not a man-and-guitar, but a complete artist, conveying all that is best in his records and adding dramatic effect of the in-person performance. Superla-tives cannot justify this man, whose inventiveness is such that he will change the same song in three following concerts, and add things no one ever noticed to such a commonplace boogie as 'It's might crazy' ['Mighty Crazy'] . . . he did a superbly original 'Wake up lady' and another boogie and all-too-soon he was gone, amid tumultuous whistling, foot stamping and encores."[113]

While Hopkins was in London, he and bluesman Little Walter Jacobs took time to pay a visit to a blues exhibition that had just been unveiled in Septem-ber. British blues scholar Paul Oliver had prepared the multimedia exhibit at the request of the American Embassy, providing context to foreign audiences' interest in buying blues records and seeing performers like Hopkins.

One of Great Britain's celebrities—Ringo Starr, the drummer for the Bea-tles—was a huge Lightnin' Hopkins fan. By the time Hopkins arrived in Eng-land in October 1964, the Beatles had toured the United States for the first time, sold millions of records, and performed on the *Ed Sullivan Show* three times. Their accolades and popularity were endless. While the media were putting the life of Ringo Starr and his fellow Beatles under a microscope, they prob-ably overlooked Starr's fascination with Hopkins. Starr was so enamored with Hopkins that he once sought to immigrate to Houston to be near him. Starr explained, "I wanted to go to Texas to live with Lightning Hopkins—the blues man, my hero. I actually went to the embassy and got the forms. . . . we filled these in and God they were hard, but when we got the second lot of forms, it was just too daunting, questions like 'Was your grandmother's Great Dane a communist?' Like teenagers, we gave in. But we got lists of jobs to go to in Houston—factories that would take us. We were pretty serious about it."[114]

Outside of his usual dislike of air travel, Hopkins seemed to have enjoyed his first trip to Europe. He told *Houston Chronicle* reporter Kay Pope, "Europe was all right. It was just fine. I just played music just like here. I wouldn't know one place from the other. They're good folk over there but their bread's too hard. When I finally got some food I liked, I eat a whoopin' of it. I found some chicken in one or two places and I'd order a whole chicken. I talked to a few people over there, them that spoke English who wanted my autograph. A few, not many. But I could make my guitar talk just like I talk. They could understand. They all jump, shout, jaw and grab me at the end. They would be happy like that if they didn't like me. They'd applaud me back and never want me to leave. I'd have to go off though on account of other people's playin' next."[115]

When Hopkins returned from touring Europe, he played at New York's famed Carnegie Hall on November 7, 1964.[116] Also on the bill were folksingers Doc Watson, Dave Von Ronk, and Phil Ochs and bluesman Mississippi John Hurt. Henrietta Yorchenco reviewed the show favorably for *Musical America* magazine and pointed out Hopkins as the highlight:

The star of the evening was the great Texas blues singer, Lightnin' Hopkins. Mr. Hopkins at his best has no rivals. His artistic palette admits no pale hues; all has the glowing color of life deeply savored. He is a master of several blues types—a recitative, free-flowing style for frustration and grief, a rollicking rhythm for delectable commentary of the pleasures of the flesh. If Hopkins did no more than sing it would be enough, but he is one of the finest blues guitarists of our time. Voice and instrument blend or complement each other in magnificent unity.[117]

While in New York, Hopkins returned to the studio to record an album for Prestige Records with Sam Charters, resulting in *My Life in the Blues*, a double album that mostly consisted of Hopkins answering Charters's questions about his life, with a few songs in between the interview tracks. Charters's essay for the album notes how much Hopkins's situation had changed since Charters first recorded him in 1959.

He was living in a shabby furnished room off Dowling Street in Houston eking out a meager living playing occasional weekend jobs in juke joints around town. He had been nervous and worried, distrustful of anyone that wanted to record his music. He had been wearing worn trousers and an old jacket. When I met him in New York, he had just gotten off a plane from a

European tour, he was wearing a new dark suit and shoes and there was a new ease and relaxation in his mood. His success had come late but it had come before he was deeply scarred by failure, and he seemed to have mellowed over the years.[118]

The 1960s were halfway over, and Hopkins's career remained busy and fruitful: he established solid touring bases on the East and West Coasts; he recorded widely; festivals and club gigs poured in; he survived a nasty business dispute with Mack McCormick; and he endured a possible nervous breakdown in Europe. Still, Hopkins lacked professional management or booking, but that did not concern him. He lived in a small room in a boardinghouse in Houston's Third Ward, where his income sufficed.

Yet turbulence rocked the United States, both at home and abroad. Twenty-three thousand American "military advisors" were stationed in Vietnam. The August 1964 March on Washington put the civil rights movement front and center as polls showed, for the first time, that a majority of Americans considered civil rights a pressing national issue. As an entertainer, Hopkins insulated himself from the financial struggles that the African American working class faced. He could walk into the largest auditorium on a segregated college campus in his hometown and perform to adoring crowds. He had performed at Harvard, America's oldest institution of higher learning, and at Carnegie Hall, with major folk icons like Pete Seeger. He appeared on Steve Allen's popular television show and toured Europe. His nightclub performances ranged from playing top-rank New York venues with heavyweight jazz artists such as John Coltrane to playing black clubs in Richmond, California. At fifty-two years old, as Hopkins faced the midpoint of the sixties, he was well positioned to benefit from the demand for his unique brand of African American blues.

S E V E N

VIETNAM WAR BLUES

Yes if Uncle Sam should call you,
Oh Lord I miss you so much I may die.

LIGHTNIN' HOPKINS, 1968

NINETEEN SIXTY-FIVE ushered in the midpoint of the 1960s, a half-decade that had seen enormous sacrifice and gain by African Americans and their allies in the struggle for civil rights. In March, Hopkins recorded in Houston for Ar-hoolie Records. While not much information survives about the St. Patrick's Day recording session, Arhoolie did release one track. Hopkins played a twelve-string guitar on "Going Back to Baden-Baden," referring to the German city Hopkins played when he was on the American Folk Blues tour in 1964. The words, however, refer not so much to the German town but to the photographer Stephanie Wiesand, who mothered Hopkins along until he was able to perform. The lyrics show Hopkins's usual witticisms, this time about a white woman:

I'm gonna see Miss Stephanie
5,000 miles overseas
When she done made her picture
She said
Please poor Lightnin' come see about me

Legendary blues songwriter, producer, and bass player Willie Dixon arranged for Hopkins to perform a run of dates in and around Chicago during April 1965, including April 17, 1965, at the Great Western Hall on the west side of Chicago, which "you could rent like for a wedding. [The] Black west side was a Jewish neighborhood in the 1920s, Benny Goodman grew up there, two blocks from

Sylvio's [nightclub]."[1] Hopkins's performance was particularly well received by blues scholar Pete Welding. In his review for the British *Blues Unlimited*, he exclaims, "The sea of sound parted, however, when the magisterial, imperturbable Lightnin' strode onstage—and took over completely. With only drummer [Bill] Stepney in support, Hopkins engendered such an undertow of rhythmic power that he had the floor crowded with dancers in no time at-all. By himself he handily out swung the entire [J. B.] Lenoir crew. (J. B. and his Abominable Ensemble . . . was the way one wag described them). Lightnin' is a commanding, fantastically exciting performer and he had the audience in the palm of his hand almost from the first note. He ran through a program of his staples—like "Katie Mae" and "Mojo Hand"—and filled innumerable requests. His voice is an astonishingly sensitive instrument and that guitar of his! I was simply rapt, couldn't believe how good he was."[2]

Charlie Musselwhite saw Hopkins play the Gary, Indiana, stop on the tour a couple of nights later. As in the show in Chicago, Hopkins followed J. B. Lenoir and his band: "I remember when I got there, J. B. Lenoir and his band was playing and he had a horn section. The place was jumping and everyone was dancing. I remember thinking, J. B.'s got a pretty good thing going, I wonder how Lightning is gonna follow it? He has a big band, and Lightning is just a solo player. Finally, it gets to the end of J. B.'s set, and they took the equipment down. It's time for Lightning. He comes walking on stage. He was wearing a black suit and . . . white socks . . . and had on his shades. And he had a drummer too. He sat down, plugged in, started playing guitar, and I tell you after about ten minutes I don't think anyone in there remembered J. B. Lenoir. He was rocking the house. Willie Dixon was in the house that night and also Mabel John was there. She was on the show too." After the gig, Musselwhite got to hang out with Hopkins. "I went there with Big Joe Williams and we sat at a table together, Joe and myself and Lightning . . . drinking and talking and laughing and having a good time."[3]

White blues guitar phenomenon Michael Bloomfield also attended the show in Gary with Williams, Charlie Musselwhite, and Roy Ruby. In his book *Me and Big Joe*, he reminisced:

> This kind of place was also known as a barrelhouse or chockhouse . . . run by an older black couple and consisted of a barbeque pit in front and a large bare room in the back. This room was only heated by body heat—when there were enough people in the room, the place got warm. . . . J. B. Lenoir and his big band came on. . . . the band backing him featured three horn players of such advanced stages of age and inebriation that they had to

lean against one another to avoid collapse. . . . J. B. played guitar and sang through a microphone on a rack around his neck. . . . he danced through the crowd as he played and sang, and Joe sat nodding his approval—he liked J. B. quite a bit. . . . Lightning . . . was as sly and slick and devilish as a man could be. He had a real high conk on his head and wore black, wraparound shades. He had only a drummer behind him, and when the blue lights hit that conk—man that was all she wrote.[4]

Back in Houston, in May 1965, John Carrick and his mother opened Sand Mountain at 1213 Richmond Avenue in the Montrose neighborhood. The alcohol-free coffee shop became a popular venue for folk musicians, who earned a percentage of the admission charge or just passed the hat. "Nobody ever made much money there," John Carrick attests. "It made enough to keep my mom interested, but there were many years my mom carried it out of her pocket."[5] Artists like Guy Clark, Townes Van Zandt, Jerry Jeff Walker, Janis Joplin, Don Sanders, and, eventually, Steve Earle played the low-key venue.

Carrick played some fraternity parties with Hopkins. On one occasion, when Carrick went to play a fraternity party, he discovered Clarence "Gatemouth" Brown on the gig: "We went in the back room to tune up and he's there playing and we're awestruck. We [said], 'What are you doing here?' [Brown said], 'You are the band, and I am the nigger.' He knew what the deal was, and he was trying to tell us in his way. The way they were treated was just appalling to us. These frat boys and girls. It wasn't really hateful, but we would never have addressed anybody that way." As for Hopkins's performances, "Lightnin' had these great, long articulated fingers. And when he played, Lightnin' would be up on a stool and the bass player over here and the drummer over here, lower and within reach. And with these long fingers, he would reach down and whack them on the back of the head. There's the eccentricity of the blues."[6]

Hopkins took opportunities to earn quick money in the recording studio. Aubrey Mayhew was working for Pickwick Records in New York City when he first met and recorded Hopkins: "J. L. Patterson and I were pretty good friends, and he told me Sam lived there [in Houston], so I thought it would be a pretty good thing to record him. So, I did. I didn't go in with the intent to record him [for a record] to be released."[7] Patterson was familiar with Hopkins because he recorded him for Prestige Records at his Gold Star Studios. Prestige hired Patterson to complete Hopkins's record contract after its relationship with Mack McCormick ended.[8]

Mayhew's liner notes to the Hopkins recordings detail his first meeting with Hopkins:

I immediately went to his house, which was a frame dwelling in a tradi-tional black neighborhood. A woman answering the door appeared to be a landlady rather than a relation to Sam. She was apprehensive and wanted to know why I wanted to see Sam. . . . After a few minutes she invited me in and guided me upstairs. . . . As I stepped inside, it was dark and sparsely furnished with only the necessities. A narrow cot was on the wall opposite the door. A man was lying on the cot. I asked if he was Lightning Hopkins. He said he was, and asked what I wanted. I told him I was a record producer and wanted to record him providing he wasn't under contract to a record-ing company. That was a silly statement and brought a smile to his face be-cause as I learned very quickly, Sam didn't sign contracts with record com-panies. I was apprehensive and a little uncomfortable because Sam didn't get up, didn't look at me and didn't initiate any conversation. He appeared very strange to me just lying there in the semi-dark room. He was dressed in pants, an undershirt and a stocking cap. . . . I was white, fully dressed in a suit and tie and wanted something. . . . He didn't seem bothered by any of this. . . . perhaps he sensed that my motives were artistic and not greed oriented. Although I had worked with and produced some of the biggest names in the business, I was never in awe of anyone, nor was I ever a fan. But sitting in that humble room with this totally unaffected man who was an unquestionable master of his art and a giant in the music, I felt strange, but privileged to be there. After my attempt at the amenities and small talk, I asked if he would allow me to produce a record of him. There was no fencing with his reply, just black and white . . . no pun intended. He wanted to know how many songs I wanted and how much I would pay. I told him I wanted twelve songs and would pay whatever he thought was fair. He told me how much and I agreed.[9]

Mayhew recalled what happened at the studio with the band he hired to back Hopkins. "I think J. L. Patterson rounded them up for me. It was nothing for-mal about anything like this. It was very casual, and hit-and-miss. That was what it was all about. I brought the musicians in, I think it was five blues musi-cians, thinking he needed a backup band, but when he saw those musicians, he asked what they were doing there. I told him they were his backup band, and he said, 'I don't play with no band.' I said you mean you just want to record solo? He said, 'Yes,' so I excused the musicians. I paid them and excused them."[10]

The liner notes pick up the rest of the story:

I . . . [took] my formal position as producer and went through the motions of announcing, "take one." He sang the first song, and I stopped the tape to prepare for the next take or song, but he kept on playing. At that point, I told the engineer to just run the tape non-stop. It was plain to see he was going to sing straight through the session. After the third song, he stopped and asked how many he had done and I told him three. He thought it was four and we had a meeting in the middle of the large room. We discussed the number of songs. He wanted to know, was I sure I had the money, and that he was going to do the agreed number of songs. At the end of the meeting, he became very friendly and kept repeating that I was going to be his main man, even if I was from New York. One of the songs on the session is "That Man from New York City," which he conjured up and sang for me. . . . I returned to the booth and let the tape run until Sam was finished. He then put his guitar away, put his coat and hat on, threw the empty gin bottle in the trash and replaced the two chairs. I gave him his money and he left.[11]

Mayhew was shocked by Hopkins's lifestyle: "I've been in the music business all my life, I knew who he was. I was only startled by the fact that he was living in poverty. . . . He was living in one room, sleeping on a cot. . . . I was not surprised that people knew him, and recognized him. A lot of blues singers, like every other segment of music, got promoters and managers that keep a high profile. He didn't have any of that, but to me, he probably was the biggest of all of them. . . . He knew his worth, but he didn't want to compete to take advantage of it. It was easier to just live like he was living and to play like he was playing than to go out and fight the world. And that was pretty much what he told me."[12]

Hopkins could have capitalized on his fame by surrounding himself with professional managers who would have helped him earn money and expand his career. Instead, he lived with a few possessions in a room in a Third Ward ghetto. "He didn't care about money," Mayhew asserts.[13] In a 1964 interview, Hopkins concurs, "I never wanted to be rich, a rich man don't get to heaven. Anyhow, how rich is a rich man?"[14] Clearly, Hopkins wanted to get paid when he recorded or traveled out of town to perform, but Mayhew understood that Hopkins cared little for the trappings of a road to success: "Well, there's a lot of people like that. Greed and seeking money as a mark of success or fame is not always true."[15] Hopkins knew, however, that though the folk blues boom garnered more attention to his art form, that did not mean he profited. The life of a traveling bluesman did not get any easier just because more opportunities flowered. In the November 1965 issue of *Ebony*, Hopkins bemoans, "Money's bein' made, but I'm just unfortunate. I don't make it. . . . People is paying more attention to the blues, they is. But it ain't never easier. It's more harder. They ain't doin' more better, they just come more and it still look like the more come, the less money I get."[16]

In addition to playing his usual Houston gigs at no-name juke joints, around 1964 or 1965 Hopkins held down a steady gig at the Bird Lounge on Shepherd Drive in the Montrose section of Houston, a chiefly white neighborhood featuring a plethora of nightclubs and restaurants. As George Lyon relates, "It was suitably trashy and regularly raided. The clientele was lily white, almost exclusively. It really wasn't a folky place, however . . . I think white trash and frat boys, solid Texans all."[17] Darryl Harris was on-site: "The Bird Lounge was a little more of a rock and rolly place. . . . He had this old Framis student-model guitar. He had a junky guitar. It was miked but I don't think it had pickups. During those Bird years he went to where he was playing full-time electric guitar. It had some D'Armond pickups across the sound hole."[18]

Mayhew taped several of Hopkins's shows at the Bird Lounge. One of the recordings was released during Hopkins's lifetime under the title *Live at the Bird Lounge*. Lyon recalled, "The LP was recorded after the club's usual hours—and the crowd would have been interested (maybe invited) persons, who'd have possibly had the time to sober up."[19] Hopkins's Bird Lounge gig was steady, but according to Mayhew, he just played for tips, earning about twenty-five or thirty dollars a night. The Bird Lounge recording amounted to a very haphazard affair, insinuates Mayhew: "You gotta understand that it was a little teeny club; hardly room to put the equipment in. The owner asked me if I had ever done that before, meaning working with Sam in the club. I said no. He said sometime he'll sing and sometime he won't. Sometime he'll sing one song and leave, and sometime he'll stay until six the next morning. That's why you had chaos in there. You never know what he was going to do. Get a bunch of his buddies in there, and they'd all start jawing at each other."[20]

Mayhew made no arrangements to hire professional musicians to accompany Hopkins on the live nightclub session. Whoever happened to be hanging out with Hopkins was included in the taping: "Curly [Lee] was his cousin and the other guys [on the recordings he made of Hopkins] were just old buddies . . . they were just people down there. See, you couldn't plan anything with Sam or people around him. They acted like you weren't even there. They just went on with their lives. You could tell them what to do or ask them, and they'd just ignore you."[21] In Mayhew's view, Hopkins enjoyed living simply, socializing with friends, and playing for little to no money. Hopkins, however, did like localized fame in his neighborhood—being respected by his social set: "That was what it was all about, they were his people. He trusted them. Trust is what it was all about. Therefore, he got his greatest pleasure from entertaining these people and being friends with them. He'd been to L.A. and New York and saw what kind of people they were, and me wearing a suit and tie gave him some kind of identification to thievery. Cuz everyone that ever cheated him had a suit and tie on."[22]

The fate of Hopkins's *Live at the Bird Lounge* recording is certainly an example of suspicious business practices. Pickwick released it, according to Mayhew, but the record carried the "Guest Star" label: "Pickwick had different labels, Guest Star . . . Premier, Mount Vernon, Diplomat . . . [they] just made them up as they go." The packaging on the Bird Lounge record was cheap, and the jacket carried only three paragraphs of liner notes, which provided few details about Hopkins or the recording. Mayhew explained, "Well, we didn't do liner notes. Most of it [what Pickwick released] was cover stuff [copies of hits], Broadway plays, soundalikes. They later got into buying old tapes. They were six or seven of those companies, they weren't inclined to history, they were just inclined to selling ninety-nine-cent records . . . They would sell from one company to another, that's why the duplication. And in those days, it was the beginning of bootlegging, and there was nobody to keep watch on them, and they didn't sell quantities that got wide exposure, so they got away with a lot of things they shouldn't have. . . . For years and years, I used to go to racks looking for bootleg records, and I'm knowledgeable and had the resources and know what I'm doing, and I didn't even scratch the surface [of how many illegal records were being manufactured and sold]."[23]

Often the material for the ninety-nine-cent records came from old 78s that the record companies merely rerecorded and repackaged. They would reissue the material on 33⅓-rpm records and not pay royalties. Hopkins's case illustrates another variation of unsavory record company dealings: Pickwick, or an affiliated company, would sell the tapes or reissue the same *Live at the Bird Lounge* recordings again and again under different labels with different artwork. After the initial release, the exact same Bird Lounge recordings turned up with the simple title of *Lightnin' Hopkins* on the Power label, which, as a nod to the black nationalism of the time, used a clenched fist as its symbol. The Power label used a cropped version of the cover photo used on the original *Live at the Bird Lounge* release and included an edited version of the liner notes from the original release. The Archives label also released the Bird Lounge recordings as *The Blues—Live*. The Archives release featured yet another version of the original cover photo, this time made to look like a drawing. The Power and Archives imprints were almost certainly bootleg labels or sublabels of Pickwick that sold records cheaply. Likely, artists never saw any royalties for such versions of their recordings. The Mayhew Bird Lounge recordings also turned up on the Storyville label in the UK as *The Blues of Lightnin' Hopkins, Live Recordings from Bird Lounge, Houston, Texas*, with yet another cropped version of the original cover photo.

As for contracts and royalties, Hopkins still preferred cash at the time: "I asked him to sign one [contract] the first time, and he told me he didn't sign anything. That's why he didn't record with a lot of people. He either trusted you or he didn't, that's what he implied. And I didn't push it. I recorded people back in the 1940s that became big stars that I didn't have contracts with. It was just a buddy-buddy thing. It wasn't like today. Jimmy Dean, Roy Clark, Billy Grammer, and Patsy Cline started down there with us, and there was no contracts with any of them."[24]

Mayhew worked in the music business for over sixty years. He doubts Hopkins ever saw any royalties from rereleases of the Bird Lounge recordings or other older records: "He probably got a few dollars from the original recordings recorded in back rooms or whatever, but once the recordings got out, those companies never paid royalties or mechanicals or anything." Mayhew doubted Hopkins was even aware that the records existed. "He has no way of knowing it, he lives like a hermit." When it was pointed out that Hopkins's Gold Star contracts provided for royalties, Mayhew commented, "But he never got it, I guarantee you. They put it in the contract as an inducement, but they never paid anyone. I think that's what instilled the mistrust [from the original recordings]. I don't think he fretted over the fact that everyone was going to get paid and he wasn't."[25]

Once, Hopkins claimed he owned copyrights on five hundred songs. Mayhew responded,

> For Sam to have claimed five hundred songs means he would have had to record five hundred songs, because Sam never sat down and wrote a song. He made it up as he recorded them. And whoever recorded him would get a songwriter contract from him. [That] goes to the distrust, so they could benefit from the royalties. But most of the songs had no substance. In other words, they could just be ramblings. We were in the studio one day, and the first words out of his mouth were "That man from New York City." And he always believed I was from New York. [Mayhew was from Nashville, Tennessee, but was living in New York City when he first met and recorded Hopkins.] Then he would go from there. I asked him, "Why don't you fly?" And he would start singing and make up words why he wouldn't

Mojo Hand

fly. And people would take those as songs . . . for the purpose of collecting mechanicals [royalties] if the record ever got out. The only way you make any money off a song is to make a big record, a big hit, or get multiple recordings. The chances of someone recording jibber jabber that Sam was putting down was nonexistent. He recorded a lot of standards and then put his name on it.[26]

Many of Hopkins's friends continued to be top-notch blues or zydeco performers. While he was on tour in England, Hopkins discussed some of his favorite Houston musicians in an interview with writers from *Blues Unlimited* magazine: "Yeah, Clifton Chenier's my wife's first cousin. I'd like to bring him over here. He's just about the best there is in Houston. There ain't no one else that can play accordion like him. Yeah, I want to bring him over here with me next time but if I don't make it, he sure should. Yeah he's something else, really great. Plays like nothing man . . . he can play anything you like, any type of music."[27]

Hopkins claimed responsibility for introducing Chenier to Arhoolie Records owner and founder Chris Strachwitz, who immediately started recording Chenier, providing a big boost to his career. Hopkins introduced the two when Strachwitz came to Houston to encourage Hopkins to join the American Folk Blues Festival tour in Europe:

One night I was hanging out with him because that was my greatest experience, just hanging out with Lightning and doing what he liked doing, going to the beer joints and watching him play. One night he wasn't doing nothing, and he said, "You want to go see my cousin?" and I said, "Who's your cousin?" "Cliff." "Cliff who?" "Cliff Chenier." Then I recalled the name. There was a record on Specialty I had that had [the song] "Aye Te Fe" [on it and] there was a "[Boppin'] the Rock" on Checker records. I thought that was R&B, and I didn't think it was low-down blues. But, any place Lightning wanted to go, I'd go. He said, "Well, come on along." So, we drove in his car toward what he called Frenchtown in Houston. That's where I saw those big rats running across the road. It was a neat area. . . . Anyway, we went to this tiny little beer joint again. . . . There was this lanky black man with a huge accordion on his chest with just a drummer behind him and singing the most low-down blues in this weird patois. I never heard anything like it. Then Lightning introduced me to Clifton and, of course, he told him I was trying to make records. He said, "Oh, let's cut one tomorrow." So, I called Bill Quinn [at Gold Star studios]. He said, "Yeah, come on over."[28]

Strachwitz retains vivid memories of the recording session:

> So, Clifton brought his band. I just wanted his accordion and the drum, but he brought the whole damn band. He said, "Chris that French stuff don't make it. . . . I gotta have a band." He brought a piano player, a guitar, an electric bass, and a drummer and him. . . . I think I wrote that up in some of the notes. I said, "I just wanted the way you sounded last night, the blues." The guitar player plugged in his guitar he had. . . . they both had these army surplus amplifiers. And the guitar player's amp literally started smoking. That was the end of that amp. From the bass player, all you could hear was pud pud pud. I said, "What's the matter with that amp?" Well the paper done come off the cone! At least we only had a piano and drums and Clifton. So, we did "Aye Yi Yi," and I forget what the other number was. But the other guys all yelled "Ay Yi Yi." I put it out [as a single] and actually sold a few because I actually got to know old man Dailey, Poppa Dailey's son, I think it was, who had Dailey Distributing. They took it to the radio station. Clifton had a name anyway from "Aye Te Fe," and we sold a few. The next year I went back and asked him to do an album.[29]

Arhoolie issued Chenier's album *Louisiana Blues and Zydeco* in 1965, the first in a long string of records that Arhoolie would release by Chenier over several decades.

Besides Chenier, another important fixture on the 1960s Houston music scene, and Hopkins favorite, was Albert Collins: "Albert Collins is my cousin. Younger than me. Sure he's very young but he plays better'n good guitar," Hopkins mentioned in a *Blues Unlimited* interview. "He was born in Leon County like me. I would have brought Albert over but he always teams up with a band and don't like to play by himself. He's gotta have the people on his songs [records] to play with him. I can play OK by myself—don't need no drums. There are so many people in his band. I don't know what they're called."[30] Collins and his band regularly played in Hopkins's neighborhood at places like the Christian Club on the corner of Dowling and Hadley Streets and the Ponderosa Club, also in the Third Ward. "I was raised with Lightning Hopkins, a cousin of mine. . . . Lightning Hopkins was my influence," insisted Collins.[31] The elder bluesman influenced Collins's single-string guitar technique, including playing in D minor and E minor guitar tunings.[32]

By 1965, Hopkins's influence spanned widely across the country, but it remained particularly fervent in Houston, including on players like Johnny Clyde Copeland. When Copeland became a teenager, his family moved to Hopkins's section of the Third Ward, where Copeland quickly became interested in Hopkins, T-Bone Walker, and Albert Collins, while also soaking up Blind Lemon Jefferson and Gatemouth Brown. Copeland enjoyed Hopkins's lightheartedness: "His blues is so humorous you couldn't listen to it without laughing. . . . He was a great brother. He was a real nice brother. I'm so used to hanging out in the Third Ward. Up on Live Oak and McGowen me and Lightning and the boys. That's were Lightning used to hang every day, Live Oak and McGowen. [I] did a lot of work with T-Bone, did a lot of work with Lightning."[33]

Austin guitar player W. C. Clark was acutely aware of Hopkins's unique guitar playing too. By the late 1950s, Clark was playing gigs at the Victory Grill on Austin's East Side. Clark eventually joined Joe Tex's band and went on to work with Austin-based Anglo players like Angela Strehli and Denny Freeman. "Lightning Hopkins, to be honest I cannot play like that. I cannot do it. That type of blues is soul, that's all soul. Those guys did not even know what note they were playing or what key they were playing in."[34]

Hopkins was an indelible part of Houston's folk scene as well, impacting budding Texas poet–cum–folk hero Townes Van Zandt. "When I saw his name, at the Bird Lounge, Lightnin' Hopkins at the Bird Lounge for three bucks. I was just floored," Van Zandt attested. "I had never been looking at him as a human . . . or much less a human that was alive at a place that I could go. I remember the first night seeing Lightning, sitting at his table afterwards. I learned from Lightnin' that you could hit different notes on a guitar as opposed to strumming."[35]

"Mrs. Carrick [owner of Sand Mountain] introduced me to Townes," bass player Rex "Wrecks" Bell said. ". . . it wasn't too long later I introduced him to Lightning."[36] Van Zandt testified, "I considered it a privilege to play with Lightning Hopkins, the last of the great blues players. The first marijuana I ever smoked was given to me by Lightning. . . . the first time I ever saw him, he fell flat back over the stool into the drum sets. Spider [Kilpatrick, Hopkins's drummer] had already left. Billy [Bizor] picked up his Gibson [guitar]. I walked over and said, 'Sir, I'd like to introduce myself.' Lightning always liked to be called 'Sir.' 'Have a seat, son,' he said. Which I did. . . . Lightning was the real driving force in that Houston scene. There was a whole bunch of 'little' guys, me included. Even though we didn't think we were important, it takes mud below the dirt to grow the flowers." Van Zandt later wrote the song "Brand New Companion" as a tribute. "I wrote it for that reason, just for Lightning. Lightning tribute, kind of a cheap imitation of Lightning."[37] In addition to having status with the folk crowd, Hopkins energized a younger generation of African American blues players in a particularly fecund manner.

Weldon "Juke Boy" Bonner, a Bellville, Texas, native, moved to Houston to work in 1947. After a stint playing juke joints in California for a few years, he moved back to Houston for good in 1957. Working as a one-man band, he played harmonica and guitar and sang his own poetry set to music. Early in his career, his music derived from Hopkins's sound. During the mid-sixties, he worked small Houston clubs like the Hayes Lounge, the Jungle Lounge, and the Family Inn. By then, he had recorded "Look Out Lightnin'," asserting he was ready for Hopkins to move aside:

> They tell me you supposed to be the last of the blues singers Lightnin'
> You've got to give some room for me
> You know it may take a long time now Lightnin'
> But I'm catching up with you by degrees

While Bonner mimicked Hopkins's musical style, even sang some of his songs, Otis Hicks, a bluesman from Louisiana, borrowed Hopkins's name to become Lightning Slim. He also drew deeply upon Hopkins's influences, like Blind Lemon Jefferson. Later, Hopkins would play and record "My Starter Won't Start," one of Lightning Slim's songs. The circle of inspiration remained unbroken.

Beatles drummer Ringo Starr had been a Hopkins fan since he was a teenager when he sought to immigrate to Houston just to live near Hopkins. Little information survives about how and where a meeting between the Beatles and Hopkins took place and what transpired, but the *Los Angeles Sentinel*, an African American newspaper, called Hopkins "The father of current day rock and roll and rhythm and blues," reporting that after the meeting the Beatles said, "We didn't believe a man with so much soul could ever exist, but, wow, he's the most soulful cat alive."[38] Rex Bell remembered Hopkins talking about this meeting: "Yeah, in fact John Lennon was all hot on meeting Lightnin'. And the Beatles were over here and Lightnin' was in California and John Lennon searched out Lightnin' to meet him and they met in L.A. But when Lightnin' would tell the story he'd say the Beatles met me."[39] Years later, Hopkins told Dallas newspaper columnist Frank X. Tolbert, "Before the Beatles amount to much I gave them a lot of help with the guitar. They say I sort of set their beat."[40]

Hopkins's biggest show of the year was in Newport, Rhode Island, where the Newport Folk Festival booked him to join an impressive lineup of top-tier talents. Music entrepreneur George Wein founded the Folk Festival as an outgrowth of his Newport Jazz Festivals. On Saturday, July 24, 1965, Hopkins took part in a workshop hosted by Chris Strachwitz. The casual afternoon workshop also featured Son House, Mance Lipscomb, Memphis Slim, Willie Dixon, and Josh White. Hopkins and eleven other acts performed later that night. Paul Butterfield Blues Band guitarist Michael Bloomfield introduced Hopkins's set, gushing, "Of all the blues singers I know, for me, I got one favorite to me that most typifies the blues . . . the king of the blues, Lightning Sam Hopkins."[41]

Hopkins's set included his staple "Mojo Hand," "Trouble in Mind," "Baby Please Don't Go," and several instrumentals. Hopkins's wit and upbeat mood are evident throughout the rambling talk before the instrumental "Come On Baby": "Ain't nobody here but poor Lightning. But I tell you what, he ain't got but one fire gun that shoots one way. I don't beg for no piece for every day, cuz I got something to keep me going on my way. No money, honey. You know what I mean, and no bad material to fight with, and things like that. But I keep my house cool. Know the reason? It's air-conditioned. Yeah. I ain't got but one thing to do, go there and set it on 60 and then it be cool, you know what I mean? Good God . . . ha ha . . . Lightning ain't popping off neither. I want you to stop by my house, 3124 Gray Street in Houston. But I got to talk to you a little bit, children. I ain't got long to lie to you but I gotta tell you . . ."[42] Hopkins's invitation to his audience to come and visit him, replete with home address, testifies to his often candid, unguarded, and earthy sentiments.

Chicago drummer Sam Lay, who later worked with Hopkins at clubs in New York City and Chicago, played with Hopkins for the first time at Newport: "Yeah, just the two of us [played the gig at Newport] and then after a while he called Willie Dixon down. Mostly me and Lightning [played] by ourselves. I'd just fall in [after Hopkins started the song]. I can follow anybody then and now. Most of the times Lightning just liked me to play with him by myself. He like[d] me to follow him. He couldn't lose me no kind of way. Matter of fact, it was funny to him. He said it just wasn't no problem for me to play with him. I understood his kind of style timing."[43]

At Newport, Lay also performed with the Paul Butterfield Blues Band, which backed Bob Dylan. No prior arrangement to play with Dylan existed. Dylan's performance at the 1965 Newport Folk Festival became one of the cultural touchstones of the 1960s. He played a solo acoustic set and then brought Butterfield's band onstage to back him while he played electric guitar. In addition to controversy over Dylan's choice to play electric, people also raised concerns about whites playing the blues at the festival. Musician Annie Johnston attended the show and remembered: "[There was a] fight between [Dylan manager] Albert Grossman and Alan Lomax. Chris [Strachwitz] missed the fight [but] I was there. It was in the afternoon. Paul Butterfield was playing. It was just a workshop. It was a great set. Those guys could play great blues. However, [later that night when Butterfield's band backed Bob Dylan, they] were introduced by Alan Lomax and his introduction was terrible. He said, 'Here's some white boys from Chicago and they think they can play blues and they're plugged in and we know it's gonna be loud.'"[44] Strachwitz also has strong memories of Newport: "I missed the fight between Alan Lomax and Albert Grossman because the night before I got drunk with Lightning. I chose apricot brandy and couldn't function the next day! But Lightning always stuck with gin. He and Willie Dixon told me about the fight when they came back to the dorm!"[45]

Though the Dylan-goes-electric controversy is the defining moment of the festival, Hopkins's set and persona are also well worth examining—he performed playing his acoustic guitar as the folkie crowd expected. Starting back in 1959 when Mack McCormick presented him at a hootenanny production at the Alley Theater in Houston, Hopkins appealed to a white audience by performing a role fitting the accepted perceptions about folksingers. Years after the Newport set, guitarist Bloomfield noted, "Lightning Hopkins had made electric records for twelve years but he didn't bring his electric band from Texas. No, sir, he came out at Newport just like they had taken him out of the fields, like a tar baby."[46] Hopkins seemed to be bolstering musical and social stereotypes, according to some.

After playing Newport, Hopkins headed north and worked two nights at Club 47 in Cambridge, Massachusetts.[47] *Blues Unlimited* ran a short commentary: "Lightning was in town and was really tired and sick. He had been to Newport, which was good. . . . Lightnin' was good down there clownin' but didn't sing blue anymore. He had that one boogie that evokes crowd reaction and little girls' orgasms, and he played to one beautiful chick who writhed every time he hit a high note. That was fine. He says yeah. The crowd says yeah. And he looked puzzled sometimes, not knowing whether they're for him or against him. He seems paranoid—but which of us isn't?"[48]

Hopkins closed out his 1965 East Coast summer tour by playing two nights at the Gaslight in the Greenwich Village neighborhood of New York City. He shared the bill with folk artist Eric Andersen and comedian Flip Wilson. According to Bob Dylan, the Gaslight was "A cryptic club—had a dominant presence on the street, more prestige than anyplace else. It had a mystique, big colorful banner out front and paid a weekly wage. . . . The Gaslight was non-booze but you could bring a bottle in a paper bag. It was shut down in the day and opened in the early evening with about six performers that rotated throughout the night, a closed drawn circle that an unknown couldn't break into. There weren't any auditions. It was a club I wanted to play, needed to. . . . I kept my sights on the Gaslight. How could I not? Compared to it, the rest of the places on the street were miserable, low-level basket houses or small coffee houses where the performer passed the hat."[49]

Dion DiMucci, leader of doo-wop group Dion and the Belmonts, and self-proclaimed "King of the New York Streets," saw Hopkins perform at the Gaslight: "I grew up with the blues. . . . there was a guy in my neighborhood, Willie Green—he had Lightnin' Hopkins records and Son House records. . . . Lightnin' Hopkins is a very soulful guy. He's one of my favorites. He used to hold court down in the Village, man, when he played at the Gaslight, and everyone would gather around and he would tell stories. He would do that in his music—he had natural soul, a true back-roads poet. He did have a style on guitar, it's hard to explain, but it really was just like lightning. His choice of notes on guitar and with his voice . . . they were just something different he brought to the table. . . . He was a confident guy, personally; he was right out front, in your face. He had a get-over-on-you style—it was like, 'I'm the *man*. What else you want to know?'"[50]

In the fall of 1965 Hopkins toured the West Coast. He worked two weeks, September 7–20, at the Ash Grove in Los Angeles and then headed to San Francisco to play a new club, the Matrix, from September 21 to 26 and again October 1–3. Marty Balin cofounded the club, which was located at 3138 Fillmore Street in the Marina district. The club opened on August 13, 1965, with the debut of Balin's band the Jefferson Airplane. The Airplane also served as Matrix's house band. They shared the bill with Hopkins from September 23 through 26. Guitarist and band member Jorma Kaukonen named the band in tribute to Blind Lemon Jefferson's name. Due to a San Francisco ordinance that only permitted dancing where food was served, the room was set up as a listening room with tables and chairs. It served beer and wine and featured a low stage. With a capacity of a little over one hundred, the club offered Hopkins intimate and up close. The former pizza restaurant became an important venue in the burgeoning San Francisco rock scene, highlighting a number of blues artists that crossed over into the psychedelic rock genre.

Rag Baby magazine's review of one of Hopkins's shows at the Matrix demonstrates his popularity with the white crowd:

The set opened with a fast rocker, and then a Chicago sounding modern blues. Slowing down the pace he played a really fine version of "Baby Please Don't Go"—the audience was beginning to yell now when he hit long notes—and then he dropped into a really slow blues. He was playing flashily: hitting slam chords at the ends of measures, picking the bass strings all the way up the neck, moving his hands all over the guitar, striking long slow "soul" notes, and making those incredible long runs which are his trademark. The audience was picking up on it. Cries of "play it baby" rang out, and J. C. Burris—a long time friend of Lightnin's—was whooping and yelling from his seat by Lightnin's wife. When the number stopped the requests began to come in, and he played "It's Mighty Crazy (how they keep on rubbing at the same old thing)"—a bawdy novelty piece. The next request was for "Rocky Mountain," a blues with mediocre lyrics, and then the set was closed with a fast finger-picking piece Lightnin' calls "The Old Folks Dance." It is a raggy song in the style of John Hurt or Mance Lipscomb, and is a half-joking put-down. Lightnin' picked so fast that the notes blended in the amplifier and sounded like a horn. The audience was wild.[51]

After his club dates in San Francisco, Hopkins returned to Los Angeles for a recording date for the MGM-owned Verve/Folkways label. On October 5 and 6, 1965, session players joined him in the studio. The rhythm section consisted of players with years of experience backing music industry luminaries. New Orleans native Earl Palmer played drums and Jimmy Bond played stand-up bass. Palmer was a key drummer in New Orleans from 1950 until February 1957, when he moved to Los Angeles to work for Aladdin Records. Palmer recorded with Fats Domino, Little Richard, Smiley Lewis, Dave Bartholomew, Lloyd Price, Ritchie Valens, Eddie Cochran, and many more. Bond jammed with Charlie Parker and gigged and recorded with Chet Baker. Palmer enjoyed the Verve sessions with Hopkins: "I'd never worked with him before then, it was very reminiscent of a Professor Longhair date! We didn't get started for maybe an hour or so because he had to get his peach brandy or something, which he drinks all the time, but we had a ball—I got into the peach brandy too! We had a ball that night. It was done over here at Wally Heider's [recording studio]."[52]

Two days of sessions resulted in enough songs for several albums: *Lightnin' Strikes* (Verve/Folkways), *Lightnin' Hopkins* (Verve/Folkways), and *Lightnin' Hopkins Volume II* (Everest Records—released in the UK by Polydor as *That's My Story: The Blues of Lightnin' Hopkins, Vol. 1*). The album cover of *Lightnin' Strikes* features a picture of the Reverend Gary Davis instead of Hopkins. Jerry Schoenbaum is credited with the rather nondescript liner notes, a sample of which reads, "This exciting new album was recorded October 4 and 5th in Los Angeles. Much of its success must be attributed to a sensitive and imaginative producer, David Hubert."[53] During the sessions for Verve, Hopkins cut yet another version of "Mojo Hand," featuring Don Crawford on harmonica. Overall, the *Lightnin' Strikes* sides represent fairly pedestrian musical fare. Furthermore, the cover featured a picture of T-Bone Walker.

Back in Houston, Hopkins continued to record more, too. In 1965, he worked sessions for Shreveport, Louisiana–based Jewel Records. Stan Lewis founded the Jewel label after years in record distribution and retail sales. After buying up five jukeboxes in black neighborhoods, in 1948 he took his savings and bought J & M Records at 728 Texas Street, which was in a black neighborhood in Shreveport. He renamed it Stan's, which became popular with noteworthy musicians, including Elvis Presley, who often stopped in to promote their records and mingle with fans. Soon, Lewis started a mail order business, distributing records to jukebox operators, record stores, and whoever was in the market. His business became a "one stop," a place where store owners and other large buyers could get all the records they wanted. Leonard Chess was his mentor.

After producing sides for other labels, Lewis started Jewel Records in 1963: "Bill Holford called me in the mid-'60s and said, 'Lightnin' is looking for some money, would you do a session on him?' I had a good relationship with Lightnin' anyway, so I said, 'Sure.' I released three albums on Lightnin' and recorded him more than any other blues artist I worked with. What a brilliant storyteller he was."[54] "We recorded in Houston. He wanted $2,500 outright. He'd give you ten or twelve songs. He would only do the song one time. He wanted to be paid in cash. I'd have to go to the bank and cash a check. I sold him very well. I had my retail stores. I felt like I could make some money with him. . . . The funniest thing I remember about Lightning was the drummer was off. He said, 'Man you better get it straight and do the beat right or I'm gonna kick your ass.' . . . Depending on the size of the band, we'd have to go out and get three or four fifths of whiskey. Of course, Lightning wouldn't give you but one take, but with the other musicians on other sessions we'd do five or six takes, so we'd be there for several hours. And Lightning wouldn't give us but ten sides."[55]

Hopkins only recorded eight songs for *Blue Lightning*, his first Jewel album. To get enough material for an entire album, Lewis borrowed two more songs from Joe Bihari at Modern Records, part of the masters the label acquired from Bill Quinn in 1951. The original record cover featured on old publicity photo of Hopkins that Lewis found around his record shop. After Hopkins expressed his displeasure with the photo, Jewel redid the cover with a different picture.

Blue Lightning included the track "Back Door Friend," Hopkins's tale of a cheating married woman making love to a man who slips out the back door when her husband comes home. Jewel also released the song as the A-side for its first Hopkins single and backed it with "Fishing Clothes." In producer Don Logan's estimation, the "45 sold well."

The theme—a back door friend or back door man—is a pungent one throughout the blues:

What you gonna do with a woman
When she got a back door friend
She just praying for you to move out
So her back door friend can move in

In 1925, Sara Martin released on the Okeh label her "Strange Loving Blues" song, which included the line:

Every sensible woman got a back door man[56]

Lonnie Johnson's "I Ain't Gonna Be Your Fool," cut for Decca in 1938, included several references to the back door man:

I worked for you, baby,
When your man was slipping in my back door
I can see for myself so take your back door man,
I won't be your fool no more

Howlin' Wolf cut the Willie Dixon tune "Back Door Man" for Chess in 1962. Moreover, Chicago blues artist Jimmy Rogers and Beaumont, Texas, native Johnny Winter both recorded versions of Hopkins's "Back Door Friend." Winter's version debuted on his self-titled first album, which Columbia Records released in 1969. Winter first heard Hopkins's music on the radio in Beaumont when he was thirteen: "He was definitely an influence on me. He did what he wanted to do when he felt like doing it. I think 'Back Door Friend' is the only song of his I ever played."[57] Winter's version is not a straight copy of Hopkins's song, particularly the lyrics, which Winter spun with his own words, but his rendition still maintains the spirit of Hopkins's song. Winter wanted to give Hopkins songwriting credit, since he believes crediting people for their work is important.[58] The album hit number 24 on the *Billboard* magazine charts, indicating substantial sales that could have generated substantial royalties for whoever was in control of Hopkins's copyright.

In an interview conducted by Earl Ofari in 1970 for the *Los Angeles Free Press*, when asked about the trend of young white bluesmen such as Johnny Winter, Mike Bloomfield, and Paul Butterfield, Hopkins replied, "Well it's pretty hard to say, when you're copying someone else it's no big thing. It's just something about that they don't agree. It's kind of like eating the wrong food. Now you know Johnny Winter and them . . . practically all the kids would get around and play with me. You know Johnny he was more successful than me. . . . I'm supposed to get the credit for a lot of things done, but I don't get it. I'm *the* bluesman. I know that. I get calls from far and low. When it comes to bread though, I'm not the man they put the bread on. The other fellow get the break. I'm just be furnishing the things that give them the ideas. Well, maybe I'll get lucky some day."[59]

In private, Hopkins voiced similar feelings about receiving less than his fair share of money. Houston bluesman Big Walter Price confided, "He would tell you this, he wasn't too particular about contracts with record companies. He said the same thing I always know, they wasn't going to treat you fair just like me and Little Richard. They been taking money from us since they've been out there."[60] As Price explained, Hopkins deeply disliked record companies' mistreatment of him. Hopkins's remedy seems valid. Signing agreements is pointless for an artist if they could not be enforced.

Hopkins had no power to force record companies to provide him with a fair accounting of sales and correctly calculated royalty payments. Hopkins obviously realized that whatever cash payment he negotiated at the time of the recording session was likely the only money he was ever going to see; therefore, he accepted that fact and did not spend time and energy chasing after record companies for payments after the service was rendered. He did not write his songs for others to record, so if someone recorded his song, and experienced some success, this did not affect Hopkins's daily routine whatsoever.

Four years after his 1970 interview for the *Los Angeles Free Press*, in a conversation between Hopkins and a reporter with the University of Texas *Daily Texan* newspaper, he did not seem embittered about Winter's song: "You know I played with Johnny Winter up on Haight Ashbury Street, and he came to me and said, 'Lightnin' I'm going to New York to cut some records.' He recorded my song 'Backdoor Friend,' which sold a million copies, and all Lightnin' said was good for him."[61] Winter has no memory of this meeting: "I heard he did not like me doing his song. It was a very good song. I liked it a lot. He was a nice guy. He was a great blues singer and a great guitar player. Nobody else sounds like Lightning. He just plays whatever he felt like. He should have been appreciated more. You can learn everything [by listening to his music]. He was a very down-home country guy. I think he had an impact, without a doubt."[62]

Darryl Harris saw Johnny Winter open for Hopkins when Winter signed his big recording contract with Columbia: "He could really be threatened by other musicians if he thought someone else was getting more attention than he was. [Winter] was the most blazing guitar player you ever saw in your life. It was a great show. Lightnin' came out [and said] why don't you turn that down? I like to hear what I'm playing. Some people make a lot of noise with their guitar, but

I like to talk with mine. He would really, really show how insecure he was. He was very uptight that someone was getting a better response. People just went crazy over him [Winter]."[63]

After Hopkins recorded "Back Door Friend" for Stan Lewis, Jewel's Su-Ma Publishing received the publishing share. Because Lewis listed his name as co-composer, Hopkins was left with only 25 percent overall royalties because the publishing company took 50 percent for publishing royalties and Lewis took 25 percent for songwriter's royalties. Whether Jewel actually paid Hopkins any royalties only Lewis and his employees know. Don Logan worked for Jewel Records: "Stan did the one with 'Back Door Friend,' that really, of all the tunes, that was the biggest one we had. That was the one Nashville played, that Wolfman Jack played."[64]

Lewis bought radio airtime for his retail store to push his products. "Since I bought the time, I could tell them what to play, so naturally I favored all these guys that helped me when I first started, blues, Atlantic, Chess, Modern, Kent, Herald. 'Shake a Hand' with Fay Adams, that was a big record for us, and Lightnin' Hopkins. I'd have the Lightnin' Hopkins special on or the Muddy Waters special on, the B. B. King special, six records for $3.98, or whatever it was."[65]

Interestingly, the *Blue Lightning* record gave Stan Lewis and Hopkins composer credit on the eight songs that Lewis's company recorded. The veracity of Lewis's claim to song authorship appears specious. The songs contained on the album provide telltale clues. "Move On Out Part 1" and "Move On Out Part 2" are instrumentals. Hopkins, who could toss off and unveil endless riffs, jams, and boogies, likely worked these out spontaneously and solo. Hopkins did play other composers' songs but usually songs with accompanying lyrics. Furthermore, Hopkins also recorded "Wig Wearing Woman," which is just a variation of his "Short Haired Woman," first recorded for the Aladdin label in the 1940s. BMI, the agency that collects license fees, gives Lewis composer credit on 620 songs, but most of the albums Hopkins recorded during the 1960s did not involve cowritten songs. For example, the four Hopkins albums Chris Strachwitz's Arhoolie label released did not have any cowritten songs, and the ten albums Hopkins recorded for Prestige/Bluesville did not include cowritten songs, except for a couple with performer Brownie McGhee.

According to Logan, Stan Lewis recorded the first two Hopkins records on Jewel, *Blue Lightning* and *Talking Some Sense*, and he recorded the last one. Logan remembered the problems he encountered when trying to find Hopkins when he went to Houston to record him for the *Great Electric Show and Dance* record:

Lightnin' did not have an address that you could send him anything. The first time I went down there, George Wild Child Butler was with me, [I] had all this money [to pay Hopkins]. We didn't know where Lightnin' was, so we started off at a grocery store, and then there's a place in Houston going out of town where the old KCOH studios used to be, and go on down there and turn to the left and there's the biggest ghetto I've ever seen, at least up to that time. And you'd drive up between the houses and there'd be a place with a Coke sign and there'd be a bar, so I'd sit out in the car. No white people down there, and George would go in the bar, course he probably had him a few cuz I gave him his money. And he'd come back, and we'd go to another grocery store. We went to at least twenty-five grocery stores and there's a grocery store [where they] said just sit out in front of the store. He's gonna come by driving a big Chrysler with a whip antenna. It was '68, he must have had a CB; he had a long whip antenna. There it passed by and I waved my hands and Wild Child waved his. That's how we told him when the session was. He talked to Stan on the phone and came to the particulars of how much money, where, and when. . . . . It was a unique experience.[66]

Logan's memories regarding the actual recording session were dimmer: "I was in the control booth part of the time. . . . I got him to repeat a few choruses. [Bill] Holford [owner and engineer of ACA Studios] had a three-track, so we were limited to what we could do. That album, [the] *Great Electric Show and Dance*, was the best of two sessions." The session almost ended in violence, since Logan cut the drummer's recording session fee: "We discharged that drummer. He kept a good steady beat, but we were going to sit there and not get anything. Lightnin' would just not follow him, and I had all that money in my pocket. I was afraid someone was going to get me if I didn't spend it and give it to Lightnin'. It was kind of a funny thing there."[67]

The fired drummer came back to settle the score later that day:

[Hopkins] wanted that drummer to follow him. He was always the leader of the band. That first session I did there was a real problem with the drummer, and I had to get another one. I didn't know it at the time, but I guess Lightnin' saved my life. This was when he was going out to Rice University to play a gig, and the drummer was kind of disgruntled that he wasn't going to get his money. And I had the big roll of money Stan had given me, but I wouldn't . . . give it to him until the end of the session. After the session was over, the drummer was waiting out there, and he had some things to say about not being included on the session. I noticed him [Hopkins] step in between me and the guy. A little bit later on Wild Child, [who] played harp on the session, said, "Man that drummer had a knife. He was going to cut you." Lord Jesus, here I am a white boy in Houston gonna wind up in a box to go home. Lightnin' said, "Come on kid, you gonna go with us out to Rice. You gonna play with us, and we'll pay you your money." It was all settled. Nobody got hurt.

[After the session] I brought Stan back some papers. But the papers I brought just had an "X." Then I had two witnesses [saying] this is Lightnin' Hopkins' signature. . . . I think he did twelve songs for us, or ten. . . . It was written out so he could read it. . . . I don't want to be accused of saying he was illiterate, but the paper I brought back to Stan did have an X on it, with two signatures on it saying [it was Lightnin's signature].[68]

Hopkins closed out 1965 with a nine-night stand at the 11th Door in Austin, Texas.[69] Bill Simonson owned the venue, which stood on the corner of Red River and Eleventh Street. *Austin Statesman* music writer Jim Langdon mentioned Hopkins's engagement in his Night Beat column: "For the finest in traditional blues catch Lightning Hopkins at the 11th Door this week. Flanked by Billy Bizor and Cleveland Chenier on rub board, the durable Houston blues guitarist has been putting on some of the best of his nightclub shows since he opened last weekend. And the response has been equally good. Manager Bill Simonson reported turning away more than 100 people Saturday night alone, and when I dropped by the club Tuesday evening there was an exceptional weeknight audience on hand digging Lightning."[70] Hopkins always drew well in Austin, and the 11th Door gigs were no exception.

By the spring of 1966, Hopkins was back in California. He started off his tour on April 5 with three nights at the Ash Grove, his West Coast anchor club. On April 15, he gigged at the Berkeley Blues Festival at the Harmon Gymnasium at the University of California. Mance Lipscomb, Clifton Chenier, and Muddy Waters joined him on the bill. Arhoolie Records impresario Chris Strachwitz and Ed Denson organized the show, under the Pretentious Folk Front moniker. Like most of Hopkins's gigs, no arrangements were made in advance for a backing band. Francis Clay drummed for Muddy Waters' band and backed Hopkins, the only time the two performed together in front of an audience: "Just about all festivals I ended up backing everybody on the show. The response was great. Lightning was a great entertainer. The more people applauded, and yelled at him, the more he'd get into it. He was very responsive, to their delight."[71] Clay later recorded several LPs with Hopkins for Arhoolie.

KAL radio recorded the show, and Arhoolie released portions of Lipscomb, Chenier, and Hopkins's performances on the album *Blues Festival*. Hopkins's set attracted some solid write-ups in the Bay Area media. *San Francisco Chronicle* writer Ralph Gleason noted, "I have never heard Hopkins sound as effective as he did Friday night, his voice dark with tragedy and his guitar evoking strange and almost mystical sounds during the accompaniment. Hopkins has now worked out a little vignette of storyline to introduce each tune, which is really a drag and quite pretentious. As he was about to sing a blues with the line 'Don't the moon look lonesome shinin' through the trees,' he told the story of a girl he loved and how 'I made this song' concerning her. But he sang very well indeed and one can forgive the make believe context because of the hard reality with which he sings his songs."[72]

After the Berkeley Blues Festival gig, Hopkins stayed in the Bay Area and worked the Savoy Club in Richmond on April 17, 1966. Ed Denson detailed Hopkins's show in his Folk Scene column, published in the *Berkeley Barb*:

The crowd was an old-time blues crowd who had come to hear the man billed as "the world's greatest blues singer," along with a go-go girl and L. C. Robinson. L. C. was acting as the MC for the show and played a few numbers on the guitar. . . . then the go-go girl came out and put on the most incredible dance I've seen. If only the Tribune knew, or the Sexual Freedom League. It was like a thirty minute orgasm during which she danced on the stage, the floor, the bar, tables, customers, everything. It really turned the crowd on for Lightning. He hit the stage after a long intro by L. C. and said, "Yeah! Oh Yeah!" and the crowd said "Yeah!" Then he began playing blues just as everyone imagines they are played—the amp distorting and the mike cutting all the highs out of his voice, the crowd dancing and yelling, women whooping and waving their arms around in the air, men replying to verses and calling out requests, the waiter flashing his light on the bottles to see if they were empty, and Lightning putting out long slow blues. Really fine, superfine.[73]

Hopkins worked from April 19 through 25 at the Matrix in San Francisco. On Sunday, April 24, 1966, he appeared at an afternoon benefit at the Matrix titled "Blues for Bogalusa," sharing the bill with the Outfit, Vince Guaraldi, and Sopwith Camel. No records of the benefit survive, but the show probably benefited the Deacons for Defense or community organizers in Bogalusa, Louisiana, a stronghold for the Ku Klux Klan. The Deacons, an armed African American political organization, protected the black community and civil rights organizations such as the Congress for Racial Equality (CORE) from racial terrorism perpetrated by the Ku Klux Klan. Stories in *New York Post* and *New York Times* on the Deacons, including a front-page report in the June 6, 1965, edition of the *Times*, brought the Deacons into the national spotlight. Repeated Klan attacks and local law enforcement's failure to enforce the law resulted in the United States attorney general's office intervening against the Bogalusa sheriff, the police chief, and Klan members.

Norman Mayell, drummer for San Francisco band Sopwith Camel, played the show with Hopkins:

> We opened the show at the Matrix for Lightning. He was dressed in a fedora and a suit, and black sunglasses, very black, big ones, couldn't see his eyes or the expression on his face. . . . Somehow he must have understood that he was sort of revered by the audience, so he asked Martin [Beard], the bass player in the Camel, and myself to sit in at the end of his set for two songs followed by Spencer Dryden and Jack Cassidy from Jefferson Airplane for two songs.
>
> We were already set up on stage. And other band members from around San Francisco were there to see Lightning Hopkins play. It was filled with musicians as well as audience. I remember we played two songs. . . . I have a feeling he was playing acoustic, and we sat in and played. I was really happy about it because I played so much blues with Michael [Bloomfield] in Chicago and that was the thing I was into. Martin, the bass player, hadn't had that much experience, and we went up on stage, and we did OK. A lot of people said, "You did fine." We had some embarrassing moments because he is inscrutable. In those days, he was just this dark unfathomable character, not necessarily friendly at all, but we were going to get the chance to play with a blues God.[74]

Hopkins followed up the Matrix club dates with April 29 and 30 gigs at the Fillmore Auditorium, where he opened for Jefferson Airplane the first night, and Quicksilver Messenger Service the second night. Promoter Bill Graham, founder of the Fillmore, recalled his logic behind booking blues and psychedelic rock acts on the same bill: "I was beginning to realize whether the supporting acts on the bill would sell any tickets on their own. I could put on not only what I wanted to but *should've* been putting on. . . . Quicksilver alone would sell out the hall. It was like a mother saying to her child 'You want the ice cream? You gotta eat the meat. You gotta eat the vegetables. . . . The meat is good for you, the vegetables are good for you. Gotta eat your meat and veggies. *Then* you get your ice cream.' The ice cream was the Grateful Dead or Quicksilver or Jefferson Airplane. But the vegetables you had to go through might be Lightning Hopkins or Junior Wells. It was like 'Go on. You'll love him. You don't think so now. But you will. When you *try* him.'"[75]

In Houston, however, some viewed Hopkins's gigs with rock 'n' roll bands unfavorably. A correspondent writing in the October 1966 issue of *Blues Unlimited* magazine opined, "Lightning Hopkins is currently playing a spot called Lou's Rickshaw Room, a semi-hippie hangout, and is sounding bad. He gives the people rock and roll for the most part and is conscious of playing for Mr. Whitey."[76]

Mack McCormick understood the difference in Hopkins's performances:

At a black club the audience are very demanding. They are not like so many people today. They are demanding of the musicians. They won't put up with foolishness. They won't put up with long intermissions. I seen a guy pick up Lightning Hopkins and carry him outside a club because he spent too much time tuning up and talking and fooling around. And Lightning came back in and then he provided the music the crowd wanted. That's at a place called Irene's in the 6th ward.

They are demanding people and the fact that someone may be well known nationally is not that impressive. They are here tonight to do what we need. And if they don't do it we'll let the jukebox do it. White people tended to put up with things when he was on stage. He had this bizarre attitude that if he could talk for an hour and only play 30 minutes that he somehow was ahead of the game. And that was his thinking. This is so unlike musicians and he would talk and talk and get drunk and then it became drunken rambling. Until it became where I began to regret that I brought him before white audiences.[77]

Modern music was in flux, and Hopkins's music, to some extent, changed with it. The blistering electric sides he recorded for Herald Records became an important milestone in his musical evolution and strong evidence that his music did not petrify. Not all successful entertainers have the luxury to play material that solely pleases their own selves. Hopkins gave audiences what they wanted, thus reaping the success of that strategy: repeat bookings and better gigs. The *Blues Unlimited* writer's sentiments sound similar to those of the "folk police" that decried Bob Dylan's electric set at the 1965 Newport Folk Festival, where Hopkins also appeared. Hopkins easily worked solo gigs with a miked acoustic guitar on the coffeehouse scene or could plug in an electric guitar, add a drummer, and rock a raucous black juke joint, sometimes on the same night. Ample evidence suggests Hopkins derived an immense amount of pleasure from playing diverse types of crowds, from Third Ward neighborhoods to bourgeois college auditoriums. Either way, he was preaching the gospel according to Sam Hopkins and living life on his own terms.

In the fall of 1966, some of the same West Coast venues he played on his spring tour beckoned his return. On September 23, he played the first of ten nights at the Ash Grove in Los Angeles, then turned north up the coast for dates at the Jabberwock in Berkeley and the Matrix in San Francisco. He followed those gigs with a ten-night run at the Matrix club, then worked the two nights of October 21–22 at the Fillmore Auditorium opening for the Grateful Dead, who were known to include Hopkins's "Katie Mae" in their sets. According to Grateful Dead member Jerry Garcia, Hopkins influenced the vocal style of the Dead's keyboard player, Ron "Pigpen" McKernan: "He can sing exactly like Lightnin' Hopkins . . . and play the guitar like Lightnin' Hopkins to the point of being completely irregular about changes and stuff, just like Lightnin' is."[78] Dead guitar player Phil Lesh noted, "Never was Pigpen more at home than with a bottle of wine and a guitar . . . playing Lightnin' Hopkins songs."[79]

The Ash Grove booked Hopkins for another ten-night run from March 17 through 26, 1967. Depending on the demand, Hopkins usually did two shows a night when he worked the Ash Grove. The second show on March 24 was recorded. Hopkins's hour-long-plus second set included Big Joe Williams's "Baby Please Don't Go," Ray Charles's "What'd I Say," "Take Me Back," "Mojo Hand," "Do the Twist," "Trouble in Mind," "Ain't It Crazy," "Rocky Mountain Blues," and several instrumentals.

During his stay in Los Angeles, Hopkins wrote a letter in longhand to his girlfriend Antoinette back in Houston. Besides confirming Hopkins's illiteracy, the letter is a window into their relationship as well as Hopkins's business affairs. Addressed to Miss Antoinette Hopkins, the personal note began, "My dear little wife." Hopkins wrote he missed his "little wife" and "she should kiss herself for me." Hopkins did not have any other dates booked in California and was waiting for a friend to arrange some: "Al Smith is supposed to get me some work for me in Frisco so I don't get something else to do I will be home." He also wrote, "A fellow was in last night want to record me" and explained he awaited news from Jimmy Bond and Carroll Peery.[80]

Hopkins's letter shows his lack of professional help in managing or booking him, leaving him dependent on friends to arrange dates for him. In the past, Harold Leventhal, known as someone who "could book (and fill) virtually any auditorium in the country with Judy Collins, the Weavers, Odetta, and Theodore Bikel, among others,"[81] booked him into Carnegie Hall in 1960. Manny Greenhill, Joan Baez's manager, also booked him for a short time in the 1960s and was certainly capable of handling Hopkins's business affairs. Chris Strachwitz also helped arrange gigs for Hopkins in the Bay Area, and Ed Pearl helped him get gigs, but neither was his full-time booking agent or manager. Hopkins had access to music business professionals and chose not to use them; he preferred to take care of his business himself, even if it meant making trips to the West Coast just to play at the Ash Grove.

Furthermore, people could not easily find Hopkins, even when they wanted to hire him. Folksinger Tim Williams worked with Hopkins in the 1960s and '70s: "I tried to book him one time and had three phone numbers for him in Houston, and they were all girlfriends. They were all women, and they were all pissed off at him. I could never track him down. The gig never did come together. It could be quite a chore if you called him from California to Texas, about '68. He had several phone numbers. You could leave messages for him."[82]

In 1967, Les Blank, a young filmmaker, convinced Lightnin' Hopkins to let him travel to Houston to shoot a film about him:

I was itching to do a film, tired of doing industrial films. [I] had gone to L.A. to do fiction, feature films. [I] had a strong interest in folk music . . . country music. Anything that came along to this club in Los Angeles called the Ash Grove. Lightnin' passed through there, and I was interested in what he was doing. One day I was watching the Lightnin' concert with my assistant, who had spent some time in Houston. He said he knew some people who knew John Lomax, Jr., who was close with Lightnin', and maybe he could help us do a film on Lightnin'. So, we went backstage and talked to Lightnin'. I showed him a film I did on Dizzy Gillespie . . . on the wall of his dressing room. He thought it was interesting. And [Lightnin'] was also interested that we had some money to pay him. My assistant had succeeded in borrowing $5,000 from his father to get a start in a film career. . . . we told Lightnin' that we had $5,000, and he said that would be just fine. We explained that we needed most of it to make the movie and could only pay him about a third of it. He accepted that $1,500. . . . I listened to all the Lightnin' albums I could get my hands on. Of course, we talked to John Lomax, Jr. He gave us a list of scenes he thought would be important to film. He would help set them up.[83]

Les Blank and his assistant, Skip Gerson, followed Hopkins. After one day of shooting, Blank realized that making the documentary was fraught with tension: "We were so eager to shoot, we spent all day shooting everything he did, and everything he said and sang and he got fed up with us and told us to go away and he wanted the rest of his money then and there."[84] The outtakes from Blank's film revealed the exchange:

> HOPKINS: Well I know I sat and did things I [was] supposed to do. Now I'm gonna ask when am I gonna get my next money? I supposed to get it. I supposed to done got it.
>
> SKIP GERSON: No. It's as soon as we're finished as soon, as we got all the stuff we need to get.
>
> HOPKINS: I give you so much. You can't get no more. I'm supposed to get my money because Saturday is two weeks. That's a hell of a long time for me and look what I done tonight . . . this is work. You got so god-damn much it ain't even funny. Things is in there I know you ain't gonna use. What the hell you gonna do with that?
>
> GERSON: Nothing.
>
> HOPKINS: That is true.
>
> GERSON: Absolutely nothing.[85]

Hopkins was accustomed to recording a set amount of songs for a set amount of money. He appeared on television shows, but that did not compare to a film crew following him around all day. Blank and Gerson finally worked out their problems with Hopkins. They "gave him a third [of the money] up front, a third halfway through filming, and a third when we were all wrapped up. Then after that [disagreement about money was settled], when we got back to being able to come over and shoot some more, we were extremely careful how long we stayed and how we pushed him."[86]

The film shoot lasted six weeks as Blank followed Hopkins: "It took a lot of false starts before I abandoned the usual documentary approach of having a narrator explaining the blues and Lightnin's place in its development. Instead, sequences are threaded together with stitches of feeling that move the film along much like the structure of music itself. With the exception of *Burden of Dreams*, all of my films since have been essentially narrator-less. And the film style tends to resemble the spirit of the music contained."[87] The final cut ran a little over forty minutes, showing Hopkins at a rodeo in Houston, playing at a barbeque, and hanging out in his apartment in Houston with his friend Billy Bizor. Some scenes reveal Hopkins back in Centerville, looking like a conquering hero as he greeted his old friends. Blank released the film in 1969, winning the Golden Hugo award at the 1968 Chicago Film Festival.

John Lomax, Jr., held a premiere at his house on Vanderbilt Street in Houston attended by Darryl Harris, Townes Van Zandt and his wife, and Hopkins and his girlfriend Antoinette. As Harris witnessed, Hopkins "tried to wheedle the Lomaxes out of this little piano they had. There was one of the scenes in the movie where he had a big thing of hair sticking out. You could tell he wasn't happy about that. He was vain. It was his first time to see it."[88] Les Blank also recalled that Hopkins did not like the scene where his hair was messy: "He said that he didn't want the scene with his hair messed up. And I told him that was the strongest scene we had. And that's the only scene we really had of him improvising and that we really wanted to keep it. He said very emphatically, 'Don't keep it.' I struggled with that, and finally I disobeyed his wishes and left it in."[89]

In October 1967, Hopkins played some of the most unusual gigs of his career. From the 13th through the 15th, the Straight Theatre, located at 1902 Haight Street in San Francisco, booked him. The poster for the performance advertised "environmental dance classes" with registration at eight p.m. and class at nine p.m. each night. The 1,500-seat theater adjoined a Masonic hall. In the summer of 1967, Reginald Williams and his partners spent $100,000 renovating the theater, adding a stage and a five-thousand-square-foot parquet dance floor that replaced twenty rows of seats. The owners secured all the necessary permits from the city except a dance permit. The police department controlled the dance permits and postponed several hearings. After their last appeal for their dance permit was turned down, the Straight called their events "dance classes" to stay within the law.

Kaleidoscope and Martha's Laundry joined Hopkins on the Straight Theatre bill. Kaleidoscope were "Arguably the most eclectic band of the psychedelic era," according to music journalist Richie Unterberger.[90] Founded by David Lindley and Chris Darrow in the mid-1960s, they took elements of Middle Eastern, folk, blues, and acid rock, melding a unique sound. Chester Crill, a member of Kaleidoscope, immersed himself in Hopkins's gigs:

The Straight Theatre was plop down in the middle of hippy-dippy Haight Street and was a large legitimate movie theatre where they had whacked out say, the first 50 rows, to make a dance floor when the movie theatre had closed. The city was not in a mood to allow another psychedelic rock show place . . . so they wouldn't give the Straight a license. To get around that, they hired some legal guys who advised [that] they open a dance instruction biz, and that was the official come-on. Between sets an "instructress" would come out for about 5–8 minutes and talk through learning some dance steps and then announce "Mr. Hopkins will now play and you can practice the steps I have just shown you" or just as offer, "This will be a free dance period so practice the steps you still have difficulty with etc."

I remember standing under the marquee looking up seeing our name over Lightnin's and thinking how unfair it seemed. We hadn't been a band for a year, and we got better billing (we sure weren't much of a draw then or ever). The Straight was only open the nights the Fillmore and Avalon weren't and frequently booked bands that had just finished a gig at one of them or was on its way to a weekend gig there. Anyway, this was when the greatest bills in rock history always seemed to have both a genuine blues player or jazz group or both with a rock band. Lightnin' was in great form. . . . I think Lightnin' got more people practicing their dance steps, if you don't count belly dancing, than us. When asked about drugs, he would always say "I bring it ins me not ons me." I still fondly remember this gig (and not too many others) for the good feelings and good music.[91]

After his San Francisco gigs, the Seattle Folklore Society, formed in the fall of 1966, booked Hopkins, notes Don Duncan: "Several folklore buffs formed a society here and ponied up $20 each. . . . Every few months, the society brings in . . . Negro blues men like Furry Lewis and Booker White and Jesse (Lone Cat) Fuller and the Rev. Gary Davis and Lightning Hopkins. Purists were open-mouthed when Lightning Hopkins, Texas based blues man, produced an electrified guitar. But Lightning was forgiven, 'Because his music was properly rooted down home.'"[92]

The Seattle Folklore Society booked Hopkins to play at Washington Hall on Saturday, October 22, 1967. The *Seattle Post-Intelligencer* ran a short preview for the gig:

"A Down Home Blues Party" for 18 year olds and older; beer and wine will be served for those over 21; Saturday Oct. 22, 8:30–1 a.m. Washington Hall, 153 14th Ave. Admission $2. Starring Lightnin' Hopkins, composer, vocalist, guitar player with a style all his own, night club performer and recording artist; Mike Russo, who will play barrelhouse piano and perhaps some Leadbelly style 12 string guitar. Folksinging, blues, dancing and chitchat informal style.[93]

John Ullman, one of the founders of the Seattle Folklore Society, helped book the Washington Hall show:

Mojo Hand

[We] found a hall in the heart of the ghetto at 14th [near] Yessler [Street]. We decided that blues music needed a beer and wine bar and space to dance . . . we got about a thousand people. It was a very diverse crowd. There was a guy that showed up with pictures of Lightning's cousins in it. There was people who heard his music with their children and never expected to see him in their lifetime. We teamed up with a radio station before[hand]. There was some law on the books that you couldn't dance and serve alcohol. The cops came and said they were gonna shut us down. One of the people involved was an attorney. One of the police[men] saw my friend Phil Williams and his wife, who were also in an old-time bluegrass band, and he was a fan of theirs, and suddenly the light went on, and he said, "Why are we shutting these people down? All they do is just play good music." So, we asked them, "Who are you supposed to shut down?" They said they didn't know, but they'd go back and find out. Then at about 10:45 the cabaret commissioner came back and he said, "I'm shutting you down," and by then we were into the last song. I asked, "Why are you shutting us down?" He said, "There's beer and wine and people under twenty-one and over eighteen." He said, "The reason I'm shutting you down is because there's dancing." I said, "You can go upstairs and see there's no room for dancing." He went upstairs and came back and said, "I'm shutting you down." I said, "Why, there's no dancing." He said, "But it said there would be dancing in the newspaper."

It was a very exciting evening. Musically it was wonderful. Since then, people said what was really going on is that you tried to get a bass player and a drummer. I spoke to someone who was an officer in the musicians union who said . . . the hall needs to have five union musicians. But we couldn't afford that and let the whole thing go and some people thought that the musicians union was against you. An alternative explanation was that there was a peace march that day and all the police had new riot gear. But it was a peaceful peace march. So one of the explanations was that the police were all dressed up and had nowhere to go.[94]

Piano player and Eugene, Oregon, resident Mike Russo worked the Washington Hall date and several more gigs with Hopkins during this time period:

I was very good friends with Brownie McGhee, and that was back in the '50s. Somehow through Brownie I got to meet Sam. We hit it off right away. [We were] kind of an odd combination, a redneck and a black musician. We clicked, and there's not much difference between country music and the blues. I played piano in his style of music. We knew what each other was talking about when we played.

So every time he came to this part of the country, we traveled together. I'd open up the show for him, and then I'd stay on stage on piano, and he'd do his thing. I knew all his licks. He was a pretty eccentric musician. He didn't stick to a set of rules. . . . I just knew what he was going to do. It was just communication, it didn't have to do with notes. I started a long time ago. . . . I recorded with Fred McDowell. He was the same way. Most people couldn't play with him. He [Hopkins] just played how he felt. I never knew when he would quit. He usually played "Baby Please Don't Go," and he usually did an encore. . . . Lightning and I played together for about two years. Once in a while, he'd get a little too drunk and play the same song over and over again. We talked about cars, drank a lot of whiskey, and did all the bad things musicians do. We had an agreement about pay. We shared the take. I took a third . . . and he took two-thirds because he was the one on top of the billing. Last note we played we wanted our money. We always got paid.[95]

On December 1 and 2, 1967, Hopkins played the Vulcan Gas Company in Austin with Conqueroo, the house band, in support. The Vulcan, located on Congress Avenue, just south of the state capitol complex, opened in October 1967. Don Hyde cofounded the club: "I got together with Gary [Maxwell], who had been booking a couple of shows with Houston [White] under the name of Electric Grandmother. They were just renting out halls, but they didn't have a permanent spot. I found the building that the Vulcan went into at 316 Congress . . . and rented it. It was a permanent place that we could do shows every week. That was when the name changed from the Electric Grandmother to the Vulcan Gas Company."[96]

The authorities' negative response to the club intimates the views held by many in the local establishment. The conservative political climate in Texas resulted in increased attention on a nightclub that attracted longhaired youth and mixed-race bands. The Vulcan did not have a liquor license, and according to Hyde, did not want one because the owners thought it was more hassle than it was worth. Vulcan's lack of liquor did nothing to stop the unwarranted attention the club received.

Don Hyde describes the issues at stake:

Local police, sheriff's department, Texas Highway Department, military police from Fort Hood, and from Bergstrom [Air Force Base], FBI, . . . Food and Drug Administration, it was just ridiculous. Every week one agency or another would sweep through the club going through everyone's guitar case looking for a [marijuana] seed or stem. You could get sent up for ten or fifteen years for a seed in Texas at that time. When it opened up . . . the police had no idea that . . . that many people leaned in that direction. In those days, if your hair touched the top of your ear it was considered to be radical. When we opened up we had a thousand people.

The first or second weekend we had the [13th Floor] Elevators and it was sold out. The local authorities went crazy over it. They couldn't believe it. At one point, we couldn't buy ads in the *American Statesman* [the Austin daily paper]. The city council passed a proclamation against the club. A lot of people didn't like it that we were booking black and white acts on the same bill. People didn't like . . . that we were identified with the antiwar movement. We had guys picketing the club with machetes drawn. These were Vietnam vets. They stood there scowling as people bought tickets, and the police didn't do anything about it. They thought it was funny. The establishment was hysterical about it.[97]

"One of the first acts that I booked in was Lightnin' Hopkins," Jim Franklin adds. "I always tried to get Mance [Lipscomb] to be on the same bill with Lightnin' Hopkins, and he wouldn't ever do it. Mance really didn't like him. He flat-out said that he wouldn't be on the same bill with Lightnin'. . . . We had a kind of policy, an agreement among us at the Vulcan, to book as many of the old blues players as possible, while they were still available."[98]

Franklin had to find Hopkins first: "I went down to Houston with Houston White, who was one of the owners of the Vulcan, to contact Lightnin'. And we knew where to go. I don't know how Houston knew who his contacts were. We went down to Dowling Street . . . there was this one bar there. Lightnin' used to hold court there, every day sitting in his car parked out front. We did the first contract . . . he's sitting in the driver's seat and Houston's kind of kneeling down outside the driver's window, negotiating the deal. He agreed to play. When he came down for the show, he brought Billy Bizor, his cousin, who played harmonica, and another cousin played drums."[99]

The first night of Hopkins's initial two-night stand at the Vulcan veered near disaster, according to Franklin: "He starts into a really keen set and the drummer's drunk. Lightning would start a song, and he would stop it right at the beginning. It was embarrassing. He launched into ["Mr. Charlie"] and told a really great lead story and when the song starts, the drummer was off. So, Lightning had to stop that one and start again. . . . the next night they were sober and dressed. The second night Lightning rescued his reputation because it came off good."[100]

Added Hyde:

We always booked him with an electronic band. We didn't book him with an acoustic act. Our house bands, Johnny Winter, Conqueroo, Shiva's Headband, would gauge their set to what was on the show. All those house acts at the Vulcan could kind of bring it down a notch when somebody like Mance or Lightnin' Hopkins or John Lee Hooker were playing, and the audience didn't have a problem with it at all. We always gave the older blues guy the headline on the show. [Hopkins] was a rascal. He didn't go out of his way to be friendly. You could get along with him. He was fairly guarded most of the time. He never stood us up for a show. He showed up when he was supposed to, very professional. He didn't mix with the backup players that much. Some guys like John Lee Hooker or Jimmy Reed or Big Joe [Williams] would mix with the other musicians a lot and go out to dinner with them and hang with them. Lightnin' was standoffish, didn't get real social with them."[101]

Chris Strachwitz recorded Hopkins in his apartment in Houston on December 18, 1967. Arhoolie released the results on the *Texas Blues Man* album, an optimum performance for his trusted friend Strachwitz. Pete Welding wrote in *Down Beat*, "Here Hopkins is in fine form, doubtless as a result of the rapport producer Chris Strachwitz has with him. The performances are relaxed, full of restrained excitement, and stamped with the authority of a master."[102] Four of the ten songs on the record dealt with African American issues. Hopkins had every reason to have the conditions of black citizens on his mind.

Earlier that year when Les Blank was shooting his movie, Hopkins related his own harassment by police in a small town near Houston:

Now you know why they put me in jail? Cuz I run up on a wreck that they was whooping a man. And I put on my brakes and it pull to the right. And here come a man running with a book, Tiny. I had a pair of shades on. He told me to put my hand on the car and I put them on the car. I had a pack of cigarettes in my pocket. He said keep 'em up there. I said yes sir. So he goes up there to take care of the other white boys up there and I'm the onliest

Negro in the bunch. He turn around and come back by me I take one hand down. Gonna get me a cigarette. He said I told you to keep your hands on the car. I said yes sir. He hit me and I ain't seen them shades since. Last thing I seen [was] them going up there. Big old Tiny he's as big as this house here. Then he take me and put handcuffs on me. And them white boys that was in there said, "Whatcha doing with this poor old Negro?" He said, "Look, man, take it out on me, he ain't done nothing but curb to the right." He said, "I don't give a damn. He's gonna curb to the left now." That's in Richmond, Rosenberg. I don't go down there anymore. They come to Houston and get me if they want. . . . You ain't gonna fool me down there no more.[103]

The songs Hopkins recorded that December day in his apartment span a century of racial issues: "Slavery" produced the defiant lines "Yes I would get my shotgun / And I wouldn't be a slave no more"; "I Would If I Could" evoked segregation; while "Tom Moore Blues," first recorded as the song "Tim Moore's Farm" for Gold Star Records in 1948, recalled the plantation era. The Strachwitz version sticks close to the original. "Bud Russell Blues" relates the story of the prison transfer agent and takes place in 1910 down on the Brazos River. Russell transferred prisoners in chains and delivered Leadbelly to the Sugarland prison farm in 1920.

Russell was known in Texas folk songs as "an evil spirit wandering the land, kidnapping men into slavery."[104] Hopkins's mentor Texas Alexander sang about Bud Russell in his "Penitentiary Moan Blues," recorded for Okeh Records in 1928. Hopkins continued the theme of defiance in "Bud Russell Blues," ending the song with:

> The next time the boss man hit me
> I'm gonna give him a big surprise
> I ain't joking neither

In "I Would If I Could," Hopkins explored segregation at movie theaters:

> I'm gonna take my baby
> We goin' the picture show
> I'm gonna make everyone get back
> Cause we gonna sit in the front row

Audiences' enthusiasm for Hopkins's performances throughout the rest of the 1960s did not wane or wilt. He capitalized on this popularity by keeping a full schedule, recording and gigging frequently, mixing nonchalantly with rock 'n' roll bands and folk enthusiasts, and tapping the frustrations of the uneasy era with topical songs placing racism back into a context of American history fraught with oppression, especially in the unrepentant South. Before the decade was over, he recorded material for dozens of albums, causing his overall LP material to dwarf the two-hundred-plus sides he recorded for the 78-rpm format from the late 1940s through the late 1950s.

E I G H T

It is a sin to be rich
You know that it's a low down shame to be poor
You know a rich man ain't got a chance to go to heaven
And a poor man got a hard way to go

LIGHTNIN' HOPKINS, 1972

DURING THE MID-1960S, psychedelic rock, influenced in part by the use, within hippie culture, of consciousness-altering substances such as LSD, mescaline, psilocybin, and marijuana, garnered attention as a distinct subgenre in an already fertile and progressive national music scene. Mixing elements of free-form jazz, Indian, and Middle Eastern music, some psychedelic bands employed Indian sitars and tablas with guitar effects from wah-wah pedals and heavy distortion to evoke fresh, trend-setting, youthful sounds exemplified by bands like the Grateful Dead, the Jefferson Airplane, Quicksilver Messenger Service, Moby Grape, and Big Brother and the Holding Company and tunes like the Electric Prunes' "I Had Too Much to Dream Last Night," the Byrds' "Eight Miles High," the Chambers Brothers' "Time Has Come Today," and "Season of the Witch" by Donovan.

Blues artists regularly shared bills with white psychedelic rock bands, fostering a cross-cultural pollination that moved in two directions. Chess Records took advantage of this opportunity to profit from the psychedelic crowd's exposure to blues acts like Muddy Waters and Howlin' Wolf—two of their most important artists. In 1968, Chess Records released Waters's new album *Electric Mud*, an attempt to appeal to a white audience. Chess added elements of psychedelia to Waters's electric blues material and brought in some Chicago jazz-rock players on the recording. Waters and his band rerecorded some of his classic songs like "I Just Want to Make Love to You," but this time abundant doses of wah-wah and fuzz guitar were added. This mixture of psychedelic rock with classic Chicago blues resulted in good sales, according to Marshall Chess, who claimed to have sold 150,000 to 200,000 copies of *Electric Mud*,[1] which became Waters's first album to appear on the *Billboard* and *Cash Box* record charts. However, according to Waters's biographer Peter Gordon, the record attracted bad reviews in America. Even Waters himself dished out harsh comments: "That *Electric Mud* record I did, that one was dogshit. They said, 'This can't be Muddy Waters with all this shit going on—all this wow-wow and fuzztone.'"[2]

In 1969, Chess followed up by adding psychedelic sounds to the style of Howlin' Wolf on *This Is Howling Wolf's New Album*, subtitled: *He doesn't like it. He didn't like his electric guitar at first either*. The subtitle text amounts to a crass marketing device. Chess repeated the formula used with Waters by including some of the same sidemen. Moreover, the producer drowned Wolf's classic Chicago blues songs in heavily wah-wahed guitar, electric saxophone, and flute, which did little to enhance Wolf's authentic blues music. During the recording sessions, Wolf told Chess records cofounder Phil Chess, "Why don't you take those wah-wahs and all that other shit and go throw it off in the lake."[3] As with Waters's record, the critics did not approve. Unlike Waters's *Electric Mud*, though, Wolf's record quickly became a sales dud.

Hopkins experienced his own commingling of the blues and psychedelic rock in the studio. In the late 1960s, Hopkins became associated with the Houston-headquartered International Artists record label. In February 1968, he entered the studio with two members of the leading Texas psychedelic rock band, the 13th Floor Elevators. Thanks to Hopkins's producer, the results were not as offensive to artists or critics as the sessions of Muddy Waters or Howling Wolf. In fact, basically, Hopkins's attempts resulted in little more than another record of his own ilk, but with white sidemen from a psychedelic Texas band backing him.

Entrepreneur Fred Carroll founded International Artists (IA) in Houston in 1965. His first release was a single by the Coastliners, a band from Baytown, an industrial city twenty-seven miles east of Houston, in October 1965. The Coastliners single "Alright" did not chart well, and Carroll sold his label to Bill Dillard, a Houston attorney. Dillard then formed the International Artists Corporation with Noble Ginther (his law firm partner), Ken Skinner, and Lester Martin as principals.[4]

The newly reconstituted IA released five more singles that also flopped. Its sixth try, the 13th Floor Elevators single "You're Gonna Miss Me," garnered some attention, and business started to progress for the label. The Elevators' single reached number 55 on the *Billboard* magazine charts and also landed the band on Dick Clark's television show *American Bandstand*. Due to the success of the Elevators, the IA principals hired Lelan Rogers, brother of country pop artist Kenny Rogers, away from his home in Los Angeles to work on production and promotion.[5] In November 1966, the label followed up the Elevators' "You're Gonna Miss Me" single with their debut album, *The Psychedelic Sounds of the 13th Floor Elevators*. IA signed more bands and issued more albums in the psychedelic vein. IA followed the Elevators' first LP with Houston psychedelic band Red Crayola's *Parable of the Arable Land* (1967), Houston band Lost and Found's *Everybody's Here* (1967), and the *Power Plant* album by Austin band Golden Dawn in early 1968. The IA releases illustrate Houston's healthy and growing psychedelic scene.

How Hopkins came to record an album for the International Artists label in February 1968 is fairly well known, but many of the details about the recording session are not as easy to determine. Mansel Rubenstein operated a business in Hopkins's neighborhood on Dowling Street and struck up a relationship with Hopkins. Rubenstein first became acquainted with Hopkins when the bluesman pawned his guitar at Mansel's Loan Office, a pawnshop Rubenstein owned near Hadley and Dowling Streets, behind Rubenstein's Department Store, also located on Dowling. As Rubenstein recalls, Hopkins was well known in the neighborhood and many locals kowtowed to him, partly due to Hopkins's star quality and everyday sense of lyricism—making vivid oral poetry from the sundry qualities of life.[6]

Although Rubenstein claimed that Hopkins did not trust white people, somehow Rubenstein was exempted from Hopkins's distrust, so he sometimes acted as a go-between for Hopkins and those who wanted to do business with him. Rubenstein informed IA producer Lelan Rogers of Hopkins's availability, and Rogers immediately took up the offer.[7] By 1968, International Artists owned a major interest in the former Gold Star Studios facility, so this is where Hopkins recorded.[8] He previously recorded at the studio, now christened International Artists Studios, while under contract with Prestige Records and other companies. After Rubenstein's initial suggestion and Rogers's acceptance, the sessions that yielded *Free Form Patterns* were soon submerged in a haze of psychedelic drugs and cheap booze; thus, they are barely recalled by players after four decades. For example, the authors of *House of Hits: The Story of Houston's Gold Star/SugarHill Recording Studios* claim in their book, cowritten by engineer Jim Duff, that Johnny Winter was the only white musician who participated in Hopkins's International Artists recording sessions. Winter, however, unequivocally denies that he had ever recorded with Hopkins.[9]

Other myths and errors regarding the Hopkins *Free Form Patterns* sessions are fairly easily dispelled. The songs "Fox Chase" and "Baby Child" are cocredited to Billy Bizor and Mansel Rubenstein, but Rubenstein denied having any role in composing them.[10] The liner notes also include a claim by Hopkins that he "played a command performance for the Queen of England," but there is no proof that ever happened. More likely, Hopkins's claim reflects self-mythologizing. In 1964, Hopkins toured England with the American Folk Blues Festival, but no evidence suggests the tour included a performance for Queen Elizabeth.

Danny Thomas, the drummer for the 13th Floor Elevators when Hopkins recorded his IA album, explains that Lelan Rogers arranged Hopkins's recording for IA: "Everyone knew already that Lightning was available because he would play at the same clubs we did . . . there was always a shared billing with the rock musicians. So there's already camaraderie in place. So it's just a natural conclusion that Lelan came to get Lightning [and] to persuade him to come in there and put some songs on tape. So he was paid a cash amount just to come in and record. . . . So Lelan said would you guys like to play with him?"[11]

Rubinstein corroborated Thomas's memory of the cash payment, saying Hopkins earned one thousand dollars to make the record.[12] Meanwhile, Rogers posits, "Lightnin' had a rule of thumb he worked by, and that was you don't pay him any royalties . . . you have all the publishing, you have everything and you give him $1,000 per song, that's it."[13] Hopkins likely received one thousand dollars for the entire session, one can presume, not for each song.

Thomas narrates how bass player Duke Davis came to join the Elevators and the Hopkins sessions: "[Bassist] Danny Galindo left the Elevators and went to play with Steve Ray Vaughan's older brother [Jimmie Lee] in the [band] the Storm in Austin. That's why Duke [Davis] was called in to play bass with me. It was basically Lelan seizing the day. He had a real good ear for sincerity in music. He saw that in Lightning and he wanted to get that on tape." One thing has remained stuck in Thomas's mind—Billy Bizor's poverty at the time they made Free Form Patterns: "Lightning came by and picked me up. He drove a fancy expensive . . . I think it was a Lincoln or a Cadillac. I just thought that was wonderful. He was just as dapper as a gentleman could be, coat and tie and a hat and sunglasses. We went over in the neighborhood where Billy Bizor lived . . . in a pretty rundown shack in one room. We went in there and there was a cot and a sink hanging off the wall. I think there was one common bathroom for everyone that lived in the house. Billy Bizor was the harmonica player. We stopped on the way at the package store and [Hopkins] picked up a pint of bourbon and stuck it in his pocket. And Duke was there and we sat down and recorded the first four songs."[14]

Duke Davis has rich memories of the Hopkins recording sessions:

I was with the Elevators. . . . we were working on the [Elevators'] *Bull of the Woods* album, and Lelan kind of pulled the plug on it. And [Lelan] came in and said we wanted to do this project with Lightning . . . and [did] I want to play on it? And of course we just jumped at the chance. . . . Lightning was very unique, he'd be playing sixteen or thirty-two blues bar pattern and all of a sudden there'd be a bar missing, [as] if it was a big train wreck or something. And rather than say, "It goes like this," he'd say, "Let's just try another one." I know we sat there for a couple of days and we must have recorded like fifty songs. . . . We never did anything twice. . . . It was a pretty relaxed thing. He'd come in and I guess Billy Bizor was his harmonica player and Elmore [Nixon] his piano player. The three of them had played together quite a bit. So, Lightning just used the same approach with Danny and I as with those guys, let's just play. He pulled out a bottle of homemade moonshine. He said we're gonna drink something first. We had a few belts of that. Danny [Thomas] and I were probably psychedelicized. We had a great time. It was just one of those magical things."[15]

IA issued the record with two different covers. The first featured a painting of Hopkins from the shoulder up in his ever-present sunglasses and wearing a large white cowboy hat in front of a red background. As Lelan Rogers tells, "After I left IA they changed the Lightnin' record cover design that had been done by Guy Clark. It was beautiful."[16] The second cover, obviously aimed at the psychedelic crowd, featured the words Freeform Patterns in white-and-red letters on a black background encircling Hopkins's name, which was within an oval with the letters in red, white, and blue. The second jacket hinted at psychedelic contents to be found within, but anyone who bought the record hoping for a mix of psychedelic rock and blues based on the artwork and Elevators sidemen would have been disappointed.

Despite the psychedelic accompaniment, *Free Form Patterns* is not inundated with special effects like the Waters and Wolf records. Chess Records intentionally added these elements to their artists' records in a purposeful attempt to attract youthful white buyers. In Hopkins's case, when Lelan Rogers got the opportunity to record Hopkins, he simply used the players already working in the studio at that time. Rogers made no attempts to psychedelicize or compromise Hopkins.

"Mr. Charlie," captured for the first time in New York City in 1960 for Bobby Robinson's Fire label, starts the record. This version is not inventive or unique, just revisited in a Houston studio eight years later. "Fox Chase," the only harmonica instrumental, features rather tame harmonica riffing that pushes up-tempo rhythms but remains stubbornly standard. "Mr. Ditta's Grocery Store" aims to capture Houston in a narrative microcosm, picturing a local corner store and offering up double entendres about "meat," both as commodity and sexual favor, to satisfy a customer who is "hungry." The psychedelic edges are muted as the tongue-in-cheek shotgun-shack blues ripples. "Got Her Letter This Morning" also tames down the psychedelia to the point of near absence, while the closer—the fiery "Mini Skirt"—is a dirty and raw tale of women's wear in the era of changing fashions. Spontaneous, upbeat, and honest, it completes the record's arc. To the casual listener, these tracks match most tracks Hopkins recorded that decade for power and consistency, and their narrative framework is similar, too.

After the recording sessions, Hopkins began to use Davis and Thomas to back him at local gigs, while Mason Romans, who worked for International Artists booking and road-managing bands, booked Hopkins as well, in addition to the 13th Floor Elevators, Bubble Puppy, the Moving Sidewalks, and ZZ Top: "A fella named Ray Rush managed some bands, did a lot of mixing. He mentioned Lightning Hopkins and told me how to get in touch. . . . a fellow named Mansel Rubenstein had a dry goods store on Dowling [Street], and that was the only way to get in touch with Lightning. I went and visited Mansel—very nice fellow. He got in touch with Lightning, and Lightning and I met there at the dry goods store. We visited for a while. After that, every time I had an opportunity to book Lightning I had to call Mansel, and Mansel would call Lightning, and I would tell him what time I would pick him up and take him to the gig. I always picked him up and dropped him off at Mansel's Dry Goods store. He was living off Dowling Street somewhere."[17]

As Romans attests, Hopkins was professional and hassle-free. In exchange for doing all the legwork, he took a 10–15 percent commission from Hopkins's guaranteed payment: "[Hopkins was] extremely easy to work with. He was very warm, very friendly. With Lightning it's strictly a guarantee [as opposed to a percentage of the take at the door]. Never had any trouble getting him paid. I got anywhere from one hundred to two hundred dollars for Lightning. He always wanted a little pint of whiskey. He kept it in his coat pocket. When he got ready to take a little snort it didn't matter where he was playing, he took a little snort. Duke was always up there. They would sit in with Lightning and would jam. I collected money and gave him the money. I never tried to chisel him. I considered it an honor to book a legend. [I] booked him into white clubs, no juke joints or anything like that. Those were where he was extremely popular at that time. I booked him at Love Street Light Circus several times."[18]

During the mid-to-late 1960s, several Houston bands became popular on a regional, national, and international basis and used these burgeoning clubs as a springboard for their careers. Of the many Houston clubs of this era, perhaps the scene at the Love Street Light Circus Feel Good Machine most closely resembled that of the vaunted psychedelic venues in San Francisco like the Avalon Ballroom, the Winterland Ballroom, and the Fillmore Auditorium. Johnny Winter described the Love Street Light Circus atmosphere as a combination of light show, dancing girls, and hippies."[19]

The Love Street Light Circus Feel Good Machine opened at 1019 Commerce Street in downtown Houston on June 3, 1967. Lasting about three years, it hosted IA artists Red Krayola (originally Red Crayola) and the 13th Floor Elevators, plus Shiva's Headband, Bubble Puppy, Johnny Winter, Fever Tree, and ZZ Top precursor bands the Moving Sidewalks and American Blues. On July 4 and 5, 1969, ZZ Top played their first gigs at Light Street. "The audiences sat at tables or in the Zonk-Out, a series of cushions with back rests."[20] David Adickes started Love Street and acted as the manager and light show projectionist for the crowds numbering up to three hundred.[21]

After the *Free Form Patterns* sessions, Hopkins worked some dates at Love Street with Davis and Thomas backing him on bass and drums.[22] "We started doing live gigs with him. [On the gigs] we'd make pocket change, forty or fifty bucks. We were working for drugs mainly. Danny and I were just thrilled to play with him," Davis says.[23] Thomas goes even further: "Lightning represented the first pure authentic warm-blooded human being that us white musicians could spend time with on a day-to-day basis and get the real information, the authentic licks from, the way that they were handed down in the . . . black culture. There were a whole bunch of great white musicians that have now become famous in Houston that lined up that tried to get with Lightning . . . who were trying to learn the music theory to make up what was called . . . the blues."[24]

Romans verifies the multiculturalism of the club as well: "One time . . . I booked Flatt and Scruggs, Lightning, the 13th Floor Elevators, and a lesser band at Love Street on a Sunday afternoon. Lightning was so popular he stole the show from Flatt and Scruggs."[25] The duo had been performing together as a bluegrass act since 1948 and issued an unbroken streak of top 40 country singles that ran from the summer of 1959 through 1968, but they could not compete with Hopkins's homegrown popularity.

Richard and Steve Ames of Ames Productions operated the Catacombs, another club where young white Houston musicians fell under Hopkins's influence. It opened in 1966, with Bob Cope as the general manager, with a "'Class C' license allowing 15–20 year olds to enter, thus no booze allowed. We also had at least four Houston Police Department officers on hand during operating hours."[26] According to Stephen Hammond, a high school student who worked there, the club was popular from the start with teens: "This was a time of transition from popular 'dance' music to concert-style. Initially, 'the skate,' the 'boog-a-loo,' and other dance forms were 'in.'"[27] The Grateful Dead, the Mothers of Invention, and the Jeff Beck Group played their first Houston shows there. Romans remembered booking Hopkins into the Catacombs. "The manager of the club did not want me to go in, he said it's strictly teenagers. I said I wanted to go in and watch Lightning. I sat down in the front row, and in walks Billy Gibbons. He sat there and was totally carried away with Lightning and the blues. I thought that [Hopkins's performance] was quite an influence on Billy in his later years. I would like to think I was influential in crossing the different types of music and making them blend. I think putting him in Love Street Light Circus or the Catacombs, the people that came there, particularly Love Street, were interested in, or had a broad enough mind to, listen to different types of music."[28]

Billy Gibbons and his ZZ Top bandmates, bassist Dusty Hill and drummer Frank Beard, later sold millions of records playing Texas-slanted, blues-based boogie. Such clubs incubated a meeting ground between artists of different races, age groups, and economic situations. Raised in the wealthy Tanglewood area of Houston, Gibbons learned about black music through his black maid's daughter, Little Stella, so he had a good grounding in Little Richard, Jimmy Reed, B. B. King, and others by the time he saw Lightnin' Hopkins.[29] Guitar player Rocky Hill, Dusty Hill's older brother and bandmate in American Blues, played with Hopkins during the late 1960s. When Hill's band American Blues dissolved and the remains evolved into ZZ Top, he started playing bass with Hopkins. Hill recalled, "Dusty wanted to play rock 'n' roll. . . . [Dusty] wanted to make some money. And he did. . . . I wanted to play some blues and I did." On his decision to work with Hopkins, Hill said, "It was a great idea, but bad financially."[30] Uncle John Turner remembered, "Rocky did a volunteer apprenticeship. Rocky attached himself to Lightnin'. Rocky served Lightnin' as his boy, carried his guitar, drove him around. Carried his amp, probably sometimes played a little bass."[31]

Rocky Hill introduced Rex Bell to Hopkins: "First time I met Lightnin' was a fellow named Rocky Hill. He was playing with Lightnin' and it was just about the time ZZ Top took off and Rocky had all these other things. So Rocky was playing bass with Lightnin' and he asked me if I wanted to meet Lightnin' and maybe become his bass player. So I went up and met Lightnin' and he took me to one of his black clubs. This was back in 1968, when you really couldn't go in any black areas. Since I was the bass player it was cool. Rocky went on [to other things]."[32]

Bell ran the Old Quarter, a club at 1402 Congress in downtown Houston, which existed from 1969 to 1974 and served beer, wine, setups, and free popcorn to small crowds of about sixty people. He advertised it as "overlooking skid row."[33] Darryl Harris remembers the downscale neighborhood: "Around the corner was a liquor store. The next door down was this really, really downscale hotel, the hotel where the desk clerk had a club hanging on the wall. It [the Old Quarter] was very soulful. It was an amazingly mixed crowd in there."[34] Texas singer/songwriter Vince Bell honed his craft there: "The Old Quarter was a run-down, two-story stucco-over-brick blockhouse of a building with iron bars across the broken, clouded windows. The entrance was ten-foot-high bar doors that could not be locked without a chain and a stout two-by-four."[35] Dale Soffar, one of Bell's partners, adds: "It had those brick walls where the plaster was coming off in places, brick floors and tables that were old sewing machines with the heads off. We had people who would come from the opera at Jones Hall—they'd be in suits and tuxedos sitting there next to hippies."[36]

Houston folksinger Don Sanders worked at the Old Quarter for several years: "The Old Quarter was a rougher venue. I was the MC there for several years, so I would work there . . . introducing the acts and playing a few songs in between. That was my gig. More or less if you looked across the parking lots you could see the [Harris County] jail. There were still residence hotels downtown at that point. So, a bunch of the winos and beeros still hung out in bars down on Congress. Mance, Lightnin' playing there [and] Juke Boy [Bonner]. Everyone passed the hat, and you had a one- or two-dollar cover charge on weekends to keep out the drunkest of the drunk. That was the basic idea."[37]

Sanders adds, "[The] Allman [Brothers] early on, when they were touring they would come and headquarter themselves at a hotel and tour out from here. On their off nights Duane and Jai Johnny [Jaimoe Johanson] would come in and jam. That's actually how I learned to play slide up close. The Old Quarter was tiny . . . and the bar took up most of one side and at the time they had a piano on top of the bar where Big Walter Price would play. Rocky [Hill] and Dusty [Hill] would play there. Dusty and Frank [Beard] would come in. Rocky and Dusty at that time had a band called American Blues, dyed their hair blue, and played in a joint on the [nearby Market] Square called the Cellar. Johnny Winter would come in and play."[38]

Rex Bell explained Hopkins's involvement: "I got to know Lightnin' well enough to ask him to play at my club. . . . whenever I hired Lightnin', I'd hire a bartender and a drummer, and I'd play bass. That's how I got in to play with Lightnin' cuz I'd hire him. He didn't really associate with white people all that much." Hopkins did, however, associate with the people who paid to see him, according to Bell: "He liked to come out between sets and talk. Sometimes at the Old Quarter he'd just stay on stage. He must have had a bladder made out of titanium. He would just stay on stage. That place was so small and so crowded. People would just talk to him so he'd just sit there and talk to them. He'd occasionally break but sometimes he wouldn't. He mainly drank whiskey, straight out of the bottle onstage."[39]

Bell remembers how he and his co-owner used to treat Hopkins like a star: "We used to go pick up Lightnin' in [a] Cadillac limousine, he'd have us stop in this alleyway and these guys would sell whiskey. It was after hours. I don't know why he would do that. He could get liquor anywhere. He just liked pulling up in his limousine. He would be in the back and he'd have couple of white guys driving. We'd bring him back to the Third Ward. He had a sense of drama. . . . He was a star. He was like being with royalty . . . being with Elvis. . . . [He] had this magic personality, he could talk to people, he could talk to the audience."[40]

Michael Point also chauffeured Hopkins: "Hopkins was . . . my employer in the early '70s when my shiny semi-new Pontiac, with me in the chauffeur's seat, was his usual means of transportation to his Houston gigs. It regularly took us four or five hours to get from his house to the venue, despite a geographic proximity of no more than a few dozen blocks, since we had to make a triumphant tour of the bars on Dowling Street before even thinking about heading toward the club. It was a labor of love on my part, although I actually did get paid a couple of times, and while it was occasionally more of a masochistic situation than I desired, it still ranks up at the top of my list of memorable musical experiences."[41]

Hopkins did not always use young white rock musicians to back him for his Houston gigs during this time period. In the *Washington Post*, Harry Summerall vividly sketched his first encounter with Hopkins:

> It was in a steamy, smoky Houston nightclub, in 1968, that I met the legendary Lightnin' Hopkins. He was my hero, or rather, the hero of my heroes, the Rolling Stones. . . . Swept up in the blues craze of the late '60s, he had become a mythic figure and I was awed. But I was quickly brought down to earth. He was sprawled across a Naugahyde couch in the dank dressing

room, a bottle of liquor at his side. Wearing a new straw cowboy hat and chomping on a soggy cigar, he rasped out ribald jokes for his ancient sidemen. There were fleeting images of gold-capped, tobacco-stained grins and lined faces etched out by the years and, yes, the blues. There were cackling laughs, deep swigs from paper cups and a feeling of warm camaraderie. They weren't myths or legends—just three feisty old men out to have a good time. Later that night, with a harmonica, a beat-up Gibson guitar and Hopkins' rambling vocals, they made music that curled my toes.[42]

Billy Bizor likely played the harmonica.

Summerall's account typifies how many young white fans tended to imagine Hopkins as a cultural artifact to be admired from afar. Often, however, when they met him or experienced his music in person, they realized how his music authentically mirrored his vexing and often bitter experience in American culture. To many middle-class white youth, such African American narratives, memories, and insights, particularly from someone of Hopkins's generation, were totally foreign and unknown. Although Hopkins was a blues singer by trade, in reality, he acted as a cultural ambassador and an educator whose music taught generations of listeners what being born black in East Texas near the turn of the twentieth century meant.

Whether in youth clubs such as the Catacombs or psychedelic hippie joints like Love Street Light Circus, Hopkins preached the African American experience, in the form of his blues songs, which transcended momentary "highs." For many teenagers, the drugs, alcohol, and need to satisfy hormonal desires may have been more important than the musical entertainment, but the history that Hopkins's songs and stage patter embodied was fertile and long-lasting.

In addition to influencing aspiring young white musicians at a variety of hometown venues, Hopkins continued to get bookings at large festivals. He was invited to the 1968 Festival of American Folklife held on the mall in Washington, DC. The festival, presented by the Smithsonian Institution, showcased some aspects of American cultural roots through demonstrations and performances. The Institute of Texan Cultures presented a full program including craft makers, foods, and musicians such as Mance Lipscomb, Robert Shaw, the Baca Band, and the Solomon Family Band.[43]

An unissued recording of Hopkins's performance on Sunday, July 7, survives in the Folklife Archive. The hyperbole the MC used while introducing Hopkins indicates the stature he was accorded at this stage of his career: "One of the greatest singers America has ever produced, one of the greatest artists who have come forth and naturally he was born in Texas. He's one of the greatest innovators of folk blues all of you know him and I'm not going to dwell at length . . . but here he is, the greatest of them all, Lightnin' Hopkins."[44]

Hopkins told the crowd about the trouble he experienced on his flight to Washington, DC: "Ladies and gentlemens, I'm kinda shook up from my ride. I was on the plane this mornin' and one of the motors went out and you know about how I feel. But here's a little song I'll sing to you that's where I went to Louisiana, got me a mojo hand. Got me a wife too." Then he sang "Mojo Hand" accompanied by his acoustic guitar. He followed it with "Trouble in Mind." The crowd on the mall enthusiastically responded, "We can hear you Sam," to which Hopkins said, "Well I hope so. This little song is 'Baby Please Don't Go.'"[45]

Hopkins was then joined by his band, which included, on harmonica, Billy Bizor, who introduced himself: "Hello ladies and gentlemen, now this is the one and only Billy Bizor harmonica blower for the Lightnin' Hopkins band, the little tune you're about to hear is the 'Harmonica Jump,' I'm going to try and do the best I can because I'm still scared from this morning as the plane went out on us. I was pretty high up there. In case I know how to do it, I'd have went down and got another motor and brought it back, so help us the good Lord fixed it so we're here now. And the pleasure is all mine, we'll try and sock it to you, you better believe it."[46]

Hopkins closed out 1968 by spending most of December in the Bay Area. He worked a weekend at the Overcast in San Francisco, another weekend at the New Orleans House in Berkeley, and several weekends at Mandrake's in Berkeley. In the spring of 1969, Hopkins worked some Texas dates with John Lomax, Jr., including East Texas State University's Student Center Ballroom in Commerce on March 6, followed by two nights at the Dallas Museum of Fine Arts, on March 7 and 8.

Hopkins stayed at the home of singer Lu Mitchell for the museum gigs. According to Mitchell, people decided that Hopkins should stay with her because they were afraid if he got out of their sight he would end up in a bar in Deep Ellum and not make the gigs: "While at our home Lightnin' regaled us with stories of his musical career. He said that in Germany the fans grabbed at him and in many cases cut off parts of his tie and shirt for souvenirs. He never understood this. He was leery of promoters who wanted use him to make money for themselves. He wore alligator shoes, and while at the house he wore a hair net. Delightful man."[47]

Sometime in the spring of 1969, Hopkins worked a session in Los Angeles for Vault Records that was issued as *California Mudslide (and Earthquake)*. Bruce Bromberg worked for California/Merit Record Distributors when the opportunity to record Hopkins developed: "One day my boss comes by and he says, 'Hey you know Lightnin' is coming to town and let's make a record . . . and you could produce it.' I said, 'I don't know Jack [Lewerke, Vault Records president]. Lightnin' sure has made a lot of records.' What an idiot, here I was getting an opportunity to record Lightnin' Hopkins. Anyways it turned out that we were gonna do it."[48] Hopkins's deal with Vault included an option to record follow-up material.

Bromberg discloses, "I pointed out to him that time [we had met] at Long Gone's, and did he remember it? He kind of grunted at me, didn't tell me he did or he didn't. The day of the session . . . we had a big mudslide and he wrote a song about it."[49] In the liner notes to a reissued version of the album, Bromberg wrote, "The session had quite a party atmosphere, which made me nervous, but didn't seem to faze Lightnin' at all."[50]

According to Bromberg, the financial arrangements for the session followed a familiar pattern: "Give Lightnin' a hundred bucks, and he'd go sing a song. Give him another hundred bucks and he'd go sing another song. Yeah, that's how he wanted to do it. That's how we did it. There were contracts, because I remember seeing them. I'm sure there was some kind of recording contract. I think he signed a song contract for every song."[51]

Louisiana native Tony Joe White was a Monument Records recording artist promoting his new record *Polk Salad Annie* in Los Angeles when Hopkins cut the session for Vault. According to Bromberg, "Tony's all-time favorite artist on the earth was Lightnin' Hopkins. So he got all excited and we said come on. So we did the session at night. [Hopkins] would record a song and then I'd say, I was very familiar with his repertoire, let's do one like that one, let's do one like this one. 'Santa Fe Blues' was one I really liked. It was on RPM, so he did a 'New Santa Fe Blues.' And he did some comparable ones."[52]

Though Hopkins recorded the record solo, Bromberg finally "talked him into one extra one where I had to play organ. It was fun. I don't know that it was the best Lightnin' record, but it was a good one and it was a big thrill for me. So after that, Tony and Lightnin' jammed. Alas Lightnin' would not let us record that. That would have been good. At the end of the session Tony wanted to play with Lightnin', so they did. Tony was one of the few honkies that could play the blues. He had the feel of it. The session was three or four hours."[53]

Bromberg was less than completely happy with the consistency and quality of the material. "And I'm ashamed to say," he recalled, "that later I tried to make a single of one of his songs, and I overdubbed a bass and drums on it. [We had] about an 80 percent success there. Even though his guitar was really good on some levels, when you have a single artist and you try to overdub, it's more difficult than you think. Anyway the single got some airplay."[54] Vault released "Easy on Your Heels" as a single, and Bromberg later wrote that it "got played on the local R&B station KGFJ and sold some records."[55]

Hopkins's releases were still so plentiful that even reviewers had difficulty keeping track of them. Mike Leadbitter, writing about *California Mudslide (and Earthquake)* and *That's My Story* in *Blues Unlimited*, noted: "Man I can't keep up with all these albums by Sam! I'm beginning to get Hopkinstipation. All I can say is predictable, well-played blues from Lightnin'. This description fits both sets, but I'll take the one on Vault. . . . our man plays solo or with bass, and drums, then has a go on organ or piano. Thus we get a different and entertaining picture of a great man. He sounds well and happy and the selection is varied enough to warrant a recommendation to his many fans."[56]

Ron Brown, writing in the UK-based *Jazz Journal*, offered similar high praise for *California Mudslide (and Earthquake)*: "A lovely recent recording by Lightning . . . The electric guitar playing is assured and compelling, and Sam sounds deeply involved in his self-composed material, particularly the title track, Hopkins' graphic description of a West Coast disaster. . . . he has a lovely touch and extracts a superb tone from the piano; his noodling in the bass is especially nice. His organ playing is less adventurous, but is appropriately churchy on 'Jesus' and swings mightily on 'Los Angeles Boogie' . . . you can buy this one with confidence."[57]

While Hopkins was in Los Angeles, he worked a benefit for the Ash Grove at the Europa Theater on May 2 and 3, 1969. The Ash Grove burned down on April 23.[58] The owner, Ed Pearl, remembered:

The first fire was in 1969, I think in February. . . . A number of the artists gathered together to do a benefit for the Ash Grove to reopen. . . . The fire was just awful and Lightning was supposed to play at the Ash Grove the week after it burned down. . . . I had started it with a baby grand piano that was given to me for a total bargain rate. Anyway it burned up. It was still standing there when Lightning came there and played on it. I think I was hoping that I could discover a recording because I remember putting a tape on it. Anyway he got done playing and walked away and the whole thing collapsed. It was really prophetic. Later on, a month or so later, this whole group of people artists . . . we called a press conference and amazing the press was there including television and everything. So they asked Roger McGuinn of the Byrds why he was doing this benefit and I swear I thought they [would] talk about this music or that music. Roger said I met my wife there. . . . And one after another every one of these young guys got up and said they had met their wives or girlfriends there. It was crazy. It wasn't political. But basically that's what the club meant to people: it really touched them personally.[59]

Right after the fire, the Ash Grove set up temporary headquarters at the Europa Theater on Beverly Boulevard.[60] Hopkins's cousin Albert Collins and his Vault Records label mate Elaine Brown joined him on the bill for shows on May 2 and 3. By now, Collins's career was thriving. In 1962, his single "Frosty" sold a million copies, but through most of the 1960s he had not been able to make a living playing music.[61] Eventually, the blues revival tide swept him up in the person of Bob Hite, a member of the boogie blues band Canned Heat, who found Collins in Houston after Hopkins told him where Collins was playing.[62] Hite brought Collins to California and took him on tour with Canned Heat. With assistance from Hite, Imperial Records signed Collins and released three of his albums, and Collins gigged at the Fillmore West in San Francisco.

At the time of the Ash Grove benefit show, Elaine Brown was serving as the deputy minister of information for the Black Panther Party, which captured America's attention when Panther leader Bobby Seale led a group of armed demonstrators into the state capitol building in Sacramento, California, on May 2, 1967, to protest a proposed law to ban carrying guns in public. While they were at the state capitol, Seale read a statement, which said in part:

Black people have begged, prayed, petitioned, and everything else to get the racist power structure of America to right the wrongs which have been historically perpetrated against black people. All of these efforts have been answered by more repression, deceit and hypocrisy. . . . The Black Panther Party for Self Defense believes that the time has come for black people to arm themselves against this terror before it is too late.[63]

Vault Records released Brown's debut album *Seize the Time* in 1969. The Black Panther Party donated the proceeds of Brown's record to its breakfast program, which provided free food to low-income youth. Houston native Horace Tapscott backed her on the record of revolutionary songs. Bobby Seale later titled his biography *Seize the Time* as well. He and Huey Newton were admirers of Hopkins, as Seale noted in the book: "Huey and I and Weasel . . . were all sitting in the car one night. We decided we wanted to buy some records by T-Bone Walker, Lightnin' Hopkins and Howlin' Wolf, these downhome brothers."[64]

After the Ash Grove benefits, Hopkins worked Mandrake's in Berkeley from May 13 through 18 with the house band Shades of Joy in support.[65] Hopkins's booking was part of Mandrake's Spring Blues Festival, which included Albert Collins working the club for six nights before Hopkins and then John Lee Hooker following Hopkins for another six nights. Mandrake's was located at University Avenue and 10th and had operated since 1965 as a pool hall with occasional music bookings. Mary Moore became partner and music booker in the club in 1968. "It was a powerhouse club for just that short period of time" and "was the birthplace for a lot of bands," reports Country Joe McDonald.[66] According to her obituary, "Ms. Moore was longtime friends with Sonny Terry and Brownie McGhee, who always drew large crowds, as did John Lee Hooker, Muddy Waters, Lightnin' Hopkins," and others.[67]

Berkeley, home of the University of California's flagship campus, was a hotbed of activism in the 1960s. During Hopkins's residency at Mandrake's, the town erupted in a dispute over university-owned land that activists used as an informal park. The university had purchased the lot, a site of demolished apartment buildings, bounded by Dwight and Haste Streets just east of Telegraph Avenue, about a year previously and reportedly planned to build a parking lot on it. On Sunday, April 20, 1969, about two hundred people armed with rakes, hoses, and shovels descended on the block of land just south of campus and began landscaping the park. The activists christened the space "Power to the People Park."[68] Less than a week later, the university announced that it would construct an intramural playing field on the site.[69] By May 13, UC Chancellor Roger W. Heyns announced that the university would go ahead with its plans to make the disputed space into an intramural park and that it would fence off the land to reinforce its ownership and keep "unauthorized persons from the site."[70]

Heyns's statement heightened the tensions between the park activists and the university. Sim Van Der Ryn, a UC professor, who sat on the just-formed committee on housing and environment, said the university "didn't seem to be very interested in negotiations" about the lot.[71] On May 15, a noon rally and march to protest the university's seizure of People's Park turned violent when police opened fire into the crowd. According to the *Daily Californian*, fifty-eight people were hospitalized and thirty-five were shot, and there were twenty-five arrests on charges ranging from felony possession of a concealed weapon to misdemeanors for throwing rocks. Police wearing flak jackets used tear gas and shotguns on the crowd. By evening, over five hundred police from nine different departments walked the streets. At the request of the mayor and city manager, Governor Ronald Reagan issued an emergency regulation establishing a curfew that ran from 10:00 p.m. to 6:00 a.m. in the City of Berkeley. The National Guard walked the streets, and a helicopter circled the city blaring out the news of the curfew. The next day the *Berkeley Barb*'s headline blared "Pigs Shoot to Kill—Bystanders Gunned Down."[72]

The unrest on the Berkeley streets and campus made Hopkins uneasy. Carroll Peery, a friend of Hopkins, remembered, "At that time the campus was full of violence and noise because they had a serious problem with the government. It made him nervous because there were police everywhere. He didn't like it . . . he was always afraid of authority . . . he did not want to go anywhere near authority. . . . A lot of people, some of the black folks, thought he was an Uncle Tom because of his fear of authority. Younger people, they had no understanding of it."[73]

Hopkins, like many black men in America, had a legitimate reason to fear authority. He was raised in a time when blacks were lynched in town squares. Fifty years after a lynching in his hometown, white supremacy still dominated Houston. Less than two years before Hopkins went through this unrest in Berkeley, the Houston police terrorized hundreds of innocent college students in Hopkins's neighborhood by firing thousands of rounds into dormitories at Texas Southern University. Many black neighborhoods often seemed on the verge of exploding with racial unrest throughout the 1960s. Hopkins's fear of getting caught in the crossfire of police forces attempting to maintain racial, political, and social "order" in a chaotic time of civil right struggles was very real. Enduring the legacy of slavery in small-town East Texas and everyday life in the Deep South impacted Hopkins's behavior and psychological makeup. Thus, in 1969, despite the gains of the civil rights movement, Hopkins's desire to steer clear of authority was not unfounded paranoia, but, in fact, a sensible survival mechanism.

After the Mandrake's gigs, Hopkins recorded on May 20, 1969, for Arhoolie in Berkeley. Francis Clay accompanied him on drums, and some members of Earl Hooker's band, including Johnny "Big Moose" Walker, piano, Geno Scaggs, bass, Jeff Carp, harmonica, and Paul Asbell on guitar, recorded a few tracks. Asbell remembers the session: "The Earl Hooker band got brought into the studio. There was no way I would say no to playing with [Hopkins. It] was an afternoon thing, three or four songs. Funny as hell to watch. I found it really easy to follow him. He didn't really trust people he didn't know, but if you played with him . . . he was really nice to me. I think he was always looking to be ripped off, cuz that was his entire life. He was always assuming someone was always trying to get an edge. Not with Chris, but no matter who it was, Lightnin' was trying to run a game. I don't think he distrusted Chris as others. Chris was paying us."[74]

Walker, as Asbell relates, almost fell asleep during the session: "[A] funny, funny moment when Lightnin' was doing a couple songs unaccompanied, where I think he was his best. A number of us were in the control room watching him through the glass. Moose was at the piano but not playing. Lightnin' was making up one of his classic free association things, Moose was slowly falling asleep, and you could see him kind of leaning over and catch himself and get upright and then snooze off. We were watching it, knowing it was a great song taking place, and if Moose had just one time gotten too sleepy and didn't catch himself, he would have fallen over on the floor into a pile of mike stands and totally ruined the take."[75]

Francis Clay recorded on many of the songs during the May 20 session: "Most times he would just start them [the songs] off. Whatever was in his mind, what he felt, and we'd join in. If he didn't drink so much, some of them would have been better. The morning we got to the session everybody would be playing wrong so he'd make them sit out. A lot of them just ended up me and him. I think one time he just told me to lay out, and he'd do it all by himself. He was the show all by himself. He start out real mellow and everybody got along fine, and then the more whiskey was drunk, he'd start getting his prima donna attitude, and it would be more of a personal thing with him. If we couldn't feel what he felt, then you were wrong. You couldn't always tell which way he was going to go. If we couldn't hear him thinkin' we were wrong."[76]

The tracks were released on a double album titled *Lightnin'!* on the Poppy label. Some of the tracks later turned up on the recording *In Berkeley*, which Arhoolie released in 1973. Many of the Poppy tracks, such as "Mojo Hand," "One Kind Favor," "Hello Central," and "Back Door Friend," were rerecordings of songs Hopkins had released earlier. Ulish Carter of the *New Pittsburgh Courier* gave *Lightnin'!* a good review, emphatically writing:

Lightnin' Hopkins is one of the old time great blues singers and has to rate in the top ten of all time. His release is entitled *Lightnin'!* and made up of a two record set composed of 20 tunes, some of his classics as well as some new releases. His release is also live and the producers Chris Strachwitz and Jim Mallory do a magnificent job of getting the best out of the musicians around Hopkins voice and guitar work. Hopkins sounds just as good on this one as he has ever sounded as he down right cooks on all of the material. Again for those into the rare blues this is it.[77]

During the session, Hopkins did record one topical song, "Please Settle in Viet Nam," which was released as a single by Joliet Records and on the *In Berkeley* record. Hopkins addressed the Vietnam War in the studio several times. Even before the Vietnam War started, Hopkins sang "War Is Starting Again," a haunting song Vee-Jay Records released on the *Lightnin' Strikes* album in 1962:

Mojo Hand

Oh you know this world is in a tangle baby
Yes I believe they fixing to start a war again
Oh you know this world is in a tangle now people
Yeah I feel they gonna to start a war again

Hopkins also addressed the war in "Viet Nam Part 1 & 2," recorded for Jewel Records in 1968. On "Please Settle in Vietnam," Hopkins's narrative reveals his opposition to the war, but also unveils a lyrical twist about a woman:

My girlfriend got a boyfriend fighting
She don't know when that man coming back home
I said I hope he'll stay forever
Cuz I ain't gonna leave that girl alone

At a 1966 Ash Grove gig, he sang,

If you want to fight and be bad
Just take yourself over to Vietnam
That's where they're raising plenty of fights
I heard one boy said . . . Who's gonna take care of my wife and child?[78]

The song deftly reveals his concern for people caught up in the plight of poverty, war, and loss.

University of Michigan students organized the inaugural three-day-long Ann Arbor Blues Festival, the first major blues-only festival in the country, on the first weekend of August 1969. They booked Hopkins to play Sunday evening, August 3. The bluesman seemed enthusiastic: "Well, I been looking forward for this for a long time. And I thought this would happen in the future and it did, so now I hope it lasts long. Fact of business is I believe it will."[79] The festival took place on the Fuller Flatlands, on the University of Michigan campus, just a few short weeks before the better-known Woodstock Music and Art Fair at Max Yasgur's farm in upstate New York. Dan Morgenstern, writing in *Down Beat*, estimated that it drew 20,000 people, not even a tenth of the 300,000 who attended Woodstock. Morgenstern's review waxed positive: "[Hopkins] was a joy to behold. . . . he seemed determined to have a good time and take the audience with him. 'It's good out here in the prairie like this,' he told them, launching into 'Mojo Hand.' Among the songs that followed in the set that ended too soon . . . the standouts were 'Don't Wanna be Baptized' and a long anecdote about a girl who stole his brand-new second hand Cadillac."[80]

In the fall, Hopkins returned to the West Coast for club gigs. He was booked into the Candy Company in San Diego from September 25 to 28, 1969, with Jack Tempchin in support. A preview in the *San Diego Door* noted, "Last time he appeared at the Candy Co. he drew the largest crowd in Candy Co. history."[81] Tom Waits, a soon-to-be-acclaimed musician and performer, attended one of Hopkins's gigs at the Candy Company. A few years earlier, the fifteen-year-old Waits experienced a Hopkins performance at a coffeehouse in San Diego, which helped spur Waits: "He was doing, I don't know, 'Black Snake Moan' or something, and I just thought, 'Wow, this is something I could do.' I don't mean I could play guitar like him, I just mean this could be a possible career opportunity for me."[82] Throughout the fall of 1969, he kept busy, completing a West Coast tour, including gigs in Berkeley, Seattle, Cotati, and Los Angeles.

Nineteen seventy did not start out well for Hopkins. On January 27, he was involved in a serious car accident and injured his neck. According to one source, Hopkins cracked a vertebra in his neck.[83] Although Hopkins had to wear a neck brace after the wreck, apparently his injury was not too severe, because he played a gig just four days later.

On February 1, 1970, Hopkins worked at the Jewish Community Center with John A. Lomax, Jr. The show was billed as a "Dialog of Blues and Folk Music," and the cover charge was $1.50 for members and $2.00 for guests. A copy of a check to Hopkins for the gig, drawn on Lomax's personal account, is preserved in the Lomax archives at the University of Texas. The amount is a mere $52.40, and a note on the check reads, "Remainder due on account ½ of JCC concert net." If half of the net refers to Hopkins receiving half of the concert's net pay, and Lomax earned the other half, Lomax's business arrangements for that concert seem suspicious. Hopkins was a natural headliner providing much of the draw, no doubt, which would certainly entitle him to more of the proceeds.

By late spring, Hopkins stopped wearing his neck brace. On April 10, 1970, Little Hattie, a seamstress who lived in Hopkins's neighborhood, sent a letter to her friend J. J. Phillips, also known as Skinny Minnie. Phillips had spent some time living in Houston in the 1960s and had an intimate relationship with Hopkins for five years.[84] Trident Press published Phillips's book *Mojo Hand* in 1966. The book was a fictional narrative, informed by Phillips's experiences with Hopkins in Houston, that featured a character named Eunice and a blues singer named Blacksnake Brown.

Hattie called Hopkins "Turkey Neck," and her letter reveals how lowly she thought of him. She wrote:

Minnie I got your letter Thurs morn and it's Fri. morning now. And can you imagine I walked out of the store and old Turkey Neck was sitting outside drinking a beer and said, "The mailman went in your place and left your mail." Yes Turkey Neck had wreck in his car had his [turkey neck] in traction for a good while. He didn't have it yesterday. I think Turkey Neck told you he had an accident, got banged up. So we both tried to contact you by phone. And about Turkey Necks' attitude toward his fellow man, pay it no mind that poor soul is just the same as always. I'll speak to them about the blk [*sic*] man.[85]

While the neighborhood woman criticized Hopkins, he toured the West Coast in June 1970, stopping at his usual venues in the Bay Area, the New Orleans House, the Matrix, and Mandrake's; playing nine nights at the Ash Grove in Los Angeles; and playing the Lincoln School Auditorium in San Francisco with Ramblin' Jack Elliott and folk musician Sandy Bull on June 6.

When Hopkins returned from his West Coast tour, the racial climate on Dowling Street and in the rest of Hopkins's Third Ward neighborhood was getting tense. More than twenty-five years after Lola Cullum plucked Hopkins off Dowling Street and took him to Los Angeles to record, the street was still a full-fledged red light district. Hopkins had worked with Black Panther Elaine Brown at benefits for the Ash Grove in May 1969. In Houston, the Black Panther–like group People's Party II was headquartered on Dowling Street, less than a mile away from the residence of Hopkins. Founded by Carl Bernard Hampton, the organization adopted a ten-point program similar to the Black Panthers' platform and set out to monitor police behavior and serve the people.

On September 5, 1970, Hopkins worked what was probably his first gig at the coffeehouse on the University of Houston campus.[86] Dalis Allen, a UH student, ran the coffeehouse. She remembered how the venue came into existence: "We just took over the ROTC building, tied-dyed a bunch of fabric, and put some carpet down on the floor. [The capacity] I'd say was not more than a hundred, if that. We just put pillows on the floor and people came and sat down. We didn't really put down chairs."[87]

Allen would often convince Hopkins to play the coffeehouse, which was less than three miles from Hopkins's apartment: "I used to go over to his house and talk him into coming over. At that time, we didn't have a very big budget, and we paid like fifty bucks. I'd just go to his house, knock on his door, and he and I would sit down and go back and forth and talk it over. I paid most people fifty dollars. That's kind of what we would argue about . . . but he would agree. He'd pretty much always come. He'd always say yes in the end, but we had to spar about it a bit. I don't even think I got anything in writing. We always had good crowds for him and Mance [Lipscomb]."[88]

Bill Haymes was a musician who worked a gig with Hopkins at the UH coffeehouse:

I was actually in NROTC. So I had pretty short hair and was learning my craft as a singer/songwriter. I get to the gig . . . early. There was a little warm-up room and there was Lightnin' and basically a guy who drove him around. This was a younger guy. I was in awe of Lightnin' Hopkins. . . . And it was a chilly night, so it must have been fall or spring. For some reason, I had half of a Styrofoam cup of hot chocolate. I introduced myself, "I'm honored to open for you." He said you gotta get your voice working right. Gotta get your voice working. I said yes, and he reached in his pocket and pulled out a little flask of vodka. So he . . . said, "Come here, I'll give you something to get your voice going." He reaches over to pour it in my cup, and I'm drinking hot chocolate. But even though I was a sophomore or junior in college, I knew enough not to refuse to drink with Lightnin' Hopkins, that was an honor. I held out my hand and he filled it up. So I got a cup that's half vodka and half hot chocolate. He goes, ". . . There's something that's good for your voice." And he wasn't making fun of me, he was sharing with me something that he in fact [thought could] make you sing better. So I stood there five or ten minutes and drank this awful concoction of curdled hot chocolate and vodka and went out and did my show. Never saw him again. He treated me like a fellow performer, where he could have been dismissive or angry, but offering to give me a drink was really sincere.[89]

On October 3, 1970, Hopkins worked the Family Hand with Houston folk artist Frank Davis.[90] Mike Condray, Linda Herrera, and George Banks ran the establishment, a restaurant featuring live music located at 2400 Brazos Street, in the Montrose neighborhood, known as a hippie and gay enclave, just south of downtown Houston. The venue attracted a lot of attention from the Houston Police Department. Bob Novotney worked at the Family Hand: "We were counterculture. It was a police state down here. You didn't see any blacks walking the streets after dark down here. If the hippies were walking the streets they would get stopped. There were frequent illegal searches [in the restaurant] every Wednesday night. It was like clockwork. It was harassment to the restaurant, because we served blacks. There would be two or three squad cars out there. They would always come in and have someone up against the wall or going through their pockets."[91]

Mike Condray adds, "I first [booked] Lightnin' at a café I owned called Family Hand here in Houston, Texas. We had home-cooked meals, served breakfast in the morning, and at night we had music. And Lightnin' played there on holidays, he played Halloween, and we closed this place on a New Year's Eve show and he was the act we used that night."[92] The police and extremists targeted the Family Hand. According to *Space City!*, the underground newspaper, the venue was "a coming together point for Houston freaks, radicals and other weirdoes."[93] Local veteran John Carrick calls it "an inner-city drug haven."[94] The police raided the Hand on May 27, 1970, and arrested seventeen people on various charges. Managers Mike Condray, Linda Herrera, and George Banks were also arrested that day. On June 24, 1970, firebombs exploded at the front of the building, causing some minor exterior damage and a broken window. Later that year, on Labor Day morning, a homemade pipe bomb exploded at the door, causing $250.00 worth of damage. A few days later, the restaurant received a "rat sheet," which was a communiqué from the United Klans of America, listing names, addresses, and phone numbers of people the Klan thought were dangerous communists, including one of the managers of the Family Hand.[95]

Aside from these incidents, the venue maintained a kind of countercultural interzone, fostering creativity and camaraderie. Frank Davis worked with Hopkins at the Family Hand: "He was very kind really. There was a whole lot of shuffling going on around him. He wanted to be very famous and all that stuff, but he would protect you from being screwed over. Lightning, by himself, was quite a guy, but when there were people around, it was a circus. You would think he would peacock around. I never saw any maliciousness. He was genuine. Everybody needed him, he needed them, and they needed him. He was always fun to be with."[96]

Hopkins finally sought professional help arranging out-of-town gigs. Sandra Getz, the vice president of Deputy Star Productions in Hollywood, began handling bookings for Hopkins from at least 1970 and continued through 1973.[97] By 1970 Cecil Harold, an African American surgeon, was handling Hopkins's affairs on the Houston end, replacing John Lomax, Jr., in this role. Rex Bell recalled, "He was a friend of his that [Hopkins] could trust. He wasn't necessarily a good booking agent, but he could trust him. He was the guy you called if you wanted to book Lightnin'."[98] Ryan Trimble worked with Harold to book Hopkins at Liberty Hall. "Dr. Harold was really a nice person. He never charged Lightnin'. He was just Lightnin's buddy."[99]

A cache of paperwork from Sandra Getz's work with Hopkins from 1970 through 1973 survives. The documents include contracts, which reveal Hopkins's earnings for various gigs, large and small. Some contracts are from gigs

Hopkins worked when he toured the West Coast from October 21 through November 8, 1970. KCET-TV booked Hopkins to play in its studio on North Vine Street in Hollywood on October 21. Hopkins received one hundred dollars payable at the taping and round-trip airfare from Houston to Los Angeles. The station taped Hopkins's appearance for the *Boboquivari* show, a series PBS broadcast in 1971. Other episodes featured performances by Tim Buckley, Odetta, Kris Kristofferson, and Ramblin' Jack Elliott.

The tape shows Hopkins wearing his ever-present dark shades, nattily dressed in a brown suit, dark yellow shirt with brown stripes, a wide, striped tie, and floppy cream-colored beret. Hopkins sat perched on a stool placed on a tiny riser surrounded by audience members. Camera close-ups show his gold pinky rings flashing as he used a fingerpick on his thumb to strum his acoustic guitar on "Questionnaire Blues," which delves into Vietnam War draft issues. Hopkins's selection was relevant. He ends his set with a rap and a song about going to see one's parents: "I never did forget to go see my parents. Go and speak well to mama." His tune "How Long Have It Been Since You Been Home" preaches about "poor mama, rocking by the window, since you been gone." Despite being a hip bluesman painfully aware of the Vietnam War and incendiary race issues, he was also genuinely family-oriented. His plea for mama is honest and endearing, not simply another blues trope.

On November 13–14, 1970, Hopkins worked his first gigs at the Armadillo World Headquarters in Austin, Texas. Tickets for $1.50 in advance or $2.00 at the door would get you in to see Hopkins supported by the band T. Tellonious Troll.[100] Shiva's Headband manager Eddie Wilson and some partners officially opened the Armadillo on August 7, 1970, booking bands from a wide range of musical genres, including folk, country, jazz, rock, and blues. National acts Captain Beefheart, Linda Ronstadt, Ravi Shankar, Iggy Pop, Bruce Springsteen, the Flying Burrito Brothers, B. B. King, Bill Monroe, and Ramsey Lewis played the 1,500-capacity venue, which closed in 1980.

Drummer Uncle John Turner worked the Armadillo gigs with Hopkins: "[It] became the main hippie concert place. It was so different for the time. When I first moved from California, me and my band Krackerjack stayed in the Armadillo. We didn't have anyplace to stay. It was the hippie days. I got called in to play. I was just there most of the time, I guess. I'd already seen him a few times. Wasn't much to it, blues wasn't important enough for that to mean much. The gig was uneventful to me except I started noticing his patterns. He wasn't actually making a mistake: he was just playing odd patterns. In other words, he just added a couple of beats here and a couple of beats there, but he always did it the same. So it wasn't really a mistake. . . . But if you didn't know it . . . it didn't fit into the standard way."[101]

Turner enjoyed Hopkins's personality in addition to his musical side: "He could get the prettiest white girls to sit with him backstage. And that meant a lot to him. And he was one of those black people that spoke in that braggadocio [third] person about how cool he was about everything. Very dapper person, always dressed, very clean, very well dressed, suit and hat, and had good hair. He was a bluesman all the way, so he took advantage of that to promote his stature, his outward appearance. You never saw him out in public without looking dapper."[102]

Kaleidoscope founding member Chris Darrow imagined Hopkins as a key player in bringing the blues to a new generation. Darrow was a close-to-the-ground musician well informed about Hopkins's music during the heady folk-blues revival. His expert point of view sums up Hopkins's presence on the American popular culture scene:

When Lightnin' went to Folkways Records in 1959, he became one of the first of the old blues guys to play the coffee house circuit and colleges. He helped to open up a new generation to his brand of American blues. Places like the Ash Grove in L.A. and the Club 47 in Boston were the venues where you could see the bluesmen up close. The folk festivals like Newport and Berkeley brought a more intellectual and academic crowd into the equation. When the English Invasion came in the mid-sixties, groups like the Rolling Stones, the Animals, Them, and the Yardbirds were doing covers of old blues standards and more modern, R&B standards. Thus, another audience opened up and allowed for blues artists to expand into a more international and contemporary scene. Many artists found themselves on their way out of America and traveling to many foreign countries to gig. The hippie generation and the sixties "anything goes" mentality put these artists, and Lightnin' in particular, on the bill with the likes of our band, the Kaleidoscope, at a place like the Straight Theater. The "free form" aspect of FM radio at the time allowed for the listener to hear Lightnin' Hopkins next to the Jefferson Airplane, on any given day, and think nothing of it. People like Mance Lipscomb, Mississippi John Hurt, John Lee Hooker and Lightnin' all became very popular artists at the time and were very comfortable at folk clubs, college concerts and psychedelic concerts. There were no barriers in those days with regard to who could play where, with whom, and when. Each and every one of these guys was grateful for the sixties renaissance. It re-energized their careers and gave a new audience to their music.[103]

N I N E

Sometimes I wonder why the black man had to be slave.

LIGHTNIN' HOPKINS, 1981

HOPKINS BEGAN 1971 with performance dates on the West Coast, including February 11 at the University of California, Berkeley, at the Science Lecture Hall; February 12 at the Student Union of the University of Southern California, Los Angeles; February 13 at College Union, Fresno State; and February 16 at Freeborn Hall, University of California, Davis. By spring, he was back in Houston.

Liberty Hall was a venue on the eastern edge of downtown Houston at 1610 Chenevert Street. It opened in March 1971, holding about six hundred people. The structure was previously an American Legion hall, and a church before that. It became the premier small venue of the 1970s in Houston. Liberty Hall booked plays like *One Flew over the Cuckoo's Nest*, musicals like *Tommy*, comedians Cheech and Chong, and a wide variety of musical performers, including Bruce Springsteen, the Ramones, the Velvet Underground, the New York Dolls, Waylon Jennings, Jimmy Reed, Muddy Waters, John Lee Hooker, Willie Dixon, and Freddie King.

Two of the former managers from the Family Hand, Mike Condray and Linda Herrera, ran it alongside Ryan Trimble. Mike Condray knew the building was ideal for a music venue: "It was perfect, it had hardwood floors, stage, air-conditioning, high ceilings, balconies, ticket box, almost just walk in and start doing shows."[1] For most acts, the producers ran two shows on Friday and Saturday. The club kept a separate phone line for community radio station KPFT, the local Pacifica affiliate, to provide live, uninterrupted broadcasts of shows.

Condray talked about booking Hopkins: "[I got to know him] through Rex Bell and Dale Soffar at the Old Quarter. And when they told me he'd play for a hundred bucks a night, I was just bowled over. That just sounded great. He was easy to work with, a lot of fun. He didn't have a phone. You had to go to his house, and you'd tell him what date you wanted. I never saw a calendar or anything, but he was always there on time and knew what he was supposed to do. If he was supposed to have a band or not a band. I put together a band for him sometimes. We got to be friends and he worked a lot at Liberty Hall."[2]

Rex Bell and Spider Kilpatrick often backed Hopkins at his Liberty Hall gigs, according to Condray:

Rex would play bass with him a lot. In fact, he could never say Rex's name. He would always call him Rick. He would rely on me to get Rick, and he showed up with a drummer a lot in the Liberty Hall days. A guy called Spider, and Spider had a very small, almost jazz drum kit, very small bass drum. He had a tom-tom, but he put his lunch on that, and he had a snare and a cymbal. He [Rex] could make the changes without Lightnin' getting upset and make it work. [Lightnin' would] make up his verses as he went along too. He was very unpredictable, hard to play with. But Rex could drop a note here or there and not miss a note. He knew what he was there for—to make this guy look good. He didn't make any big deal about any missed changes. Rex plays good guitar too, so he could follow Lightnin' on the fret board and see what was going to happen next or hope to be able to anticipate was going to happen next. He would always ask for Rex. That was part of the deal, and he would depend on me to contact Rex.[3]

From May 12 to 15, 1971, Hopkins worked Liberty Hall with Big Mama Thornton and George "Harmonica" Smith. She did not get along with Hopkins, Ryan Trimble attested: "Some of her relatives were married to some of his relatives, and there was a little animosity there. I think they were jealous of Lightnin' because he was successful. People liked Lightnin', the young white people. [Thornton and Hopkins] got into a thing there, and I had to get in between them and tell her to leave him alone."[4] Mike Condray agreed: "For some reason during that thing she pushed Lightnin' down on his ass. I'm talking about when the show's not on cuz they were offstage. For some reason, I looked around and there Lightnin' was back flat on his back and Big Mama Thornton, who was bigger than he was by a long mile, probably had gone back to her business. They were like two kids. Pushed him down and went and got a drink. But again, no incident, no big deal, if you haven't seen it, it was over with before you knew it."[5]

"There were a few nights of shows when Lightnin' Hopkins shared a gig with Mama Thornton. She was on first. Her band comes on," adds Darryl Harris. "They started playing some of these hot up-tempo numbers, in the middle of it one of them steps up to the mike and says, 'And now Willie Mae Thornton,' and she jumps in and gives it everything. Lightnin' comes on and he was playing with Rex [Bell]. Rex was on the verge of comatose. Lightning says, 'I guess ain't nobody is gonna introduce me.' It was [Hopkins's] insecurity. It was hilarious and embarrassing. It was hard to be embarrassed for Lightning Hopkins. He stood up to play, which he never did. He didn't have a strap. And he ended up lying on his back, kicking his legs up in the air while he played."[6]

By August 1971, Hopkins gigged a series of dates in California, where he played the Head Band in Goleta on the 31st. Before that, on August 7 and 8, he worked the Ash Grove in Los Angeles; on August 16, Funky Quarters in San Diego; and August 19, In Your Ear in Palo Alto. Ed Michel recorded Hopkins on May 16 and 17, 1972, at Village Recorders in Los Angeles. Michel had worked with Hopkins on the *Down South Summit Meeting* record in 1960. The current recording deal was set up through Dr. Cecil Harold. Michel picks up the story:

Bill Syzmczyk . . . was my pal. He had the office across the hall. I was running Impulse, and he was a hot pop producer. . . . [He] got a considerable hunk of money from Gulf and Western and formed Tumbleweed, which lasted a couple of years and sunk without a trace. So, this was a project recorded for them.

Lightnin' shows up in the studio and says, "OK, roll the tape." And you roll the tape and you get a take or you don't get a take. If you want a second take of the same thing, too bad. It's not gonna be a second take of the same thing because Lightnin' doesn't work that way. You say, "gee, do another," and one, he's gonna sing something different or start out the same way and go off on its own path, which is very nice from an artist point of view, but rough if you're trying to get a smoothly put together take of something with a bad mistake in it. The other thing is that Lightnin' frequently is a little bit out of tune, and he doesn't really rehearse with the guys he's playing with. So, you gotta get people who sort of have a sense for a feel for what he's gonna do and will follow his patterns. And he also had a kind of sadistic way. There are places where you're playing the blues where you can go to a four chord or a five chord, he'll sort of wait until a guy he's playing with will commit himself, and then he'll give the guy a nasty smile and go the other way. He used to do that to let everyone know he was the boss, and he was the boss. He was very strict about, OK, I'm gonna record this amount of tunes, and that's what I'm getting paid for, and that's all I'm gonna record. But if you say, hey, three of them aren't usable, let's do it over again. He would say no. There was no arguing with him.[7]

Michel provided a number of studio musicians for Hopkins over the two days of recording. No fewer than four drummers, four guitar players, two bassists, and one violinist, jazz musician Michael White, worked with Hopkins. The most-well-known player was John Lee Hooker, who brought two guitarists from his band—Luther Tucker and Charlie Grimes. Michel did not arrange for John Lee Hooker to be on the session: "John just showed up. He wasn't invited, but he was a pal, so it wasn't necessary to throw him out. The first thing he sings on, he didn't have a microphone, and you don't get another take for a couple of reasons."

Hopkins's recording methods were better suited to musicians familiar with his idiosyncrasies. The material seems inferior, like half-gestated songs, plus the core players do not synch with him. "He drank and he got drunk, he drank and got less functional. He didn't drink incessantly," Michel observes. "He didn't drink like an alcoholic. He didn't drink till he was shit-faced. Oh and it took a lot of editing and manipulation to get it to only that sloppy. Lightnin' wasn't that cooperative in telling the other musicians what he was going to do, so it was a question of getting four or five others to get what he was going to do."

Luckily for Hopkins, the record label fell apart, so the sessions were not released until long after his death. Michel concludes, "At the point they [Tumbleweed] were sinking without a trace so since I didn't get paid for it, they said why don't you just keep the masters. . . . He never asked why the recordings never came out. He got paid reasonably for it. The five thousand dollars [over twenty-six thousand dollars today] was a pretty realistic number for that time. The guys involved with Tumbleweed, we'd all been seriously involved in corporate existence and five grand was not much to pay an artist. And the nature of the recording was going to be a lot different [from when Michel recorded him in 1960 for the *Down South Summit Meeting* sessions]. It wasn't going to be three hours in one day, it was going to be a couple of days in a multitrack studio, I believe we did sixteen tracks and a lot more musicians, a lot more people involved."[8]

In August, Hopkins traversed Southern California for a short stint, working the 25th–27th at Ash Grove in Los Angeles. On August 28, he was featured at the Lighthouse in Hermosa Beach, and by August 29, he was back at the Ash Grove for a September 1–3 engagement.

Hopkins played more gigs at Liberty Hall on November 26 and 27. Guitarist Jimmie Vaughan played in the band Storm, who opened for Hopkins on those dates. "I remember that Liberty Hall gig," said Vaughan. "We were backstage and there was some guy back there with him. It was Frankie Lee Sims."[9] Sims recorded with Hopkins years before when he was still with the Gold Star label.

Vaughan was a big fan of Hopkins, seeing him often, including a Valentine's Day gig, when all the songs referenced women, matters of the heart, and Valentine's Day.

Hopkins was arrested in Houston in February 1973 for possession of a weapon, a pistol, resulting in a $400.00 bond. The misdemeanor charge was later dropped by Carol Vance, the district attorney of Harris County. This was the first record of Hopkins's involvement in the criminal justice system since he violated gaming laws in Houston in 1947.

From February 19 through 23, 1973, Hopkins played the Egress in Vancouver, British Columbia. Buzz Wright ran the club, which was located at 739 Beatty Street. With a capacity of about two hundred, the club booked blues, rock, and folk acts like Albert Collins, Muddy Waters, Bo Diddley, Tim Buckley, Phil Ochs, and Mimi Farina. Folksinger Tim Williams, who had worked with Hopkins in Southern California, opened the Egress gigs for Hopkins: "They hired a jazz rhythm section to play with him, and they couldn't hang and wait for him to indicate the changes. He was pretty blunt about getting rid of the rhythm section but very nice to me and several other Vancouver musicians that knew him at that point. [He was] very gracious . . . laid back to the point of being lazy. One of the funniest things I remember was the club owner trying to get him off the phone and on the stage because it took him fifteen minutes to say goodbye to whatever family he had on the phone. The club owner's got a packed house. They're sitting on each other's shoulders. Sam moved at his own time. You didn't hurry him. He was a very charming guy. I shared a few bottles of scotch with him."[10] Also, "He was an outrageous flirt. His attention was generally on the prettiest girl in the room."[11]

In the spring of 1973, Hopkins worked the Vermont Blues Festival in the Patrick Gym at the University of Vermont in Burlington. Held on April 28, the event featured Otis Rush, Hound Dog Taylor, Ry Cooder, Mance Lipscomb, and Sleepy John Estes. The *Vermont Cynic*, the university paper, called Hopkins "a living legend in today's blues world" and the "elder legend of the festival" who "draws SRO crowds everywhere he performs."[12]

Dick Waterman booked Hopkins for the festival. Waterman, a former journalist, was a photographer, agent, promoter, and record producer. He founded Avalon Productions to book and manage traditional bluesmen who were not making a living playing music. Waterman managed Skip James and was involved in finding Son House and getting his career restarted in the 1960s. Waterman first encountered Hopkins when he photographed him at the Newport Folk Festival in 1965.

Waterman went through Dr. Cecil Harold to book Hopkins and remembered the difficulty of working with Harold: "We never argued on the money or the airfare. It was just that Dr. Harold talked to you really slowly and treated you like an idiot child. And he would say, 'You folks, you been doing wrong by Lightnin' all these years and now it's Lightnin's chance, it's Lightnin's turn to get a little money.' He would do this thing and you would just hold the phone and let him talk. And after he scolded you for racial inequalities for a while, then he got around to the business and the money and made the deal. But you had to hold the phone and let him talk awhile."[13]

Judging by Waterman's experience with him, Harold did not seem to have acute skills for the music business. Because of Harold's efforts, Hopkins was paid $2,500 cash and airfare for the gigs Waterman booked, but Hopkins had to fly halfway across the country to do one gig instead of multiple engagements. Waterman insisted, "You see, he wasn't really skilled as a music negotiator. I would say to him I just saw that Lightnin' played in New York, and if he's going to play in New York and I'm in Boston, why don't you let me have the night before or the night after? Why have Lightnin' go from Houston to New York and play one night and go home? Let me know and I'll pick up half the airfare and get him to play in Boston, double the money in the northeast. He couldn't quite understand this or didn't want to understand this. In other words, it didn't make sense for Lightnin' to come from Houston to Boston and to play an hour and go back to Houston."[14]

Despite the booking hassles with Dr. Harold, Hopkins pleased the mostly white audiences, putting a unique spin on each show: "Lightnin' also appealed to hippie types, but he personified cool, laid-back behavior like the Miles Davis muse. I always felt that he made it up. It was very free form, he had certain verses and stanzas . . . but he had floating verses that he would pull in and make up rhyming verses for the city he was in or the situation he was in. He was certainly not locked into a dozen songs."[15]

Waterman noticed a distinct difference between Hopkins and other bluesmen he worked with during the folk blues revival:

The guys I worked with—Son House, Skip James—were much more intense in their deliveries. The important thing is that most bluesmen in the 1960s were rural. Son House came from Mississippi and Fred McDowell, Mississippi. Mance Lipscomb, they were rural guys. Lightnin' was a city guy and had city ways. That's a real big difference, a profound difference. All those guys played acoustic, and Lightnin' played amplified with a pickup. So, both the way he carried himself as an urban man and played his blues amplified made him very different from Skip [James] and Bukka [White] and Fred [McDowell] and Robert Pete [Williams]. He came from a very different place socially and musically. He was very cool. Some of the others [bluesmen] would be overly polite and respectful around white people, but Lightnin' didn't have any of that. Lightnin' would just treat everyone the same, and if anything he carried himself with a sense of confidence and almost arrogance. He was Lightnin' Hopkins.[16]

At some point in 1974, Sam Charters came to Houston to record Hopkins. Charters had first recorded Hopkins for Folkways in 1959. The Folkways recording played a major role in Hopkins's career comeback. By now, Charters was living and working in Sweden. He worked for Sonet, a small Swedish label. Charters successfully proposed that Sonet release a series of blues records called "Legacy of the Blues." Charters recorded Hopkins for the series, which was originally released only in Sweden.

According to Larry "Bones" McCall, Charters made arrangements with Dr. Cecil Harold to record Hopkins, with McCall on drums:

He played at my father's club one time. My dad owned the Copper Kettle in the Fifth Ward. I held a mic for him during his entire gig. That was the only experience I had with him. [Later] I got referred to Samuel Charters, so he contacted me and asked me to find a place where I could work with Lightnin'. I got together with the bass player I knew. And we set out to do a session. . . . I never recorded with Lightnin' before . . . I didn't know Lightnin's style of recording. But I learned about it very quickly. He would record songs and named them after he finished recording them. So, later on when I was twenty-four or twenty-five I played the session with him. He recruited the bass player Ozell Roberts. So, Charters paid him for the session. Lightnin' started playing, and then he fell in after him. It was spontaneous. He was traveling with the harmonica player, a white guy who was more hip to what he was doing. That harmonica player played a session. He offered me a drink, a Jax beer. I never will forget him drinking a Jax beer . . . hot [laughs]. He had a half pint of some kind of whiskey. He wasn't drunk. Professional alcoholic. We took the first take. He wouldn't redo it.[17]

The players, as critic Steve Leggett writes, "try to make sense of Hopkins' personalized sense of rhythm as best they can, and together with Hopkins' skewed, half improvised lyrics, they manage to make a few things work here, including the conversational 'The Hearse Backed Up to the Door,' the metaphor-filled 'I

Been Burning Bad Gasoline,' and the brisk instrumental, 'Doin' My Boogie,' one of two bonus tracks included in this reissue. Most of these songs, though, feel like the kinds of things a band plays before actually recording a take, when little things like tempo and rhythm are still being worked on, and the end result seems even more ragged and random than the typical ragged and random Lightnin' Hopkins session."[18] Although the session, which lasted only an afternoon, does feel piecemeal, the recording is sharp, the songs tuneful, and Hopkins's easygoing swing is charming, especially on rev-ups like "Don't You Call That Boogie." Bonus tracks found on the 2005 reissue offer fine blues distillations neglected on the original version, like "Born by the Devil," a traditional-styled urban lament.

Like Dick Waterman, Charters expressed displeasure with Cecil Harold: "What a son of a bitch he was to work with. I must say nobody ever put me through that kind of shit in my life. That's the way he was. I was made to feel like I was something on the level of Al Capone with everything I was proposing."[19] For this session, Charters paid Hopkins five thousand dollars, which Harold insisted be paid in cash in the form of small bills, which concerned Charters: "They had booked me into a studio that they knew about which was really near Dowling Street and it was [a] very rough [neighborhood]. By the time the session finished [the studio] was surrounded outside by some really tough dudes. [They were] looking in the windows and hanging around the doors and everything. So, I said in a loud voice as we signed the contracts, 'We did all that, got the contract signed, and here is the five thousand dollars in cash.' [They had] this stunned look on their faces, Lightning and the doctor. There was this sudden surprised look on the guys hanging inside the windows and doors, and so Lightning and the doctor went into the bathroom and stuffed money inside their socks, inside their drawers, and then leaped into his car and got the hell out of there. So, that was some way to deal with the fact that I'd been put through shit."[20]

The August 1975 edition of *Ebony* magazine ran a piece claiming Hopkins was dead. In the article, titled "Culture," *Ebony* ran photos of Muddy Waters, Leadbelly, and Hopkins with a caption stating, "The blues over the years has become sophisticated and merged with other singing. But when it was pure and 'country' no artists interpreted better than Muddy Waters, and the late Sam (Lightnin') Hopkins, and Huddie (Leadbelly) Ledbetter."[21]

Hopkins sent a letter to the editor of *Ebony*, declaring, "I am not dead, I am playing and singing nationally. Will you please take steps to correct this damaging blunder?" and signed it Sam Lightnin' Hopkins.[22] In addition to publishing Hopkins's letter, the editors ran a short piece on their error in the Backstage column: "Two separate editors had checked their sources and came up with the affirmation that Mr. Hopkins was no longer with us. . . . We were happy to learn that Mr. Hopkins is continuing his career and that he is being aided by Dr. Cecil G. Harold, a black surgeon who calls himself Hopkins' 'unpaid manager.' A long time friend and admirer of Lightnin' Hopkins, Dr. Harold helps him avoid some of the contractual pitfalls that have cost him considerable money in the past. Now 63 years old, Lightnin' is currently singing in Texas but is scheduled for a tour of California in November and has signed to record an album for Blue Labor records later in New York. Mr. Hopkins does little radio or television work, according to Dr. Harold, because of some bitter experiences in early years. When he is not on the road, Hopkins lives quietly with his wife Antoinette in their Houston home."[23]

In October 1975, Hopkins toured briefly across Canada, starting at the Playhouse Theater in Winnipeg, Manitoba. The itinerary included dates at the University of Saskatchewan, University of Regina, and Simon Fraser University, and in the cities of Lethbridge, Edmonton, and Vancouver. The tour concluded in Victoria, British Columbia.[24] Canadian singer/songwriter Don Freed, who had appeared in a documentary with Johnny Cash in 1968 and recorded an unreleased album for Capitol Records, opened on tour dates for Hopkins: "In the mid-'70s, I used to get calls from time to time because I would be a cheap and easy opening act. So, in 1975 there were some people in my hometown that asked if I would go on tour with Lightnin' Hopkins."[25]

Freed went to meet Hopkins and start the tour: "I remember going down to Winnipeg and going to the airport and meeting him. He looked kind of bewildered, [and he was with] his wife. Her name was Antoinette, beautiful woman, very churchy woman. Every night he basically did the same show. The thing that I remembered was that he had to get paid every night in American twenty-dollar bills, cash, and his wife Antoinette would take that roll of twenties and stick it in her purse and she hung onto that purse until the end of the tour."[26]

As was his usual custom, Hopkins worked with a pickup band, noted Freed: "He picked up a bass player and drummer in Winnipeg. Two young guys—long hair and beards. He didn't want to rehearse with them . . . he just figured they'd just fit in with him. But he would drop bars and add bars every night. So, this drummer and bass player were always on edge because they didn't know what he was gonna do because he was used to playing with people who were used to playing that kind of style. But he changed things around every night. I remember he wore these western suits with spangles, not as garish as Nashville people, and he wore a hat like a Stetson hat. And he would tell the same jokes and do the same kind of almost corny patter in his performance."[27]

On this tour, according to Freed, Hopkins had better conditions than his backing band: "The long distances he and his wife would fly in an airplane, but the shorter distances we would travel in a Winnebago. One time we were traveling from Calgary to Edmonton, I think it was in early November and the first snowfall had come kind of like a light dusting, it wasn't anything really serious. And I guess they weren't used to seeing snow. So, we passed a couple of cars on the highway, a couple of cars in the ditch. And they were sitting right across from me kind of like knee to knee and they see these cars in the ditch and she opens her purse and pulls out her rosary and starts praying and he reaches in his overcoat and brings out a bottle of whiskey and starts drinking. I swear to you I had to go into the bathroom and laugh. One is sitting there praying, and the other is sitting there drinking. We didn't want them to see us laughing."[28]

Hopkins's habit of not rehearsing with sidemen resulted in a terrible show at Simon Fraser University, the fourth stop on the tour. Brian Gibbard reviewed the show, titled "Lightnin' Letdown," for the *Ubyssey*, the college newspaper:

The problem lay not so much with Hopkins as with his "band." The man is a sixty-ish guitarist and singer from the southern states. It was a shock therefore when he appeared on stage with two young white sidemen on bass and drums. They were competent enough musicians. Unfortunately they were completely unfamiliar with the material they were to play. The evening became a mental battle. I tried to concentrate on Hopkins' simple but nonetheless effective guitar style. The mistakes, especially the drummer's inability to follow the leader's rhythm whims, spoiled the attempt. The evening alternated between slow blues and instrumental boogie. "Rock Me Baby," "Lightnin's Boogie" and "Baby Please Don't Go" all showed Hopkins' talents fairly well. The evening was marred by a disastrous instrumental version of Ray Charles' "What'd I Say."[29]

By April 1976, Hopkins found himself back in New Orleans. Photographer John Gibbs Rockwood caught him playing sets on the 10th at the Warehouse, joined by Albert King, Muddy Waters, and Johnny Shines, and on the 11th at the New Orleans Heritage and Jazz Festival: "Lightnin' just showed up with a couple of locals. Not particularly players either. But I'll tell you, he was awesome. Ripped the place apart. I mean he destroyed those other guys. Played them—and remember who we're talking about now—right off the stage. The next day when I saw him at the festival I told him I'd seen the show. 'Did you like it?' he asked. I told him he was incredible. So he said, 'What do you think I am gonna do today?' I told him I thought he'd be great. He just looked at me, you know, with a little bit of a smile behind the weird sunglasses you see here and said quietly, 'I'm gonna fuck 'em up today.' And he did."[30]

Hopkins played the Village Gate on February 3 and 4, 1977, with jazz legends Art Blakey and Sonny Stitt. Art D'Lugoff, the Village Gate owner, hired New York guitar player Robert Ross to back Hopkins. Because there was not enough money to hire Ross's three-piece band, Ross played bass and hired drummer George Morales from his band. Ross also found Hopkins a hotel room:

I picked him up at the airport and the first thing he wants to do is go to a liquor store. I drove him to a liquor store and he gets a pint of Jack Daniel's. Mind you it's eleven a.m. So, he's happy with the bottle. Then it's like I need something to eat. There's a diner near the motel he's going to be staying. He's finishing the pint as we're parking the car. He just finished a pint . . . in twenty minutes from the airport. Then he turns around and looks at me and says, "You got any poultry in this car?" He goes "I smells chicken." He says, "You got any poultry in this car?" He reaches in his pocket and opens up his wallet, and he's flashing me a badge, poultry inspector 1030901 or whatever. It looked very official. I don't know the guy. I know Bo Diddley is a sheriff. For a second, he really had me going. He looks at me and goes, "Lightning got you." We had a really good laugh. We really hit it off.[31]

However, the first time Ross played with Hopkins he was not acquainted with his style or what he wanted out of a sideman:

When I was playing with him the first time, I noticed right away. The first time around the first twelve bars or thirteen or fourteen bars, I would lay back on the bass and wait to see what's happening. I don't know this tune, so you just listen. First time around I would listen. The second time, OK I got it now. By the third time around I'm playing much stronger now, I'm no longer laying back. I know what's happening, I know where the changes are gonna be. So I started to play . . . more aggressively. And when I did that, I noticed he would trip me up. He would wait an extra beat or an extra two beats or an extra bar before making the change. . . . This is like, OK, I got ya, just lay back, stay out of his way. So, that became the modus operandi after that point: he wants you to play way behind the beat and not play aggressively, not show off. Let him do his thing. I don't even know why I'm there. I'm in the background, and that's the way it's gonna be. He was nice enough not to mention anything. He let you know, just by his playing, he wanted you to play a certain way. . . . one night at the Village Gate . . . he said over the microphone that I played pretty good for being a white guy, or a white boy.[32]

In Centerville, Texas, his hometown, Hopkins was arrested for drunk driving and speeding on October 8. Although checked into the jail, he was released by 5:00 p.m. because the jail closed, and the Leon County jailer and judge went home. The paperwork was processed a few days later. According to official county records, Hopkins paid $256.00 for driving under the influence (along with fees associated with the charge) and $32.00 for the speeding violation, which he covered from the $783.67 in cash he had on hand. While another published account suggests Hopkins was arrested with a weapon on hand, no court documents support such a conjecture.

During 1977, Hopkins headed to California to play in Hermosa Beach. The gigs included bassist Larry Taylor as backing band member. "I was playing in a band in L.A. called the Hollywood Fats Band," he recalls.

We had a band going in 1977. We were the first playing that old-style '50s, '60s Chicago style. We played at a place called the Lighthouse, in Hermosa Beach. We were on about four or five gigs with him, and with Bonnie Raitt gigs with him. . . . Every time [Hopkins] come through the Lighthouse, he'd use me and Richard Innes. . . . [Hopkins] sort of had a child-like sort of attitude, but it was kidding more than anything else, as if trying to trip you up. You either knew what he was doing or you didn't. If you were aware of his music and had listened to him as a musician listening to other musicians you'd know automatically what he was gonna do just because of the phrases. I wasn't 100 percent but I had a clue because I had listened to his music over the years. I had seen him at the Ash Grove when I was a kid. You knew sorta by doing it more than one time what he was going to do by the feel, the tempo, and the words. His personality was . . . a little sarcastic. He wasn't the friendliest person in the world until you actually ended up in a really good situation, then he turned into a really friendly person. . . . I remember playing the gig with Bonnie Raitt at the Santa Monica Civic [Auditorium] and my wife just had a baby and she was in the backstage with the stroller. He was in the back in the dressing room rocking the stroller with my kid in it. He must have loved kids.

[It was] me and Richard, real simple, upright bass. Sometimes he'd [Hopkins] get a little loud. I'd just go back and turn it down. He was in front so he couldn't see. He didn't notice. He was playing electric, that particular era. His own material was country, country blues. His way [of playing] got a lot of signs of early artists, real back porch, when he was just acoustic. He played the same songs [in Santa Monica]. He went over better than she [Raitt] did. They went totally nuts over it. Two gigs I played, one in Santa Monica, another one in Santa Barbara, the night after. Both places they totally went nuts over the guy. They were really appreciative of what he did. The only thing he'd like to do was drink Pearl beer. I knew a place that sold it. I'd go there every time before the gig and bring him a six-pack. You couldn't get it at a regular liquor store. He loved us. He'd got to love us after a few gigs. He'd just presented himself that way. He went all out to show who he was. He'd do funny little things with his hand. He'd do little things with the fingerboard with his right hand. He was a showman.

A Japan tour commenced on February 10, 1978. Hopkins took Flight 959 from Houston International Airport to Los Angeles, where he picked up a flight to Tokyo via Hawaii. They reached Japan and were met by flower givers and media. Whisked away in limousines chauffeured by black-suited drivers to the Hotel Prince, they were soon surrounded by Japanese gardens with pagodas.

During the next morning, snow pelted down. Sonny Terry and Brownie McGhee arrived that morning, met their interpreter and drummer Donald Bailey, and went to a studio for rehearsal. They went over songs only in rough sketches, since Hopkins didn't want the band actually to record anything. Limousines took them to Tokyo and Yokohama, and McGhee rode with Hopkins and assistant David Benson. Several music writers interviewed Hopkins, but Benson answered questions.

The crowds at the gigs, which took place from six to nine p.m., numbered around 1,500. On one occasion, the band took a bullet train from Tokyo to Osaka. Hopkins was skeptical at first about the cutting-edge traveling, but he settled in once the swift train started, soaking up the scenery and buying beers and lunch. Later, Hopkins wouldn't leave his hotel rooms except for gigs. He depended on room service for food, but he did leave his room to go to the hotel coffee shop in order to save a room service charge. Hopkins had a bridge of gold in his mouth and couldn't eat very well. As a result, he was self-conscious, believing everyone would look at him.

Hopkins watched the Ali-Spinks fight in Osaka and provided a blow-by-blow commentary for McGhee, who was blind. Brownie McGhee and Sonny Terry didn't speak to each other; they talked to Hopkins and Benson separately. No one knows why, but Hopkins suspected the problem arose due to Terry's wife. McGhee had a history of fooling with other men's wives.

At Nagoya, Hopkins finally came out of seclusion, rocking the show heavily enough, and titillating the foreign audience, who were favored with two encores. The next stop was Sapporo. They flew on ANA from Nagoya, with VIP treatment—like being whisked around behind the scenes and seated on the plane after everyone else. Benson joined Donald Bailey at a coffee shop, where Bailey bitched about how Hopkins treated him on stage. Benson said, that's classic Hopkins. He treated everyone like shit at times—Antoinette, Harold, and him too.

At one meal, Hopkins didn't understand the use of utensils. After hearing Benson's instructions, Hopkins angrily said, "I'd rather travel with a dog." Benson pressed, "You think I'm lower than a dog? I'll knock your old ass out." "You'll have to knock me out every time," Hopkins retorted. The meals cost forty dollars. Even though Hopkins didn't pay for them (they were covered by the per diem), his vitriol was evident. Benson's promise to pay him back calmed down Hopkins. Benson, though, never paid him the forty dollars. They soon left Sapporo for Sendai. Staying at a nice modern hotel downtown, Hopkins knew the end of the tour was imminent. That night, a sense of relief shaped his performance: happiness almost exuded from his guitar playing, according to Benson.[33]

Hopkins taped an appearance on the *Austin City Limits* television show on October 9, 1978. Terry Lickona produced the show, which also featured the Neville Brothers and Robert Shaw. Lickona remembered wanting to get Hopkins to perform: "Ron Wilson called me, I had no idea who to contact regarding Lightnin'. He had been on my wish list. Ron approached me. . . . [He] was playing some gigs with Lightnin'. He pitched the idea of doing a show and we said yes. Ron was really the one that took the ball and ran with it. He had to convince Lightnin' to do it. It took a while until we got commitment from him to do it. And until the day he showed up to do it, no one knew whether he would do it or not."[34]

Hopkins was particular about getting his money before he played, posing a challenge for Lickona:

At some point during the day, Ron asked me about the payment. We had had a previous conversation, it's usually sent two weeks after the performance. It depends how long they rehearse and tape. It's broken down in fifteen-minute increments. That's why we couldn't pay in advance. I think Lightnin' must have said something to Ron, and that's why Ron brought it up with me. And I reminded him of the situation of paying within two weeks. He kind of scratched his head and said if there was any way you could pay Lightnin' before the show I guarantee that you will get a better show out of him. And I thought to myself, how much difference could four hundred dollars make? And even back then for Lightnin' I thought for sure he was getting paid better than that. Ron said it was the principle as much as the amount and Lightnin' just didn't trust anybody no matter what the situation was. It was a Sunday, so the banks were closed. Our accounting department was closed, so it wasn't just like I could just have somebody cut a check. I took up a collection from the staff . . . to try and get enough to pay him, and we did. We made him feel that much better and got a better show as a result.[35]

Dressed in a western-cut, two-tone blue leisure suit, with a fedora cocked slightly off-center, Hopkins was covered with "bling" before it became a tag word and cliché. His jacket was customized with rhinestone initials on the front. The camera angle caught the back of it, showing light glinting off the inset metal studs set in a free-flowing design. With his gold tooth flashing, matching his gold-rimmed prescription glasses, Hopkins started the set with "Mojo Hand." He kept looking back at his bass player, Ron Wilson, as if he was out of synch and tune. As the center of attention under the glare of studio lights, with a beer in a plastic cup beside him on a stool, Hopkins clearly enjoyed himself and rose to the occasion. When he played "She Ain't No Cadillac," he used a wah-wah pedal to great effect. And, for the first time in the set, he stood up to play "Rock Me Baby." For a player who first hit the stage as an eight-year-old, this sixty-five-year-old version of Hopkins was no wizened bluesman eking out rote chords, but an ever-vibrant master leaving the rapt, hooting, and hand-clapping audience wanting more. The cameras might have offered him a national television audience, but this flavorful down-home set was magical, personal, and intimate, culminating in the raucous farewell of "Good Night Blues."

In February 1980, Hopkins came to the aid of premier zydeco performer Clifton Chenier, who was suffering from kidney ailments that required dialysis. He had also had a foot removed, and these medical procedures resulted in major medical bills. In response, some of Chenier's fellow musicians joined each other for two nights at the iconic blues club Antone's in Austin, Texas, for a fund-raiser. Friday, February 1, featured Hopkins with the Cobras. Saturday, February 2, featured Chenier's backup Red-Hot Louisiana Band, along with the Red Beans and Rice Revue from Lafayette, Hopkins himself, Big Walter Price, and others. Hopkins's set burned bright and long on Saturday, according to local reports, while his donation to the cause also included five hundred dollars

Hopkins paid for a set of rare records, including one of his own 78s. Chenier was well loved, and taken care of, that night by the circle of friends.

On June 1, Hopkins joined Dexter Gordon at the Spoleto Festival at the College of Charleston in Charleston, South Carolina. Paying him, prior to the gig, one thousand dollars cash and coach round-trip airfare for a one-hour set, the festival also provided the backing band, guitar, and amp, and hotel as well. Official documents for the event suggest that race was still an ever-present issue in the local community, to the degree that the college pondered whether the "welcome" of Sarah Vaughan would help or hurt relations with Charleston's black community. Furthermore, the college realized that jazz, often associated in the region with white audiences during this period, was not the favored art form of local music lovers. Officials acknowledged a need to balance public taste with the college's mission to highlight jazz and create a multicultural event: "If a significant audience from the black community is desired, we must mix the better-known forms with jazz in a tasteful and intelligent fashion. . . . The booking of Lightnin' Hopkins was a step in this direction." In this case, Hopkins seems to have been a token blues player, used to satisfy the public's yearning for "low" art forms—the folk, blues, and boogie of the streets.[36] "Hopkins showed that he still possesses a firm handle on country blues and field shouts that have marked him as perhaps the leading national resource for the blues," read the account from the *News and Courier*, which noted he also displayed a "gravelly delivery and a simple but rocking guitar style, served up with intensity and wit."[37]

In August 1980, Hopkins started working at Tramps in New York. Dublin, Ireland, native Terry Dunne migrated to New York in 1968 and opened Tramps at 125 East 15th Street in Greenwich Village in 1975. "When I opened the bar in the East Village, I thought it would be a great idea to make it a blues bar and see if I could revive the blues, which wasn't doing so well at the time," Dunne related.[38] By 1979, *New York Times* music critic Robert Palmer described Tramps as one of the clubs that was responsible for New York's blues renaissance. Tramps had a booking policy that mostly featured blues acts. Other clubs like the Lone Star on Fifth Avenue and 13th Street (where Hopkins played in 1979), the Bottom Line at 15 West Fourth, and the Village Gate also booked a wide variety of blues acts.

After Hopkins played Tramps, Dunne noted,

One night it was in August, probably about 1980. It was really hot outside, it was like August weather, really humid, our air-conditioning broke down. There was Lightnin' on stage dressed in a beautiful ruffled shirt and lovely jacket and the large, heavy black hat he wore. He looked fantastic.

He started to play, and it was so hot in the room because we had no windows, in this back room where he was playing. He was sweating and it was pouring in torrents off him. He had all his clothing on. He didn't take off his hat or his jacket. Meantime the audience they were so hot, women were literally stripped down to their brassieres. It was an amazing night of blues. When the show was finished Lightnin' came up to the counter and ordered his drink, which was Canadian Club straight up. He said to me, "You know, Terry, you guys are doing a nice job here but it's a little hot up there tonight." It was so funny. It was unbelievable. He was a trooper. He did a couple of sets that night.[39]

Dunne enjoyed treating his performers well. "We booked them into . . . the Gramercy Park Hotel. The whole idea was to make them feel good, and feel at home. Your place had to have a reputation. We took great pleasure in looking after them," Dunne said. Hopkins drew a good crowd and worked two shows a night. "He packed the house, every time. Ninety people capacity in the cabaret room. But I had it opened up so the people at the bar . . . [could hear]. There was also a crowd at the bar that could see it," Dunne said.[40] A typical Tramps booking for Hopkins was Friday, October 31, through Sunday, November 2, 1980, when he worked nine o'clock and midnight shows each night. The cover charge was only seven dollars, with a two-drink minimum at tables.

Dunne also hired the backing band for Hopkins. Robert Ross, who had played with Hopkins at the Village Gate, also backed Hopkins at Tramps. Ross's band would open the show and then play behind Hopkins. Ross depicts Hopkins's transformation before he took the stage: "There were times when he looked tired and thin. He looked his age. I was a little worried about him. The guy drinks like a fish and he's jet-lagged. He's gotta be feeling the heat. He should be feeling the heat. I'm feeling it. I was supposed to pick him up late. He was gonna take a nap. I dropped him off at the hotel. I went to pick him up four hours later to go to the show. He was wearing this leather rawhide kind of a suit, like Daniel Boone or somebody. It looked unbelievable on him. He looked like [he was only] forty-five. It just filled him out, straightened him up, added like twenty pounds, squared his shoulders. Puffed him up. That was like a transformation. Performers gotta get psyched up to get in front of a crowd. He was ready to kill."[41]

Johnny Copeland's memory of Hopkins's farewell Tramps gig is still keen:

I saw his last performance at Tramps. I was getting ready to go to Europe. I said I'm not going to see him tonight. So, I called to talk to him . . . and we talked a little while and I said "Man, I don't think I'm going to be able to get down to your show tonight. I'm going to Europe tomorrow. I'm flying out to Europe tomorrow. I need to get myself together for that." He said "Well, OK." He said, "You have a good trip and have a good time." And he said, "You know I've been sick." It was something about the way he said it. He said, "You know I've been sick." I said, "You been sick?" He said, "Yeah, I've been real sick, really sick." I said, "OK. I'll be on down there." So, I went and got my friend, and we drove on down there, and we sat with him all night, and that turned out to be his last performance. It was something about the way he said it that I knew I had to go. I didn't want to miss it in the first place. I knew I had a lot to do the next day you know.[42]

Throughout 1981, Hopkins kept playing out, though only in Texas, where he gigged at Manor House in Austin and Rock House in Houston, the latter of which found him holding court with bassist Larry Martin and drummer Andy McCobb. Some of the hometown tracks were captured and released as *Forever: Last Recordings*. The recording's live slices, though not exactly boasting stellar fidelity, do capture, in stripped-down performance and rough hues, Hopkins revisiting tunes with ample sly style. The album, not released until 1983, bears witness to Hopkins's long-lasting musical mannerisms. In addition, the rereleased compilation *Lightnin' Strikes Back* (Vee-Jay Records, 1962) hit the market in England on Charly Records, and the single "War Is Started/Louisiana Woman," both songs credited to songwriter S. Joseph, was manufactured by Jewel Records.[43] Most likely, the tracks are actually misidentified versions of Hopkins's "War Is Starting Again" and "Got Me a Louisiana Woman," cocomposed by Lee Ivory Semien, featured on the album *Lightnin' Strikes*, released by the label Stateside in 1962 as well.

During the same year, Jeff Todd Titon published the compendium *Downhome Blues Lyrics: An Anthology from the Post–World War II Era*, which featured transcriptions of Hopkins's "War News Blues," "Coffee Blues," "Candy Kitchen," "Lonesome Home," "Short Haired Woman," and "Give Me Back That Wig."[44] Behind the live performances, outpouring of material, and academic documentation of Hopkins's lyrical craft, a shadow lurked. Hopkins was gravely ill. Just a year earlier, Robert Palmer glowingly captured the bluesman's persona and historic import in a piece in the *New York Times* celebrating his sixty-eighth year: "Mr. Hopkins is a real folk poet, a chronicler of his life and his community who's the closest thing to the 'griots' of West Africa and Alex Haley's *Roots* that one can find in the United States."[45] Such continued legendry aside, the coarse, witty, and cool-headed Hopkins, whose pliant, elastic rhythm and off-the-cuff word-slinging continued to challenge players onstage with him, entice fans, and prompt his induction into the Blues Foundation Hall of Fame in 1980, was suffering cancer's corrosive impact.

By January 1982, Hopkins required hospitalization. St. Joseph's Medical Center in downtown Houston admitted him on January 27. Arthur Shaw worked in the housekeeping department at St. Joseph's: "Lightning was a pretty regular patient at St. Joe's. I recall about three occasions where the staff would say Lightning was in the hospital. Members of the housekeeping, nursing, everyone would walk down the corridor of the floor where he was at, hope to see him. Sometimes his door was opened. Sometimes it was closed. We knew Lightning was in there. I can't say I ever heard any music passing by cuz people thought maybe he might be singing or have his guitar in there. Lightning . . . was world-famous . . . this hospital didn't get many celebrities of that stature. There was a very large African American composition of the hospital staff at St. Joseph's, at all levels. All the black employees knew of him. More than just blacks, a good number of whites, they knew who he was, where he was, and what was wrong with him."[46]

Several of Hopkins's friends were summoned to his deathbed. Harmonica player Tommy Dardar worked many gigs with Hopkins in the 1960s and 1970s. He was called to Hopkins's hospital room: "He was a great guy. I got along pretty well with him, for the most part, pretty good. I was surprised . . . he asked me to come to see him before he died. We were all pretty cool with him at that point. Actually, I was rather surprised that he thought of even wanting to see me then. Cuz . . . we did a lot of arguing with him, maybe that's why he liked me. David [Benson] was the guy that drove him around cuz Lightnin' wasn't getting around real well then. I don't know . . . he told David to have Tommy Dardar come to see him. So, David took me up there before he died. Went up and paid my respects, got to see him before he passed and it was a good meeting, and I'm glad I did it."[47]

Ryan Trimble drew close to Hopkins when hired to play with the icon at Liberty Hall in the 1970s. Trimble had an experience at Hopkins's hospital deathbed similar to Dardar's:

Lightnin' was a really unique individual, and then when he was dying, Dave called me. Dave Benson, he said Ryan you want to see Lightnin' before he dies, you better go over there right now. And he was at St. Joseph's hospital. . . . I went over to St. Joe's. It was real quiet down there and the door was shut, [I] kinda knocked [on] it and I kinda pushed it open and man, there was about fifty black people in that room. They were all packed around

Lightnin', little people, older people, men, women, all kinds of black guys and girls. So I said, "Is Lightnin' here?" And Lightnin' heard me, he said, "Come on in Ryan." He could barely talk. He had throat cancer. They had to part me an aisle so I could walk over to his bed, and they were all just staring at me. So, I walked over there and we talked about fifteen or twenty minutes about the old times. And then he says, "You know I'm not gonna be able to sing when I get out of here." I said, "Maybe you can," he said, "No I'm not going to be able to," he said, "Can you get me a job, can you get me some work Ryan?" I said, "Yeah man, you can work for me." He was really glad he had him a job, but I knew he was gonna die, but I guess they didn't tell him that he was dying. It was really kind of sad man, couldn't hardly stand it. No one ever said a word. That was the last time I saw him. I tell you, I couldn't hardly stand that time. Cuz I really cared for Lightnin'. It really broke me up. I said my goodbyes right there. It wasn't too long after that he died. It was really sad man. Lightnin' was well liked. He treated me really nice.[48]

Hopkins died in St. Joseph's hospital on January 30, 1982. The cause of his death was pneumonia, a complication caused by his cancer of the esophagus. According to Dr. Cecil Harold, the bluesman's last words were "Doc, something's got to be done."

The wake took place at Johnson's Funeral Chapel on McGowen Street in Houston. The service began in the early evening as a line of one thousand attendees stretched around the building, where photographers were not allowed access. The room was small, the casket open, and the people were quiet and reserved in front of the wreaths and family members—Antoinette and four children. Rocky Hill, younger brother to Dusty Hill of ZZ Top fame, was on hand with guitar and launched into "Amazing Grace." He also lamented that the world lost the equivalent of a Picasso.[49] Billy Gibbons from ZZ Top, along with local bluesman Little Rose, were in the audience as well. The funeral took place the following day as a private affair, in accordance with Hopkins's last wishes.

Hopkins's will was probated on February 18, 1982. He bequeathed his Chevrolet truck, clothes, and $100.00 to his son Charles Lewis Hopkins. His daughter, Celestine Hopkins, in turn, received $2,000; daughter Anna Mae Box was given $3,000, plus quarterly royalty payments of $100.00; and Antoinette Charles was provided the house at 357 Knoxville in Houston, cash savings and certificates of savings from the South Main Bank and Houston United Bank, and his 1977 Cadillac. Meanwhile, his jewelry, household furniture, and personal effects were freely distributed by Antoinette Charles, the executor of the will. At the time of his death, Hopkins owed St. Joseph's hospital over $11,000, federal tax money in the amount of $3,400, and insurers $712.00, while his funeral expenses amounted to over $5,000. His assets at the time amounted to no more than $25,500 in cash, $12,000 in real estate, and a few thousand in personal effects.[50]

However, four people contested the veracity of the will, Anna Mae Box, Celestine Hopkins, Darnelle Hopkins, and Charles Lewis Hopkins, who claimed that the official county documents did not constitute an authentic will. The signature *is* unusual, for Hopkins typically signed documents using a signature reading "Sam Hopkins" or "Lightnin' Hopkins." The will, though, shows only the abbreviation "S H" twice, each scrawled in a different style.[51]

He died three days after the will was signed. Therefore, the contestants argue Hopkins did not exhibit the mental capacity to make sound judgments: "Deceased became largely, if not solely, dependent on Proponent and her agents, for all of his needs and medical care, and Deceased was dominated by Proponent in many of his activities and decisions. Proponent controlled deceased as to where he went, whom he visited, who he talked with, who was to be his housekeeper, who was permitted to be alone with him, and who was not."[52] The court, in turn, found for Antoinette Charles. The dispute only adds mystery to the final days of a beloved and beleaguered bluesman caught in the crosshairs of family, financial, and legal disputes.

EPILOGUE

Don't forget poor Lightnin'
After he is dead and gone
Please don't forget poor Lightnin'
Peoples after poor Lightnin' is dead and gone.
LIGHTNIN' HOPKINS

"I'D HATE TO THINK of not having a Lightning Hopkins. The blues would never have been what it turned out to be because he was a great player. He didn't put sugar on anything, he just played it," B. B. King said almost thirty years after Hopkins's death.[1]

The first successful attempt to memorialize Hopkins began in January 2002, when a few hundred residents and visitors saw a concrete statue molded around a steel frame of Hopkins's likeness sitting on a bench displayed in Crockett, Texas. Hopkins never lived in the community, though his own hometown, Centerville, sits just a few miles down a country lane. Carved by sculptor Jim Jeffries, who was paid through private, not municipal, funds, the statue was unveiled at an event attended by Hopkins's offspring Anna Mae Box, along with her daughter. Other local luminaries included Rex "Wrecks" Bell, the owner of Old Quarter Acoustic Café from Galveston—plus intermittent bass player for Hopkins in the 1970s—who played some tunes and offered anecdotes. For instance, Hopkins always referred to him as Rick, despite their longtime acquaintance, he quipped. Pip and Guy Gillette, owners of local business Camp Street Café, located across the street from the statue, spearheaded the effort to lionize the "irascible" bluesman, which was well-intended.

The second successful attempt to immortalize Hopkins in Texas public history projects emerged through the plans and outreach of Eric Davis, a native of Illinois who ventured to Houston in the early 1990s. Davis was able to fund-raise on behalf of a large state historical marker that celebrates Hopkins's life in Houston, which previously had only been publicly acknowledged on a tombstone. Blues history author Roger Wood, a professor at Houston Community College who spoke at the dedication ceremony, which also offered performances by Texas Johnny Brown, Diunna Greenleaf, and Milton Hopkins, aided the campaign. Commercial chain restaurant House of Blues donated hot dogs, while local press coverage included interviews with Justin Townes Earle and members of ZZ Top, who were not on hand for the event, but discussed the influence of Hopkins. Overall, the event, held twenty-two years after his death, seemed to contradict Hopkins's own wishes that no large ceremony should honor him.

Lightnin' Hopkins undoubtedly had a major impact on American popular culture. One trip to a well-stocked record store will show how many guitar players and bands have been influenced by African American blues guitar players and singers, especially Sam "Lightnin'" Hopkins, one of the most important bluesmen of the twentieth century. A quick search for Lightnin' Hopkins on Amazon.com shows 192 matches in music, 909 matches in books, and 1,343 MP3 downloads available.[2] Knowing this, one might also argue that the amount of his music product available only shows that there is a profit to be made selling Hopkins's music. That evidence of commercial popularity alone does not speak to influence. Even ignoring the large amount of his music still available almost thirty years after his death, though, one is still left with his 909 occurrences in literature.

A literature review quickly proves that arguing Hopkins's influence is a very legitimate part of music history discourse. Most scholars, journalists, musicians, and musicologists agree: Hopkins had a large influence spanning multiple generations. One way to frame or narrow down Hopkins's specific impact is to look at a few of the major guitar players whom he influenced. Then we can trace his influence through the guitar players who incorporated his style into their own. For example, Hopkins influenced his cousin, Albert Collins, and Chicago blues guitarist Buddy Guy.[3] Albert Collins, Buddy Guy, and Albert King influenced Jimi Hendrix.[4] By any measure, Jimi Hendrix, known to have "stacks of Hopkins" records in his collection,[5] powerfully shaped American popular music, particularly through his guitar playing, which partly borrows from performers Hopkins influenced.

Author Maury Dean wrote that Hendrix was "influenced by Sam Lightnin' Hopkins," while Hendrix biographer Keith Shadwick saw several parallels between Hendrix's later career and Hopkins's and Arthur Crudup's careers.[6] Shadwick captured the Hopkins parallel perfectly when he wrote, "Hendrix was a person who thrived on spontaneity and who was capable of incorporating any given event of the moment into his performing routine." Hopkins was known for improvising songs on the spot. Shadwick concluded, "Hendrix may not have copied Lightning Hopkins but he came from the same American minstrel tradition and was proud of that fact."[7] David Dicaire, however, sees that "The high level energy of his [Hopkins's] blazing fingers was copied by countless guitar players, especially in the styles of blues-rockers Jimi Hendrix and Alvin Lee. . . . his popularization of the boogie woogie accompaniment can be found in the music of such early rockers as Chuck Berry and Elvis Presley as well as fellow Texans Johnny Winter, ZZ Top, and the late Stevie Ray Vaughan."[8]

In many cases, guitar players picked up Hopkins's style through secondary or tertiary sources, through musicians Hopkins influenced, or right from Hopkins; therefore, Hopkins influenced them in several ways. Stevie Ray Vaughan, who picked up Hopkins's influence through Hendrix, lifted his song "Rude Mood," nominated for a Grammy Award for Best Instrumental, from Hopkins's song "Sky Hop." Vaughan's brother Jimmie noted correctly, "I don't think there could be a B. B. King, or a Buddy Guy, or Jimi Hendrix or a Stevie Ray Vaughan without Lightnin' Hopkins."[9]

Hopkins influenced many bluesmen, some well known, and some long forgotten. A very truncated list, according to Gerard Herzhaft's *Encyclopedia of the Blues*, includes Louisiana Red, R. L. Burnside, Baby Tate, Peppermint Harris, L. C. Robinson, Johnny Fuller, Philip Walker, Carolina Slim, and Tarheel Slim.[10] Hopkins also took Long Gone John and Bernie Pearl under his wing. Jas Obrecht, author of *Rollin' and Tumblin': The Postwar Blues Guitarists*, pointed out the profound influence of Hopkins on other musicians, from B. B. and Freddie King to Muddy Waters, Son Thomas, and R. L. Burnside."[11]

The music Hopkins made in the immediate post–World War II period also provided space for others to produce music in that vein. Author Herzhaft wrote, "In the face of the tremendous commercial success of some Texas singers, much more primitive, such as Lightning Hopkins and Smoky Hogg, he [Lowell Fulson] was able to record in 1949 a series of titles in the same style as theirs."[12] Blues scholar Paul Oliver takes it a step further. Oliver said that Hopkins inspired a whole regional style of the blues. Oliver cited Muddy Waters, Robert Johnson, and Lightnin' Hopkins's influence on a "whole retinue of imitators." Oliver suggested that a dominant musician who has the ability to influence others is then the basis of a regional style.[13] According to blues encyclopedia author Herzhaft, Hopkins also influenced Louisiana swamp blues producer J. D. Miller, who "joined [the sound of] Lightning Hopkins with that of Jimmy Reed."[14] The Louisiana swamp blues Herzhaft refers to is defined by Slim Harpo but also practiced by Lightning Slim and Lazy Lester.

Hopkins's influence can be seen in many rock 'n' roll bands. One promi-
nent example is the Grateful Dead, the original "jam band," who often played
Hopkins's music. Ron "Pigpen" McKernan, a founding member of the Grateful
Dead and a Lightnin' Hopkins nut,[15] sang Hopkins's song "She's Mine" in his
solo part of their live sets.[16] The Grateful Dead influenced the jam bands following in their wake, like Phish, who included Hopkins's song "Shaggy Dog" in
their live show from 1986 to 1988.[17]

Hopkins's sharp style and cool demeanor became woven into the fabric of
American popular culture. As Peter Case notes, "You could do a whole book on
the clothes of Lightning Hopkins. He looked beautiful. He always had these
really great jackets, great shirts, always dressed cool, shades, a sense of style
that not many other blues guys had. He had an amazing look. Not only did he
know how he wanted to sound, he knew how he wanted to look too, when I
saw him, he was wearing a suit, the shades, he had it."[18] ZZ Top guitarist Billy
Gibbons, himself a "sharp-dressed man," declares, "He was a real flashy guy,
always dressed in the finest of the fine."[19] Multi-instrumentalist solo artist and
Jackson Browne sideman David Lindley concurs: "He also had fabulous poly-
ester clothes, sharp shoes and was always well dressed and neat. We got along
great. I always wanted to be Lightnin' Hopkins, clothes and all."[20] All the views
testify to Hopkins's keen sense of self-regard.

Few published pictures reveal Hopkins without sunglasses—Hopkins's
trademark look, evidenced in the *Blues Brothers* movie released in 1980 featuring
two Caucasian actors portraying bluesmen, replete with costumes combining
dark suits, ties, and black sunglasses. Many of the top-tier African American
bluesmen besides Hopkins wore suits and ties, especially during the 1960s.
Hopkins, however, is the only nonblind African American bluesman whose
trademark image included dark shades, which soon became popular in Hollywood depictions of "bluesmen."

A multitude of songs lament, evoke, or pay homage to Hopkins. Brownie
McGhee's "Letter to Lightnin' Hopkins" lightheartedly calls Hopkins out and
recognizes his stature in the music field. Juke Boy Bonner's "Look Out Lightnin'" showed Bonner's struggle to try and attain Hopkins's stature. Louisiana
Red's "I Met Lightning Hopkins" reveals a younger bluesman wanting to be
associated with the better-known Hopkins. In 1987, Athens, Georgia, band
R.E.M., one of the most popular bands in the world, released their commercial
breakthrough album *Document*. It included the song simply titled "Lightning
Hopkins." Other Hopkins tribute songs released since his death include "Lightning Hopkins Goes Surfing" and "To Lightning Hopkins Blues."

In *Blues Singers: Biographies of 50 Legendary Artists of the Early 20th Century*, author David Dicaire summed up Hopkins's impact thus: "In the long illustrious American folk music tradition, Hopkins occupies a regal position. He is in the same company as Huddie 'Leadbelly' Ledbetter, Pete Seeger, Woody and Arlo Guthrie, Joan Baez, Bob Dylan, Brownie McGhee, Sonny Terry, Harry Chapin, Don McLean and others who wrote political and social songs that mattered to their country. Hopkins reflected the life of the poor, common black persons in his songs, and he fostered awareness of their plight. When a Who's Who of folk singers is compiled, Hopkins is a natural selection."[21]

His songs did not fit neatly into twelve-bar blues patterns; he spoke and sang in vernacular, impromptu, and off-the-cuff poetry. While many musicians emulated his style, from Bernie Pearl, a Jewish Caucasian from Los Angeles, California, to Juke Boy Bonner, an African American from Brenham, Texas, few share the living history rooted in his American music. Musician Dave Alvin said it best: "I can play Lightning Hopkins' stuff, I can't play Lightning Hopkins, [because] part of the greats, any kind of music, the way they play is the same way that they walk and talk and the way they sing, there's no disconnect between the way the guy is and their art, it's the same thing."[22]

Hopkins tapped into the life and experiences, the rapture and the rancor, of African Americans in the twentieth century. Deep down in the blood-thickened grooves of his songs, listeners can catch glimpses, shards, and shadings of sorrow songs found on slave and sharecropper plantations, prison work fields, and infamous chain gang highways, not to mention endless juke joints, front porches, and coffeehouse folk clubs. Hopkins's sorrow songs constitute a living fabric, a commanding version of history as his-story. More so, his music is an intrinsic portion of what W. E. B. Du Bois identified as the three gifts of African Americans to this country: song and story, sweat and brawn, and spirit.[23] Hopkins exuded all three in his life.

Ethnomusicologists, guitar magazine writers, journalists, fans, and musicians can argue indefinitely about Lightnin' Hopkins's historical value. However, as the erudite scholar Cornel West noted, "Bluesmen aren't sanitized. Bluesmen aren't deodorized. Bluesmen are funky. Bluesmen got soul."[24] Most would agree that there was nothing about Sam "Lightnin'" Hopkins that was deodorized, sanitized, or edited. Sam Hopkins had raucous soul and left much of it, free and fiery, in his indelible music.

Lightnin' Hopkins, 1972. Photo by Philip Melnick.

Lightnin' Hopkins with Bernie Pearl, 1967. Photo by Philip Melnick.

Lightnin' Hopkins with Alan Lomax in Dallas, Texas, March 1969.
Photo courtesy of Lu Mitchell.

Lu Mitchell with Lightnin' Hopkins in Dallas, Texas, March 1969.
Photo courtesy of Lu Mitchell.

Lightnin' Hopkins in Dallas, Texas, March 1969.
Photo courtesy of Lu Mitchell.

Peter Case, Project Row Houses, Houston, Texas, July 2011. Photo by David Ensminger.

Dr. Robert Murphy, Houston, Texas, July 2011. Photo by David Ensminger.

Lightnin' Hopkins's gravestone, Houston, Texas, January 2012. Photo by David Ensminger.

NOTES

CHAPTER I

1. Liner notes, *My Life in the Blues*, Prestige PR 7370, 1965.
2. Randolph B. Campbell, *An Empire for Slavery: That Peculiar Institution in Texas, 1821–1865* (Baton Rouge: Louisiana State University Press, 1991), p. 231.
3. Library of Congress Slave Narratives, Texas Narratives, vol. 16, part 1, "Uncle Willis Anderson," http://memory.loc.gov/cgi-bin/ampage?collId=mesn&fileName=16 1/mesn161.db&recNum=26&itemLink=D?mesnbib:1:./temp/~ammem_2 UtZ (accessed February 19, 2006).
4. Mance Lipscomb, interviewed by Allan Turner, Center for American History, University of Texas at Austin, Allan Turner Collection, 1972–2009.
5. Amos Keeler, "From Buffalo," *Jewett County Messenger*, December 13, 1889.
6. Released on *Early Recordings*, Arhoolie 2007, 1963.
7. Les Blank, *The Blues According to Lightnin' Hopkins*, Flower Films, 1969, outtakes disc 16, track 3.
8. Ibid., outtakes disc 14, track 1.
9. Lightning Hopkins, "Mama and Papa Hopkins," *Autobiography in Blues*, Tradition Records TLP 1040, 1960.
10. *Grapeland Messenger*, May 20, 1915.
11. Lightnin' Hopkins, "My Family," *My Life in the Blues*.
12. Blank, *Blues*, outtakes disc 6, track 2.
13. Ibid., outtakes disc 7, track 3.
14. Ibid., outtakes disc 8, track 4.

15. Ibid., outtakes disc 3, track 5.
16. Ibid., outtakes disc 4, track 1.
17. Lightnin' Hopkins, from documentary *Artists in America*, 16-mm film, KUHT Film Productions, University of Houston, 1971.
18. Lightnin' Hopkins, "I Learn about the Blues," *My Life in the Blues*.
19. Ibid.
20. Blank, *Blues*, outtakes disc 10, track 5.

CHAPTER 2

1. Frank X. Tolbert, "The Loose Caboose Not a Wild Joint," *Dallas Morning News*, February 6, 1972.
2. Mack McCormick, "A Conversation with Lightnin' Hopkins," *Jazz Journal* 13 (December 1960): 23.
3. Les Blank, *The Blues According to Lightnin' Hopkins*, Flower Films, 1969.
4. Lightnin' Hopkins interview with Sam Charters, "I Growed Up with the Blues," *My Life in the Blues*, Prestige PR 7370, 1965.
5. Andy Silberman, "Lightnin', Doc Draw Praise at Folk Festival, Phoenix Press Conference," Swarthmore College *Phoenix*, April 9, 1963.
6. O'Brien's interview with Nat Dove, 2009.
7. Larry Willoughby, *Texas Rhythm, Texas Rhyme: A Pictorial History of Texas Music* (Austin: Texas Monthly Press, 1984).
8. Arnold Shaw, "After Hours, Gitars, Folk Songs, and Halls of Ivy," *Harper's Magazine*, November 1964, p. 43.
9. Charles R. Townsend, *San Antonio Rose: The Life and Music of Bob Wills* (Urbana: University of Illinois Press, 1976), p. 4.
10. Mance Lipscomb, interviewed by Allan Turner, Center for American History, University of Texas at Austin, Allan Turner Collection, 1972–2009.
11. Jim O'Neal and Amy Van Singel, eds., *The Voice of the Blues* (New York: Routledge, 2002), p. 139.
12. Paul Swinton, "A Twist of Lemon," *Blues and Rhythm*, no. 121, p. 4, http://www.bluesandrhythm.co.uk/documents/121.pdf.
13. Comment on a panel discussion at the Ponderosa Stomp music conference, New Orleans, Louisiana, April 27, 2009.
14. *Chicago Defender*, July 26, 1926.
15. Giles Oakley, *The Devil's Music: A History of the Blues* (New York: Da Capo Press, 1997), p. 115; *Blind Lemon Jefferson, Classic Sides*, Jsp Records, B000085BE, March 18, 2003.
16. O'Brien's interview with Ray Dawkins.
17. Blank, *Blues*, outtakes disc 10, track 5.
18. Lightnin' Hopkins interview with Charters.
19. Blank, *Blues*, outtakes disc 10, track 5.

20. O'Brien's interview with Barbara Dane.
21. For a thorough discussion of gospel and blues see James H. Cone, *The Spirituals and the Blues: An Interpretation* (New York: Seabury Press, 1972); see also John Michael Spencer, "The Theologies of the Blues," in *Blues and Evil* (Knoxville: University of Tennessee Press, 1993), pp. 35–67.
22. Blank, *Blues*, outtakes disc 15, track 1.
23. John Rodgers, "'King of the Blues,' 'It's Like a Cool Breeze,'" *Daily Californian*, September 23, 1965.
24. Mack McCormick, "A Conversation with Lightnin' Hopkins," *Jazz Journal* 14 (January 1961): 18.
25. Blank, *Blues*, outtakes disc 8, track 3.
26. McCormick, "A Conversation with Lightnin' Hopkins," *Jazz Journal* 13 (December 1960): 24.
27. Ibid.
28. Blank, *Blues*, outtakes disc 15, track 2.
29. Ibid., outtakes disc 6, track 3.
30. "Crockett, David," *The Handbook of Texas Online*, Texas State Historical Society, http://www.tshaonline.org/handbook/online/articles/fcr24 (accessed December 17, 2010); "Houston County Was Created in 1837," *Grapeland Messenger*, July 1, 1937.
31. Blank, *Blues*, outtakes disc 8, track 3.
32. Ibid., outtakes disc 6, track 3.
33. Ibid., outtakes disc 8, track 3.
34. Ibid., outtakes disc 8, track 1.
35. Robert Palmer, *Blues & Chaos: The Music Writing of Robert Palmer*, ed. Anthony DeCurtis (New York: Simon and Schuster, 2009), p. 53.
36. Lightnin' Hopkins interview, "I Learn about the Blues," *My Life in the Blues*.
37. O'Brien's interview with Ray Dawkins, 2005.
38. Paul Oliver, liner notes to *Texas Alexander Vol. 2 (1928–1930). Complete Recordings in Chronological Order*, Document Records MBCD 2002, 2000; McCormick, "A Conversation with Lightnin' Hopkins," *Jazz Journal* 13 (December 1960): 23.
39. Paul Oliver, liner notes to *Texas Alexander Volume 1 (11 August 1927 to 15 November 1928). Complete Recordings in Chronological Order*, Document Records MBCD 2001, 1995.
40. Ibid.
41. Sheldon Harris, *Blues Who's Who: A Biographical Dictionary of Blues Singers* (New York: Da Capo Press, 1981), p. 29.
42. Lightnin' Hopkins interview with Sam Charters, "I Meet Texas Alexander," *My Life in the Blues*.
43. Ibid.
44. Blank, *Blues*, outtakes disc 1, track 6.

CHAPTER 3

1. Paul Oliver, *Conversation with the Blues* (Cambridge: Cambridge University Press, 1997), p. 44.
2. Les Blank, *The Blues According to Lightnin' Hopkins*, Flower Films, 1969, outtakes disc 15, track 2.
3. O'Brien's interview with Ryan Trimble, 2008.
4. John Lightfoot, "Early Texas Bluesmen," in *The Roots of Texas Music*, ed. Lawrence Clayton and Joe W. Specht (College Station: Texas A&M University Press, 2003), p. 108.
5. O'Brien's interview with Tomcat Courtney, 2010.
6. Blank, *Blues*, outtakes disc 14, track 1.
7. Stephen Calt, *I'd Rather Be the Devil* (New York: Da Capo Press, 1994), pp. 69–71, 85–86, 127.
8. Texas State Department of Health, Bureau of Vital Statistics, Standard Certificate of Birth, Leon County records.
9. Lightnin' Hopkins interview, "I First Come to Houston," *My Life in the Blues*, Prestige PR 7370, 1965.
10. Nathaniel "Bill" Barnes interview, Nathaniel "Bill" Barnes Collection, Collection Number MSS 441, Houston Metropolitan Research Center, Houston Public Library.
11. O'Brien's interview with Tomcat Courtney.
12. Lightning Hopkins, "When My First Wife Quit Me," *The Complete Candid Recordings Otis Spann/Lightning Hopkins Sessions*, Mosaic 139, 1992. Lightnin' recorded this in November 1960 for Nat Hentoff's Candid label. John Lee Hooker recorded "When My First Wife Left Me," also known as "When My First Wife Quit Me," which had a similar theme but different lyrics, for Modern Records in 1949.
13. Chattel Mortgage Docket, Trinity County 1911, p. 220, County Records Collection, Newton Grisham Library, Sam Houston State University, Huntsville, Texas.
14. Ibid., p. 194.
15. Armistead Albert Aldrich Papers, 1835–1945, Box 2L 228, Miscellaneous Legal Papers folder, Center for American History, University of Texas at Austin.
16. O'Brien's interview with Ray Dawkins, 2005.
17. Ibid.
18. Mack McCormick, "A Conversation with Lightnin' Hopkins," *Jazz Journal* 13 (November 1960): 23. When Hopkins is discussing his wife when he was on a chain gang (probably Elamer Lacy, who gave birth to his daughter Anna Mae), the interviewer asks, "Is this your first wife?" Hopkins replied, "No, it wasn't my first one." See also Lightnin' Hopkins interview, "I Learn about the Blues," track from *My Life in the Blues*, for his mention of his "girl" Ida Mae.
19. Lightning Hopkins, *Texas Thunderbolt*, Proper Box 123, 2007.
20. Liner notes, *My Life in the Blues*, Prestige PR 7370, 1965.

21. Lightnin' Hopkins, "Tim Moore's Farm," *All the Classics 1946–1951*, JSP Records JSP 7705, 2003.

22. Glen Alyn, "Mance Lipscomb: Fight, Flight or the Blues," in *Juneteenth Texas Essays in African American Folklore*, ed. Francis Edward Abernathy et al. (Denton: University of North Texas Press, 1996), p. 84.

23. O'Brien's interview with Ola Mae Kennedy, 2010.

24. Alyn, "Mance Lipscomb," p. 99.

25. Chris Strachwitz, liner notes to *Lightning Hopkins, Early Recordings Vol. 2*, Arhoolie 2010, 1971.

26. McCormick, "A Conversation," p. 17.

27. Neil Slaven, liner notes to *Lightnin' Hopkins, All the Classics 1946–1951*, JSP Records JSP 7705, 2003.

28. Lightnin' Hopkins interview with Sam Charters, "I Meet Texas Alexander," *My Life in the Blues*; Sheldon Harris, *Blues Who's Who: A Biographical Dictionary of Blues Singers* (New York: Da Capo Press, 1987), p. 29.

29. Liner notes, *My Life in the Blues*.

30. Paul Oliver, *Conversation with the Blues* (Cambridge: Cambridge University Press, 1997), p. 57.

31. Mack McCormick, liner notes to *Country Blues*, Tradition Records TLP 1035, 1959.

32. Andy Silberman, "Lightnin', Doc Draw Praise at Folk Festival, Phoenix Press Conference," Swarthmore College *Phoenix*, April 9, 1963.

33. McCormick, "A Conversation," p. 23.

34. The January 25, 1912, edition of the *Crockett Courier* mentions an Arch Baker being elected to the board of directors of the First National Bank of Crockett, http://www.rootsweb.ancestry.com/~txhousto/articles_stories_etc/couriergleanings_jan25_1912_localnews.htm (accessed August 18, 2009). For documentation about, and Hopkins's memories concerning, Houston County sheriffs, see http://www.rootsweb.ancestry.com/~txhousto/sheriffs.htm (accessed August 18, 2009); *Epitaph for a Legend*, Charly Records Ltd LIKD 52, 1989.

35. Mack McCormick, liner notes to Mance Lipscomb, *Texas Sharecropper and Songster*, Arhoolie F1001, 1960.

36. *Lightnin' Hopkins: Rare Performances, 1960–1979*, Vestapol 13022, 2001.

37. Ibid.

38. Giles Oakley, *The Devil's Music: A History of the Blues* (New York: Da Capo Press, 1997), p. 41.

39. McCormick, "A Conversation," p. 23.

40. Lightning Hopkins, "Selling Wine," released on *Lightning Hopkins in Berkeley*, Arhoolie Records 1063, 1972.

41. Pete Welding, "Arthur 'Big Boy' Spires: A Bio-Discography," *Blues Unlimited*, no. 28 (December 1965): 3.

42. Kip Lornell, "Part Two: Albany Blues," *Living Blues*, no. 15 (Winter 1973–1974): 22–23.

43. Glen Alyn, comp., *I Say Me a Parable: The Autobiography of Mance Lipscomb Texas Bluesman* (New York: W. W. Norton and Company, 1993), p. 224.
44. Ibid., pp. 202, 223.
45. Barbara Dane Collection, AFC 1980/001: SR 17, 1961, track 4, Archive of Folk Culture, American Folklife Center, Library of Congress, Washington, DC.
46. Alyn, *I Say Me a Parable*, pp. 223, 224.
47. Lightnin' Hopkins interview, "I First Come to Houston," track from *My Life in the Blues*.
48. Jackie Hoyer and Brook Griffin, "Houston's Fourth Ward: Old Neighborhood, New Life," *Banking and Community Perspectives*, issue 2 (2002): 1–8.
49. O'Brien's interview with Tomcat Courtney.
50. Mack McCormick, "A Conversation with Lightnin' Hopkins," *Jazz Journal* 15 (February 1961): 19.
51. Bernadette Pruitt, "For the Advancement of the Race: African-American Migration and Community Building in Houston, 1914–1945" (PhD diss., University of Houston, May 2001), p. 317.
52. Ibid., p. 319.

CHAPTER 4

1. "Angry Crowd Kills 1 Officer Beats Another," *California Sentinel*, August 29, 1946.
2. Ibid.
3. Horace Tapscott, *The Musical and Social Journey of Horace Tapscott*, ed. Steven Isoardi (Durham, NC: Duke University Press, 2001), pp. 1–2.
4. O'Brien's interview with Ola Mae Kennedy, 2010.
5. Lightnin' Hopkins interview, from documentary *Artists in America*, 16-mm film, KUHT Film Productions, University of Houston, 1971.
6. Les Blank, *The Blues According to Lightnin' Hopkins*, Flower Films, 1969, outtakes disc 12, track 1.
7. Lightning Hopkins interview, *Artists in America*.
8. Ibid.
9. Steve Tracy, "That Chicken Shack Boogie Man," Part 1, *Blues Unlimited*, no. 83 (July 1971): 7–8.
10. Lightnin' Hopkins interview, "I Do My First Record and Get My Name," *My Life in the Blues*, Prestige PR 7370, 1965.
11. Ibid.
12. Barbara Dane interview with Lightnin' Sam Hopkins, Barbara Dane Collection, AFC 1980/001: SR 12 & SR 13, American Folk Life Center, Library of Congress, Washington, DC.
13. Frank X. Tolbert, "In Remembrance of Texas Bluesmen," *Dallas Morning News*, March 1, 1982.
14. O'Brien's interview with Doyle Bramhall, 2005.
15. David Honeyboy Edwards, *The World Don't Owe Me Nothin'* (Chicago: Chicago Review Press, 1997), p. 173.

16. O'Brien's interview with Texas Johnny Brown, 2005.

17. O'Brien's interview with Ray Dawkins, 2005.

18. O'Brien's interview with Tomcat Courtney, 2010.

19. Shaw Artists Corporation promotional material for Amos Milburn, Amos Milburn Vertical File, Institute of Jazz Studies, John Cotton Dana Library, Rutgers, The State University of New Jersey.

20. O'Brien's interview with Texas Johnny Brown.

21. Dick Shurman, liner notes to *Goree Carter and His Hepcats: Rock Awhile*, Blues Boy BB-306, 1999.

22. Ibid.

23. O'Brien's interviews with Jacqueline Beckham, 2004, 2010.

24. O'Brien's interview with John Hightower, 2009.

25. O'Brien's interviews with Jacqueline Beckham.

26. Edwards, *World Don't Owe Me*, p. 170.

27. O'Brien's interview with Texas Johnny Brown.

28. "A. Milburn 'Smash Hit' on Tour of One Nite Stands," *Los Angeles Sentinel*, November 23, 1950.

29. Forms number 150409 and 150410, Justice of the Peace Records, Harris County Archive, Houston, Texas.

30. Lightnin' Hopkins interview, *Artists in America*.

31. Blank, *Blues*, outtakes disc 1, track 6.

32. Ensminger's interview with Peter Case, June 28, 2011.

33. Jas Obrecht, ed., *The Postwar Blues Guitarists: Rollin' & Tumblin'* (San Francisco: Miller Freeman Books, 2000), p. 74.

34. Jimmie Lee Vaughan interview, http://www.wherelightninstrikes.com/html/jv_wmv.html (accessed March 17, 2006).

35. Denny Freeman, e-mail correspondence with O'Brien, April 14, 2010.

36. O'Brien's interview with Texas Johnny Brown.

37. Mike Leadbitter, "I Know Houston Can't Be Heaven: Don Robey," *Blues Unlimited* 46 (September 1967): 4.

38. John Broven, *Record Makers and Breakers: Voices of the Independent Rock 'n' Roll Pioneers* (Urbana: University of Illinois Press, 2009), p. 258.

39. Ibid., p. 259.

40. Barbara Dane interview with Brownie McGhee, Barbara Dane Collection, AFC 1980/001: SR62, American Folk Life Center, Library of Congress, Washington, DC.

41. Huey P. Meaux Papers, 1940–1994, box 96-384/23, Center for American History, University of Texas at Austin.

42. Curtis Amy oral history, Beyond Central Collection, Center for Oral History Research, UCLA Library, Los Angeles.

43. Ibid.

44. Hank Davis, liner notes to Peppermint Harris, *I Got Loaded*, Route 66 Records KIX-23, 1983.

45. Buddy Gheen, liner notes to Peppermint Harris, *Being Black Twice*, Homecooking Records HCS-116, 1989.

46. Davis, liner notes to Peppermint Harris, *I Got Loaded*.

47. Chris Strachwitz, liner notes to *Lightning Hopkins Early Recordings Vol. 2*, Arhoolie 2019, 1971.

48. *Chicago Defender*, July 23, 1949.

49. *Atlanta Daily World*, October 5, 1947.

50. *Billboard*, June 4, 1949, p. 122.

51. *Billboard*, August 13, 1949, p. 35.

52. John Minton, "Houston Creoles and Zydeco: The Emergence of an African American Urban Popular Style," *American Music* 14, no. 4 (Winter 1996): 501–502.

53. Recording contract dated December 16, 1950, Huey P. Meaux Papers, box 96-384/23.

54. Ibid.

55. Dane interview with Hopkins.

56. O'Brien's interview with David Honeyboy Edwards, 2009.

57. Edwards, *World Don't Owe Me*, pp. 169–170.

58. Ibid., p. 172.

59. Cilia Huggins, "The Calvin Owens Story," *Juke Blues* 35 (Summer 1995): 11–12.

60. O'Brien's interview with Big Walter Price, 2005.

61. Frank Kofsky, *John Coltrane and the Jazz Revolution of the 1960s* (New York: Pathfinder, 1998), p. 110.

62. O'Brien's interview with Aubrey Mayhew, 2006.

63. E. B. Rea, "Encores and Echoes," *Baltimore Afro American*, January 20, 1951.

64. Phil Johnson, "DISCS: BLUES. Hello Central: The Best of Lightnin' Hopkins, COLUMBIA LEGACY," *The Independent on Sunday*, July 11, 2004.

65. Joel Whitburn, *Joel Whitburn's Top R & B Singles, 1942–1988* (Menomonee Falls, WI: Record Research Inc., 1988).

66. Hal Webman, "Rhythm and Blues Notes," *Billboard*, February 9, 1952, p. 39.

67. Dane interview with Hopkins.

68. Johnny Otis Collection, EC 10" 2536, track 10, Archives of Traditional Music, Indiana University; Leslie Carter, liner notes to Long Gone Miles, *Country Born*, World-Pacific 1820, 1964.

69. Johnny Otis Collection; Leslie Carter, liner notes to Long Gone Miles, *Country Born*.

70. O'Brien's interview with Earl Gilliam, 2008.

71. Michael Lydon, *Man and His Music: Ray Charles* (New York: Riverhead Books, 1998), pp. 93, 104.

72. Ibid.

73. Allmusic.com, http://allmusic.com/cg/amg.dll?p=amg&sql=17:1312293 (accessed September 23, 2009).

74. O'Brien's interview with Peter Case, 2004.

75. Dane interview with Hopkins.

76. *Billboard*, March 2, 1957, p. 62.

77. *Billboard*, October 26, 1959, p. 50.

78. Ren Grevatt, "On the Beat," *Billboard*, April 14, 1958, p. 14.

79. "Diskeries in Blues Switch," *Billboard*, August 18, 1958, pp. 16, 22.

80. George Cole, *The Last Miles: The Music of Miles Davis, 1980–1991* (Ann Arbor: University of Michigan Press, 2007), p. 121; Ian Carr, *Miles Davis: The Definitive Biography* (London: HarperCollins, Ltd., 1992), p. 395.

CHAPTER 5

1. Ronald D. Cohen, *"Wasn't That a Time!": Firsthand Accounts of the Folk Music Revival* (Metuchen, NJ: Scarecrow Press, 1995), pp. 145–146.

2. Francis Davis, *The History of the Blues* (New York: Hyperion, 1995), p. 14.

3. Ray B. Browne, "Field Hands First Cried Out the Blues," *Washington Post*, April 24, 1960.

4. O'Brien's interview with Sam Charters, 2005; liner notes to *Lightnin' Hopkins*, Folkways 3822, 1959.

5. Sam Charters letter to Marian Disler dated January 16, 1959, Sam Charters file, Moses and Frances Asch Collection, Smithsonian Center for Folklife and Cultural Heritage, Washington, DC.

6. O'Brien's interview with Chris Strachwitz, 2005.

7. Steve Cushing, *Blues before Sunrise: The Radio Interviews* (Urbana: University of Illinois Press, 2010), p. 56.

8. O'Brien's interview with Mack McCormick, 2005.

9. "'Hootenanny' Scores Hit," *Houston Chronicle*, undated clipping, Lightnin' Hopkins file, Arhoolie Record Company Files.

10. "'Hootenanny' Singers Win Applause at Alley Program," *Houston Post*, undated clipping, Lightnin' Hopkins file, Arhoolie Record Company Files.

11. Anonymous liner notes to *Lightnin' Hopkins Strums the Blues*, Score Records 4022, 1958.

12. O'Brien's interview with Sam Charters.

13. John S. Wilson, "Lightning Hopkins Rediscovered," *New York Times*, August 23, 1959.

14. Ensminger's interview with Robert Murphy, June 30, 2011.

15. Lightning Hopkins letter to Moe Asch and Folkways Records dated November 26, 1959, Lightning Hopkins file, Moses and Frances Asch Collection.

16. O'Brien's interview with Mack McCormick.

17. Moses Asch letter to Lightning Hopkins dated December 4, 1959, Lightning Hopkins file, Moses and Frances Asch Collection.

18. Lightning Hopkins letter to Moe Asch dated December 12, 1959, Lightning Hopkins file, Moses and Frances Asch Collection.

19. O'Brien's interview with Mack McCormick.

20. O'Brien's interview with Ed Badeaux, 2006.

21. David King Dunaway, *How Can I Keep from Singing? The Ballad of Pete Seeger* (New York: Villard Books, 2008), p. 193.

22. Mack McCormick, liner notes to Sam Lightnin' Hopkins, *The Rooster Crowed in England*, 77 Records 77LA12/1, 1959.

23. D. K. Wilgus, Record Reviews, *Journal of American Folklore* 76, no. 299 (1963): 87–90.

24. Ensminger's interview with Robert Murphy.

25. Mack McCormick, liner notes, *Smokes Like Lightning*, Bluesville 1070, 1963.

26. Mack McCormick, "A Conversation with Lightnin' Hopkins," *Jazz Journal*.

27. Mack McCormick, liner notes to *The Unexpurgated Folk Songs of Men*, Raglan Records, 1960.

28. Undated five-page letter to Chris Strachwitz from Mack McCormick, Lightnin' Hopkins file, Arhoolie Record Company Files.

29. Robert Shelton, "An Earthy Shirt-Sleeve Type of Folk Art," *New York Times*, January 31, 1960.

30. Barbara Dane interview with Lightnin' Sam Hopkins, Barbara Dane Collection, AFC 1980/001: SR 12 & SR 13, American Folk Life Center, Library of Congress, Washington, DC.

31. O'Brien's interview with Chris Strachwitz.

32. Ann Holmes, "Lightnin', Balladeer of Dowling Street," *Houston Chronicle*, May 12, 1960.

33. Pete J. Welding, "Lightnin'," *Down Beat*, July 20, 1961, p. 64.

34. Ensminger's interview with Andy Bradley, July 1, 2011.

35. O'Brien's interview with Bill Greenwood, 2009.

36. John Lomax, Jr., letter to B. J. Connors, Lomax papers.

37. Mack McCormick undated letter to Sam Charters, Samuel and Ann Charters Archives of Blues and Vernacular Music, Folder IC1-2, Thomas J. Dodd Research Center, University of Connecticut, Storrs, Connecticut.

38. Grover Lewis, "Lookin' for Lightnin': A Blues Odyssey," *Village Voice*, January 2, 1969, January 9, 1969.

39. Lewis, "Lookin' for Lightnin'," January 23, 1969.

40. John Lomax, Jr., letter dated June 11, 1960, to Bess Lomax, Box 3D318, James Avery Lomax Family Papers, Center for American History, University of Texas at Austin.

41. Alfred Frankenstein, "UC's Folk Festival Is Skillfully Shaped," *San Francisco Chronicle*, July 4, 1960.

42. O'Brien's interview with Ed Pearl, 2005.

43. O'Brien's interview with Barbara Dane, 2005.

44. O'Brien's interview with Ed Pearl.

45. Ed Michel, liner notes to *Down South Summit Meeting*, World Pacific Records WP-1296, 1960.

46. Dan Aykroyd and Ben Manilla, *Elwood's Blues: Interviews with the Blues Legends and Stars* (San Francisco: Backbeat Books, 2004), p. 91.

47. Lightnin' Sam Hopkins Interview, KPFK, Reel 1 and Reel 2, 1960, Barbara Dane Collection, AFC 1980/001: SR 12 & SR 13.

48. John Lomax, Jr., letter to Barry Olivier, early 1960, Box 3D218, Lomax papers.

49. Lightnin' Sam Hopkins Interview, KPFK.

50. O'Brien's interview with Mack McCormick.

51. Robert Shelton, "'Lightning' Strikes," *New York Times*, October 15, 1960.

52. "A Pattern of Words and Music," press release dated November 4, 1960, Lightnin' Hopkins vertical file, Institute of Jazz Studies, Rutgers, The State University of New Jersey, John Cotton Dana Library, Newark, NJ.

53. O'Brien's interview with John Sebastian, Jr., 2009.

54. *Texas Blues Guitar*, Grossman's Guitar Workshop 13041DVD, 2003.

55. Mark Humphrey, liner notes to *Lightnin' Hopkins: Rare Performances, 1960–1979*, DVD, Vestapol 13022, 2001, p. 13.

56. Nat Hentoff, liner notes to *Lightnin' in New York*, Candid 9010, 1960.

57. Les Blank, *The Blues According to Lightnin' Hopkins*, Flower Films, 1969, outtakes disc 16, track 3.

58. John Broven, "Bobby's Happy House of Hits, Part 2: The Story of Bobby Robinson and His Famous Labels," *Juke Blues*, no. 16 (Summer 1989): 10–11.

59. Ibid.

60. John Broven, "Behind the Sun Again," *Juke Blues*, February–March 1974, pp. 15–16.

61. *Billboard*, January 23, 1961, p. 40.

62. While Hopkins's situation improved greatly from early 1959, when Charters found and recorded him, until late 1960, when he returned from his triumphant trip to New York City, the African American population in Houston experienced ongoing segregation and abuse. On March 4, 1960, thirteen students from Texas Southern University (formerly Texas State University of Negroes) marched from a flagpole on campus to a Weingarten's grocery store seven blocks away on Alameda Road in Third Ward, where they sat in at a lunch counter. The students did not get served, but their actions marked the beginning of the sit-in movement west of the Mississippi River.

    The demand for racial equality also led to a white backlash, which included violent hate crimes. On March 7, 1960, just three days after the first sit-in, two masked white men kidnapped Felton Turner at gunpoint. They tied him to a tree and beat him with a chain and carved "KKK" into his stomach in two places. The attackers said they were hired because the students at TSU were getting too much publicity. They threatened to kill him if he tried to escape. Less than two weeks later, Hopkins played a hootenanny in downtown Houston at the Alley Theater.

CHAPTER 6

1. Reviews of This Week's Singles, "Lightnin' Hopkins, Mojo Hand," *Billboard*, January 23, 1961, p. 40.
2. Frank X. Tolbert, *Tolbert's Texas* (New York: Doubleday and Company, 1983), p. 7.
3. Les Blank, *The Blues According to Lightnin' Hopkins*, Flower Films, 1969, outtakes disc 13, track 2.
4. Peter D. Goldsmith, *Making People's Music: Moe Asch and Folkways Records* (Washington, DC: Smithsonian Institution Press, 1988), p. 268.
5. Undated five-page letter to Chris Strachwitz from Mack McCormick, Lightnin' Hopkins file, Arhoolie Record Company Files.
6. *Dirty Linen*, no. 62 (February / March 1996).
7. Kenneth S. Goldstein and Pete Narvaez, "Producing Blues Recordings," *Journal of American Folklore* 109, no. 434 (Autumn 1996): 454.
8. Lightning Hopkins Prestige Records Contract, Prestige Records Company files, Berkeley, California.
9. O'Brien's interview with Mack McCormick, 2005.
10. Undated five-page letter to Chris Strachwitz from Mack McCormick.
11. O'Brien's interview with Mack McCormick.
12. Skea.
13. Leonard and Mary Gaskin Papers, 1910–1999, Series 1, Business records, Box 1, folder, itineraries, Archives Center, National Museum of American History, Washington, DC.
14. Mack McCormick, liner notes to *Last Night Blues*, Prestige / Bluesville 1029, 1960.
15. Blank, *Blues*, outtakes disc 12, track 2.
16. Leonard and Mary Gaskin Papers, 1910–1999, Series 1, Business records, Box 1, folder, itineraries.
17. O'Brien's interview with Ed Badeaux, 2006.
18. *Rice Thresher*, March 3, 1961.
19. O'Brien's interview with Ezra Charles, 2005.
20. O'Brien's interview with Uncle John Turner, 2005.
21. Bill Hampton, "Hopkins to Sing the Blues," *Daily Texan*, March 29, 1961.
22. Gilbert Shelton, "Folk Singing Rates Ovation while Lightnin' Strikes UT," *Daily Texan*, March 30, 1961.
23. O'Brien's interview with Don Sanders, 2008.
24. Goldstein and Narvaez, "Producing Blues Recordings," p. 455.
25. Mack McCormick, liner notes to *Blues in My Bottle*, Bluesville 1045, 1961.
26. Ibid.
27. Ibid.
28. Robert Murphy interview with John Wheat, in possession of authors; also at Center for American History, University of Texas at Austin.
29. Ibid.

30. Ensminger's interview with Robert Murphy, June 30, 2011.
31. Taj Mahal with Stephen Foehr, *Taj Mahal: An Autobiography of a Bluesman* (London: Sanctuary Publishing, 2001), pp. 72–78.
32. Ibid.
33. O'Brien's interview with Ed Pearl, 2005.
34. O'Brien's interview with Bernie Pearl, 2005.
35. O'Brien's interview with Dave Alvin, 2004.
36. Ibid.
37. Dave Alvin, "Ashgrove," *Ashgrove*, Yep Roc Records YEP 2075, 2004.
38. *Blues Hoot*, Horizon Records SWP-1617, 1963.
39. O'Brien's interview with Dave Alvin.
40. O'Brien's interview with Mack McCormick.
41. O'Brien's interview with W. L. Bane, 2005.
42. Craig Harris, "Ramblin' Jack Elliott," Allmusic Guide, http://allmusic.com/artist/ramblin-jack-elliott-p73798/biography (accessed December 27, 2010).
43. O'Brien's interview with Ramblin' Jack Elliott, 2010.
44. Dale, Nightclub Reviews, Ashgrove, Los Angeles, Oct. 20, "Lightnin'" Sam Hopkins, Jack Elliott, *Variety*, November 1, 1961.
45. O'Brien's interview with Bruce Bromberg, 2005.
46. Gene Robertson, "On the Beam," *Sun-Reporter*, November 11, 1961.
47. O'Brien's interview with Mose Allison, 2008.
48. Mike Leadbitter and Neal Slaven, *Blues Records 1943–1970: A Selective Discography* (London: Record Information Services, 1987), p. 608.
49. Mack McCormick, liner notes to *Walking This Road by Myself*, Bluesville 1057, 1962.
50. http://www.johnglennhome.org/john_glenn.shtml (accessed November 16, 2009).
51. McCormick, liner notes to *Walking This Road by Myself*.
52. Mack McCormick interview, Allan Turner Collection, 1972–2009, Center for American History, University of Texas at Austin.
53. *Billboard*, April 14, 1962, p. 40.
54. O'Brien's interview with Jim Franklin, 2010.
55. O'Brien's interview with Ed Badeaux.
56. Ibid.
57. Ibid.
58. Ibid.
59. Ibid.
60. Bill Cole, *John Coltrane* (New York: Da Capo Press, 1993), p. 84.
61. Robert Shelton, "Two Guitarists at Village Gate: Sam Hopkins Sings Negro Folk Blues with Wry Humor," *New York Times*, March 31, 1962.
62. Nina Simone with Stephen Cleary, *I Put a Spell on You: The Autobiography of Nina Simone* (New York: Da Capo Press, 2003), pp. 67–68.
63. *Los Angeles Sentinel*, July 5, 1962.

64. O'Brien's interview with John Sebastian, Jr., 2009.

65. Ibid.

66. Ibid.

67. Ibid.

68. Mack McCormick, liner notes to *Smokes Like Lightning*, Bluesville LP, 1070.

69. Mack McCormick interview, Allan Turner Collection.

70. O'Brien's interview with Sam Charters, 2005.

71. Letter from Sam Charters to Mack McCormick dated December 24, 1963, Lightning Hopkins file, Prestige Records, Berkeley, California.

72. O'Brien's interview with Sam Charters.

73. Letter from Mack McCormick to Robert Weinstock, undated, Lightning Hopkins file, Prestige Records, Berkeley, California.

74. Letter from Sam Charters to Mack McCormick dated December 24, 1963.

75. Letter from Richard Asher to Mack McCormick dated November 20, 1963, Lightning Hopkins file, Prestige Records, Berkeley, California.

76. O'Brien's interview with Sam Charters.

77. Letter from Sam Charters to Mack McCormick dated February 27, 1964, Lightning Hopkins file, Prestige Records, Berkeley, California.

78. O'Brien's interview with Sam Charters.

79. Blank, *Blues*, outtakes disc 10, track 5.

80. Ibid.

81. Mike Leadbitter, "An Interview with Juke Boy Bonner," *Blues Unlimited* 79 (1971): 20.

82. Mack McCormick interview, Allan Turner Collection.

83. O'Brien's interview with Sam Charters.

84. Chris Strachwitz, liner notes to *Lightning Hopkins with His Brothers Joel and John Henry and with Barbara Dane*, Arhoolie F1022, 1966.

85. O'Brien's interview with Chris Strachwitz, 2005.

86. Ibid.

87. John Davis, "Folk Songs: New Music That Tries to Be Old Plagues Houston," *Daily Cougar*, September 3, 1963.

88. O'Brien's interview with Mack Webster, 2011.

89. John A. Lomax, Jr., liner notes to *Look, It's Us*, Jester Records, Inc., 1963.

90. O'Brien's interview with Mack Webster.

91. Ibid.

92. O'Brien's interview with Darryl Harris, 2010.

93. O'Brien's interview with Mack Webster.

94. Eric Von Schmidt and Jim Rooney, *Baby Let Me Follow You Down: The Illustrated Story of the Cambridge Folk Years* (Amherst: University of Massachusetts Press, 1994), p. 121.

95. May 13, 1964, contract.

96. O'Brien's interview with Chris Strachwitz.

97. O'Brien's interview with Carroll Peery, 2005.
98. O'Brien's interview with Barry Hansen, 2005.
99. Ibid.
100. Ibid.
101. O'Brien's interview with Barbara Dane, 2005.
102. *Steve Allen Show*, June 25, 1964, UCLA Film and Television Archives, Powell Library, UCLA, Los Angeles, California.
103. Ibid.
104. Carolyn Hester e-mail to O'Brien, December 30, 2008.
105. Rod Kennedy, *Music from the Heart* (Austin: Eakin Press, 1998).
106. O'Brien's interview with Chris Strachwitz.
107. Blank, *Blues*, outtakes disc 3, track 1.
108. Kay Pope, "The European Odyssey of Lightnin' Sam Hopkins," *Houston Chronicle*, November 22, 1964.
109. Stephanie Wiesand, liner notes to *American Folk Blues Festival 1962-1966*, Reeling in the Years Productions, 2003.
110. O'Brien's interview with Bob Koester, 2010.
111. Ibid.
112. Ibid.
113. Simon A. Napier, "The Third American Folk-Blues Festival," *Blues Unlimited*, November 1964, p. 3.
114. Beatles, *The Beatles Anthology* (San Francisco: Chronicle Books, 2000), p. 37.
115. Pope, "European Odyssey."
116. Henrietta Yorchenco, "Folk Song '64," *Musical America*, December 1964, p. 263.
117. Ibid.
118. Sam Charters, liner notes to Lightnin' Hopkins, *My Life in the Blues*, Prestige PR 7370, 1965.

CHAPTER 7

1. O'Brien's interview with Bob Koester, 2010.
2. Pete Welding, "To Chicago—Ten April Days 1965," *Blues Unlimited*, no. 23 (June 1965): 9.
3. O'Brien's interview with Charlie Musselwhite, 2010.
4. Michael Bloomfield with S. Summerville, *Me and Big Joe* (San Francisco: RE/SEARCH Productions, 1980).
5. O'Brien's interview with John Carrick, 2009.
6. Ibid.
7. O'Brien's interview with Aubrey Mayhew, 2006.
8. Letter from Sam Charters to Mack McCormick dated February 27, 1964, Lightning Hopkins file, Prestige Record Company, Berkeley, California.
9. Aubrey Mayhew, liner notes to Lightnin' Hopkins, *The Lost Texas Tapes Volume 1*, Collectables Records COL CD 5205, 1990.

10. O'Brien's interview with Aubrey Mayhew.
11. Mayhew, liner notes to Lightnin' Hopkins, *The Lost Texas Tapes Volume 1*.
12. O'Brien's interview with Aubrey Mayhew.
13. Ibid.
14. "Lightnin' Will Still Be Wailin'," *Melody Maker* 39 (October 31, 1964).
15. O'Brien's interview with Aubrey Mayhew.
16. Louie Robinson, "Rock and Roll Becomes Respectable," *Ebony*, November 1965, p. 55.
17. George W. Lyon, letter to the editor, *Blues Unlimited*, January / February 1971, p. 13.
18. O'Brien's interview with Darryl Harris, 2010.
19. Lyon, letter to the editor.
20. O'Brien's interview with Aubrey Mayhew.
21. Ibid.
22. Ibid.
23. Ibid.
24. Ibid.
25. Ibid.
26. Ibid.
27. Charles Radcliffe, "Lightnin'," *Blues Unlimited* 18 (January 1965): 9.
28. O'Brien's interview with Chris Strachwitz, 2005.
29. Ibid.
30. Radcliffe, "Lightnin'," p. 9.
31. Charles Shaar Murray, *Boogie Man: The Adventures of John Lee Hooker in the Twentieth Century* (New York: St. Martin's Press, 2000), p. 135.
32. John Swenson, *Rolling Stone Jazz and Blues Album Guide* (New York: Random House, 1999), p. 68.
33. Johnny Copeland interview, Tamara Saviano Collection, Box #1007, Johnny Copeland (CD 3272 2112 3851), July 31, 1996, Wittliff Collections, Albert B. Alkek Library, Texas State University, San Marcos.
34. W. C. Clarke interview, Tamara Saviano Collection, Box #1007, W. C. Clarke (CD 3272 2112 4420), December 24, 1988, Wittliff Collections, Albert B. Alkek Library, Texas State University, San Marcos.
35. Townes Van Zandt, *Last Rights*, Track 9, compact disc, Gregor 41290, 1990.
36. Robert Earl Hardy, *A Deeper Shade of Blue: The Life and Music of Townes Van Zandt* (Denton: University of North Texas Press, 2008), p. 62.
37. Kathleen Hudson, *Telling Stories, Writing Songs: An Album of Texas Songwriters* (Austin: University of Texas Press, 2001), p. 71.
38. "The Beatles Say 'Man Has Soul,'" *Los Angeles Sentinel*, May 8, 1966.
39. O'Brien's interview with Rex Bell, 2004.
40. Frank X. Tolbert, Tolbert's Texas, "Lightnin' Hopkins 'Electrifies' People," *Dallas Morning News*, February 1, 1972.
41. Lightnin' Hopkins, *Live at Newport*, Vanguard Records UV 067, 1965.

42. Ibid.

43. O'Brien's interview with Sam Lay, 2007.

44. O'Brien's interview with Annie Johnston, 2006.

45. Chris Strachwitz, liner notes to *The Journey of Chris Strachwitz: Arhoolie Records 40th Anniversary Collection, 1960–2000*, Arhoolie 491, 2000, p. 64.

46. Greil Marcus, *The Old Weird America: The World of Bob Dylan's Basement Tapes* (New York: Picador, 1997), p. 14.

47. *Broadside of Boston* 4, no. 11 (July 21, 1965).

48. P. G., "Boston Blues," *Blues Unlimited*, November 1965.

49. Bob Dylan, *Chronicles Volume 1* (New York: Simon and Schuster, 2005), pp. 15–16.

50. Dion, "Dion's Bluesy Dozen," eMusic, http://www.emusic.com/lists/showlist.html?lid=682259 (accessed December 21, 2010).

51. *Rag Baby* 1, no. 2 (October 1965), as posted at Rock Archaeology 101, http://rockarchaeology101.blogspot.com/search?q=lightnin+hopkins (accessed January 2, 2011).

52. John Broven, *Rhythm and Blues in New Orleans* (Gretna, LA: Pelican Publishing Co., 1978), p. 8.

53. Liner notes to *Lightnin' Strikes*, Verve Forecast FV/FVS-9022, 1962.

54. Stan Lewis, liner notes, *The Jewel/Paula Records Story: The Blues, Rhythm & Blues and Soul Recordings*, Capricorn Records 9 42014-2, 1993.

55. O'Brien's interviews with Stan Lewis, 2006, 2008.

56. Paul Oliver, *Blues Fell This Morning: Meaning in the Blues* (Cambridge: Cambridge University Press, 1990), pp. 87, 110.

57. O'Brien's interview with Johnny Winter, 2010.

58. Ibid.

59. Earl Ofari, "Sam Lightnin' Hopkins: Past, Present and Future," *Los Angeles Free Press* 7, issue 32 (August 1970): 55.

60. O'Brien's interview with Big Walter Price, 2005.

61. *Daily Texan*, June 18, 1974.

62. O'Brien's interview with Johnny Winter.

63. O'Brien's interview with Darryl Harris.

64. O'Brien's interview with Don Logan.

65. O'Brien's interview with Stan Lewis.

66. O'Brien's interview with Don Logan, 2008.

67. Ibid.

68. Ibid.

69. Jim Langdon, Night Beat, *Austin Statesman*, December 1, 1965.

70. Jim Langdon, Night Beat, "Catch Lightning Hopkins for Traditional Blues," *Austin Statesman*, December 8, 1965.

71. O'Brien's interview with Francis Clay, 2005.

72. Ralph J. Gleason, "On the Town," *San Francisco Chronicle*, April 18, 1966.

73. Ed Denson, "The Folk Scene, But Only the Best," *Berkeley Barb*, April 22, 1966.

74. O'Brien's interview with Norman Mayell, 2009.

75. Bill Graham and Robert Greenfield, *Bill Graham Presents* (New York: Dell Publishing, 1992), p. 177.

76. "Blues News," *Blues Unlimited* 37 (October 1966): 13.

77. Allan Turner Collection, 1972–2009, Box 2X89, Mack McCormick, Houston, TX, 2009, compact disc 1, Dolph Briscoe Center for American History, University of Texas at Austin.

78. Ralph J. Gleason, "Jerry Garcia, the Guru," in *The Grateful Dead Reader*, ed. David Dodd and Diana Spaulding (New York: Oxford University Press USA, 2001), p. 32.

79. Phil Lesh, *Searching for My Sound: My Life with the Grateful Dead* (New York: Little Brown & Company, 2005).

80. Lightning Hopkins letter dated March 24, 1967, John Davis Williams Library, Blues Archive, University of Mississippi, Oxford, Mississippi.

81. David King Dunaway, *How Can I Keep from Singing: The Ballad of Pete Seeger* (New York: Villard, 2008), p. 264.

82. O'Brien's interview with Tim Williams, 2007.

83. O'Brien's interview with Les Blank, 2006.

84. Ibid.

85. Les Blank, *The Blues According to Lightnin' Hopkins*, Flower Films, 1969, outtakes disc 8, track 1.

86. O'Brien's interview with Les Blank.

87. Les Blank, "On the Making of *The Blues According to Lightnin' Hopkins*," http://www.lesblank.com/art/lh.htm (accessed February 2, 2011).

88. O'Brien's interview with Darryl Harris.

89. O'Brien's interview with Les Blank.

90. Richie Unterberger, Kaleidoscope, Allmusic Guide, http://allmusic.com/artist/kaleidoscope-p4654/biography (accessed December 22, 2010).

91. E-mail correspondence to O'Brien from Chester Crill, December 3, 2008.

92. Don Duncan, "Driftwood Diary," *Seattle Times*, June 30, 1968.

93. *Seattle Post-Intelligencer*, Area 206 section, October 20, 1967.

94. O'Brien's interview with John Ullman, 2008.

95. O'Brien's interview with Mike Russo, 2010.

96. O'Brien's interview with Don Hyde, 2010.

97. Ibid.

98. O'Brien's interview with Jim Franklin, 2010.

99. Ibid.

100. Ibid.

101. O'Brien's interview with Don Hyde.

102. Pete Welding, "Blues 'n' Folk," *Down Beat* 30 (April 3, 1969).

103. Blank, *Blues*, outtakes disc 1, track 3.

104. Charles K. Wolfe and Kip Lornell, *The Life and Legend of Leadbelly* (New York: Da Capo Press, 1999), p. 79.

CHAPTER 8

1. Mark Humphrey, liner notes to *Electric Mud*, Chess MCA CHD 9363, 1996; Richie Unterberger, review of *Electric Mud*, Allmusic Guide, http://allmusic.com/album/electric-mud-r108932 (accessed December 27, 2010).

2. Robert Gordon, *Can't Be Satisfied: The Life and Times of Muddy Waters* (Boston: Little, Brown, 2002): pp. 206–207.

3. James Segrest and Mark Hoffman, *Moanin' at Midnight: The Life and Times of Howlin' Wolf* (New York: Thunder's Mouth Press, 2004), p. 248.

4. Patrick Lundborg, "The International Artists Record Label," Lysergia.com, http://www.lysergia.com/LamaWorkshop/IAlabel/IAstory.htm (accessed December 27, 2010).

5. Ibid.

6. O'Brien's interview with Mansel Rubenstein.

7. Ibid.; liner notes to *Free Form Patterns*, orig. International Artists, reissue Fuel 2000 #302 061 315 2, 2003.

8. Paul Drummond, *Eye Mind: The Saga of Roky Erickson and the 13th Floor Elevators, the Pioneers of the Psychedelic Sound* (Los Angeles: Process Media, 2007), p. 308.

9. O'Brien's interview with Johnny Winter, 2010; Andy Bradley and Roger Wood, *House of Hits: The Story of Houston's Gold Star/SugarHill Recording Studios* (Austin: University of Texas Press, 2010), p. 175.

10. O'Brien's interview with Mansel Rubenstein.

11. O'Brien's interview with Danny Thomas.

12. O'Brien's interview with Mansel Rubenstein.

13. Drummond, *Eye Mind*, p. 308.

14. O'Brien's interview with Danny Thomas.

15. O'Brien's interview with Duke Davis, 2010.

16. Savage, p. 35.

17. O'Brien's interview with Mason Romans.

18. Ibid.

19. O'Brien's interview with Johnny Winter.

20. Love Street Light Circus Feel Good Machine, "1960s Texas Music—Houston Live Music Venues," *1960s Texas Music*, http://www.scarletdukes.com/st/tmhou_venues2.html (accessed December 28, 2010); Allen Box, "Houston Music History, Part One: Our Heritage," *Space City!* 2, no. 11 (October 31–November 13, 1970): 21.

21. Love Street Light Circus Feel Good Machine, "1960s Texas Music—Houston Live Music Venues"; O'Brien's interview with Mason Romans.

22. O'Brien's interviews with Mason Romans, Duke Davis, and Danny Thomas.

23. O'Brien's interview with Duke Davis.

24. O'Brien's interview with Danny Thomas.

25. O'Brien's interview with Mason Romans.

26. Stephen Hammond interview, *1960s Texas Music*, http://www.scarletdukes.com/st/tmhou_hammondint.html (accessed December 13, 2010).

27. Ibid.

28. O'Brien's interview with Mason Romans.

29. Stanley Booth, *Rhythm Oil: A Journey through the Music of the American South* (London: Jonathan Cape, 1991), p. 171.

30. Andrew Dansby, "Houston Guitarist Rocky Hill Dies at 62," *Houston Chronicle*, April 13, 2009, http://www.chron.com/entertainment/music/article/ZZ-Top-member-s-brother-Houstonian-Rocky-Hill-1608919.php (accessed January 12, 2011).

31. O'Brien's interview with Uncle John Turner, 2005.

32. O'Brien's interview with Rex Bell, 2004.

33. *Daily Cougar.*

34. O'Brien's interview with Darryl Harris, 2010.

35. Vince Bell, *One Man's Music: The Life and Times of Texas Songwriter Vince Bell* (Denton: University of North Texas Press, 2009), p. 10.

36. Claudia Feldman, "Houston's '60s Night Scene: Joplin Sang Here for $20 a Night," *Houston Chronicle*, August 13, 1989, Texas Magazine section, p. 14.

37. O'Brien's interview with Don Sanders, 2008.

38. Ibid.

39. O'Brien's interview with Rex Bell.

40. Ibid.

41. Michael Point, "CD Set Preserves Lightnin's Legacy," *Austin American-Statesman*, November 21, 1991.

42. Harry Summerall, "Screamin' Nighthawk: Portrait of a Blues Man," *Washington Post*, December 11, 1980.

43. Smithsonian Institution, *1968 Festival of American Folklife* (for Institute of Texan Cultures, see pp. 35–36; Hopkins mentioned on pp. 19, 24, and 28), http://folklife.si.edu/resources/Center/Archives/Finding_Aids/Festival/FAF1968_Program_Book.pdf (accessed May 9, 2012).

44. Smithsonian Folklife Festival Documentation Collection, Ralph Rinzler Folklife Archive and Collection, Series 2 Audio Recordings from the production of the program, FP-1968-10RR-0012 (68.101.12) and FP-1968-10RR-0013 (68.101.13), Smithsonian Institution, Washington, DC.

45. Ibid.

46. Ibid.

47. Lu Mitchell, http://www.lumitchell.com/lm_images22.html (accessed January 18, 2011).

48. O'Brien's interview with Bruce Bromberg, 2005.

49. Ibid.

50. Bruce Bromberg, liner notes to *California Mudslide (and Earthquake)*, Vault SLP-129, 1969.

51. O'Brien's interview with Bruce Bromberg.

52. Ibid.

53. Ibid.

54. Ibid.

55. Bromberg, liner notes to *California Mudslide*.

56. Mike Leadbitter, Reviews, *Blues Unlimited*, no. 67 (November 1969): 27.

57. Ron Brown, review of *The California Mudslide and Earthquake, Jazz Journal*, February 1971, pp. 35–36.

58. Pete Johnson, "Benefit Concerts to Aid Ash Grove," *Los Angeles Times*, May 27, 1969.

59. O'Brien's interview with Ed Pearl, 2005.

60. *Los Angeles Times*, April 30, 1969, H17.

61. Richard Skelly, Albert Collins biography, http://allmusic.com/artist/albert-collins-p6321/biography, (accessed January 13, 2011).

62. Denis Lewis and Cilla Huggins, "A Long Conversation with Collins," *Blues Unlimited*, nos. 135/136 (July/September 1979): 4–11; Skelly, Albert Collins biography.

63. Bobby Seale, *Seize the Time: The Story of the Black Panther Party and Huey P. Newton* (New York: Random House, 1970), pp. 153–166, Seale quotation on p. 162; David Hilliard and Lewis Cole, *This Side of Glory: The Autobiography of David Hilliard and the Story of the Black Panther Party* (Boston: Little, Brown and Company, 1993), p. 122.

64. Seale, *Seize the Time*, p. 27.

65. *Berkeley Barb*, May 16–22, 1969, p. 19.

66. Charles Burress, "Mary Moore—Founder of Berkeley Nightclub Mandrake's," *San Francisco Chronicle*, December 28, 2001.

67. Burress, "Mary Moore."

68. Craig Oren, "Would-be University Parking Lot Becomes 'Power to the People Park,'" *Daily Californian*, April 22, 1969.

69. Craig Oren, "UC to Build Playing Field on Site of 'People's Park,'" *Daily Californian*, April 28, 1969.

70. Jerry Popkin, "Park to Become Fenced-in Field," *Daily Californian*, May 14, 1969.

71. Ibid., 12.

72. *Berkeley Barb*, May 16–22, 1969.

73. O'Brien's interview with Carroll Peery, 2005.

74. O'Brien's interview with Paul Asbell.

75. Ibid.

76. O'Brien's interview with Francis Clay, 2005.

77. Ulish Carter, "If Rotgut Blues Is Your Thing, Here It Is," *New Pittsburgh Courier*, September 22, 1979.

78. Hopkins performance, May 6, 1966, available at http://www.wolfgangsvault.com/lightnin-hopkins/concerts/ash-grove-may-06-1966-1st-set.html.

79. Michael Erlewine, e-mail correspondence with O'Brien, June 15, 2008.

80. Dan Morgenstern, *Down Beat*, October 1969, p. 29.

81. "Lightnin' Hopkins," *San Diego Door*, September 25, 1969, p. 14.

82. Barney Hoskyns, *Lowside of the Road: A Life of Tom Waits* (New York: Broadway Books, 2009), p. 41.

83. Alan Govenar, *Lightnin' Hopkins: His Life and Blues* (Chicago: Chicago Review Press, 2010), p. 194.

84. Ibid., p. 163.

85. Little Hattie letter to Minnie dated April 10, 1970, courtesy of Jane Phillips.

86. *Space City!* 2, no. 7 (September 5–18, 1970): 25.

87. O'Brien's interview with Dalis Allen, 2005.

88. Ibid.

89. O'Brien's interview with Bill Haymes, 2006.

90. *Space City!* 2, no. 9 (October 3–16, 1970): 17, 23.

91. O'Brien's interview with Bob Novotney.

92. O'Brien's interview with Mike Condray, 2005.

93. "Family Hand Firebombed," *Space City!* 2, no. 8 (September 19–October 3, 1970): 4.

94. O'Brien's interview with John Carrick, 2009.

95. "Family Hand Firebombed."

96. O'Brien's interview with Frank Davis, 2010.

97. Sandra Getz documents, courtesy of Mary Katherine Aldin, Folklore Productions, Santa Monica, California.

98. O'Brien's interview with Rex Bell.

99. O'Brien's interview with Ryan Trimble, 2008.

100. Armadillo World Headquarters display ad, *Austin Statesman*, November 13, 1970.

101. O'Brien's interview with Uncle John Turner; see http://www.unclejohnturner.com/photos.html for a picture of Turner playing the Armadillo with Hopkins.

102. O'Brien's interview with Uncle John Turner.

103. Chris Darrow e-mail correspondence with O'Brien, December 3, 2008.

CHAPTER 9

1. O'Brien's interview with Mike Condray, 2005.

2. Ibid.

3. Ibid.

4. O'Brien's interview with Ryan Trimble, 2008.

5. O'Brien's interview with Mike Condray.

6. O'Brien's interview with Darryl Harris, 2010.

7. O'Brien's interview with Ed Michel, 2006.

8. Ibid.

9. Hugh Gregory, *Roadhouse Blues: Stevie Ray Vaughan and Texas R&B* (San Francisco: Backbeat Books, 2003).

10. O'Brien's interview with Tim Williams, 2007.

11. Tim Williams, e-mail correspondence with O'Brien, July 21, 2006.

12. "Blues Greats Converge on Burlington for Festival," and "Blues Workshops Provide Talk with the Greats," *Vermont Cynic*, April 23, 1973.

13. O'Brien's interview with Dick Waterman, 2007.

14. Ibid.

15. Ibid.

16. Ibid.

17. O'Brien's interview with Larry "Bones" McCall, 2011.

18. Steve Leggett, review of *The Sonet Blues Story: Lightnin' Hopkins*, http://www.allmu sic.com/album/the-sonet-blues-story-r850127/review (accessed March 15, 2011).

19. O'Brien's interview with Sam Charters, 2005.

20. Ibid.

21. Alex Bontemps, "Culture," *Ebony*, August 1975, p. 114.

22. *Ebony*, October 1975, p. 19.

23. Ibid., p. 22.

24. O'Brien's interview with Don Freed, 2007; *Winnipeg Free Press*, October 8, 1975; *The Sheaf*, October 1975; *The Carillon* 17, no. 7 (October 17, 1975); *The Ubyssey*, October 31, 1975, Friday section, p. 2.

25. O'Brien's interview with Don Freed.

26. Ibid.

27. Ibid.

28. Ibid.

29. Brian Gibbard, *The Ubyssey*, October 31, 1975, Friday section, p. 2.

30. John Gibbs Rockwood, *Witness to the Blues* (Toledo, OH: Radio Room Press, 1999).

31. O'Brien's interview with Robert Ross, 2010.

32. Ibid.

33. O'Brien's interviews with David Benson, 2005, 2010.

34. O'Brien's interview with Terry Lickona, 2006.

35. Ibid.

36. Michael Grofsorean, letter dated April 14, 1980, Spoleto Festival Archives, 1956–1989, Marlene and Nathan Addlestone Library, College of Charleston, Charleston, South Carolina.

37. Jack Dressler, "'Jazz at Spoleto' Terrific, Effective," *News and Courier*, June 2, 1980.

38. O'Brien's interview with Terry Dunne, 2010.

39. Ibid.

40. Ibid.

41. O'Brien's interview with Robert Ross.

42. Johnny Copeland interview, Tamara Saviano Collection, Box #1007, Johnny Copeland (CD 3272 2112 3851), July 31, 1996, Wittliff Collections, Albert B. Alkek Library, Texas State University, San Marcos.

43. Lightnin' Hopkins, "War Is Started/Louisiana Woman," 7" single, Jewel 857, 1981.

44. Jeff Todd Titon, *Downhome Blues Lyrics: An Anthology from the Post–World War II Era* (orig. 1981; Champaign: University of Illinois Press, 1991).

45. Robert Palmer and Anthony DeCurtis, *Blues & Chaos* (New York: Simon and Schuster, 2009), p. 52.

46. O'Brien's interview with Arthur Shaw, 2011.

47. O'Brien's interview with Tommy Dardar, 2009.

48. O'Brien's interview with Ryan Trimble.

49. Marty Racine, "Things Are Tough Enough—We Just Got the Blues," *Houston Chronicle*, February 7, 1982.

50. Last Will and Testament, Probate Court Number 1, Harris County, Texas, February 3, 1982.

51. Ibid.

52. Will Contest, Filed in Harris County Probate Court Number 1, Harris County, Texas, March 8, 1982.

EPILOGUE

1. "Texas Blues Legend Sam Lightnin' Hopkins—Where Lightnin' Strikes," http://www.youtube.com/watch?v=IQfcxn_ViVc (accessed December 15, 2010).

2. Results from entering "Lightnin' Hopkins" search string on Amazon.com (accessed November 30, 2009).

3. For Hopkins influence on Collins also see Holly George Warren et al., eds., *The Rolling Stone Encyclopedia of Rock and Roll* (New York: Fireside, 2001), p. 197.

4. Charles Shaar Murray, *Crosstown Traffic: Jimi Hendrix and the Post-War Rock 'n' Roll Revolution* (New York: St. Martin's Press, 1989), pp. 138, 143.

5. Johnny Black, *Jimi Hendrix: The Ultimate Experience* (New York: Da Capo Press, 1999), p. 39.

6. Maury Dean, *Rock and Roll Goldrush: A Singles Un-Cyclopedia* (New York: Algora Publishing, 2003), p. 245; Keith Shadwick, *Jimi Hendrix: Musician* (San Francisco: Backbeat Books, 2003).

7. Shadwick, *Jimi Hendrix*, p. 24.

8. David Dicaire, *Blues Singers: Biographies of 50 Legendary Artists of the Early 20th Century* (Jefferson, NC: McFarland, 1999), pp. 162–163.

9. Jimmie Lee Vaughan interview, http://www.wherelightninstrikes.com/html/jv_wmv.html (accessed March 17, 2006).

10. Gerard Herzhaft, *Encyclopedia of the Blues* (Fayetteville: University of Arkansas Press, 1992), pp. 47, 103, 135, 147, 214.

11. Jas Obrecht, ed. *Rollin' and Tumblin': The Postwar Blues Guitarists* (San Francisco: Miller Freeman Books, 2000), p. 78.

12. Herzhaft, *Encyclopedia of the Blues*, p. 122.

13. Paul Oliver, liner notes to *Blind Boy Fuller with Sonny Terry and Bull City Red*, Blues Classics No. 11, cited in Barbara Allen and Thomas Schlereth, eds., *Sense of Place: American Regional Cultures* (Lexington: University of Kentucky Press, 1990), p. 121.

14. Herzhaft, *Encyclopedia of the Blues*, p. 213.

15. Jeffrey Pepper Rogers, *Rock Troubadours* (San Anselmo, CA: String Letter Publishing, 2000), p. 71.

16. Oliver Trager, *The American Book of the Grateful Dead: The Definitive Encyclopedia of the Grateful Dead* (New York: Fireside, 1997), p. 337.

17. Mockingbird Foundation, *The Phish Companion: A Guide to the Band and Their Music* (San Francisco: Backbeat Books, 2004), p. 221.

18. O'Brien's interview with Peter Case, June 13, 2004.

19. John Milward, liner notes to *Lightnin' Hopkins Live at Newport*, Vanguard Records UV 067, 1965.

20. David Lindley e-mail to O'Brien, 2008.

21. Dicaire, *Blues Singers*, p. 163.

22. O'Brien's interview with Dave Alvin, 2004.

23. W. E. B. Du Bois, *The Souls of Black Folk* (New York: Bantam Classics, 1989), p. 186.

24. "Cornel West: 'Being True to the Funk of Living,'" http://today.msnbc.msn.com /id/34157251/ns/today-today_books/ (accessed December 1, 2009).

INDEX